MW00586152

THE
PATRIARCH NICEPHORUS
OF CONSTANTINOPLE

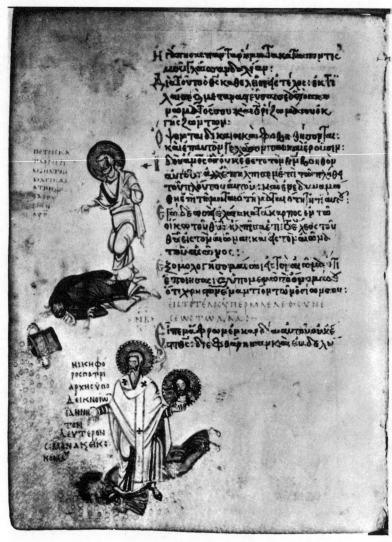

Chludov Psalter, fol. 51 v.

Text of *Psalms* 51 & 52

(Moscow, *Russian Historical* Museum 129, ninth century)

THE
PATRIARCH NICEPHORUS
OF CONSTANTINOPLE

ECCLESIASTICAL POLICY
AND IMAGE WORSHIP IN THE
BYZANTINE EMPIRE

BY

PAUL J. ALEXANDER

OXFORD
AT THE CLARENDON PRESS

OXFORD
UNIVERSITY PRESS

Great Clarendon Street, Oxford OX2 6DP

Oxford University Press is a department of the University of Oxford
It furthers the University's objective of excellence in research, scholarship,
and education by publishing worldwide in

Oxford New York

Athens Auckland Bangkok Bogotá Buenos Aires Cape Town
Chennai Dar es Salaam Delhi Florence Hong Kong Istanbul Karachi
Kolkata Kuala Lumpur Madrid Melbourne Mexico City Mumbai
Nairobi Paris São Paulo Singapore Taipei Tokyo Toronto Warsaw

and associated companies in Berlin Ibadan

Oxford is a registered trade mark of Oxford University Press
in the UK and in certain other countries

Published in the United States
by Oxford University Press Inc., New York

© Oxford University Press 1958

The moral rights of the author have been asserted

Database right Oxford University Press (maker)

Special edition for Sandpiper Books Ltd., 2001

All rights reserved. No part of this publication may be reproduced,
stored in a retrieval system, or transmitted, in any form or by any means,
without the prior permission in writing of Oxford University Press,
or as expressly permitted by law, or under terms agreed with the appropriate
reprographics rights organization. Enquiries concerning reproduction
outside the scope of the above should be sent to the Rights Department,
Oxford University Press, at the address above

You must not circulate this book in any other binding or cover
and you must impose this same condition on any acquirer

British Library Cataloguing in Publication Data

Data available

Library of Congress Cataloging in Publication Data

Data available

ISBN 0-19-826401-1

1 3 5 7 9 10 8 6 4 2

Printed in Great Britain
on acid-free paper by
Biddles Ltd.,
Guildford & King's Lynn

TO THE MEMORY
OF MY PARENTS

PREFACE

THIS book deals with the Iconoclastic Controversy in the Byzantine Empire. My interest in this subject goes back to my student days in Paris when my friend Dr. Erich Weil first called my attention to Byzantine history and to the Iconoclastic Movement. Later at Harvard University I was for several terms a member of the late Professor R. P. Blake's seminar on Byzantine history and literature in which he devoted considerable attention to the sources of the Iconoclastic Period. At the time my curiosity was stimulated by Ehrhard's remark that the principal work of the Patriarch Nicephorus, his *Refutatio et Eversio*, was still unedited. With that enthusiasm and helpfulness remembered by all who ever came in contact with him, Professor Blake ordered microfilms of the two surviving manuscripts of this work and later had prints made of them. At that time I had known the Patriarch primarily as a chronicler. I had therefore expected that his *Refutatio et Eversio*, written by one who had witnessed the stirring years of the Second Iconoclastic Controversy from an exceptionally favourable post of observation, would shed light on the events of the period. When I deciphered the manuscripts of his work my first reaction was disappointment. The *Refutatio et Eversio* deals exclusively with theological polemics and supplies little information on the political and ecclesiastical history of the period. Only gradually did I come to see the true importance of the Patriarch Nicephorus. In the first place, as an historical figure, he invites reflection on the course of events that might have ensued if his moderate views, rather than those of the more radical Theodore of Studios, had prevailed. Secondly, the Patriarch Nicephorus is practically alone in having preserved documents emanating from the Iconoclasts: precious fragments from the writings of the Emperor Constantine V, as well as the Dogmatic Definition and patristic florilegium issued by the Iconoclastic Council of St. Sophia. The views and tendencies of the Iconoclasts can thus be reconstructed and analysed. Finally, his theological works, and especially his *Refutatio et Eversio*, while perhaps lacking in historical concreteness, depth, and originality, are, as it were, the *summa* of the Controversy, being far more systematic than the works of

Theodore. They give the most complete picture of the issues involved in the great struggle about religious images.

It is my privilege to thank publicly the many institutions and individuals who at various stages of my work have helped or advised me. Work on my book began at Harvard University where my late teacher, Professor R. P. Blake, as well as Professor George La Piana, encouraged me to submit a first version of parts of this book as my doctoral dissertation. Both gentlemen made innumerable suggestions, and the book owes much of what may be valuable to their tireless advice. My work on the book was continued during two happy years when I worked as a Junior Fellow at Dumbarton Oaks Research Library and Collection of Harvard University, under the inspiring direction of Harvard's Professor Wilhelm Köhler. He has remained the kindest and wisest of counsellors and friends ever since. Several chapters or sections were first tried out at the annual symposia held at Dumbarton Oaks and I am in debt for suggestions and criticisms made at these meetings. I am also grateful to Dumbarton Oaks for several summer grants which enabled me to continue my work. The war, and afterwards my teaching duties at Hobart and William Smith Colleges (Geneva, N.Y.), interrupted my work on this book, but the stimulus of a scholarly and enthusiastic faculty, of an interesting and comprehensive curriculum, and of responsive students broadened my intellectual horizon immeasurably. Above all it was my privilege, during my nine years at Hobart and William Smith Colleges, to profit from an almost daily exchange of ideas and information with my colleague and friend Professor Brooks Otis whose personality, scholarship, and general outlook have had a profound impact on my thinking. Furthermore, in 1951–2, a John Simon Guggenheim Memorial Fellowship and a membership at the Institute for Advanced Study in Princeton enabled me to devote an entire academic year to this book in an intellectually stimulating and carefree atmosphere. During my stay at the Institute, I received valuable help from Professors Harold Cherniss, Ernst Kantorowicz, and Michael Cherniavsky. For a great number of years Professor Ernst Kitzinger, now Director of Studies at Dumbarton Oaks, has helped me by discussing with me the difficulties found in my work. In presentation and style the book owes a debt of gratitude to an (anonymous) reader of the Oxford

University Press whose constructive criticism led to the rewriting of parts of the manuscript. In this revision of the book I received valuable assistance from Dr. George Nadel, of Harvard University, for whose skill and patience I have the highest admiration. My colleague Dr. Henry Popkin of Brandeis University rendered me a similar service with regard to the Appendix. I cannot conclude this brief account of my indebtedness without mentioning Werner Jaeger, University Professor at Harvard, in whose Institute for Classical Studies I learned a great deal more than philology and palaeography. He had a decisive influence on my interests and development and has at various critical stages of my life helped and advised me in the most generous way. To all these scholars, and to others whose past help may at present escape me, I wish to record here my heartfelt gratitude.

Bibliography and footnotes will make clear the extent of my reliance on other scholars. Among them J. B. Bury, George Ostrogorsky, and V. Grumel have had perhaps the greatest influence on my book. Two publications appeared when work on it was already too far advanced to consider them in detail. One of them is A. J. Visser's monograph entitled *Nikephorus und der Bilderstreit* (Haag, 1952). In my opinion it overlaps only slightly with my biography of the Patriarch. I wish to mention especially Visser's two sections on Nicephorus' ecclesiology and christology (pp. 86–108) which are not treated in my book. I regret even more that Ernst Kitzinger's brilliant memoir on 'The Cult of Images in the Age before Iconoclasm' (*Dumbarton Oaks Papers*, viii, 1954, 83–150) appeared after the completion of my work. My first chapter especially would have profited greatly from Kitzinger's conclusions. Many libraries and librarians have put up with my demands for out-of-the-way titles and other time-consuming requests. I mention in particular the Harvard College Library; the library of Andover–Harvard Divinity School; the librarians at Dumbarton Oaks and especially Mrs. N. Scheffer whose knowledge of Russian bibliography has frequently rescued me from black despair; Miss Elizabeth Thalman and her able associates at Hobart and William Smith Colleges who never lost their patience; the scholarly librarian at the Institute for Advanced Study, Miss Judith Sachs, and her kind assistants; the Princeton University Library and the

remarkable and generous library of the Princeton Theological
Seminary; and finally the librarians of Brandeis University.
The Administration of Brandeis University also contributed
to the expense of typing the final draft of the book. I also
wish to express my obligation to the staff of the Clarendon Press
for their assistance in seeing the book through the press.

As soon as circumstances permit, I plan to edit the Greek text
of the *Refutatio et Eversio*.

P. J. A.

22 April, 1957

CONTENTS

ABBREVIATIONS

AA. SS.   *Acta sanctorum quotquot toto orbe coluntur* etc. (Antwerp, 1643 ff.).

A.B.   *Analecta Bollandiana* (Paris, 1882 ff.).

B.H.G.   *Bibliotheca hagiographica graeca* (ed. 2, Brussels, 1909).

B.Z.   *Byzantinische Zeitschrift* (1892 ff.).

C.S.H.B.   *Corpus scriptorum historiae byzantinae*, ed. B. G. Niebuhr, etc., vols. i–li (Bonn, 1828–97).

D.A.C.L.   *Dictionnaire d'archéologie chrétienne et de liturgie*, publié par le R. P. Don Fernand Cabrol, avec le concours d'un grand nombre de collaborateurs (Paris, 1903 ff.).

D.T.C.   *Dictionnaire de théologie catholique*, &c., ed. by A. Vacant and P. Mangenot (Paris, 1923 ff.).

É.O.   *Échos d'Orient* (1897/8 ff.).

M.G.H.   *Monumenta Germaniae Historica.*

N.P.B.   Angelo Mai, *Novae Patrum Bibliothecae*, vols. i to x (Rome, 1844–1905).

P.G.   Jacques Paul Migne, *Patrologiae cursus completus, Series Graeca*, vols. i to clxi (Paris, 1857–66).

P.L.   Jacques Paul Migne, *Patrologiae cursus completus, Series Latina*, vols. i to ccxxi (Paris, 1844–64).

P.O.   *Patrologia Orientalis* (Paris, 1903 ff.).

R.E.   *Paulys Real-Encyclopädie der classischen Altertumswissenschaft*, ed. 2, by G. Wissowa and others (Stuttgart, 1894 ff.).

T.U.   *Texte und Untersuchungen zur Geschichte der altchristlichen Literatur*, edd. Oscar von Gebhardt and Adolf Harnack (Berlin, 1882 ff.).

V.V.   *Vizantiiskii Vremennik* (St. Petersburg, 1894–1927). New Series, vols. i ff. (1947 ff.).

I

RELIGIOUS IMAGES: PRACTICE AND OPPOSITION[1]

THE Iconoclastic Controversy of the eighth and ninth centuries was concerned with the legitimacy of Christian images and with the degree of respect that was to be paid to them. While it raged, both sides, friends as well as foes of religious images, naturally thought, spoke, and wrote of that stage and type of Christian art with which they were familiar: the religious art of the Eastern Roman Empire in the eighth and ninth centuries. The study of the Iconoclastic Controversy thus has to begin with the question: How had this religious art come into being and what was its character?

There are a number of problems about the origins of Christian art—the date of the earliest catacomb paintings in Rome, their derivation from local traditions or Oriental models (Egyptian, Syrian, Mesopotamian)—upon which the opinions of scholars are divided, and which cannot be dealt with here. On the other hand, the study of early Christian art has produced results on which there is some measure of agreement. In the first place, there seems to have been no Christian art, at Rome or elsewhere, before the second half of the second century A.D.—or even later. Secondly, even when this art began, notably in the Roman Catacombs, the primary purpose of the earliest paintings was 'argumentative' (Elliger): it was meant to demonstrate, by way of historical reminders, the hope of resurrection and of a future life, by illustration either of suitable episodes in the biblical narrative (resurrection of Lazarus, &c.) or of the sacraments (the Baptism and Eucharist) or of Christian symbols (the Fish, the Good Shepherd). It is also clear, at least to this writer, that in the earliest catacomb paintings, which seem to date from the

[1] The purpose of the two introductory chapters is to sketch the development of the principal issue which was to engage the attention of Nicephorus as Patriarch. Obviously the procedure will be eclectic as this book does not pretend to give a history of religious images in the Church. The attempt will be made to summarize briefly the main phases of the development and to emphasize those that have a bearing on the Iconoclastic Controversy of the ninth century.

second half of the second century, there is a marked reluctance to portray Christ. The earliest representation of the resurrection of Lazarus in the *Cappella greca*, to take only the most striking example, shows the tomb of Lazarus, the dead Lazarus, the risen Lazarus, and one of the sisters, but not Jesus Christ Himself, who had performed the miracle. Later painters representing this subject as well as others in the Roman Catacombs freed themselves from such scruples, but the art of the Catacombs preserves the memory of an early period when Christian painters shied away from portraying Christ—unquestionably under the impact of the Old Testament prohibitions (Exod. xx. 4, &c.).

This early hesitancy is not visible in another monument of early Christian art: the Christian chapel at Dura-Europus. Here, as in Rome, symbolic and real representations are found together: the fresco of the Good Shepherd on the west wall is a symbol of Christ's saving power but on the north wall Christ Himself is represented healing the paralytic and walking upon the waters of the lake, 'the earliest known representation of our Saviour'.

The end of the persecutions and the christianization of the Empire gave a fresh stimulus to Christian art. Now that Christianity could emerge from its subterranean or otherwise hidden burial chambers and places of worship, and now that the emperors themselves built splendid Christian basilicas, artistic decoration came to be regarded as indispensable. As early as the fourth century authors describe entire cycles of church decoration, and by the time of the outbreak of the Iconoclastic Controversy many a church presented to its congregation some part of the sacred story in visual form.[1]

---

[1] The Roman Catacombs and their decoration are conveniently described in C. M. Kaufmann, *Handbuch der christlichen Archäologie* etc., 3rd ed., Paderborn, 1922, 113–41. On 'The Paintings in the Christian Chapel at Dura' see P. V. C. Baur, in *The Excavations at Dura-Europos*, Fifth Season (New Haven, 1934), 254–88, esp. 262–6. The literary evidence for early Christian art is examined by Hugo Koch, *Die altchristliche Bilderfrage nach den literarischen Quellen*, Forschungen zur Religion und Literatur des Alten und Neuen Testaments, xxvii, 1917, and by Walter Elliger, *Die Stellung der alten Christen zu den Bildern in den ersten vier Jahrhunderten*, Studien über christliche Denkmäler, xx, 1930. In a more recent book the last author has attempted to co-ordinate the archaeological and literary evidence (which must indeed tell the same story), to elaborate on the factors favouring or retarding the development of a Christian art, and to define the contributions of the various regions of the Empire to it: *Zur Entstehung und frühen Entwicklung der alt-christlichen Bildkunst*, ibid. xxiii, 1934. Another book which has helped in the writing of this chapter is Ernst von Dobschütz's *Christusbilder*, Texte und Untersuchungen zur

It would be wrong, however, to think exclusively of the decoration of sacred buildings in connexion with the Iconoclastic Controversy. The figures of Jesus, of the Virgin, and of the martyrs appeared on all sorts of liturgical objects, pilgrim's souvenirs, and personal ornaments. Of these the most important, from the point of view of this book, were the 'icons' in the proper sense of the word. The most ancient icons preserved date from the sixth century but there may have been earlier ones. The earliest examples, most of them from the monastery of St. Catherine on Mt. Sinai and now in the museum of the Ecclesiastical Academy at Kiev, are painted in wax colours on small wooden tablets. Some of them portray more than one person: a husband and a wife who both died a martyr's death; or the Saints Sergius and Bacchus; or John the Baptist, Christ and the Virgin. The representations on these icons, like the pagan funerary portraits from which they are descended, have large, profound, and staring eyes, and show a slight turn of the head against an extraordinary distribution of the light, and the nimbus.

In some ways these icons are even more important for the study of image worship than the 'argumentative' art of catacombs and churches. In the first place, they were small and portable, and thus no legislative or administrative act could easily suppress them. Any Christian might own one or several icons. Secondly, there existed a very special relationship between the owner and the icon. The frescoes and mosaics in the churches were educational and, in addition, they might or might not become the object of veneration. The mere fact of the existence of small icons, obviously intended to be kept not in churches but in private and secular buildings or even to be carried about, demonstrates a strong wish, on the part of private individuals, to possess a portrait of the person represented. The owner of an icon would normally make it the object of personal, in some cases superstitious, devotion. When early in the fourth century the Empress Constantia, the sister of Constantine the Great, asked Eusebius to have copied for her a certain image which she believed

Geschichte der altchristlichen Literatur, N.F., III, 1899. This deals primarily with a special category of Christian images, images of Christ 'not made by human hands', but repeatedly discusses general questions connected with religious images. I have also profited greatly from André Grabar, *Martyrium, Recherches sur le culte des reliques et l'art chrétien antique*, 2 vols. and album, Paris, 1946; ii. 1–38 are especially pertinent in the present context.

to be that of Christ, it is obvious that her demand was motivated by a very keen desire to 'own' what she revered. Similarly, around A.D. 400 the author of the (Syriac) *Doctrina Addai* wrote that King Abgar of Edessa rejoiced at the image of Christ painted during his lifetime by Hannan 'with choice paints' and placed it 'with great honour in one of his palatial houses'. This again shows that there were some who desired to see where earlier generations had been satisfied to read and to hear. Every attack upon the images therefore became a burning issue because it threatened not only the art of the churches but also the personal piety of many an inhabitant of the Byzantine Empire. Finally, the icons differed from the narrative decoration of the churches in that they were actionless portraits showing the physical features of Christ or of the Saints. Thus, like the pagan cult statues, which they resemble in this respect, they were apt to evoke in the beholder feelings of awe and even to inspire him to acts of worship.[1]

The discussion of the icons has led from the question of the existence of a Christian art to the quite different problem of image worship. In the Gnostic sect of the Carpocratians, the 'crowning' of paintings and sculptures of Christ, as well as the observation of other pagan rites before His image, were practised as early as the second part of the second century. Into the Church the worship of images was introduced at a later date. Isolated instances of image worship may have occurred earlier, but about the middle of the fifth century it began to spread all over the Empire. This development is part and parcel of a more general phenomenon which J. B. Bury called the 'pagan transmutation of Christianity'. Incense, lights, flowers, the cult of martyrs, of saints, and of images now became part of the liturgy. It has been pointed out that as long as churches were merely houses of assembly, to be distinguished carefully from pagan temples where the deity was thought to reside, image worship could hardly emerge.

In the fourth century, however, the concept of the *res sacra* was accepted by Christians, and conditions were now favourable to the spread of image worship. This practice seems to have started with images which, in the thought of some of the faithful, had an extraordinarily close physical connexion with the divine

[1] See Note A, p. 232.

power. The Stylites of Syria, in the fifth and sixth centuries, were considered and considered themselves to be particularly close to God inasmuch as their pillars diminished the physical distance from Heaven. For that reason they were in a favoured position to obtain God's grace for others and to communicate it to them by all manner of physical contact, staves, 'sacred dust', or any other object that had been in physical touch with their bodies. The Stylites were in the habit of giving their visitors clay tablets with portraits of themselves impressed upon them. Since the clay of which the tablet was made was nothing but the 'sacred dust' or the dirt and sweat which the Saint had scraped from his body and which had been moulded into an image of the Saint, the power of God, as granted through the Saint, was soon considered to reside in the image on the clay tablet. The 'images not made by human hands' experienced a similar development. These were images of Christ or of a Saint, thought to have originated by physical contact (drying of the face on a towel, impression upon a cloth) with the person represented. As in the case of the Stylites' images, the miraculous power of the model was seen manifest in the image. Finally, the powers thought to reside in the relic of a Saint, or in a locality which had witnessed an event of sacred history, were believed to be active, also by way of physical contact, in the reliquary or other container in which the relic of the Saint or the dust from a sacred locality was kept. If the container was adorned with a representation of the Saint or the event, even the image on the container seemed to be endowed with miraculous power. Students of the Stylite movement, of the 'images not made by human hands', and of the cult of relics have come to the same conclusions: at the root of image worship lay the concept that material objects can be the seat of divine power and that this power can be secured through physical contact with a sacred object. The images thus became sacred objects of a secondary kind, by virtue of past contact with a sacred object of the primary type (dust, cloth, container, &c.). Only gradually was this materialistic concept spiritualized so that any sacred image, irrespective of past contacts, would be the bearer of supernatural power.[1]

[1] Carpocratians: texts in Dobschütz, *Christusbilder*, 98*. It is often argued that the Nestorian Church knows of no image-worship and that, since it seceded from the Orthodox Church after the First Council of Ephesus (431), the spread of image-

Within the Byzantine Empire the legitimacy of Christian religious art was questioned by individual theologians, but it was not until the eighth century that iconoclastic sentiment obtained the support of the Emperor and subsequently developed into an iconoclastic movement.

The precise origins of this movement have been the subject of much discussion. Some Byzantine sources connect it with iconoclastic measures taken in the Moslem realm. These accounts are based on a statement made at the Seventh Council of Nicaea by a monk John, the representative of the Eastern Patriarchates. This monk told of a Palestinian Jew Tessarakontapechys (Forty-Cubits-High) who promised the Khalif Yazid II (720–4) a reign of thirty years if he would destroy 'every representational painting, whether on tablets or in wall mosaics or on sacred vessels and altar coverings, and all such objects as are found in all Christian churches . . . and so also all representations of any kind whatever that adorn and embellish the market places of cities . . .'. John said further that the Khalif yielded to this advice and that his orders were carried out. When the Bishop Constantine of Nacoleia and his followers, so John concluded, heard of the acts of Yazid, they 'imitated' them. Some aspects of this story may belong to the realm of legend, but there can be no doubt that the Khalif Yazid II embarked on an iconoclastic programme; for no sooner had the monk John finished his story at the Council of

worship must have begun after that date (see Karl Holl, 'Der Anteil der Styliten am Aufkommen der Bilderverehrung', *Gesammelte Aufsätze zur Kirchengeschichte*, ii (Tübingen, 1928), 388–98, esp. 388 note). It seems, however, that the early Nestorian Church worshipped images as intensely as the Orthodox Church and abolished image-worship only in modern times; see Laurence E. Browne, *The Eclipse of Christianity in Asia from the Time of Mohammed till the Fourteenth Century* (Cambridge, 1933), 79 f., 'Pagan Transmutation of Christianity': J. B. Bury, *History of the Later Roman Empire* etc. i (London, 1923), 372. Adolf Harnack, *Lehrbuch der Dogmengeschichte*, ii (ed. 4, Tübingen, 1909), 467, speaks of a 'Christentum zweiter Ordnung', Holl, loc. cit. 397, of 'Ethnizismus', Elliger, *Zur Entstehung*, 272 and *passim*, of 'Ethnisierung'. Churches as sacred objects: Koch, *Die altchristliche Bilderfrage*, 93–99. On stylites and the worship of their images see Holl, loc. cit. On the relation of 'images not made by human hands' with image-worship see Dobschütz, *Christusbilder*, 277–9 and *passim*. Cf. p. 277: 'So hat man im Bilderstreit die Bilder als solche als Träger heiliger göttlicher Kräfte verteidigt . . . übernatürlichen Ursprung hat man für sie nicht in Anspruch genommen.' On the connexion between the cult of relics and images see Grabar, *Martyrium*, vol. ii, chap. viii, 'Des reliques aux icones', ii, pp. 343–57. Dobschütz holds that the cult of ordinary images pushed the cult of 'images not made by human hands' into the background, and Grabar thinks that it developed at the expense of the cult of relics (see also Grabar, i. 391–3). These views are perhaps somewhat exaggerated.

Nicaea than it was confirmed by an eyewitness. The historicity of Yazid's destruction of images, therefore, seems above suspicion, but it is very difficult to determine what influence, if any, it had on the Byzantine Empire.[1]

To clarify this question it is necessary to consider the archaeological evidence for Yazid's campaign against images. At various places in Palestine and Transjordania, both in churches and in synagogues, there have been found floor mosaics on which all representations of living beings were destroyed but where the rest of the ornamentation was left intact. An interesting instance is the mosaic decoration of the Byzantine church at Maïn (Transjordania) discovered in 1937. The floor of its nave (and that of an annex) was originally decorated with mosaics showing geometric designs, animals, fruits, Noah's Ark, hunting scenes, pictures of Palestinian church buildings, and a lion and an ox grazing peacefully together in the Messianic Age (cf. Isaiah xi. 7). These mosaics were later subjected to a selective process of destruction: all living creatures were eliminated, but not so successfully that traces of one kind or another did not remain. A mosaic inscription commemorates the repair of these mosaics in 719/20, indiction three.[2] The destruction must have occurred either in the

---

[1] On this problem, as on others, I have received valuable help from Professor Ernst Kitzinger, of Dumbarton Oaks. The literature is listed in the article by K. A. C. Creswell, 'The Lawfulness of Painting in Early Islam', *Ars Islamica*, xi/xii (1946), 159–66 (to which Dr. Richard Ettinghausen kindly called my attention). The narrative of John of Jerusalem: Mansi, xiii. 196–200 = *P.G.* cix. 517–20 (where it was reprinted from an edition by Combefis who in turn had based his text on one of the most interesting and complex of Greek manuscripts, the *Paris. gr.* 1115, see Melioranski, *Georgii Kiprianin*, &c., 84, and *Harvard Theological Review*, xlv (1952), 177 n. 2). Confirmation of destruction by eyewitness: Mansi, xiii. 200B: ὁ ἁγιώτατος ἐπίσκοπος Μεσσήνης (Latin translation: *Messanae*) εἶπε· κἀγὼ παιδίον ἤμην ἐν Συρίᾳ ὁπήνικα ὁ τῶν Σαρακηνῶν σύμβουλος τὰς εἰκόνας κατέστρεφεν. This passage was, so far as I can see, first adduced by K. A. C. Creswell. It seems decisive evidence for Yazid's iconoclastic campaign. On p. 164 Creswell wrongly emends (Mansi, xiii. 200B) the name of Οὐλιδος (= Walid), the Khalif who punished Yazid's Jewish adviser, into Hisham; Hisham (724–43) was the brother, Walid II (743–4) the son, of Yazid II, and it is not at all impossible that the Jew Tessarakontapechys (Forty-Cubits-High), if he really existed, was punished only during the reign of Walid II. On the campaign of revenge with which Walid II began his reign see Julius Wellhausen, *Das arabische Reich und sein Sturz* (Berlin, 1902), 221.

[2] R. de Vaux, 'Une Mosaïque byzantine à Ma'in (Transjordanie)', *Revue Biblique*, xlvii (1938), 227–58. On plate xi, no. 1, a mosaic from the northern annex, one sees clearly the tail and hind legs of an ox while the rest of the animal is replaced by a tree-trunk (see pp. 233 f. of the article). Similarly, on the mosaics in

reign of Yazid's predecessor Umar II (died 9 February 720) or in the first month of Yazid's reign.[1] The damage in other churches and in the synagogues cannot be dated as in Maïn, but it shows the same practice of selective destruction.[2]

This last feature is of importance for the problem under consideration. Whatever its basis may have been, it reveals a hostility to the representation of living creatures which was unknown to Byzantine Iconoclasts.[3] Byzantine Iconoclasm was both more radical and more moderate than the destruction in the Arab realm would suggest. The Byzantine Iconoclasts did not limit their destruction to representations of living creatures. Their attack was directed against any representation of religious subjects in churches or elsewhere. On the other hand, they did not object in the least to secular art whether it represented living beings or inanimate objects. In fact the iconoclastic period witnessed considerable artistic activity so far as secular objects were concerned. It is instructive to compare the mutilation of the mosaics at Maïn with what the *Life of St. Stephen the Younger* relates of Constantine V's treatment of the church of the Virgin at Blachernae at Constantinople. This church had been adorned before with murals (διάτοιχα) from the life of Christ: the Incarnation, various miracles, the Resurrection, the Pentecost. They were destroyed and replaced by mosaics (περιμουσοῦν) of trees, birds, animals, ivy, cranes, crows, peacocks, and other secular subjects (ἄλλα τινὰ ἐγκύκλια).[4] Consequently, even if at the beginning of the Iconoclastic Controversy the Byzantine Iconoclasts should have been influenced by events in the Khalifate, there can be little question that these 'imitators' were inspired by different motives and followed different lines from those of their masters.[5]

the nave several animals, as well as the dove sent out by Noah, are obliterated (p. 236). Of a hunting scene (p. 237 and plate xii), there are still traces of a hunter's javelin in the process of wounding a panther. The nave inscription (p. 239) is badly mutilated and the readings are far from certain, but there can be little doubt that it commemorates the repair of the mosaic floors by an unknown presbyter in the year 719/20, indiction three.

[1] See Note B, pp. 232 f.

[2] Other cases of selective destruction of floor mosaics: De Vaux, p. 258, n. 1; J.-B. Frey, 'La Question des images chez les Juifs à la lumière des récentes découvertes', *Biblica*, xv (1934), 265–300, esp. 298 f. Selective mutilation of paintings and sculptures at the Monastery of Apa Jeremias at Saqqara: J. E. Quibell, *Excavations at Saqqara (1908–9, 1909–10)* IV (Cairo, 1912), p. iv.

[3] See Note C, pp. 233 f.   [4] See Note C*, p. 234.   [5] See Note D, pp. 234 f.

Leo III may have had his personal reasons for embracing Iconoclasm. He was almost certainly a native of Syrian Germanicea or Mar'ash, on the border of Syria and Asia Minor. In this city there was a large Moslem population, and discussion with Infidels may well have convinced Leo that image-worship was difficult to justify. Yet there is no reason to believe that such considerations applied to any of the other Iconoclasts, except perhaps to Leo's *aide* Beser, who had been in Arab captivity before the days of Byzantine Iconoclasm. The outbreak of Iconoclasm at Byzantium must be considered a new and most powerful eruption of ancient opposition to images within the Church rather than as an 'imitation' of foreign attitudes.[1]

The correspondence of the Patriarch Germanos I of Constantinople, who was forced to resign in 730 because of his staunch defence of the images, makes it clear that the movement began with the agitation of two bishops from Asia Minor, Constantine of Nacoleia and Thomas of Claudiopolis. They found a most important ally in the Emperor. Yet even before Leo III intervened for the first time, in 726, iconoclastic propaganda had succeeded in stirring up confusion in various cities and among the masses of the population. Then from 726 on, the Emperor began to talk about the issue, perhaps even to preach against the 'idols', in other words, to appeal to the laity over the heads of the clergy—a policy that his son Constantine V was to inherit from him. With one or two possible exceptions it does not seem that any images were destroyed before 730, but in that year, on 17 January, the Emperor held a *silention* and issued an edict ordering 'the destruction of the images of the Saints'.[2]

Information on the implementation of the edict of 730 and on the persecution of image-worshippers under Leo III is meagre.

---

[1] See Note E, p. 235.

[2] On the outbreak of Iconoclasm see the detailed study of George Ostrogorsky, 'Les Débuts de la querelle des images', *Mélanges Charles Diehl*, i (Paris, 1930), 235–55. The author examines carefully the chronology of the problem and emphasizes the importance of Germanos' letters. On the results of iconoclastic propaganda see the letter to Thomas of Claudiopolis, *P.G.* xcviii. 184c: νῦν δὲ πόλεις ὅλαι καὶ τὰ πλήθη τῶν λαῶν οὐκ ἐν ὀλίγῳ περὶ τούτου θορύβῳ τυγχάνοντες. On the Emperor's talks (sermons?) cf. Nicephorus, *Breviarium*, p. 57, 26 (de Boor); *Vita Stephani*, *P.G.* c. 1084B; Theophanes, p. 404, 3–4 (de Boor); Louis Bréhier, 'Sur un texte relatif au début de la querelle iconoclaste', *Échos d'Orient*, xxxvii (1938), 17–22. On the edict of 730 cf. Nicephorus, p. 58, 19 sqq.; Theophanes, p. 408:31. See Ai. Christophilopulu, 'Σιλέντιον', *B.Z.* xliv (1951), 79–85.

Theophanes mentions specifically that Leo III combined Iconoclasm with a disbelief in the intercession of the Virgin and of the
Saints and with a hatred of martyrs' relics. The Patriarch Germanos of Constantinople (died 733) speaks of the monks as
special targets of the Iconoclasts who ejected them from their
monasteries and mutilated their bodies. The *Breviarium* of Nicephorus states that 'from that time [i.e. from 730] on, many of the
pious who did not approve of the edict suffered very many
penalties and tortures'. The seriousness and determination of the
Emperor can perhaps be gauged most clearly from the reactions
which his measure produced inside and outside the Empire. Even
before the edict of 730 an attempt on the part of certain men
connected with the court (βασιλικοὶ ἄνθρωποι) to destroy an
especially popular icon had led to their murder by an enraged mob.
More serious had been the revolt of the Helladic theme (Greece
and the Cyclades) which though unsuccessful had resulted in a
naval battle between the rebels and the loyal part of the fleet somewhere near the capital in April 726. But historically the most
ominous consequence of the new doctrine was that it initiated
a deterioration of Byzantine relations with the Papacy, which in
the next generation was to result in the alliance of the Papacy
with the Frankish rulers and the secession of Italy from the
Byzantine Empire.[1]

Iconoclasm reached its highest point under Leo's successor
Constantine V (741–75). To his contemporaries, as well as to
later generations, Constantine V seemed blessed beyond ordinary
mortals: he inherited the throne from his father, was able to put

[1] On Leo's disbelief in the Saints and his hatred of martyrs' relics see Theophanes, 406, 22 ff. On the persecution of Iconophiles under Leo III see Germanos,
De Haeresibus et Synodis, 42, *P.G.* xcviii. 80B; Nicephorus, *Breviarium*, 58, 25 (de
Boor); Theophanes, 409, 18 (de Boor). The scantiness of the information for this
period is especially marked if it is compared to the wealth of materials for the
period from Constantine V on. It should be noted, however, that even for the later
period, only one major Greek source dates from the eighth century (the *Breviarium*
of Nicephorus, on which see below, p. 156 ff.), and all the other Greek sources, especially the Saints' lives, from the ninth century (the *Life of St. Romanos the Younger*
was originally written in Arabic, see below, p. 16f.). It seems clear that the lack of
information for the reign of Leo III is connected with what Karl Krumbacher,
Geschichte, pp. 12 f., once called the 'ungeheure Lücke' of the seventh and eighth
centuries. On the incident of the icon above the Chalke Gate see Theophanes,
405, 5 (de Boor). The later embellishment of this story (*AA.SS. Augusti*, ii. 428–
48) was written in A.D. 870 at the earliest. Revolt of Helladic theme: Theophanes
405, 14 (de Boor).

down the dangerous revolt of his brother-in-law Artavasdos early in his reign, ruled for more than thirty years, won resounding victories over Arabs and Bulgarians, and at his death left the dynasty firmly established on the Byzantine throne. In view of such prosperity, it is not surprising that Constantine V became a hero of legend and apocalypse. Moreover, Constantine's great successes were an embarrassment to the iconophile party for many generations to come, and his subjects wondered whether a ruler so obviously favoured by God could really be the monstrous heretic whom the image-worshippers made him out to be.[1]

The Emperor Constantine V composed several *opuscula* on the image problem which he himself read to assemblies of the clergy. In addition, in 752/3, he arranged *silentia* in several places during which he explained, or had his sympathizers explain, his theological views. In other words like his father before him, Constantine was appealing to his subjects over the heads of the hierarchy.[2]

The record of one of these propaganda meetings is preserved in the *Admonition of the Old Man Concerning the Holy Images*. In the second part of this work, which dates from between 750 and 754, the Emperor is said to 'have sent out heralds of his wickedness everywhere'. One of these, Cosmas, probably bishop of Germanicea, publicly interrogated the hero of the story, Georgios, who was an iconophile stalwart and in all probability a Cypriot monk. In the minutes of this dialogue Georgios accused his iconoclastic opponent of impiety. For him the images were an institution of Christ Himself, and the claim that the Church was worshipping idols therefore implied that Jesus Christ established idols. The argument led to an impasse, although Cosmas later on in the dialogue answered Georgios' query by pointing out that the new 'idols' were not established by Jesus but were due to a later paganization of the Church. Cosmas next referred to the Old Testament prohibitions of the image-worship. As in the treatises against the Jews, this gave rise to the usual discussion as to the validity of the Law in the Church, and Georgios took the position that the Second Commandment and similar texts were

---

[1] On Constantine V as epic hero see N. Adontz, 'Les Légendes de Maurice et de Constantin V, &c.', *Annuaire de l'Institut de Philologie et d'Histoire Orientales*, ii (1934), 1–12, esp. 9–12. Add the remarkable scene described by Theophanes, 501, 3 ff. (de Boor). Constantine V in apocalyptic literature: see Note D, pp. 234 f.

[2] Above, p. 9. *Silentia:* Theophanes, 427, 19. See Ai. Christophilopulu, '*Σιλέντιον*', *B.Z.* xliv (1951), 79–85.

superseded by the Incarnation.[1] Finally, both parties attempted to support their views by scriptural and patristic evidence. It is perhaps worth noting that some of both Georgios' and Cosmas' evidence was very questionable indeed. It is striking that in the *Admonition* there is no trace of Constantine's writings. Cosmas does not avail himself of the iconoclastic *florilegium* which Constantine had prepared and which would have supplied Cosmas with much better patristic authority than he had; nor did he use the argument from Christ's divine and human natures, which Constantine handled with so much dexterity. The two parties argued very much as Christian and Jew had argued for a long time in the anti-Jewish literature.[2]

In 754 the Emperor assembled a Church Council which was to pronounce on the icons. The Iconoclastic Council of 754, which called itself the Seventh Ecumenical, held a number of meetings in the imperial palace of Hiereia, which lay beyond the Straits south of Chalcedon, and its formal and concluding meeting, probably in the presence of the Emperor Constantine V and of his family, in the church of the Virgin Mary in the quarter of Blachernae at Constantinople. It was attended by 338 bishops, a fact which implies that Leo III and Constantine V had succeeded in appointing their partisans to practically all the bishoprics of the Empire. Of the deliberations of the Council we know only the formal *Definition* or *Horos*. By a stroke of dramatic cruelty

[1] Below, pp. 33 ff.

[2] Constantine's *florilegium*: below, p. . *Νουθεσία*: ed. B. M. Melioranski, *Georgii Kiprianin i Ioann Ierusalimlianin*, Zapiski Istoriko-Filologicheskago Fakulteta Imp. S. Peterburskago Universiteta lix (1901), pp. v–xxxix (with elaborate historical commentary). Important review by Ed. Kurtz, *B.Z.* xi (1902), 538–43. The author was a disciple, called Theosebes. He was arrested together with Georgios and later fled to Syria (p. xxxix). Parts II and III of the *Admonition* were written between 750 and 754, the first part after 766 and probably between 770 and 775 (pp. 33 ff.). On the validity of the Second Commandment Georgios says, p. xii: πάντα ὅσα ἐλάλησεν Μωσῆς περὶ τῆς ἐνσάρκου οἰκονομίας ἔχομεν αὐτὰ χειραγωγούμενοι δι' αὐτῶν εἰς τὴν ἡμῶν σωτηρίαν· ὅσα δὲ διετάξατο τὸν λαὸν τοῦ Ἰσραὴλ καὶ ἅπερ παρέδωκεν ἤδη φυλάττειν, αὐτὰ χρείαν οὐκ ἔχομεν. Cosmas on paganization of Church: p. xix. Georgios refers not only to the usual stories about miraculous images of Christ, such as the legend of Abgar of Edessa (pp. xxi f.), but also to an unknown Petrine fragment where the Apostle Peter is said to have 'illustrated' his acount of the Transfiguration on a wax tablet. It probably comes from the *Vita Pancratii*, fragments of which are frequently quoted in the course of the Controversy. Cosmas refers to texts of Epiphanius (which Georgios declares to be a Novationist forgery, see below, p. 177 n. 1), to (the Arian) Georgius of Alexandria, and to (the Monophysite) Severus of Antioch.

the most prominent among the repentant Iconoclasts, Gregory bishop of Neocaesarea, who had himself attended the Council of Hiereia, was asked to read it sentence by sentence more than thirty years later at the Seventh Ecumenical Council of Nicaea in 787—to have it refuted by a treatise composed probably by the Patriarch Tarasius himself. About the *Horos* of 754 it must suffice to say that in general it incorporated the iconoclastic ideas of the Emperor who had assembled it.[1]

After having thus received the sanction of a Church Council for his theological doctrines, the Emperor proceeded to implement its decision. He required the army to take an oath that they would not worship images, hold communion with the monks, or even greet them.[2] His persecution and destruction of religious art soon was coupled with a persecution of its most energetic defenders, the monks, so much so that a modern writer speaks of Constantine's 'monachomachism'. Constantine referred to the monks publicly as the 'Unmentionables' (ἀμνημόνευτοι) or as 'the Lustful' (λάγνοι), to the nuns with a similar epithet (μάχλαι), and to monasteries in general as 'the order of darkness' (σκοτίας δόγμα). The *Admonition of the Old Man concerning the Holy Images*, which was mentioned above, contains in its first part a prophecy *ex eventu* describing the persecution under Constantine V in general terms:

---

[1] On the iconoclastic Council of 754 see primarily Nicephorus, *Breviarium*, 65 f., and Theophanes, 427 f. On the imperial palace of Hiereia: R. Janin, *Constantinople byzantine* (Paris, 1950), 147–9. On the church of the Virgin: Alfons M. Schneider, 'Die Blachernen', *Oriens*, iv (1951), 102–5. *Definition (Horos)* of 754 edited among the *Acts* of the Seventh Council of Nicaea (787), where it was read and refuted: Mansi, xiii. 205–364. Ostrogorsky, *Studien*, 16–29, has shown that the Council based its *Definition* on the writings of Constantine V but purged his formulations of elements that might be considered heretical or incautious from the christological point of view.

[2] Oath required by Constantine V: *Adversus Constantinum Caballinum* (*P.G.* xcv. 337C); *Vita Stephani Iunioris* (*P.G.* c. 1112A) (oath imposed on ἅπαντα . . . τὸν ὑπ' αὐτοῦ λαόν); Nicephorus, *Breviarium*, 73 (de Boor) (oath imposed on all subjects) and *Refutatio et Eversio*, fol. 195a (B) (oath imposed upon army); Theophanes, 437 (oath imposed on all subjects). The *Vita Stephani* claims that the oath included a prohibition of holding communion with the monks or even greeting them, and this is supported by Nicephorus' *Refutatio et Eversio*, fol. 195ʳ (B), παρακελευόμενος . . . τοὺς δ'οὖν τοῦ μονήρους βίου ὡς ἄγος τι ὁρᾶν καὶ μηδ' ὁπωσοῦν πελάζειν ἢ προσομιλεῖν τὰ εἰς εἰρήνην παντάπασιν αὐτοῖς. See Dölger, *Regesten*, no. 324. 'Unmentionables' and other epithets: *Νουθεσία*, ed. Melioranski, p. vi; *Vita Stephani Iunioris*, *P.G.* c. 1112A; *Vita S. Romani martyris recentioris*, ed. P. Peeters, *Analecta Bollandiana*, xxx (1911), 417.

Antichrists and godhaters will be found (how could it be otherwise?) who will lay hands upon the same assembly [the monks] and will inflict upon it dishonour, threats, and finally most bitter death, the cutting of limbs, the gouging out of the eyes, robberies and dispersions; and some are drowned in the sea, others are placed upon pillories, others are made to perish from hunger, others are dragged by the mobs, mocked, maltreated, criticized as prostitutes and haters of Christ; others again are ordered to mate with women. Why do I say so much? The Enemy employs all his power to eradicate and ruin the apostolic gathering assembled by God [the monks].

Another document is evidence for the nascent animosity between the persecuted monks and the secular clergy. While most of the latter made their peace with the iconoclastic government, the monks did not give in, largely because it was in the monasteries that the most famous icons and their shrines were located. How they felt about the secular hierarchy can perhaps be seen best from a passage which occurs in the *Adversus Constantinum Caballinum*, an anonymous treatise written between 765 and 787:

But the bishops of this generation care for nothing but horses and cattle and herds and field and hoards of gold. [They care] at what price they will distribute the wine, how they will weigh the oil, how they will do business with wool and silk, and they consider nothing carefully except the stamp on the coin and its weight. And daily they covet the Sybaritic tables and fragrant wine and great fish, but they neglect their flock and they care for their bodies but neglect their soul. In truth, as it is said, the shepherds of this generation have become 'wolves'. And if they notice that some of their flock have committed some trifling sin they readily rise up against [them] and issue one penalty after the other. And although they do not consider the strictness (ἀκρίβεια) of their dignity of shepherd, they examine daily their flock, not as shepherds, but as hirelings.[1]

---

[1] *Adversus Constantinum Caballinum*, P.G. xcv. 329D. The explanation given here for the resistance of the monks is due to a suggestion made to me by Professor George La Piana. It seems that the passage alludes to the affair of the Simoniac bishops (below, pp. 81 f.). At any rate we find the slogans of the Sabbas group in this passage (ἀκρίβεια, μισθωτοί), which makes me think that the author probably belonged to that group. I. Andreev, 'Sv. Tarasii, Patriarkh Konstantinopol'skii', *Bogoslovskii Vestnik*, June 1899, 143–80, esp. pp. 174 f., explains the failure of the secular clergy to resist Iconoclasm by the lack of a developed theory of religious images prior to the Seventh Council: under the Iconoclastic emperors the Iconophiles were prevented from circulating even the writings of John of Damascus and they were thus defenceless in face of the imperial propaganda. This, however, is hardly the whole story, and the pressure of the government on the bishops must account for a large part of their weakness.

The persecution was general, and although the monks were Constantine V's special target, iconophile bishops and laymen likewise often had to flee, lost their property, or were subjected even to physical injury. One of the most prominent martyrs under Constantine V was St. Stephen the Younger. The *Vita* of this Saint, written by Stephen the Deacon in 806, tells how his mother prayed before the famous icon of the Virgin in the church of the Virgin at Blachernae (this icon was later destroyed by Constantine); how under Leo III many of the iconophiles at Constantinople left the capital and emigrated 'to the orthodox village-towns'; how his parents brought the sixteen-year-old Stephen to the abbot of the monastery on Mt. Auxentius in Bithynia; how Stephen, who at the age of thirty-one became abbot of his monastery, suffered from the persecutions under Leo III and especially under Constantine V; how after prolonged efforts on the part of Constantine V to win Stephen over to Iconoclasm Stephen was finally arrested and put in the public jail at Constantinople, which he found filled with 342 monks from all parts of the Empire, all mutilated in various cruel ways by their persecutors; how he was finally slain at the express order of the Emperor and his body mutilated by the city mob. All this is so well told in the *Vita* and has so often and so skilfully been retold by modern writers that it is permissible to be brief on this subject. Another lively account of the persecution may be found in the *Acta SS. Davidis, Symeonis et Georgii Mitylenae in Insula Lesbo*. There the oldest of the saintly brothers, David, is described as descending in 761/2 from his hermitage on Mt. Ida. Somewhere in the fields he meets the bishop of the neighbouring see of Galgala (?) who is hiding from his iconoclastic persecutors, and who ordains David a presbyter.[1]

[1] *Vita S. Stephani Iunioris, P.G.* c. 1067–1186; on it see Charles Diehl, 'Une Vie de saint à l'époque des empereurs iconoclastes', *Comptes Rendus de l'Académie des Inscriptions*, 1915. On its sources, J. Gill, 'The Life of Stephen the Younger by Stephen the Deacon. Debts and Loans', *Orientalia Christiana Periodica*, vi (1940), 114–39. The bishop of Galgala hiding before the persecutors: 'Acta graeca SS. Davidis, Symeonis et Georgii Mitylenae in insula Lesbo', *Analecta Bollandiana*, xviii (1899), 216 f. In *AA.SS. Octobris*, tomus viii (Brussels, 1853; Paris and Rome, 1866), 127, will be found a very useful list of the seven principal martyrs of the persecution under Constantine V, but the persecution was actually much more general than such a list would make one suppose. Gabriel Millet, '*ΠΑΡΑΣΤΑΣΕΙΣ ΣΥΝΤΟΜΟΙ ΧΡΟΝΙ-ΚΑΙ*. Essai sur la date', *Bulletin de Correspondance Hellénique*, lxx (1946), 393–402, esp. 396–8, has recently called attention to another martyr, the monk Anastasius. I. Andreev, 'Sv. Tarasii, Patriarkh Konstantinopol'skii', *Bogoslovskii Vestnik*, June

An earlier and perhaps even more interesting source for the persecutions is the *Life of St. Romanos*; it is preserved only in Georgian but was originally written in Arabic, certainly before 787, and thus is, with the exception of the *Admonition*, of the *Adversus Constantinum Caballinum*, and possibly of Nicephorus' *Breviarium*, the oldest source for the Iconoclastic Controversy. The background of this *Life* is formed by the border warfare between the Byzantine Empire and the Arabs under Constantine V and one of the early Abbassid khalifs, Abu Jafar, better known under his surname Al Mansur (754–75). The hero of the *Life* was a native of Galatia who in 771 was captured by an Arab force while on a journey on behalf of his monastery and jailed in the recently (764) founded city of Baghdad. It is interesting to see how the controversy about the images and the persecution of monasticism made themselves felt far beyond the confines of the Empire and reached even the dungeons of Baghdad. There St. Romanus was soon joined by two monks, John and Symeon, who had both been deacons at Constantinople and become monks near Seleucia Sidera in Phrygia. In Phrygia the persecution raged perhaps even more violently than elsewhere, because this area was governed by one of Constantine's most energetic and brutal lieutenants, Michael Lachanodracon. It is known from the *Vita S. Stephani* that on one occasion St. Stephen advised the monks of Mt. Auxentius to flee to one of three regions not affected by the heresy: to the north shore of the Black Sea and the Caucasus area, to Italy south of Rome, or to the Mediterranean shores from Lycia to Palestine including the island of Cyprus. To be safe from the persecution the iconophile monks then had to escape to lands no longer effectively controlled by the Empire. The monks John and Symeon, since they were residents of Phrygia, not unnaturally fled eastward to Arab territory. They came to an Arab fortress which they were permitted to enter after the garrison had taken a solemn oath that they would remain unharmed. This was undoubtedly the usual way of escape for Byzantine Iconophiles, and under normal conditions the fugitives would have been granted the freedom of practising their religion in the Arab

1899, 167, 170, is inclined to restrict the extent of the persecution. According to him, only the 'mixed' monasteries at Constantinople were closed, and there were only six martyrs and confessors under Constantine V. To the present writer this thesis seems to contradict the sources quoted in the text which speak of a general per-
.secution of the monks.

dominions. In the case of John and Symeon, however, things did not follow the normal course. The garrison wanted to ingratiate itself with the Khalif. They jailed John and Symeon and later sent them together with another captive, a high imperial official called Georgius, to Al Mansur at Baghdad pretending that they were regular captives of the Arab-Byzantine border warfare. In Baghdad they shared the jail with St. Romanos and many other Christians and Moslems. Now it happened that Georgius was a fanatical Iconoclast, and from this time onward, throughout the nine long years of St. Romanos' stay in various Arab prisons, continuous arguments and clashes took place in jail between St. Romanos, John, and Symeon on the one hand, and Georgius and his iconoclastic majority on the other. On one occasion Georgius even incited his followers to murder their iconophile fellow-prisoners and fellow-Christians, and the plot would have succeeded if at the last moment the Iconophiles had not been aided by some Moslem prisoners who in all probability were delighted to see the routine of prison life enlivened by a free-for-all. The *Life of St. Romanos* thus illustrates the normal course of a flight from the Byzantine to the Arab dominions, as well as the fierceness of the struggle between Iconoclasts and Iconophiles which persisted with such violence even inside an Arabian prison.[1]

In A.D. 775 Constantine V Copronymus died and was succeeded by his son, Leo IV the Khazar (775–80). Constantine had thought that Iconoclasm could be victorious only if the monks were defeated. Leo IV had been brought up as an Iconoclast and even the influence of his iconophile wife, Irene the Athenian, apparently did not alter his convictions on the problem of images. However, he abandoned the anti-monastic policy of his father. Not only did he release all the prisoners and exiles of the latter's rule, but he even appointed metropolitan bishops from among the abbots whom his father had persecuted. This latter measure,

---

[1] Life of St. Romanus, ed. P. Peeters, 'S. Romain le néomartyr (†1 mai 780) d'après un document géorgien', *Analecta Bollandiana*, xxx (1911), 393–427 (with Latin translation). This fascinating text has been unduly neglected by students of the Iconoclastic Controversy. No Greek original: p. 405. Date: 780–7, see p. 403. Michael Lachanodracon: Theophanes, 445. Areas of refuge: *Vita Stephani, P.G.* c. 1117c. Arrest of John and Symeon, *Life of St. Romanos*, 414: *Advenerunt ad arcem quandam Saracenorum acceptoque ab iis iure iurando inter eos ingressi sunt. Tum qui ius iurandum dederant, fidem eorum fallentes, comprehenderunt eos et in carcerem coniecerunt, eo consilio ut in Syriam mitterent.* The text (ibid.) calls Georgios principem quendam ex aula regia. The plot in prison: pp. 418 f.

combined with his iconoclastic persecutions, makes clear his attitude towards monasticism: he used sugar where the whip had failed. The failure was admitted, but the policy itself was not dropped.[1]

Leo probably was aware of the dangers involved in such a sudden change of tactics. He died in 780 and was succeeded by his son Constantine, who was still a minor and for whom his mother Irene was regent. Irene was anxious to restore image-worship and to make peace with the image-worshippers. It was at this time that the Iconoclasts made their great mistake. Irene had sent out the summons for an Ecumenical Council which was to assemble on 1 August 786. Shortly before that date

the majority of bishops wallowing about in the heresy of the accusers of the Christians (οἱ δὲ πλείους τῶν ἐπισκόπων τῇ αἱρέσει τῶν χριστιανο-κατηγόρων ἐγκαλινδούμενοι) plotted with laymen, many in number, to the effect that the holding of a council should not be tolerated, but that they should agree to the overthrow and violence against the venerable icons; and they stirred up not a few phratries and whispering campaigns (ψιθυρισμοί) against the Patriarch Tarasius so that they even formed illegal meetings (παρασυναγωγαί).

Tarasius pointed out to them that this was uncanonical and succeeded in intimidating them. On the day before the Council was scheduled to meet for the first time in the church of the Holy Apostles, the troops garrisoned at Constantinople assembled in the atrium of the church and made it clear that they would not tolerate it. Tarasius drew up a report on these disturbances for the information of the Emperors, but they saw no reason to cancel the meeting. The next morning the Council assembled under the presidency of Tarasius, in the presence of Emperor and Empress. Proceedings had scarcely started when the soldiers began to make noise outside. According to the *Acta* they were instigated (ἐξ ὑποβολῆς) by the iconoclastic bishops in the assembly, but according to Theophanes the troop was stirred up by its own commanders and the memory of their great Emperor Constantine V.

---

[1] Methodius, *Vita Theophanis*, ed. B. Latyshev, *Zapiski Rossiiskoi Akademii Nauk*, VIIIᵉ série, xiii. 4 (Petrograd, 1918), 7, calls Leo IV ὁ χλιαρώτατος καὶ εἰς ὁπότερον, ἀγαθόν τέ φημι καὶ χεῖρον, ἀνέκβατος and p. 10 ὁ ἀλωπεκόφρων. Agapius of Menbidj, *Universal History*, *P.O.* viii. 547: 'Il mit en liberté tous ceux qui se trouvaient dans la prison de son père et rappela tous ceux qu'il avait exilés.' Abbots appointed to bishoprics: Theophanes, 449.

The Empress decided to postpone the meeting and the bishops dispersed. Some of the bishops, however, when leaving the church sided with the soldiery and proclaimed the Council of Hiereia as the 'Seventh Council'. Meanwhile the soldiers had become hungry and withdrew.[1] An almost incredible intrigue was now set on foot. A rumour was spread that the Arabs were making a raid. Under this pretext the garrison of Constantinople was taken to Malagina, the first standing camp (ἄπληκτον) on the main military road to Cilicia. In the meantime the capital was occupied by troops who had been stationed in Thrace. An order was issued to the soldiers at Malagina to hand over their arms. The chronicler expresses surprise that they obeyed without even attempting resistance: 'they became foolish by (the act of) God and gave them (the arms).' The families of the soldiers were exiled from the city and everybody was told to return to his birthplace. The Empress, thereupon, built up a new force with officers obedient to her.[2]

While there were good reasons for the outbreak of Iconoclasm in the beginning of the eighth century the historian is at a loss to

---

[1] Chief sources: (1) Συγγραφὴ σύντομος δηλωτικὴ τῶν πραχθέντων πρὸ τῆς συνόδου, Mansi, xii. 990 f.; (2) Theophanes, 461 f. For an interpretation of the events see F. I. Uspenski, 'Voennoe ustroistvo vizantiiskoi imperii', *Izvestiia Russkago Arkheologicheskago Instituta v Konstantinopolie*, vi (1900), 157 ff. The wording of the Συγγραφή does not indicate whether the majority of *all* the bishops, or only the majority of the iconoclastic bishops, was opposed to the holding of a council. Yet a remark of Tarasius at the Council of Nicaea makes it clear that the latter assumption is correct. Mansi, xii. 999E: the mob were ἔχοντες εἰς συμμαχίαν καί τινας εὐαριθμήτους ἐπισκόπους ὧν τὰ ὀνόματα ἑκὼν ὑπερβήσομαι ὡς παρὰ πάντων γινωσκόμενα. On the church of the Holy Apostles see A. Heisenberg, *Grabeskirche und Apostelkirche*, &c. (Leipzig, 1908), vol. ii; on the meaning of λουτήρ, pp. 136 f.

[2] Rumour of Arab raid: Theophanes, 462. There was indeed an Arab raid that year, see Tabari, A.H. 170, translated *English Historical Review*, xv (1900), 740. On Malagina: W. M. Ramsay, *The Historical Geography of Asia Minor* (London, 1890), 199–206. Irene and her *chef de cabinet* Stauracius from the very first had been anxious to get rid of the old guard of Constantine V Copronymus. A great many officers had been removed in 780 for having participated in the plot of the ex-Caesar Nicephorus, among them the general of the Armeniac theme (Theophanes, 454). One year later the general of Sicily, Elpidius, fell into disgrace and took refuge with the Arabs (ibid. 455). In the same year (781–2) the Armenian prince Tatzates, who had been in Byzantine service since 759/60 and was now general of the Bucellarian theme, went over to the Arabs (ibid. 456; cf. Ghevond, *Histoire des guerres et des conquêtes des Arabes en Arménie*, French translation by Chahnazarian (Paris, 1856), 153. It may be supposed that the events of 786 were but the last step in this gradual purge. The *Vita Nicetae Mediciensis* by Theosterictus mentions the event as follows: (Irene) τοὺς ταύτῃ [i.e. τῇ ἀληθείᾳ] ἀντιλέγοντας, λύσασα τὰς τούτων ζώνας, ἐξέωσε τῆς πόλεως.

account for its collapse in 786. The new outbreak of 815 proved that the forces of Iconoclasm were not exhausted, yet the army allowed itself to be disbanded and disarmed, its leaders made no subsequent attempt to reorganize it, and the iconoclastic bishops made no firm stand for their beliefs. It would seem that in the balance of forces in the critical years from 780 to 787 many accidents and many human and personal factors played a decisive role. Otherwise it could not be explained why Iconoclasm which in 787 was in possession not only of the churches but also of the armed forces gave in so meekly. The scenes in the church of the Holy Apostles and later at Malagina mark some of the missed opportunities in history.

Only after the iconoclastic opposition had been deprived of its armed protectors could the Seventh Ecumenical Council begin its deliberations. Three hundred bishops and many abbots and monks participated. It held seven meetings at Nicaea, in the church of St. Sophia, extending from 23 September to 13 October 787, and a final ceremonial gathering in the presence of the Emperor Constantine VI and his mother Irene on 22 October, at the imperial palace of Magnaura. The Acts of this Ecumenical Council are preserved.[1] They are the official minutes of the deliberations of the Council, and as such they present the proceedings in the light in which the iconophile party wanted them to be viewed. In spite of their official character they make fascinating reading for anyone able to read between the lines.

The image question, for the sake of which the Seventh Ecumenical Council had been convoked, was discussed at its fourth, fifth, sixth, and seventh sessions after preliminaries and procedural items had been disposed of. At the sixth meeting there was read a long and elaborate document entitled: 'Refutation of the Definition stitched up and lyingly so named by the assembled rabble of the accusers of the Christians.' This was a work divided into six tomes and containing a refutation of the *Definition* of the Iconoclastic Council of Hiereia (754), the text of which is quoted almost in its entirety. It was in all probability written by the

---

[1] Acts of the Seventh Ecumenical Council: Mansi, xii and xiii. The Acts of this most important Council cry out for a critical edition. Number of participants: Mansi, xiii. 455B. The dates of each meeting are recorded there. On the palace of Magnaura which was a part of the Great Palace but lay to the south-west of the palace proper see R. Janin, 'Constantinople byzantine', *Archives de l'Orient chrétien*, iv (1950), 117–19.

Patriarch Tarasius and is important as the fullest statement of iconophile views made between the works of John of Damascus and those of the Patriarch Nicephorus.[1] It was used by all later iconophile writers including Nicephorus.

The seventh meeting of the Seventh Ecumenical Council witnessed the reading of its own relatively brief *Definition* which repeated in dogmatic form the principal tenets of Tarasius' *Refutation* and was signed by all the members of the Council. The decisive part of this *Definition* reads as follows:

We define with all accuracy and care that the venerable and holy icons be set up like the form of the venerable and life-giving Cross, inasmuch as matter consisting of colors and pebbles and other matter is appropriate in the holy church of God, on sacred vessels and vestments, walls and panels, in houses and on the roads, as well as the image of our Lord and God and Saviour Jesus Christ, of our undefiled Lady the Holy Mother of God, of the angels worthy of honour, and of all the holy and pious men. For the more frequently they are seen by means of pictorial representation the more those who behold them are aroused to remember and desire the prototypes and to give them greeting and worship of honour—but not the true worship of our faith which befits only the divine nature—but to offer them both incense and candles, in the same way as to the form of the venerable and life-giving Cross and to the holy gospel books and to the other sacred objects, as was the custom even of the Ancients.[2]

The rule of Irene (780–802) and Constantine VI was characterized by an iconophile policy which benefited particularly the monks and the monasteries. The iconophile sources, therefore, outdo themselves in praising Irene and glossing over the various defeats, diplomatic and military, which the Byzantine Empire suffered during her reign. During this period it was on the whole the civil bureaucracy that ruled the Empire. Although in the army the officers were appointed by Irene and therefore were Iconophiles, the rank and file were in favour of Iconoclasm and

---

[1] Ἀνασκευὴ τοῦ καττυθέντος καὶ ψευδῶς ὀνομασθέντος ὅρου παρὰ τῆς ὀχλαγωγη-θείσης πληθύος τῶν χριστιανοκατηγόρων, Mansi, xiii. 205–364. Pope Hadrian I thought that its author was Tarasius, see K. Hampe, 'Hadrians I. Vertheidigung der zweiten nicaenischen Synode gegen die Angriffe Karls des Großen', *Neues Archiv für ältere deutsche Geschichtskunde*, xxi (1896), 113. Tarasius' authorship is further rendered probable by general considerations as well as by the contents of the treatise, see I. Andreev, 'Sv. Tarasii, Patriarkh Konstantinopol'skii', *Bogoslovskii Vestnik*, August 1899, 460–72.

[2] Mansi, xiii. 377D–E.

were biding their time. It is characteristic that when Constantine VI tried in 790 to make himself independent of the guardianship of his mother, he found much support in army circles. The Armeniac theme began, and other themes followed suit; they deposed the generals appointed by Irene and swore allegiance to Constantine. But as soon as there were indications that Constantine VI was again under the influence of his mother and her underlings, the Armeniac theme revolted again and the Emperor had to lead a punitive expedition against the rebels. They were defeated after their rebellion had lasted for more than a year. When Constantine VI tried to win over the Patriarch Tarasius to agree to his divorce, he put pressure behind his request by threatening to restore Iconoclasm. But by estranging the army circles Constantine had isolated himself. His mother deposed and blinded him (797). The echo of this inhuman crime was heard all over the world. From far-away Tours Alcuin wrote in 799 to Charlemagne: 'quam impie gubernator imperii illius depositus sit, non ab alienis, sed a propriis et concivibus, ubique fama narrante, crebrescit.' But the events which occurred in Rome a year later make it probable that Alcuin's remarks were not prompted by humanitarian considerations alone.[1]

Irene was overthrown in 802 by the former Minister of Finance Nicephorus. The principal source for the period, Theophanes, deals very harshly with the Emperor Nicephorus (802–11) and particularly his fiscal policy, but nowhere does Theophanes criticize the Emperor's attitude towards religious images. Nicephorus, then, must have respected the decisions of the Seventh Ecumenical Council, though he seems to have been somewhat lukewarm in its support.[2] When in 806 Nicephorus became Patriarch of Constantinople, religious images and their worship were restored, yet large and influential sections of the population looked back longingly to the great days of the Isaurian emperors and to their iconoclastic policies.

---

[1] See below, pp. 105 ff.

[2] Iconophile policy of Irene: Theophanes, 454, 457–9, *passim*. The most striking dithyramb on the Empress Irene will be found in Methodius' *Life of Theophanes*, xi f. (ed. V. V. Latyshev, *Zapiski Rossiiskoi Akademii Nauk*, VIIIe série, xiii. 4 (Petrograd, 1918), 13–15). It occupies almost two quarto pages and constitutes an extended pun on 'peace', the meaning of Irene's name. Diplomatic and military defeats and army revolts: Ostrogorsky, *Geschichte des Byzantinischen Staats*, 147. Constantine VI threatens return to Iconoclasm: *P.G.* xcix. 1852D.

II

RELIGIOUS IMAGES: THEORY AND COUNTER-THEORY

RELIGIOUS images had played an important role in Greco-Roman paganism as well as in the Christian Church. Their legitimacy was often attacked and often defended in literary works. Here the discussion will centre on three aspects of the religious image which were to be prominent in the ninth century and especially in the writings of the Patriarch Nicephorus. Of these the oldest was the notion of the image as symbol of the religious subjects represented on it. This 'symbolic' concept, originally used by pagans in defence of their cult statues, was later transferred to Christian images and in the hands of the Iconophiles played an important role throughout the Iconoclastic Controversy. According to another concept the true image revealed the essence of its model. This 'essential' function of the image loomed large on the iconoclastic side. Opponents of artistic images relied on it to prove that the artistic image was unsuited to reveal the essence of a sacred figure. Finally there was the connexion of the image of Jesus Christ with christological doctrine. This relation was emphasized by the opponents of religious images, who used it forcefully from the fourth century onward. In a different way it was also appealed to by Iconophiles including the Patriarch Nicephorus. In many authors these three aspects of the theory appear blended with one another, but to facilitate analysis it is advisable to consider them separately.

1. *The Symbolic Function of the Image*

The issue of a religious art arose late within the Christian Church, yet its peculiar difficulty and urgency derived from the fact that the Early Church, and Judaism before it, had taken a vigorous stand against pagan cult statues (ἀγάλματα) and their worship. In Antiquity literary discussions on pagan cult statues had occurred in several contexts: in philosophical treatises (Plutarch), in general attacks upon the pagan pantheon (Lucian, the Cynics), in the oratory of the Second Sophistic Movement (Dio Chrysostom), and in the polemical writings of Christians and Pagans.[1] In the last type of literature, which is particularly instructive, three groups of writings may be distinguished: (1) the Christian Apologists, chiefly those of the second century A.D.; (2) general pagan works directed against the Christians; (3) special pagan treatises concerned with the defence of cult statues and entitled περὶ ἀγαλμάτων.

The Christian Apologists of the second century were not satisfied with defending their own religion. Convinced that offence was the best defence[2] they made continuous attacks on the religion of their pagan persecutors, especially their worship of idols. Their writings show not only the Christian weapons of attack, but they sometimes also mention certain defensive arguments used by the pagans in order to refute them. Even the earliest writer of the group, Aristides, argues that God does not need outward manifestations, but that men need Him.[3] Egyptians, Chaldaeans, and Greeks have erected cult statues to their gods and deified mute and insensate idols.[4] Do they not know, Aristides asks, that these 'gods' of theirs are worked upon with the saw and the axe, are mutilated, burnt, shaped, and transformed into any shape whatever by the craftsman? If they are not even powerful enough to take care of their own salvation, how could they provide for men? Aristides records his opponents' defence:

But mistakenly their poets and philosophers, too, have claimed concerning them [the cult statues] that they are gods, *things like these which*

---

[1] For the theory of religious images in pagan antiquity see J. Geffcken, *Zwei griechische Apologeten* (Leipzig und Berlin, 1907), esp. pp. xx–xxiv; 'Der Bilderstreit des heidnischen Altertums', *Archiv für Religionswissenschaft*, xix (1916–19), 286–315; and *Der Ausgang des griechisch-römischen Heidentums* (Heidelberg, 1920) (see index, s.v. 'Götterbilder'); Ch. Clerc, *Les Théories relatives au culte des images chez les auteurs grecs du IIme siècle après J.-C.* (Paris, 1915). Valentin Müller's article 'Kultbild', *R.E.*, Suppl.-B. v. 472–511, is primarily archaeological, but see coll. 473–5.

[2] Julian, *Contra Christianos*, pp. 163 f., ed. Neumann, is aware (afraid?) of this Christian strategy: μέλλων δὲ ὑπὲρ τῶν παρ' αὐτοῖς [i.e. τοῖς Γαλιλαίοις] λεγομένων δογμάτων ἁπάντων ποιεῖσθαι τὸν λόγον ἐκεῖνο βούλομαι πρῶτον εἰπεῖν ὅτι χρὴ τοὺς ἐντυγχάνοντας, εἴπερ ἀντιλέγειν ἐθέλοιεν, ὥσπερ ἐν δικαστηρίῳ μηδὲν ἔξωθεν πολυπραγμονεῖν μηδέ, τὸ λεγόμενον, ἀντικατηγορεῖν, ἕως ἂν ὑπὲρ τῶν παρ' αὐτοῖς ἀπολογήσωνται.

[3] i. 4, p. 4: οὐ χρῄζει θυσίας καὶ σπονδῆς οὐδέ τινος πάντων τῶν φαινομέων, πάντες δὲ αὐτοῦ χρῄζουσιν. Unless stated otherwise, the early Christian Apologists will be cited from the edition of E. J. Goodspeed, *Die ältesten Apologeten* (Göttingen, 1914).

[4] xiii. 1, p. 16.

are made for the honor of God Almighty. And mistakenly they want them to resemble God, of whom nobody ever saw whom He resembles, and whom none can see.[1]

In spite of the difficulties of the text it seems clear that in the clause set in italics Aristides is alluding to a philosophical theory according to which the cult statues are not the gods but their images.[2]

Justin Martyr repeats Aristides' arguments against the 'soulless and dead' idols which according to him have not the shape of God but the form of evil demons. He hints vaguely at a counter-claim of his opponents that the shape of cult statues is an imitation in honour of the gods—obviously the same argument which occurs in Aristides.[3] It is Athenagoras' *Supplicatio pro Christianis* which is the most elaborate source for pagan and early Christian views on religious images. Christians, Athenagoras remarks, distinguish between Matter and God, thereby implying that the pagans confuse the two.[4] There follow accusations, criticisms, and stories about cult statues known from pagan authors: remarks about their being 'wood and stones', about artist and artifact, about world and Creator, and the recent invention of the art of portraiture (chs. xvi and xvii). So recent an invention are the idols that a craftsman can be named for each god. Athenagoras then draws up a well-known catalogue of famous cult statues with the names of the artists who produced them. All of them were made by man, all of them are younger than their makers, all of them needed men and the arts to come into existence: all are stone

---

[1] xiii. 3, p. 17. Goodspeed translates the Syriac original as follows: 'Sed etiam poetae et philosophi apud eos errantes de his introduxerunt haec esse deos quae in honorem dei omnipotentis fiant. Et errantes ea deo similia efficere conantur, qui nemo umquam vidit cui similis sit; et quem nemo videre potest.' The translation in the text is that by J. Rendel Harris, *Texts and Studies*, i. 1 (Cambridge, 1893), 46. Geffcken, *Zwei griechische Apologeten*, 19, translates: '. . . daß sie Götter sind, also solche Dinge, welche gemacht sind zur Ehre des allmächtigen Gottes.' Harris seems to render the complicated syntax of the Syriac clause more accurately.

[2] Geffcken, *Zwei Griech. Apol.* 77 f.

[3] Justin Martyr, *Apol.* ix. 1, pp. 31 f. (Goodspeed): ἄψυχα καὶ νεκρὰ ταῦτα γινώσκομεν καὶ θεοῦ μορφὴν μὴ ἔχοντα (οὐ γὰρ τοιαύτην ἡγούμεθα τὸν θεὸν ἔχειν τὴν μορφήν, ἥν φασί τινες εἰς τιμὴν μεμιμῆσθαι), ἀλλ' ἐκείνων τῶν φανέντων κακῶν δαιμόνων καὶ ὀνόματα καὶ σχήματα ἔχειν.

[4] iv. 1, p. 319: ἡμῖν δὲ διαιροῦσιν ἀπὸ τῆς ὕλης τὸν θεὸν καὶ δεικνύουσιν ἕτερον μέν τι εἶναι τὴν ὕλην ἄλλο δὲ τὸν θεὸν καὶ τὸ διὰ μέσου πολύ . . . μή τι ἀλόγως τὸ τῆς ἀθεότητος ἐπικαλοῦσιν ὄνομα; The implication becomes explicit xv. 1, p. 329 (Goodspeed): ἐπεὶ οἱ πολλοὶ διακρῖναι οὐ δυνάμενοι τί μὲν ὕλη τί δὲ θεὸς πόσον δὲ τὸ διὰ μέσου αὐτῶν.

and matter and superfluous art. Like Aristides, Athenagoras does not fail to mention the pagans' reply to these criticisms:

> But since it is affirmed by some, [he says], that although these are only likenesses, yet there exist gods in honour of whom they are made; and that the supplications and sacrifices presented to the likenesses are to be referred to the gods, and are in fact made to the gods; and that there is not any other way of coming to them, for "'tis hard for man to meet in presence visible a God' (*Iliad* XX. 131)....[1]

For Athenagoras the images are Matter (not God) formed by human hands. To this the pagans reply that the ἀγάλματα are mere images (i.e. of the gods) and that worship offered to them is 'referred' to the gods themselves. Thus at least as early as the second century A.D. enlightened paganism considers the cult statues as mere εἰκόνες of the gods, not as the gods themselves. It is this *symbolic* and anagogical interpretation of religious art which was to serve later as a defence for Christian images.

In another literary genre, that of the polemical writings of pagans against Christians, the same arguments and counter-arguments found in the Christian Apologists were used. In his *True Word*, written around A.D. 178, Celsus reported that the Christians criticize the pagan ἀγάλματα for being made by human hands.[2] Celsus replied that the Christians were not better, in fact worse, than the pagan philosopher Heraclitus of Ephesus who in Celsus' interpretation had rejected the cult offered to statues only as long as the worshipper did not realize the true nature of gods and heroes:

> Thus spoke Heraclitus, but they [the Christians] utterly disdain the statues. If they do so on the ground that stone or wood or bronze or gold which such or such an artist produced is not god, such wisdom is ridiculous; for who but an utter fool considers them gods rather than dedications and statues for the gods? If, however, the Christians

---

[1] xviii. 1, p. 332 (Goodspeed): ἐπεὶ τοίνυν φασί τινες εἰκόνας μὲν εἶναι ταύτας, θεοὺς δὲ ἐφ' οἷς αἱ εἰκόνες, καὶ τὰς προσόδους ἃς ταύταις [τούτοις the manuscript, em. Otto] προσίασιν καὶ τὰς θυσίας ἐπ' ἐκείνους ἀναφέρεσθαι καὶ εἰς ἐκείνους γίνεσθαι μὴ εἶναί τε ἕτερον τρόπον τοῖς θεοῖς ἢ τοῦτον προσελθεῖν (χαλεποὶ δὲ θεοὶ φαίνεσθαι ἐναργεῖς) . . .. Translation from *Ante-Nicene Fathers*, ii. 137. I suggest keeping the τούτοις of the *codex unicus* and amending ταῦτα for ταύτας. This emendation is even gentler than that of Otto and refers to the ταῦτα at the end of chapter xvii: γῆ ταῦτα καὶ λίθοι καὶ ὕλη καὶ περίεργος τέχνη.

[2] Celsi Ἀληθής Λόγος, ed. O. Glöckner, Kleine Texte für Vorlesungen und Übungen 151 (Bonn, 1924), fr. 5, p. 1.

disdain them on the ground that they ought not even to be supposed to be divine likenesses for the reason that the shape of the god is different . . . they forget that they are contradicting themselves when they claim that 'God made His own likeness and His form similar to Himself'.[1]

Thus Celsus held the same view of the cult statues as 'divine likenesses' (θεῖαι εἰκόνες) which his contemporary, Athenagoras, combated so energetically. It should be borne in mind that the arguments for and against the images were formulated before Neo-Platonism appeared on the scene.

About a century later, shortly after the death of his teacher Plotinus (A.D. 270), Porphyry stated in his famous work *Against the Christians* that

. . . those rendering proper worship to the gods do not believe the god to be in the wood or stone or bronze from which the image is built . . .; for the statues and the temples were built by the ancients as reminders so that those who went there might be at leisure and be pure hereafter and might come to think of the god; or that they might approach it and offer prayers and supplications each asking him for what he needs. For even if someone makes a portrait of a friend, he does not believe the friend himself to be in it nor that the limbs of his body are confined within the parts of the painting, but that the respect for the friend is shown through the portrait.[2]

After this assertion of the symbolical character of the pagan statues Porphyry continued:

But even if one of the Hellenes would be so light-minded as to think that the gods dwell inside the statues, his understanding would be much purer than that of a person believing that the Divine entered the womb of the Virgin Mary, became a foetus, was born and wrapped in swaddling-clothes, full of blood of the membrane, bile, and things even much stranger than these.[3]

The extant fragments of Julian's *Contra Christianos* preserve no trace of an apology for image-worship. But in a famous letter addressed to the archpriest Theodorus and written shortly before

---

[1] Celsus, viii. 62, p. 62 (Glöckner). The reference is to Heraclitus, frg. 5 in Diels–Kranz, *Vorsokratiker*, ed. 5, i, p. 151 f.

[2] Ed. A. von Harnack, *Porphyrius. Gegen die Christen etc.*, Abhandlungen der Kgl. Preußischen Akademie der Wissenschaften, Phil.-Hist. Kl., 1916, no. 1, frg. 16, pp. 92 f.

[3] Ibid., frg. 77. For a similar argument see Celsus' comparison of Christ with the pagan pantheon, iii. 42, p. 18 (Glöckner): αἱ ἀνθρώπιναι τοῦ 'Ιησοῦ σάρκες φθαρτότεραί εἰσι χρυσοῦ καὶ ἀργύρου καὶ λίθου καὶ μιαρώτεραι.

the publication of the *Contra Christianos*, the Emperor expounded his theory of religious images:

. . . our fathers established statues and altars, and the maintenance of undying fire, and generally speaking everything of the sort as symbols of the presence of the gods, not that we should regard such things as gods, but that we may worship the gods through them. For since we are corporeal it was in bodily wise that we must needs perform our service to the gods, though they are themselves without bodies; they therefore revealed to us in the first images the class of gods second in rank to the first, even those that revolve in a circle about the whole heavens. But since not even to these can due worship be offered in bodily wise—for they are by nature not in need of anything—a third class of images was invented on the earth, and by performing our worship to them we shall make the gods propitious to ourselves. For just as those who make offerings to the statues of the emperors, who are in need of nothing, nevertheless induce goodwill towards themselves thereby, so too those who make offerings to the images of the gods, though the gods need nothing, do nevertheless thereby persuade them to help and to care for them . . ..

Therefore, when we look at the images of the gods, let us not indeed think they are stones or wood, but neither let us think they are the gods themselves; and indeed we do not say that the statues of the emperors are mere wood and stone and bronze, nor that they are the emperor themselves, but that they are images of the emperors. He therefore who loves the emperor delights to see the emperor's statue, and he who loves his son delights to see his father's statue. It follows that he who loves the gods delights to gaze on the images of the gods and their likenesses, and he feels reverence and shudders in awe of the gods who look at him from the unseen world.[1]

Here is once again the symbolical view of religious art but in a more complicated form than hitherto noticed: the celestial (astral) gods are the 'first images' ($\pi\rho\hat{\omega}\tau\alpha$ $\dot{\alpha}\gamma\acute{\alpha}\lambda\mu\alpha\tau\alpha$) of the intelligible gods and the cult statues are the images of the latter. It will be seen presently that this more complex system of symbolism can be traced back to Porphyry.

Porphyry not only wrote a most comprehensive and successful general work directed against the Christians, but he also discussed the question of cult images in a special treatise entitled $\pi\epsilon\rho\grave{\iota}$

---

[1] Ed. J. Bidez, *L'Empereur Julien. Œuvres complètes*, tome i, 2ᵉ partie: *Lettres et fragments*, Paris, 1924, no. 89b, 160–2. The translation is taken from that of W. C. Wright, Loeb series, ii. 309 (with a few unimportant changes).

ἀγαλμάτων, fragments of which may be found in the third book of Eusebius' *Evangelical Preparation*.[1] The work of Porphyry was written before he joined the school of Plotinus at Rome (A.D. 263); it was composed during his stay at Athens with Longinus or even earlier and can in no way be called a Neo-Platonic treatise. Eusebius does not merely quote fragments from Porphyry; he also indicates on various occasions the general tendencies of his work: Porphyry 'endeavored to combine the doctrines concerning a creative mind of the universe and those concerning incorporeal ideals and intelligent rational powers . . . with the theology of the ancients. . . .'[2] 'They used', he says in another passage with regard to Porphyry, 'to refer all the secret and more mysterious doctrine on these subjects in a metaphorical sense to incorporeal powers, so as to appear no longer to apply their deification to the visible part of the world, but to certain invisible and incorporeal powers. . . .'[3] Clearly then Porphyry was protesting in this work that he did not deify (θεοποιεῖν) any visible part of this world but only the invisible and incorporeal powers that were beyond it.

Indeed, it is this symbolic interpretation which Porphyry set forth with what Eusebius branded as 'boastfulness' in the introduction to his work:

> I speak to those who lawfully may hear:
> Depart all ye profane, and close the doors,

Porphyry began, quoting an Orphic poem.[4] From Eusebius' anxious protests[5] it may be gathered that Porphyry had the Christians in mind when he asked 'ye profane' to depart. Porphyry continued:

> The thoughts of a wise theology, wherein man indicated God and God's powers by images akin to sense, and sketched invisible things in visible forms, I will show to those who have learned to read from the statues as from books the things there written concerning the gods. Nor is it any wonder that the utterly unlearned regard the statues as wood

---

[1] On Porphyry see J. Bidez, *Vie de Porphyre le philosophe néoplatonicien etc.* (Gand et Leipzig, 1913). Edition of the fragments περὶ ἀγαλμάτων, Appendix, pp. 1*–23*.

[2] Eusebius, *Praeparatio Evangelica* (edited and translated by E. H. Gifford, 5 vols., Oxford, 1903), iii. 6, p. 97c. The translations given in the text are those of Gifford.

[3] Ibid. iii. 13, 118b (Gifford), cf. also ibid. 121d.

[4] Bidez, frg. 1 = Eusebius, iii. 7, 97d–98a (Gifford).

[5] Eusebius, iii. 13, 118a.

and stone, just as also those who do not understand the written letters look upon the monuments as mere stones, and on the tablets as bits of wood, and on books as woven papyrus.

After this introduction Porphyry entered upon the main subject of his inquiry. Here two ideas were combined. On the one hand, Porphyry claimed that the invisible deity (τὸ θεῖον) led men to the conception of its fiery nature through the material of the statues.[1] On the other hand, the statues of the gods were expressions of the astronomical (astrological) character of the gods.[2] As stated above, Julian systematized these two leading ideas of Porphyry's work by establishing a threefold process of representation: with him the sidereal world became the image of the first class of gods and the statues in their turn represented the stars. In Porphyry's work the symbolic theory of religious images had reached its climax. They were not what the 'utterly unlearned' called them: wood or stone.[3] They were images suited for human perception, images that lead the spectator on to the conception of the deity.

The next step in the development of the symbolic theory of images occurred in a type of writings closely related to the apologetic literature of the Early Church, namely, in anti-Jewish literature. Long after the actual contacts between Church and Synagogue had ceased, Christianity had found itself compelled to face the Jews for a second time. In the seventh century, during the life and death struggle which the Byzantine Empire had to wage first against the Persians and then against the Moslems for the possession of Egypt, Palestine, and Syria, the Jews had come to occupy a position of considerable importance. During the wars against Persia, the Jews, oppressed as they were by the Byzantine government, had openly favoured the Persians, and after the Byzantine reconquest massacres of the Jewish population seem to have taken place in many places.[4] Once again

---

[1] Bidez, frg. 2 = Eusebius, iii. 7, 98a.

[2] Bidez, *Porphyry*, 21, 152f. Here the origin of these theories is discussed.

[3] Frg. 1 Bidez: τοὺς ἀμαθεστάτους. M. Bidez thinks that the Jews and Christians are meant. They are not excluded, but in view of frg. 77 of the Κατὰ Χριστιανῶν (above p. 27, n. 3) he may also be thinking of uneducated pagans.

[4] See, for instance, A. J. Butler, *The Arab Conquest of Egypt* (Oxford, 1902), 59 and n. 2; A. Pernice, *L'Imperatore Eraclio* (Firenze, 1905), 59 f.; R. P. Blake, 'Ob otnosheniiakh evreev k pravitel'stvu Vostochnoi Rimskoi imperii v 602–634 gg. po R. Kh.', *Khristianskii Vostok*, iii (1915), 175–94.

the Jews took the same hostile attitude towards New Rome when the Arabs approached,[1] and this time the Byzantine Emperor was unable to reconquer the occupied countries. Thus it came about that during the period of the Persian occupation and again after the establishment of Moslem rule the Church was faced (as it had been in the earliest days of its existence) with a serious Jewish opposition which it was compelled to meet on even terms; both Christians and Jews depended, for better or for worse, on the tolerance of their Arab masters. This renewed tenseness in the relations between Christianity and Judaism was bound to find its expression in literature.

Discussions between representatives of the two religions must have taken place frequently during these critical times and there grew up a literature in which the principal points of such discussions were analysed. It seems to begin with a fragmentary work of Iohannes, Bishop of Thessalonica from 610–49, dated to around A.D. 630. The fragments were read at the Seventh Council of Nicaea in 787 and form part, it would seem, of a comprehensive work, *Contra Paganos et Iudaeos*.[2] The first fragment read at the Council represents a discussion between a Pagan and a Christian. Nothing illustrates better than this fragment the change that Christianity had undergone since its early days. The Pagan (ὁ Ἕλλην) who is evidently defending his cult statues discusses Christian image-worship. 'In the same fashion', he asserts, 'you may believe that we too when cherishing the images do not worship them but through them the incorporeal power honored through them.' To this the Christian replies that unlike his opponent he is using images of historical personalities, of the martyrs and of Christ, and that as the Pagan himself points out, he is worshipping not the images but those persons revealed by

[1] Butler, *Arab Conquest*, 160 f.

[2] Mansi, xiii. 164–8. On the date of the author see M. Jugie, *Échos d'Orient*, xxi (1922), 293–307, and the same, *D.T.C.* viii. 1, cols. 819–25. To Jugie belongs the credit for having called attention to this long-forgotten writer. Ostrogorsky (*Studien*, 79) was the first to use the fragments as the earliest evidence for the christological theory of images. Jugie assumes that the fragments belong to a series of homilies on the gospel, mainly because the *incipit* (μέχρι τότε πειράζων τὸν κύριον ἡμῶν καὶ θεὸν Ἰησοῦν Χριστόν) seems to necessitate such a hypothesis. Yet the Old Latin translation of the Council has a fuller text for this *incipit*: 'Usque *nunc* Dominum nostrum et Iesum Christum tentans *perseverat inimicus in eremo*.' Together with the dialogue form of the fragments themselves, it would thus appear more natural to consider the work as being of the type usually called *Contra Paganos et Iudaeos*.

the paintings. The Pagan goes on to discuss the Christian images of angels, trying to establish a parallel between them and the pagan gods. All in all the pagan arguments remind us very much of Porphyry (the already cited parallel between angels and pagan gods), but the decisive difference is that now Pagan and Christian agree on the justification of image-worship on the basis of the symbolic theory. This same justification is repeated in the second fragment where a Jewish interlocutor objects to images on the basis of the Old Testament prohibitions: their purpose is said to be that of a reminder (ὑπόμνησις).[1]

The same Council preserved fragments of the fifth λόγος ὑπὲρ τῆς Χριστιανῶν ἀπολογίας κατὰ τῶν Ἰουδαίων by Leontius of Neapolis in Cyprus. The author belonged to the circle of John the Compassionate, Patriarch of Alexandria (610–19), and wrote his biography. Now Iohannes Moschus stated in the *Pratum Spirituale* that a prominent member of this circle was a certain Cosmas Scholasticus who was not only the owner of the largest private library at Alexandria, but was also devoting his life to the conversion of Jews.[2] To this end, he wrote constantly against the Jews and, moreover, persuaded Iohannes Moschus (and probably others) to proselyte the Jews with disputations and sermons. It is, therefore, reasonable to suppose that Leontius' work *Against the Jews* represents just such a missionary effort in literary form. It adheres to the tradition of anti-Jewish literature but springs from a desire of refuting and converting a real opponent. Like the work of Iohannes of Thessalonica that of Leontius was written in dialogue form. Almost all the iconophile arguments later found in the works of John of Damascus may be read in the fragments of Leontius.[3]

There is no need to discuss the anti-Jewish literature further. Many authors who wrote against the Jews touched on the problem of images and all of them used the same arguments in favour

[1] This second fragment bears the title: Ἐκ τῆς διαλέξεως Ἰουδαίου καὶ Χριστιανοῦ and is read at the Council by a person other than the first. Jugie does not question, however, that the two belong together, and indeed the dialogue form of both fragments renders the alternative view highly improbable. On the literary type called *Contra Paganos et Iudaeos* see below, pp. 33 f.

[2] *P.G.* lxxxvii. 3, 3040c–3041b. See Heinrich Gelzer, *Leontios' von Neapolis Leben des heiligen Johannes des Barmherzigen*, Sammlung ausgewählter kirchen- und dogmengeschichtlicher Quellenschriften 5 (Freiburg i. Br. and Leipzig, 1893), p. xi.

[3] *P.G.* xciii. 1597–1610.

of image-worship that were found in the writings of the early apologists.[1]

In the writings of Johannes of Thessalonica and Leontius of Neapolis can be found the earliest traces of the symbolic argument in defence of Christian image-worship, roughly a century before John of Damascus. There remains, as in so many other cases, the critical gap between late Antiquity and the Early Middle Ages, between the writings of Porphyry and those of Johannes of Thessalonica. This cannot be bridged except by hypothesis. At some time between the third and the seventh century, Christians took over the pagan argumentation. Arguments which theretofore had been used by pagan writers in defence of pagan cult statues were in the seventh century cited in writings directed against the Jews and Pagans in defence of Christian images. What needs explanation, therefore, is first the connexion between Christian apologetic literature and Byzantine anti-Jewish literature, and second, the shifting of the entire system of symbolic argumentation from the pagan to the Christian side.

As to the first point it is important to form a clear idea of the antecedents of anti-Jewish literature; these have been elucidated in a penetrating essay by A. von Harnack.[2] The general trend of his remarks, in an altogether too summary form, is the following. From the very beginning, i.e. even before the fixation of the New Testament canon, Christianity explained the activity of its founder on the basis of prophecies in the Old Testament. This explanation, however, arose at a time when the actual contacts between Church and Synagogue had already come to an end, and was addressed to those Christians who had come from the Gentile camp rather than to Jewish Christians. It consisted of two parts:

---

[1] Other examples: *Trophées de Damas*, vi, p. 245 ff., ed. G. Bardy, *Patrologia Orientalis*, xv. 2 (Paris, 1920) (composed around 680) ; Anastasius Sinaita (probably after 700), *Disputatio Adversus Iudaeos*, *P.G.* lxxxix. 1233c ff.; *Dialogue between a Christian and a Jew etc.*, ed. A. C. McGiffert (Marburg, 1899), 51 f. (the earliest recension dates around A.D. 700, but the pertinent passages may be a later addition). See Schwarzlose, *Bilderstreit*, 128 : 'Sie (i.e. Leontius, Gregentius, Anastasius Sinaita) sind als Vorläufer der eigentlichen Bilderapologeten anzusehen; ein großer Teil des später verwandten Beweisapparats ist von ihnen zuerst in Anwendung gebracht worden.'

[2] *Altercatio Simonis Iudaei et Theophili Christiani, nebst Untersuchungen über die antijüdische Polemik in der alten Kirche*, Texte und Untersuchungen I. 3 (Leipzig, 1883), esp. 56–84. For more recent works on anti-Jewish literature see Wilhelm Levison, 'Konstantinische Schenkung und Silvesterlegende', *Miscellanea Francesco Ehrle*, ii, Studi e Testi 38 (Rome, 1924), 159–247.

de Christo and *de lege*. Accordingly it did not take into account the actual objections of Judaism against the new religion, but served rather, at least after the creation of a rational theology in the period of the Apologists, to refute under the opprobrious name of Judaism, pagans and heretics (Marcion, Gnosis). It was meant to reassure the Christian soul which was divided in itself and to defend it against the pagans outside the Church rather than to refute or convert Jews. This polemic literature of the Early Church, though by its title directed against the Jews, was therefore not a literary genus by itself but formed an organic whole with the apologetic literature, the only difference being that works against the Jews often were composed in the form of an extremely artificial dialogue. Few parts of Christian literature showed such continuity of tradition as that addressed to the Jews; even the dialogue form survived into the Byzantine period. This branch of literature was independent to a considerable degree of the dogmatic development of Christianity and constituted one of the few connecting links between the earliest Christian literature and that of Byzantine Christianity. What Harnack failed to see (because he was interested primarily in the literature of earliest Christianity) was that the period of the Persian and Arab conquests revitalized this literary genus, since the Jews had gained a political importance which they had not possessed for many centuries. From Iohannes of Thessalonica onward the writings of Christian writers indicate clearly that the old literary form had to be adapted to a real opponent and thus to new problems, the most important of which was that of religious images.

So much then for the close connexion between apologetic and anti-Jewish literature. It now remains to explain how in this body of literature a group of arguments changed from the pagan to the Christian side. The reason for this shift lies in the transformation which occurred in the field of Christian religious practice: the introduction of the worship of images itself. At one time, surely later than the beginning of the cult of images itself, Christian authors active in the field of apologetic and anti-Jewish literature became aware that their attacks against pagan cult statues could be turned against the use of images in the Church. Since the problem is mentioned for the first time in the anti-Jewish writings after the Persian and Arabic wars, it is reasonable to suppose that the new contact between Christianity and Judaism, which was brought about by these events, was responsible for this new awareness. At that moment it became imperative for Christian writers of treatises *Adversus Iudaeos* to insert a discussion *de imaginibus*. Since in the past these treatises had dealt with the validity of the Law (*de lege*) and since idol-worship had been forbidden in this law, such a discussion was inevitable in this context.

It was in this embarrassing situation that a Christian writer deliberately must have taken the decision to adopt the symbolic argumentation of the pagans. At first there may have been some hesitations. To give but one example: in the above-mentioned fragment of Iohannes of Thessalonica—the earliest treatise *Adversus Paganos et Iudaeos* to mention the issue of Christian images— the symbolic defence of Christian images is suggested not by the Christian but by the Pagan, and the Christian merely expresses his approval.[1] As time went along all scruples were forgotten and in the writings of John of Damascus the arguments of men like Celsus, Porphyry, or Julian, appear with absolute ease in their Christian garb.

When and where did this change occur? It must have happened after the spread of image-worship. More especially a passage from Iohannes Philoponus' *De opificio mundi*, written between 529 and 543, and after the writer's conversion to Christianity, seems to indicate that Iohannes still considered the symbolic theory of images a pagan characteristic. In this passage Iohannes argued against an interpretation of Genesis i. 26 by Theodore of Mopsuestia according to which men honour God by honouring man created in God's likeness. Against this Iohannes invoked several biblical passages and then proceeded:

> If he [Theodore of Mopsuestia] should say that the worship offered to man is referred to God, let him know that those who worship the idols as gods also say this. Therefore they [the pagans] address them [the idols] also by names of the gods to whom they are set up. . . .[2]

Iohannes could not have written this if he had already known the Christians to use the symbolic argument in favour of their images. While this is no obstacle to the use of the symbolic theory by an individual Christian writer unknown to Iohannes Philoponus, it

[1] Mansi, xiii. 164C. See the words of the Pagan, above, p. 31. Thereupon the Christian remarks: . . . ἀλλὰ καὶ προσκυνοῦντες οὐ τὰς εἰκόνας, ὡς καὶ σὺ προεῖπες, ἀλλὰ τοὺς διὰ τῆς γραφῆς δηλουμένους δοξάζομεν.

[2] Ed. W. Reichardt, Leipzig, 1897, vi. 10, p. 251.

renders any general use by earlier Christian authors highly improbable. It is therefore after the year 529 and prior to the work
of Iohannes of Thessalonica that the change took place. It is impossible to say who was responsible for it. One might feel tempted
to guess that it was one of the Alexandrian colleagues or successors of Iohannes Philoponus who were steeped in pagan tradition,
more particularly a man like Stephanos of Alexandria who received a chair at the university of Constantinople where he
exercised great influence.[1] However, all such suggestions are pure
guesswork, and the name of the divine who took this natural but
(in view of the long pagan tradition) bold step remains unknown.

Yet the development of the symbolic argument is clear. A
direct tradition leads from the pagan theory of images to that of
the Byzantine Christians. Indeed, the Iconophiles of the eighth
century themselves were aware of the derivation of their principal
arguments from anti-Jewish literature. In a letter addressed to
Thomas of Claudiopolis, which deals with the defence of image-
worship, the Patriarch Germanos of Constantinople (715–30)
wrote:

> This you ought to realize first that not only now but often both the
> Jews and the adherents of veritable idol-worship [i.e. pagans] have
> brought forth such things against us in reproach.
> . . . Not ignobly some of our elders whose labours we have not at
> hand have rejected these from the fold of Christ like dumb dogs bark-
> ing, in the words of the Scriptures, to no avail.[2]

Evidently the writers 'whose labours we have not at hand' would
have been of great help to Germanos in composing his plea for
the images.[3] They had been writing against Jews and pagans.

The principal literary monuments from the reign of Leo III
are the works of the iconophile writers John of Damascus (*c.* 675–
749) and Germanos of Constantinople (Patriarch from 715 to 730).[4]

---

[1] Hermann Usener, *Kleine Schriften*, iii. 248–50, 210.

[2] *P.G.* xcviii. 168A–B.

[3] The Patriarch Nicephorus, several generations later, shows that he is aware
of the fact that the apologies for images are based on the earlier writings against
Jews and Pagans. When in his *Adversus Iconomachos etc.* vi (Pitra, iv. 250 ff.) he discusses the iconoclastic attack on ecclesiastical tradition, he remarks (pp. 251 f.):
προσῆκε δ' ἂν αὐτοὺς [the Iconoclasts] εἰς τὰ προεξητασμένα παρὰ Χριστιανοῖς καὶ
Θεῷ ἱερωμένοις ἐπιμελῶς διαγυμνάσασθαι ἡνίκα πρὸς Ἰουδαίους καὶ Ἕλληνας τὰς
διαμφισβητήσεις ἐποιοῦντο καὶ τὸν ὀρθὸν λόγον δεξιῶς καὶ ἀπεξεσμένως διεπέραινον.

[4] John of Damascus's treatises on images: *P.G.* xciv. 1231–1420. *De Fide
Orthodoxa*, iv. 16: ibid. 1167–76. See H. Menges, *Die Bilderlehre des hl. Johannes von*

The former expounded his ideas about images in three famous treatises concerning the images (πρὸς τοὺς διαβάλλοντας τὰς ἁγίας εἰκόνας) and summarized them in his work *De Fide Orthodoxa*. Of the writings of Germanos there are preserved a number of letters concerned with the image problem, as well as a brief discussion in his *De Haeresibus et Synodis*. As one examines these writings and studies the argumentation of friends and foes of religious images, one is constantly reminded of pagan ideas of cult statues and of Christian apologies for religious images in the literature *Contra Iudaeos et Paganos*. It appears from the works of the eighth-century Iconophiles that the Iconoclasts objected to images of Christ, of the Virgin Mary, and of the Saints on the grounds that they were idols. They quoted the Old Testament prohibitions of idol worship. They held that the images were made of vile matter and as such deserved no veneration. They claimed that the Iconophiles were worshipping the images like gods. Image worship for them had no basis in Scripture, and religious images were of recent origin within Christianity. Some of the Iconoclasts, it appears, did not object to images of Jesus Christ and of the Virgin but to those of the Saints. Characteristic of the attitude of the early Iconoclasts was the result of a heated discussion which their leader, Constantine Bishop of Nacoleia, had with the Patriarch Germanos. Constantine took leave from Germanos, so the latter tells us, with the assurance that he would neither say nor do anything against images of the Lord and of His Saints but would 'only put forth the scriptural teaching, to the effect that one should not hold any created thing worthy of divine honour'. This formula was clearly a compromise and like all such formulas it lent itself to different interpretations. Constantine of Nacoleia interpreted it, probably in good faith, as a licence for an iconoclastic campaign.[1]

Damaskus, Diss. Münster i. W., Kallmünz, 1937; Johannes M. Hoeck, 'Stand und Aufgaben der Damaskenos-Forschung', *Orientalia Christiana Periodica*, xvii (1951), 5–60. Correspondence of Germanos of Constantinople: *P.G.* xcviii. 147–222. *De Haeresibus et Synodis*: ibid. 39–88, esp. 77–88.

[1] Images as idols: John of Damascus, *P.G.* xciv. 1233A–B; Germanos, *P.G.* xcviii. 77C. Old Testament prohibitions: John of Damascus, 1233D–1236C, 1321A–B; Germanos, 176C ff. Images made of matter: John of Damascus, 1245A, 1297B; Germanos, 173D. Images not warranted by Scripture: John of Damascus, 1256B, 1301C. Images a recent invention: John of Damascus, 1305B. Images of Saints objectionable to some Iconoclasts: John of Damascus, 1249B. Compromise between Germanos and Constantine of Nacoleia: Germanos, 164B.

To the attacks of the Iconoclasts John of Damascus replied
that he did not worship matter but the maker of matter.[1] The
Law, he argued, as well as the entire cult consisted of holy objects
made by human hands which through matter led to the immaterial God.[2] 'Our worship', he continued, 'is not addressed to
matter, but through them (the images) to those represented by
them.[3] The images should be worshipped as representations (ὡς
εἰκόνας), and imitations, and likenesses, and books for the uneducated.'[4] Again and again he proclaimed that the image-
worshippers did not honour the images as gods.[5] Furthermore,
there is a series of arguments scattered throughout the three ora-
tions *De imaginibus*, but very conveniently grouped together in one
particular passage:

> And perceptibly we set up His figure everywhere, and we hallow the
> first [sense] (for sight is the first of senses) as we also [hallow] the sense
> of hearing by speaking; for the image is a memorial. And what the
> book is to those initiated to the letters, that the image is for the illiter-
> ate; and what the speech is to hearing, that the image is to sight:
> spiritually we are united with God through it.[6]

In this one short passage is found a set of arguments which
occur in one form or the other in the writings of John of Damascus
and of all the later apologists of image-worship. The images are
'memorials', they are set up to remind us of the divine activity.[7]
They preserve 'the memory of the past'.[8] These same ideas of the
image as a memorial and a reminder, and of its service as *laicorum
litteratura* (this is the term of later Western scholasticism) occur
also, though less conspicuously, in the writings of the Patriarch
Germanos—the images serve as a reminder only and a demonstration of the Saints' manly virtues.[9] It is evident then that at the

[1] John of Damascus, *De Imaginibus*, i. 16, 1245A: οὐ προσκυνῶ τῇ ὕλῃ, προσκυνῶ
δὲ τὸν τῆς ὕλης δημιουργόν.

[2] Op. cit. ii. 23, 1309C: . . . καὶ ὁ νόμος καὶ πάντα τὰ κατ' αὐτὸν πᾶσά τε ἡ καθ'
ἡμᾶς λατρεία χειροποίητά εἰσιν ἅγια, δι' ὕλης προσάγοντα ἡμᾶς τῷ ἀύλῳ Θεῷ.

[3] Op. cit. iii. 41, 1357C: προσκυνοῦμεν οὖν ταῖς εἰκόσιν, οὐ τῇ ὕλῃ προσφέροντες τὴν
προσκύνησιν, ἀλλὰ δι' αὐτῶν τοῖς ἐν αὐτοῖς εἰκονιζομένοις.

[4] Op. cit. iii. 9, 1332B: . . . ἀποδέχεσθαι καὶ τιμᾶν ὡς εἰκόνας καὶ μιμήματα καὶ
ὁμοιώματα καὶ βίβλους τῶν ἀγραμμάτων καὶ ὑπόμνησιν.

[5] See above, n. 1.   [6] Op. cit. i. 17, 1248C.

[7] Ibid. 1248D: . . . ὡς θείας ἐνεργείας ὑπόμνησιν ἄγουσαι.

[8] Op. cit. iii. 23, 1341C: πρὸς μνήμην τῶν γεγονότων, cf. i. 13, 1241D.

[9] Germanos, *De Haeresibus et Synodis*, 41, P.G. xcviii. 77D: . . . εἰς μόνην ὑπόμνησιν
καὶ ἀνδρείας ἐπίδειξιν . . . .

beginning of the Iconoclastic Controversy the Iconophiles were using in defence of their images all the arguments derived from the symbolic concept of the image which had been previously used by pagans in favour of their cult statues.

2. *The Image as Essence*

In the Old Testament and most conspicuously in the decalogue (Exod. xx. 4 and kindred texts) the strict prohibition of all artistic imitations of nature was proclaimed. The early Christians, in competing with Judaism for the souls of the Gentiles, struggling with pagan idol-worship, and living in expectation of an immediate Second Coming of the Lord, did not think of portraying Jesus or the Apostles. A formal prohibition in the New Testament was thus unnecessary. The New Testament used the word 'image' (εἰκών) in two meanings. In a few passages where portraits of the pagan Emperors (Mark xii. 16; Apoc. xiii. 14) are referred to, it meant a pictorial representation of the person represented. Otherwise, the New Testament, following the usage of the Septuagint and even of some pagan writers, used εἰκών in the figurative sense of the very essence of a thing made visible in its 'image'.[1] That seems to have been for the Greek reader the sense of man being created 'in God's image', of the Law having 'the very image of things', and of Man being 'conformed to the image of his Son'—and also of the visible world being the visible image of Plato's intelligible Forms (*Timaeus* 92c).[2] This 'essential' concept of the 'image' which seems to have been held in the Greek-speaking world by some Christians and some pagans, was hardly reconcilable with artistic images of religious personalities. It was bound to affect attitudes towards Christian art.

Opposition to Christian art continued to make itself heard to the eve of the Iconoclastic Controversy. If one musters the arguments used by the opponents of the use and worship of images in the Church, the Old Testament prohibitions while not always

---

[1] Gerhard Kittel, *Theologisches Wörterbuch zum Neuen Testament*, ii (Stuttgart, 1950), verbo εἰκών (Kleinknecht), 386: ' "Bild" kann bedeuten eine Ausstrahlung, ein Sichtbar- und Offenbarwerden des Wesens mit substantieller Teilhabe (μετοχή) am Gegenstande.' Kittel, ibid., p. 393: 'Im Neuen Testament ist durchweg in dem 'Bilde' das Urbild selbst, die abgebildete Gestalt selbst, als in ihrem Wesen sichtbar gedacht.'

[2] Gen. i. 26; Heb. x. 1; Rom. viii. 29.

quoted (Tertullian, Clement of Alexandria, Eusebius, and others emphasize their validity) are unquestionably one of the main-springs of this opposition.[1] The thesis that the Devil created 'sculptors, painters, and producers of all kinds of portraits' (Tertullian), or at least that he taught them their art so that in the pagan cult statues the uneducated 'might have models of licentiousness' (Theodoret of Cyrus), seems to have been viewed as a corollary to the fact that the God of the Old Testament had rejected the arts. In addition to explicit or implied references to the Old Testament, the reader of passages from early Christian literature notices the frequent use of one other line of argumentation against the images. To be sure, it may appear combined with the Old Testament prohibition or may occur as a philosophic justification of it, yet its origins seem to lie outside the sacred books of Judaism and Christianity. The Alexandrian fathers were especially fond of it. Clement of Alexandria, for example, drew a formal distinction between Truth and Art. Truth lies only in what is intelligible ($\tau\grave{a}$ $\nu o\eta\tau\acute{a}$); the worshippers of material images dishonour the intelligible substance of God. As he explains in a telling passage:

This Gnostic [i.e. the Christian] then may be he who is worth much, who is precious to God, in whom God has taken up residence, i.e., in whom the knowledge of God has been sanctified. Here we may also find the image ($\tau\grave{o}$ $\mathring{a}\pi\epsilon\iota\kappa\acute{o}\nu\iota\sigma\mu a$), the divine and holy statue ($\mathring{a}\gamma a\lambda\mu a$), in the just soul if it is blessed (as having been purified before) and performs blessed works. Here is both [the image] which has been taken as a residence and that which is about to be taken as a residence—the former in the case of those who are already Gnostics, the latter with those who can become Gnostics . . . ; for all that is about to believe is already faithful to God and set up as a statue full of virtues to honor [him], erected before God ($\kappa a\theta\iota\delta\rho\upsilon\mu\acute{e}\nu o\nu$ $\epsilon\mathring{i}s$ $\tau\iota\mu\grave{\eta}\nu$ $\mathring{a}\gamma a\lambda\mu a$ $\mathring{e}\nu\acute{a}\rho\epsilon\tau o\nu$, $\mathring{a}\nu a\kappa\epsilon\acute{\iota}\mu\epsilon\nu o\nu$ $\Theta\epsilon\mathring{\omega}$).[2]

The just soul or the virtuous man is God's true image—such is the view that occurs again and again in the works of Clement and of many later opponents of the use and worship of Christian images —an argument that the Alexandrian Fathers and their successors had in common with the pagan Porphyry.[3] One further very clear

[1] For literary discussions of Christian art see the works of Koch and Elliger, cited above, Ch. I, p. 2, n. 1.

[2] *Stromata*, vii, ch. V. 5, pp. 21 f., ed. Staehlin.

[3] Hierocles, *Commentarius in Aureum Carmen* (ed. Mullach, *Fragmenta Philosophorum*

expression of this attitude must suffice. The pagan philosopher Celsus had accused the Christians of avoiding cult statues. Origen replied:

[Our] cult-statues and fitting offerings to God are not fabricated by uneducated craftsmen but are rendered clear and formed within us by the Word of God: the virtues, which are imitations of 'the first born of all creation' (Col. i. 15) in Whom are the patterns of justice, prudence, courage, wisdom, piety, and the other virtues. Therefore cult-statues are in all those who, in accordance with the Divine Word, provide themselves with justice and courage and wisdom and piety and the furnishings of the other virtues. . . . And in each of those who, to the best of their ability, imitate Him even in this respect there is the cult-statue 'in the likeness of the Creator' (Col. iii. 10) which they furnish by contemplating God with a pure heart when they have become 'imitators of God' (Ephes. v. 1). And in short, all Christians attempt to erect the aforesaid altars and the cult-statues mentioned before, not those that are without soul and without perception and containing greedy deities residing in statues without soul, but those containing the spirit of God, resting as upon his own upon the aforementioned cult-statues of virtue and upon Him who is 'in the likeness of the Creator'; thus the spirit of Christ will also settle upon 'those who are made like him' (οἱ σύμμορφοι, cf. Rom. viii. 29), to use that expression. . . .[1]

This view of the just and virtuous creature as the true image of the Creator is shared by later Fathers such as Methodius of Olympus, Arnobius, and Asterius of Amasea.[2] It was foreshadowed in St. Paul's warning to the Corinthians, 'Do you not know that you are God's temple (ναός) and that God's spirit makes its house in you?', but the reference to the cardinal virtues gave it a peculiarly Greek twist. It was clearly an adaptation of what was called above the 'essential' concept of the image.[3]

Graecorum, i. 420 f.): μόνος γὰρ οἶδε τιμᾶν ὁ τὴν ἀξίαν μὴ συγχέων τῶν τιμωμένων, καὶ ὁ προηγουμένως ἱερεῖον ἑαυτὸν προσάγων, καὶ ἄγαλμα θεῖον τεκταίνων τὴν ἑαυτοῦ ψυχήν, καὶ ναὸν εἰς ὑποδοχὴν τοῦ θείου φωτὸς τὸν ἑαυτοῦ κατασκευάζων νοῦν. E. Norden, *Agnostos Theos* (Leipzig and Berlin, 1923), 345, makes it probable that this position goes back to Porphyry.

[1] *Contra Celsum*, viii. 17–19 (ii. 234 ff., ed. Koetschau).

[2] Asterius of Amasea, *De Divite et Lazaro* (*P.G.* xl. 168B): μὴ γράφε τὸν Χριστὸν (ἀρκεῖ γὰρ αὐτῷ ἡ μία τῆς ἐνσωματώσεως ταπεινοφροσύνη ἣν αὐθαιρέτως δι' ἡμᾶς κατεδέξατο . . .). The past 'humiliation' of Christ is, of course, the Incarnation, and a representation of Christ on people's garments constitutes a new 'humiliation'. Asterius seems to have protested against sacred images on garments, but he did not object to religious images in general.

[3] 1 Cor. iii. 16. Hypatius of Ephesus, in the age of Justinian, mentions that some

In the Late Roman Empire this concept was not forgotten, but became the inspiration for a schismatic movement on the borders, in Armenia and Caucasian Albania, at the turn of the seventh century.[1] Dissatisfied with the political manoeuvrings of the Armenian clergy between Byzantium and Persia, the leaders of this group retired to the desert, practised extreme forms of asceticism and waged a campaign against religious images. Their Iconoclasm was the corollary to their insistence on personal holiness. Accordingly these Armenian ascetics seem to have objected to religious images on grounds like those of Clement and Origen. This group of Iconoclasts gained a large following in northern Armenia and on the Albanian frontier. They must have remained a very powerful movement in other parts of Armenia too. In fact, in 714 George, a (monophysitic) bishop of the Arab tribes on the Syrio-Mesopotamian border, wrote a letter from Syria to the presbyter Isho, who lived in a village named Anab. Isho had been arguing with an Armenian. The latter had told him that Gregory the Illuminator, the apostle of Armenia, had prohibited the admixture of water in the wine of the Eucharist. Bishop George informed his correspondent that Gregory had never prohibited this, just as he had not ordered 'that they should make no images in their churches, although they report that he did'. George implied that the use of pure wine in the Eucharist, as well as the absence of religious images, were simply old traditions of the Armenian Church which his [Isho's] Armenian interlocutor had been trying to authenticate by tracing them back to Gregory the Illuminator. George was exaggerating in conveying that Armenian churches contained no images, but it is interesting that at the beginning of the eighth century a prominent and learned monophysitic bishop could make such a blunder. The Armenians whom he knew must have been Iconoclasts, and his letter thus is evidence for the persistence of iconoclastic sentiment among Armenians down to the eighth century.[2]

theologians considered this a decisive argument against the legitimacy of Christian art, see *Harvard Theological Review*, xlv (1952), 180, n. 28.

[1] On this movement see my article 'An Ascetic Sect of Iconoclasts in Seventh-Century Armenia', *Late Classical and Medieval Studies in Honor of Albert Matthias Friend Jr.* (Princeton, 1955), 151–60. The remarks in the text are a summary of this article.

[2] Bishop George's letter to the Presbyter Ishŏ': translated by V. Ryssel, *Theologische Studien und Kritiken*, lvi (1883), 278–371. The relevant passage, pp. 345 f.: 'Ferner aber hat ihnen [i.e. the Armenians] Gregor gar nicht befohlen . . . daß sie

By the time of George, the Bishop of the Arabs, the leading Armenian Iconoclasts had long been expelled by the Albanian Catholicus. Some of their followers had allied themselves, somewhere on the confines of Armenian territory, with a new heresy which was to play an important role in medieval and modern times: the Paulicians. It was the last act in the fascinating and tragic story of the Armenian Iconoclasts as an independent sect.[1] Their views on religious images were destined to influence in the ninth century the Iconoclasts in the Byzantine Empire.

3. *The Image and Christology*

The theories of images considered in the preceding sections either justified or rejected all religious portraiture. In the Christian Church the images of Jesus Christ naturally had particular importance and were examined in connexion with christological doctrine. Eusebius of Caesarea seems to have been the first author to reject artistic images of Christ on christological grounds.

The Empress Constantia, step-sister of Constantine the Great and wife of his co-Emperor Licinius, had asked Eusebius for an image of Christ. In his reply Eusebius asked what kind of an image Constantia desired. Christ had two 'figures' ($\mu o\rho\phi\alpha\iota$), a divine and a human 'figure'. The divine figure was known only to the Father and could therefore not be represented. Even Christ's human figure, the Flesh, had been mixed with the glory of His divinity, and 'the mortal [element] has been swallowed by the Life'. For Eusebius these christological considerations did not permit the portrayal of the Christ after His Transfiguration. As to portraying Jesus prior to the Transfiguration, this was impossible because of the Old Testament prohibitions. After recounting and condemning the use of images among uneducated and heretical Christians, Eusebius concluded:

To us such practices are forbidden. We confess that the Lord our Saviour is God and we prepare to see him as God by cleansing with all diligence our own hearts so that we may see him—after we have been cleansed, for 'blessed are the pure in heart, for they will see God'

nicht Bilder in ihren Kirchen machen sollten, wenngleich sie dies von ihm berichten. . . .' On Bishop George see A. Baumstark *Geschichte der syrischen Literatur* (Bonn, 1922), p. 257.

[1] See my article quoted above (p. 42, n. 1), p. 159.

(Matt. v. 8). But if you people yourselves, out of supererogation (?, ἐκ περιουσίας), have a high opinion of the images of our Saviour, before seeing and beholding Him face to face in the future, what better painter could we have than the Word of God itself?[1]

The peculiar christology of this passage, the connecting of christology with the problem of images of Christ, the insistence upon the superiority of the message written and heard over the image seen—all these elements betray an Origenist inspiration of Eusebius.

Not only the christology of Origenists, however, could produce iconophobia. It may be suggested as a general proposition that christological systems emphasizing the divine nature of Christ at the expense of His human nature were apt to lead to the rejection of religious images.[2] An early example of this attitude is that of the monophysitic bishop Philoxenus (= Xenaias) of Hierapolis (Manbidj) in Syria (+523), ally of Severus of Antioch. He objected to pictorial representations of Christ, of the angels, and of the Holy Spirit in the form of a dove, and waged a violent campaign against such images. There is no evidence that he opposed images of saints and martyrs. His position on images, then, was a logical corollary to his theological views: the angels and the

[1] I am using the text of the letter as printed in *P.G.* xx. 1545–50. It should be noted that this is not a critical edition of the text. The letter has been dealt with in an interesting article by George Florovsky (see, Note A, p. 232) who calls it 'composed in an Origenist idiom'. From the beginning of the letter one gets the impression that Constantia had asked Eusebius for transmission of a copy of a *specific* portrait which Constantia believed to be of Christ, but which Eusebius did not recognize as such. The original would obviously be located in Palestine, perhaps near Eusebius' Caesarea, and this would explain why the Empress had to address herself to a Palestinian bishop to get it copied. Is it conceivable that Constantia had read Eusebius' own account of the woman who shed blood and of the statue of Jesus Christ which she was supposed to have erected in her native Paneas (Eusebius, *Hist. Eccl.* vii. 18)? Eusebius had seen this piece of sculpture and had not denied its authenticity in his *Ecclesiastical History*.

[2] Two scholars from whose writings I have profited greatly, von Dobschütz (*Christusbilder*, 33) and Walter Elliger, 'Zur bilderfeindlichen Bewegung des achten Jahrhunderts', *Forschungen zur Kirchengeschichte und zur christlichen Kunst* (Festgabe Johannes Ficker), Leipzig, 1931, 40–60, have expressed a view different from that taken in the text. According to von Dobschütz, the theology of Cyril of Alexandria favoured the images. Elliger (51 ff.) connects the Iconophiles of the eighth century with the Monophysites, and with great difficulty represents the Iconoclasts as the heirs of the Antiochene School. Ostrogorsky (*Studien*, 24–28) has clearly demonstrated the connexions between Iconoclasm and Monophysitism, and I have dwelt in the text on its connexion with Origenism.

Holy Spirit were clearly incorporeal and, in Philoxenus' mono-physitic theology, Jesus Christ was first and foremost God.[1]

Meanwhile proponents of orthodox christology had discovered the pictorial representation of Christ as an important means of asserting their views. There is one official text of the late seventh century which reflects, positively as well as negatively, most of the attitudes towards religious images which have been described here so far. It is the eighty-second canon of the Trullan Council (692). This canon runs as follows:

In some of the paintings of the venerable images there is represented the Lamb to which the finger of the Precursor[John the Baptist] points. It was accepted as the type of Grace and as showing to us in anticipation the True Lamb, Christ our God. We embrace the ancient types and foreshadowings as being handed down to the Church as symbols and patterns of the Truth, but we prefer the Grace and the Truth and accept it as the fulfilment of the Law. Now in order that perfection be represented before the eyes of all people even in paintings, we ordain that from now on the human figure of Christ our God, the Lamb who took on the sin of the world, be set up, even in the images, instead of the ancient lamb. Through this figure we realize the height of the humiliation of God the Word and are led to remember his life in the flesh, his suffering and his saving death, and the redemption ensuing from it for the world.[2]

---

[1] On Philoxenus see E. Tisserant, *D.T.C.*, xii. 1509–32. What we know about his iconoclastic campaign is due to the (lost) *Ecclesiastical History* of Theodore Anagnostes who in turn relied on that of Iohannes Diacrinomenos. On Theodore Anagnostes, see H. G. Opitz, *R.E.*, Zweite Reihe, x, 1869/81, esp. on the fragment concerning Philoxenus coll. 1873, 1877, 1879 f. At the Seventh Ecumenical Council (Mansi, xiii. 180D–181B) the deacon Demetrius read an excerpt from Theodore Anagnostes' *Ecclesiastical History*, which contained biographical information on Philoxenus and made it perfectly clear that he was a monophysite—and perhaps unbaptized. Thereupon another reader, the deacon Stephanus, read a fragment from Iohannes Diacrinomenos's *Ecclesiastical History*. Since this last passage was read by another reader, not the one who read the passage from Theodore Anagnostes and therefore, presumably, from a different manuscript, I doubt that the passage from Iohannes Diacrinomenos was quoted in Theodore's work (against Opitz, col. 1879). In our present text of Theophanes (p. 134, de Boor) the 'angels' (ἄγγελοι) whose pictures Philoxenus (ed. E. Miller, *Revue Archéologique*, N.S. xxvi (1873), 402) opposed have been corrupted by a scribal error into 'Saints' (ἅγιοι).

[2] Text of Canon 82 of the Trullan or Quinisext Council: Mansi, xi. 977E–980B. George Florovsky, loc. cit. (see Note A, p. 232), p. 19 emphasized the importance of this text for the christological justification of religious images. On the disciplinary legislation of this Council in general see Louis Brehier, in A. Fliche and Victor Martin, *Histoire de l'Église*, v (1947), 471–4. In this connexion Professor Ernst Kitzinger referred me to the Chair of Bishop Maximian (546–56) at Ravenna

The precise significance of this canon is perhaps not clear in all details, but the christological emphasis is obvious. The other canons of the Council are directed against real abuses: disregard for the church building or other sacred objects, immorality, pagan festivals, magic, &c. The new images were to have a function which the old symbolic representations did not fulfil: they emphasized the Incarnation. Both the old and the new images reminded the spectator of Christ, but the new images put before him the *human* nature of Christ. Who needed such a reminder? The only explanation is that the members of the Quinisextum thought of certain quasi-monophysitic currents in the Church which were inclined to exalt Christ's divine nature at the expense of his human nature. In such quarters one would naturally suppose a tendency to cling to the early symbolic representations of Christ and to reject representations of Christ as a human being. In this interpretation the eighty-second canon of the Quinisextum lends support to the view that in the seventh century there existed in the Byzantine Empire monophysitic tendencies opposed to the portrayal of Jesus Christ.

Thus at the Quinisextum pictorial images of Christ were used to support christological orthodoxy. Only one generation later, in the writings of John of Damascus, the appeal to orthodox christology served to validate the images of Christ. For John the pictorial representation of Christ was legitimate because of Christ's human nature. On this basis he developed a theology of image-worship by investigating systematically the concepts of image and worship. Against the objections of the Iconoclasts based on the Old Testament prohibitions of idol-worship, he worked out the basic difference between pagan idols and Christian images. All those prohibitions were meant for the Jews, who were at any moment likely to backslide into idol-worship or the deification of matter. But then the Incarnation had not taken place. With the Incarnation everything had changed, since at that time the invisible divine being became visible. The Incarnation made religious art possible.

On the iconoclastic side christological arguments seem to have played no role either among the Armenian Iconoclasts or in the Byzantine Empire during the reign of Leo III. The iconoclastic

where St. John the Baptist is represented pointing heavenwards with his right hand, and holding in his left a medallion of the Lamb.

contentions of the first generation in the Byzantine Empire may be inferred from the writings of the orthodox such as John of Damascus and Germanos of Constantinople, but these authors are unaware of a christological basis for Iconoclasm. It has been claimed that as early as the reign of Leo III the Iconoclasts objected to images of Jesus Christ on christological grounds.[1] This view is mistaken. It is based on a passage in the first of the treatises on the images where John of Damascus disclaimed the thesis that to worship Christ's body is identical with the introduction of a fourth person into the Trinity and consequently with Nestorianism. It is true that, particularly in this first treatise, John of Damascus sometimes argued against iconoclastic positions without expressly identifying them as such. Yet the passage in question, read in its context, does not refer to artistic images but simply rejects in a routine fashion Monophysitism and Nestorianism as christological doctrines. Against the biblical quotations advanced by the iconoclastic theologians of Leo III, John stated his creed. He defined first of all his conception of the Trinity and then explained his christology: 'Together with the King and God I worship the purple of the body, neither as a robe nor as a fourth person—far be this from me—but as being God also and becoming without alteration what the anointing [thing] was.' After supplying his reasons for the preceding statement, he continued: 'Therefore I boldly represent the invisible God, not as invisible, but as having become visible because of us, etc.'[2]

From this there can be no doubt that John himself connected

---

[1] Ostrogorsky, *Studien*, 22 f.: 'Die Leistung Konstantins bestand vor allem darin, daß er das Bilderproblem in den Rahmen der christologisch-dogmatischen Fragen hereinstellte. Er ist sicher nicht der erste gewesen, der das tat. Eine Stelle aus der ersten Rede des Johannes Damascenus gegen die Bilderstürmer, welche eine Antwort auf die allerersten bilderfeindlichen Maßnahmen unter Leon III. darstellt, bezeugt, daß zu jener Zeit schon der Streit von den Bilderfeinden in den Kreis christologischer Divergenzen gelenkt und der Satz proklamiert worden ist, daß durch ein Abbilden Christi der Dreieinigkeit eine vierte Person beigefügt werde. Diese Idee ist also mindestens um ein Vierteljahrhundert älter als die Schrift Konstantins.'

[2] *P.G.* xciv. 1236B: συμπροσκυνῶ τῷ βασιλεῖ καὶ Θεῷ τὴν ἁλουργίδα τοῦ σώματος, οὐχ ὡς ἱμάτιον οὐδὲ ὡς τέταρτον πρόσωπον, ἄπαγε, ἀλλ᾽ ὡς ὁμόθεον χρηματίσασαν καὶ γενομένην ὅπερ τὸ χρῖσαν ἀμεταβλήτως . . . . διὸ θαρρῶν εἰκονίζω Θεὸν τὸν ἀόρατον, οὐχ ὡς ἀόρατον, ἀλλ᾽ ὡς ὁρατὸν δι᾽ ἡμᾶς γενόμενον, μεθέξει σαρκὸς καὶ αἵματος. . . . The passage reappears in the third treatise, 1325A–B. In John of Damascus, *De Fide Orthodoxa*, iii. 8 (*P.G.* xciv. 1013C–1016A), e.g. the phrase οὐ γὰρ τέταρτον παρεντίθημι πρόσωπον ἐν τῇ Τριάδι occurs in a context where there is no thought of images. So far as I can see, there is also no other evidence to prove that the Iconoclasts relied on christological arguments prior to Constantine V.

the image of Christ with christology, but this does not hold true for John's opponents. Where John speaks of a fourth person, he is rejecting Monophysitism which regarded the flesh as a mere 'robe' which the Logos put on, and then Nestorianism which was believed to make Christ's humanity a fourth person. Both expressions 'robe' and 'fourth person' are the conventional slogans with the help of which Greek theologians branded their opponents as heretics, Monophysites or Nestorians. But to infer from this that at the time when John of Damascus wrote his three works *De imaginibus* the Iconoclasts were already considering the issue of images as a christological problem would be erroneous. It is true that one generation after John of Damascus the iconoclastic Emperor Constantine V was to argue that an artistic image of Jesus Christ could be justified only by Nestorians or Monophysites. Yet the above passage from John of Damascus cannot be used as evidence that Constantine's iconoclastic argument was known under Leo III. In it John was merely rejecting the Monophysitic and Nestorian christology and justifying portraits of Christ by a reference to the Incarnation.

There is no evidence, then, that the powerful christological dilemma against images ('either you circumscribe the divine nature alongside with the human, or you separate the two natures') existed before Constantine V, and that Constantine (as Ostrogorsky thinks) did no more than support a doctrine which was developed before his time. Constantine's adaptation of the christological argument of his iconophile opponents to serve his own iconoclastic ends, a generation later, was an act of genius.

Constantine V's theological position can be studied in the fragments preserved from his writings. Altogether the Emperor appears to have published thirteen works on the image problem but the extant fragments all seem to derive from one of them, subdivided into two πεύσεις or 'questions'. It is clear first of all that the imperial author was not a convinced Chalcedonian so far as his christology was concerned, but tended towards monophysitic views. He avoided the Chalcedonian formula 'in two natures' and in general attempted to weaken and dilute the Chalcedonian terminology of the Incarnation. Secondly, Constantine defined the term 'image' (εἰκών) in a very precise way: a true image must be consubstantial (ὁμοούσιος) with the original. This definition of the 'image'—and this is a point that is not sufficiently stressed in the literature—seems to derive ultimately from the 'essential' concept of the image. The corollary to Constantine's definition was his further thesis that the only genuine image of Christ was the consecrated bread and wine of the Eucharist. Finally, Constantine V was the first among the Iconoclasts to emphasize the christological implications of Christ's portraits. The painter—this is the first alternative—represents Christ's flesh alone. Then he assigns the flesh a separate personality and adds a fourth person (the flesh) to the Trinity. The (unstated) implication is that such an assumption is Nestorian. The other alternative is that Christ's divine nature is circumscribed together with his human nature; this would be a confusion of the attributes (the divine nature is not circumscribable, the human nature is) and, again by implication, Monophysitism. 'My opponents are either Nestorians or Monophysites'—thus one could paraphrase Constantine's thesis, with which he had lifted the discussion to a christological and fundamental level. Constantine did not dare in his written works to express his hostility towards the cult of Saints, of martyrs' relics, and of the Virgin Mary. He denied, like his father before him, the concept of images as sacred objects, the concept of sainthood and the efficacy of the Saints' intercession. In the latter part of his reign he objected publicly to the belief in the Saints as well as to the images, as is known from chroniclers and hagiographers. He may have even promulgated an edict to this effect.[1]

Thus the christological argument against images of Christ had received an incisive and ingenious formulation in the days of Constantine V. This does not mean that the use of the christological dilemma by the Emperor is without a pattern in earlier thought. Like many ingenious inventions it was amazingly simple. In essence it meant that by representing Christ, the painter either separated the two natures or did to one (the divine) nature what was germane only to the other (the human). The Council of

[1] Fragments of Constantine's works: George Ostrogorsky, *Studien zur Geschichte des byzantinischen Bilderstreits*, Historische Untersuchungen 5, Breslau, 1929, 8–11 (with full discussion 11–29). His monophysitic tendencies, ibid. 24–28. Definition of the εἰκών: frg. 2. Consecrated bread and wine as true image: frgs. 19–22. Constantine's famous dilemma ('Nestorianism or Monophysitism'): frgs. 4–15. Constantine's theological achievement appraised by Ostrogorsky, op. cit., 22 f. and *Geschichte des byzantinischen Staates* (2nd ed., Munich, 1952), pp. 138 f. Constantine's opposition to the cult of Saints, martyrs' relics, and the Virgin Mary: Ostrogorsky, *Studien*, 29–40.

Hiereia stated expressly that both the painter and the worshipper of the image of Christ are guilty of these alternative 'blasphemies'.[1] A similar argument is recorded and refuted by Iohannes of Damascus in *De Fide Orthodoxa*: 'Against those who claim: "If Christ [has] two natures, you either adore likewise creation when worshipping a created nature, or you claim one nature to be worthy of worship and the other not".'[2] It is evident that the argument here reported resembles that used by Constantine Copronymus, especially in the form given to the latter argument by the Council of Hiereia. Both concern worship, the former of Christ, the latter of Christ's image. Both start from the dyophysitic doctrine. Both distinguish two alternatives for the particular worship (of Christ—of Christ's image) with which they are concerned: either one separates the two natures and worships or represents only one of the two natures (the opponents of Iohannes of Damascus: the divine; Constantine V: the human), or one offers to one nature (the opponents of John: to the human; Constantine V: to the divine) what is due to the other. The similarity in the two positions is even more evident if one bears in mind that the Council of Hiereia condemned not only the painting but also the worship of images.

Once this resemblance is established, it becomes important to determine the source of the argument refuted by John of Damascus. Its purpose is evident from its wording: it was advanced to disprove the dyophysitic christology by means of a *reductio ad absurdum* and thereby to confirm the monophysitic doctrine. If the assumption of two natures in Christ led to a paradox, the doctrine of one nature must be correct. Hence it is clear that the argument refuted by John of Damascus was monophysitic in tendency. Essentially, this was recognized by the editor of Iohannes of Damascus, Michel Lequien, who remarked in his edition of 1712: *Apollinaristae sic olim argumentati erant.*[3] He was thinking of certain writings of Apollinarian origin but circulating in the Church under the names of orthodox authorities like those of Gregory Thaumaturgus, Iulius of Rome, Athanasius,

---

[1] Mansi, xiii. 252: ταῖς αὐταῖς οὖν καὶ ὁ προσκυνήσας βλασφημίαις ὑποβέβληται.

[2] Iohannes Damascenus, *De Fide Orthodoxa*, iv. 3 (*P.G.* xciv. 1105A–B): Πρὸς τοὺς λέγοντας· εἰ δύο φύσεις ὁ Χριστός, ἢ καὶ τῇ κτίσει λατρεύετε φύσιν κτιστὴν προσκυνοῦντες, ἢ μίαν φύσιν προσκυνητὴν λέγετε ἢ μίαν ἀπροσκύνητον. (The text is uncertain.)

[3] *P.G.* xciv. 1105, n. 61.

&c.—the famous Apollinarian frauds. In fact, when in the second of his remarkable *Dissertationes Damascenicae*, Lequien demonstrated the Apollinarian origin of the *Epistulae ad Prodocium* which circulated under the authorship of Iulius of Rome, he remarked:

Nihil tam Catholicis Apollinarius objiciebat, quam quod hominem adorarent, aut aliam naturam adorando, aliam non adorando, eundem adorarent simul, et non adorarent, aut Christum in duos dividerent: adeoque indesinenter inculcabat, Verbum cum sua carne adoratione una colendum esse[1]

evidently precisely the argumentation reported by Iohannes of Damascus. Now in this dilemmatic form the argument is found, as far as I can see, only in one work of Apollinarian origin, the *Anacephalaeosis* by the Laodicean himself. Here the great heretic argued against the view that in Christ the Man was merely 'connected' (συμπέπλεκται) with the God:

Do we likewise [like the angels] worship the Man [in Christ] or not? But if we shall not worship Him, why shall we believe in His [the Man in Jesus'] being united [with the God] and why are we baptized unto His death? If however we shall worship Man and God alike, we shall act impiously by treating equally creator and creature.[2]

In other words, Apollinarius, in order to disprove the view of two natures in Christ, showed, just like the opponents of John of Damascus, that Christ's worship leads either to a negation of the union of the two natures or to a worship of Christ's human nature.

It would seem, then, that Constantine V adapted to his iconoclastic purposes an argumentation originally used by Apollinarius against dyophysites. For this purpose Constantine had to substitute the painting of the image of Christ for the worship of Christ Himself and to exchange the roles which the two natures played in Apollinarius' argument. The reason for the second modification was that, unlike the worship of Christ which was due primarily to His divinity, His artistic representation was connected first of all with His humanity.

---

[1] Ibid. 271.
[2] Ed. Hans Lietzmann, *Apollinaris von Laodicea und seine Schule*, vol. i (Tübingen, 1904), 28, p. 245: καὶ ἡμεῖς δὲ προσκυνήσομεν τὸν ἄνθρωπον ἢ οὔ; ἀλλ' εἰ μὲν οὐ προσκυνήσομεν, πῶς ἡνῶσθαι νομιοῦμεν αὐτὸν καὶ πῶς εἰς τὸν θάνατον αὐτοῦ βαπτιζόμεθα; εἰ δὲ προσκυνήσομεν ὥσπερ τὸν θεὸν οὕτω καὶ τὸν ἄνθωπον, ἀσεβήσομεν κτίσμα κτίστῃ ἐν ἴσῳ τιθέντες. Characterization of this work, p. 144: '. . . der in knappe syllogistische Form gebrachte Extract aus einem größeren Werke.'

Now objections may be made to this theory of the Apollinarian origin of Constantine's argumentation. It would seem much more probable that Apollinarius' dilemma reached Constantine through Apollinarius' heirs, namely the 'Monophysites' in the proper sense of the term. This seems both plausible and probable, but so far the writer's search in this direction has been in vain. Until an appropriate anti-Chalcedonian text is found, the derivation of Constantine V's argument from the writings of Apollinarius, from the *Anacephalaeosis* or another of his numerous works, must stand.[1]

Whether Constantine's dilemma is modelled on an Apollinarian or a later anti-Chalcedonian argument, the fact remains that the purpose of the model must have been frankly monophysitic. This agrees with Ostrogorsky's findings. This scholar called attention to the monophysitic tendency of Constantine's writings: they do not mention the proper Chalcedonian formula ἐν δύο φύσεσιν but are satisfied with statements like ἐκ δύο φύσεων which were accepted even by the moderate Monophysites of the Severan type. At the same time Constantine placed particular emphasis on the unity of Christ; in general his formulations went as far as a Byzantine monarch could go without attacking openly the Chalcedonian Council and the subsequent pronouncements of orthodoxy.[2] Going beyond Ostrogorsky's findings one may add that even the famous Constantinian dilemma is an adaptation of a monophysitic (Apollinarian) argument to the image problem.

The views advanced by Constantine made the problem of religious images a dogmatic issue of the first order. If the Iconophiles had long seen in the existence, production, and worship of Christian images a corollary to the Incarnation and thereby a confirmation of the dyophysitic doctrine as established by the Ecumenical Councils, Constantine's attack had shaken the foundation of their position. Outwardly he accepted the orthodox christology, but in fact he and his adherents were questioning once more and undermining what the Church had striven to answer authoritatively in the course of many centuries. Before Constantine Iconoclasm had been a movement opposed to the worship of images because of religious conservatism, and had been raised into prominence by recruiting amongst its members

---

[1] The monenergetic views of a seventh-century author, Theodore of Pharan, are said to have been influenced directly by Apollinarius.

[2] Ostrogorsky, *Studien*, 24–29.

the dynasty of Leo III. The Early Church had been opposed to religious images because they seemed a characteristic of paganism. They were introduced at a comparatively late date and were therefore objectionable on the same grounds as the pagan cult statues. With Constantine the iconoclastic movement received a new theological foundation. Now the worship of Christ's image was criticized not only as a return to paganism but also as a christological heresy.[1]

The impact of Constantine's ideas can be felt throughout all later discussions of the image problem. The iconoclastic side appropriated Constantine's position, and especially his christological dilemma, in the *Horos* of the Iconoclastic Council of Hiereia but only in essence; in form, the works of Constantine, which were cumbersome in their arrangement, vague, inaccurate, or often outright heretical in their theological vocabulary, required and received a complete *remaniement*.[2] The official orthodox answer to Constantine's christological attack, in the form given to it by the Council of Hiereia, may be found in Tarasius' refutation read at the Nicaean Council of 787. Yet, when in the ninth century the Patriarch Nicephorus set out on his systematic literary campaign against the iconoclastic doctrine, he commenced the long series of his dogmatic works with a refutation of Constantine's pronouncements in the *Apologeticus atque Antirrhetici*. Constantine V remained the great enemy.

In conclusion it may be said that at the beginning of the ninth century Iconoclasts and Iconophiles had examined several basic implications of Christian art. On the iconoclastic side the strongest weapons were the prohibitions of the Old Testament, the essential concept of the image and the christological dilemma first proposed by Constantine V. The iconophile theoreticians, on the other hand, relied chiefly on the symbolic theory of the religious image, which Christianity had inherited from paganism, and on the arguments from the Incarnation.

---

[1] Andreev, I., 'Sv. Tarasii, Patriarkh Konstantinopol'skii', *Bogoslovskii Vestnik*, August 1899, 459–504, esp. pp. 471 f., holds that by basing his attack on christological rather than traditional grounds, Constantine V weakened the impact of Iconoclasm on the masses who could not understand the new line of argumentation. This hypothesis is refuted by the later development of the Iconoclastic Controversy where Constantine and his writings remained the great enemy. Andreev seems to have underestimated the capacity of the Byzantines for theological argument.   [2] Ostrogorsky, *Studien*, 15–22.

III

NICEPHORUS THE LAYMAN[1]

1. Birth and Parents

NICEPHORUS was born under the rule of the Emperor
whose religious views and policy he was to combat during
his entire life: Constantine V Copronymus (A.D. 741–75).
The Bollandist G. Henschen states that Nicephorus' birth occurred around A.D. 758. This remark is based on a passage of the
Synaxarium Constantinopolitanum where it is said that Nicephorus
died in the thirteenth year of his exile after the completion of his
seventieth year.[2] A remark in one of Nicephorus' works shows
that he must at least have reached the age of intelligent childhood when he witnessed a terrible punishment meted out by the
government of Constantine to those who were unable to pay
their taxes.[3] On the other hand he seems to have no personal
memories of the bubonic plague which ravaged Constantinople
from A.D. 745 to 747, for he relies on other witnesses for his
account of this event.[4]

The place of his birth was Constantinople, and his parents were
called Theodore and Eudocia. He had several brothers. His

---

[1] Short biographical essays on Nicephorus: Gass, 'Nicephorus', in Herzog and
Plitt, *Real-Encyklopädie für protestantische Theologie und Kirche*, 2nd ed. (Leipzig, 1882),
x. 537 sq.; A. Ehrhard, 'Nicephorus', in Wetzer und Welte, *Kirchenlexikon*, 2nd
ed. (Freiburg i. Br., 1895), ix. 249–59; idem, in Karl Krumbacher, *Geschichte der
byzantinischen Litteratur etc.*, 2nd ed., Handbuch der klassischen Alterumswissen-
schaft ix. 1 (München, 1897), 71–73; E. von Dobschütz, 'Nicephorus', in Hauck,
Realencyklopädie für protestantische Theologie und Kirche, xiv. 22–25; R. Janin, 'Nicéphore de Constantinople', *D.T.C.* xi, pt. i (Paris, 1931), 452–5; G. Moravcsik,
Byzantinoturcica, i (Budapest, 1942), 278–81. After the conclusion of my research
there appeared A. J. Visser, *Nikephoros und der Bilderstreit. Eine Untersuchung über die
Stellung des Konstantinopler Patriarchen Nikephoros innerhalb der ikonoklastischen Wirren*
(Haag, 1952), on which see Preface.

[2] Henschen in *AASS. Martii*, vol. ii, col. 293F, reprinted in *P.G.* c. 39A: post
conciliabulum Copronymi circa annum 758. Cf. *Synaxarium Constantinopolitanum*,
ed. H. Delehaye, col. 725, line 12.

[3] Nicephorus, *Antirrheticus*, iii. 75, *P.G.* c, 516A: εἶδον ἔγωγε τῶν τελεσμάτων
χάριν ἀνθρώπους ἀθλίους δένδρεσιν ὑψηλοῖς τε καὶ εὐμήκεσι χειρῶν ἐξημμένους ἐκ-
κρεμεῖς ὡς ἐπὶ τὸν ἀέρα ἐπὶ πολὺ μετεωρίζεσθαί τε καὶ ταύτην πικρὰν καὶ βιαίαν δια-
φέροντας τιμωρίαν ἀπορίᾳ τῶν δημοσίων φόρων.

[4] Nicephorus, *Antirrheticus*, iii. 65, *P.G.* c. 496A.

father was an Imperial Secretary under Constantine V and came from a noble family.[1]

Nothing is known about Theodore's tenure of his office except the circumstances of his dismissal from it. From the *Vita Nicephori* it would seem that Theodore was denounced for worshipping images of Christ, the Virgin Mary, and the Saints.[2] Constantine summoned the Imperial Secretary to the palace, and Theodore, it is said, obeyed as if he were going to a banquet not to a trial. The charge was proved and Constantine tried to convert Theodore to his iconoclastic ideas by means of threats and tortures. Theodore remained adamant; he was deprived both of dignity and office[3] and banished to the fortress of Pimolissa[4] in Pontus, on the River Halys, in the northern part of the district of Amaseia.

When did these events take place? Only conjectures are possible. During the first decade after his victory over his rival Artavasdos Constantine V did not come out openly for Iconoclasm. It even took seven years after the Council of Hiereia before the persecutions began. About the year 761 the first martyrs are

---

[1] Apart from Nicephorus' own writings, his *Life* written by Ignatius the Deacon is the main source for his biography. It was edited by C. de Boor, *Nicephori* . . . *Opuscula Historica* (Leipzig, 1880), 139–217. See P. Alexander, 'Secular Biography at Byzantium', *Speculum*, xv (1940), 194–209, esp. 204. For his parents see *Vita Nicephori*, p. 142. His brothers are mentioned by Theodorus Studita, *Epistulae*, ii. 18 (*P.G.* xcix. 1173C). They seem to have died during Nicephorus' patriarchate. On Theodore's position, Ignatius, *Vita Nicephori*, p. 142 says: ἔλαχε . . . Κωνσταντίνῳ . . . τὴν τοῦ ὑπογραφέως ἀποπληροῦν χρείαν καὶ τοῖς βασιλείοις μυστηρίοις ὑπηρετεῖσθαι. This is a circumlocution for the Latin *a secretis*, cf. ibid., p. 144. On the office of ἀσηκρῆτις cf. J. B. Bury, *The Imperial Administrative System in the Ninth Century*, The British Academy Supplemental Papers I (London, 1911), 97 f., and Louis Bréhier, *Les Institutions de l'Empire Byzantin*, L'Évolution de l'Humanité xxxii *bis* (Paris, 1949), 167 f. On Theodore's connexions: *Synaxarium Constantinopolitanum*, col. 723: . . . ἐκ εὐπατρίδων καὶ εὐωνύμων.

[2] Ignatius, *Vita Nicephori*, p. 142: πικρῶς διαβάλλεται ὡς Χριστὸν ἐν εἰκόνι καὶ τὴν αὐτοῦ μητέρα τὴν ἄχραντον καὶ πάντας τοὺς ἁγίους σεβάζεται.

[3] This is my interpretation of the words of the *Vita*, p. 143: καθήρει τῆς περικειμένης χλαίνης καὶ ἀξίας. ἀξία would be the office and χλαῖνα would be one of the insignia denoting his rank in the imperial hierarchy. The difficulty, however, is that the holder of the office of ἀσηκρῆτις was of protospathar rank at best (Bury, *Imp. Adm. Syst.* 97) and nothing which might correspond to the χλαῖνα is among the insignia of this dignity. The χιτών begins only at a much more elevated rank of the hierarchy (cf. Philotheos, *Kletorologion*, ed. Bury, ibid., p. 135, line 13).

[4] *Vita*, p. 143. For the identification cf. Ramsay, *Asia Minor*, pp. 328 sq. The *Synazarium Constantinopolitanum*, col. 723, gives the fortress of Μύλασσα as the place of exile. This is clearly only a variant reading, not an actual divergence in our information. Pimolissa is probably correct since it was a fortress in the eleventh century (Cedrenus, ed. I. Bekker, vol. ii, p. 626), whereas Mylassa in Caria never was one, cf. W. Ruge, *R.E.* xxxi. 1046–64.

mentioned.[1] When in 763/4 St. Stephen the Younger was imprisoned in the Sacred Praetorium at Constantinople, he found there 342 monks 'from various countries' all of whom had been tortured for refusing to condemn the images.[2] The death of St. Stephen on 20 November 764 was followed by wholesale punishments of dignitaries who professed image-worship; some of them were banished.[3] The story of these banishments resembles that of Theodore so closely that it is safe to assume that he was not banished before 761.

Theodore's first exile did not last long. 'After some time had elapsed' Constantine asked Theodore to return to the imperial palace. He hoped that the hardships of exile would have made Theodore change his mind. But Constantine was mistaken. Theodore clung to his iconophile views. He was tortured once more and then taken to Nicaea in Bithynia. There he lived for six more years under great hardships.[4] Thus Theodore must have died in 767 or later.

The *Vita* does not give much information about Nicephorus' mother, Eudocia. She shared all the hardships of exile with her husband; after his death she lived for some time with her son. Not long after Nicephorus was appointed Imperial Secretary she entered a convent. She witnessed the brilliant career of her son at the court and lived to see him become Patriarch of Constantinople. Nicephorus paid her due respect throughout her life; she died some time during his patriarchate.[5]

2. *Childhood and Education*

Very little is known about Nicephorus' childhood, and even his medieval biographer had little specific information about it. It is not clear whether Nicephorus accompanied his parents into exile or whether the child remained in the capital, perhaps in the

[1] J. B. Bury, *A History of the Later Roman Empire from Arcadius to Irene* (London and New York, 1889), ii. 463; Edward James Martin, *A History of the Iconoclastic Controversy* (London, n.d.), 53 sq.

[2] *Vita S. Stephani Iunioris*, P.G. c. 1160c. On the chronology, cf. Ch. Diehl, 'Une Vie de saint de l'époque iconoclaste', *Académie des Inscriptions et Belles-Lettres, Comptes Rendus*, 1915, 149.

[3] Theophanes, p. 437, also p. 438, lines 2 to 26; Nicephorus, *Breviarium*, p. 72.

[4] This is one of the few biographical facts which is known only from the *Synaxarium Constantinopolitanum*, col. 723. It is not mentioned in the *Vita*.

[5] Theodorus Studita, *Epistulae*, ii. 18 (*P.G.* xcix. 1174c).

charge of some relative or friend. His father's courageous stand against the Emperor, his sufferings for the cause of image-worship, and his death in exile cannot have failed to make a lasting impression on the boy.

There is little detail in the *Vita* about Nicephorus' education. Shortly before his father's death Nicephorus had begun his 'general education' (ἐγκύκλιος παιδεία) in Constantinople and had been appointed Imperial Secretary. In the course of this general education,

he tuned the musical lyre, but not that of Pythagoras of Samos, or the impostor Aristoxenos, but rather the one with one hundred and fifty strings [i.e. the Psalter]. Continually, when playing upon it, he protected the subjects from the disease of Saul. He won the favor of the cruellest tyrant, who was throttled by the spirit of wrong opinion and acted like a drunkard unrepentantly against the dispensation of Christ; he saved the flock from his maltreatment.[1]

From these two passages, it results that Nicephorus began his general education and was appointed Imperial Secretary possibly under Constantine V, more probably under Leo IV,[2] at some time between A.D. 770 and 780. Nicephorus' appointment shows the Emperor anxious to win over to his side even the son of an official exiled for having been an obstinate advocate of image-worship. It also shows that Nicephorus did not hesitate to accept office from an iconoclastic emperor. He accepted it, and at the same time continued his general education.

What kind of education did Nicephorus receive? His medieval biographer felt that he could not omit this *topos* required by the canons of the hagiographical genre. On the other hand, he seems to have lacked specific information. Consequently he inserted a brief sketch of the educational curriculum of the day and paid no attention to Nicephorus' personal experiences.[3] In view of this silence of the sources the modern biographer must reconstruct

---

[1] *Vita*, p. 144: αὕτη (Eudocia) μετὰ τὴν τοῦ συνοίκου (Theodore) μακαρίαν τελείωσιν ἐφ' ἱκανὸν χρόνον τῷ παιδὶ συμβιώσασα ἄρτι τότε τῆς ἐγκυκλίου παιδείας ἐφαπτομένῳ καὶ τὴν διὰ χειρῶν καὶ μέλανος τέχνην πονουμένῳ· ἠρέθη γὰρ ὑπογραφεὺς τοῖς τῶν κρατούντων μυστηρίοις ὑπηρετούμενος, οὕτω γὰρ παρὰ τῇ Αὐσονίδι διαλέκτῳ τὸ Ἀσηκρῆτις ὄνομα. . . . The passage on general education is found in *Vita*, p. 150.

[2] Agapius of Menbidj, *Histoire universelle*, ed. and transl. by A. Vasiliev, *P.O.* viii. 547 (cited Chapter I, p. 18, n. 1 above).

[3] *Vita Nicephori*, pp. 149–51. The passage p. 150, line 15 to p. 151, line 13 reads like the ἀνακεφαλαίωσις (or list of chapter headings) of an elementary handbook of logic and physics. In fact, it is clearly a quotation as it lacks the double dactyls

the probable schooling received by Nicephorus from the general knowledge of Byzantine education in the eighth century.[1] Normally a child's elementary education began between the ages of six and eight years. An elementary teacher would instruct the child in reading and the rudiments of grammar. After the completion of this elementary course a young boy was expected to begin his general education. It began with a study of advanced grammar, poetry, and rhetoric. The next step was the *quadrivium* (τετρακτύς) of astronomy, geometry, music, and arithmetic. Finally, the young man would study philosophy.

It is not certain in which school Nicephorus may have received an education of this kind. It would seem probable, however, from the *Vita* that there existed a court school destined to train the officialdom of the Empire for their task. It is hard to understand how by singing the Psalter Nicephorus won the favour of Constantine V or Leo IV; perhaps he was a member of the choir in one of the imperial chapels. He certainly was in the Emperor's immediate entourage and at work in the Imperial Secretariate while at the same time receiving an education.

To judge from the *Vita*, Nicephorus' training was primarily secular, though biblical studies are mentioned. On the other hand, it is clear from his literary works that at some time during his life he must have studied theology, for he writes like a trained theologian. Like St. Stephen the Younger he may in his early childhood have listened to the lector in the church reciting the lives of martyrs and saints or the writings of the Fathers.[2] Like Constantine the Apostle of the Slavs, he may have studied and memorized Gregory Nazianzen,[3] or John Chrysostom like Stephen

---

which are characteristic for the clausulae of the *Vita*. In spite of much searching I have been unable to identify this handbook. Professor Otto Neugebauer, of Brown University, kindly called my attention to J. L. Heiberg's *Anonymi Logica et Quadrivium*, Det Kgl. Danske Videnskabernes Selskab, Historisk-Filologiske Meddelelser xv. 1 (Copenhagen, 1929). See the elaborate review by K. Praechter, *B.Z.* xxxi (1931), 82–96. This treatise, in its logical parts, shows indeed some agreements with the passage of the *Vita Nicephori*, but it does not deal with physics and includes the *quadrivium* instead.

[1] On this subject see Eduard Norden, *Die antike Kunstprosa* (Leipzig and Berlin, 1909), ii. 670–9; Friedrich Fuchs, *Die höheren Schulen von Konstantinopel im Mittelalter*, Byzantinisches Archiv VIII (Leipzig and Berlin, 1926), 41–45; Fr. Dvornik, *Les Légendes de Constantin et de Méthode vues de Byzance*, Byzantino-Slavica, Supplementa I (Prague, 1933), 25–33; Louis Bréhier, *La Civilisation byzantine*, L'Évolution de l'Humanité XXXII ter (Paris, 1950), 456–503.

[2] *P.G.* c. 1081c. [3] Dvornik, *Les Légendes*, p. 351.

the Younger.[1] Yet probably he made the same discovery as
Constantine, namely that self-instruction was not altogether satisfactory and that 'he could not understand the profound sense' of
what he was studying. In that case Nicephorus must have made
up for his lack of theological training in his later years. It is difficult to define precisely Nicephorus' intellectual and spiritual
relationship to Tarasius under whom he worked in the Imperial
Secretariate and whom he was to succeed as Patriarch. It is
more than likely, however, that, like their common biographer
Ignatius Diaconus,[2] he learned from him in some way. Furthermore, the biographer tells us that in the monastery which Nicephorus founded in the days of his retirement he devoted himself
to hymn-singing, to the reading of Holy Scripture, and to learning
in general.[3] Indeed, in a letter of the year 811 Nicephorus himself
admits that at the beginning of his patriarchate the evil spirits
'did not yet know that he was trained in matters spiritual and
divine'.[4] Although this remark may have been due in part to
modesty, it is plausible to suppose that Nicephorus' theological
knowledge increased during his patriarchate and exile.

3. *The Courtier*

Young Nicephorus' activities at court were not very well remembered when the Deacon Ignatius wrote his biography. In the
Imperial Secretariate Nicephorus was the subordinate of the
First Secretary (πρωτοασηκρήτης) Tarasius[5] who was to become
Patriarch of Constantinople in 784. The biographer states in the
conventional way that Nicephorus took a courageous stand in
disputations on image-worship which took place at court. If,
however, the biographer is right in saying that Nicephorus won
the favour of Constantine or Leo,[6] it is probable that Nicephorus
adopted an attitude more diplomatic than bold.

---

[1] *P.G.* c. 1081D.

[2] Ignatius Diaconus, *Vita Tarasii*, ed. I. A. Heikel, Acta Societatis Scientiarum
Fennicae XVII (1891), 423.

[3] *Vita Nicephori*, p. 148: νύκτωρ τε καὶ μεθ'ἡμέραν ταῖς εὐκτικαῖς ἱερολογίαις ἐγκαρ-
τερῶν καὶ τῷ ἀρίστῳ μέτρῳ τῆς ἐγκρατείας κατεντρυφῶν τῇ ἀναγνώσει τῶν θείων
προσεῖχε καὶ τοῖς μαθήμασι.

[4] *P.G.* c. 176C: οὔπω γάρ με τοῖς πνευματικοῖς καὶ θείοις παιδοτριβούμενον ἔγνωσαν.

[5] *Vita Tarasii*, ed. Heikel, p. 397: πρῶτος ὑπογραφεὺς τῶν βασιλικῶν μυστηρίων.
Vita Ioannis episcopi Gotthiae, AA. SS. Iunii, v. 191 (= *Iunii* vii. 167–71): Ταράσιος
δὲ ὁ πρωτοασηκρήτης.   [6] Above, p. 57.

Nicephorus came into prominence for the first time at the Seventh Ecumenical Council of Nicaea. On his participation there are three reports:

1. In the *Vita Nicephori* Ignatius says:

Nicephorus also was honored above many equal in age by travelling together with these select leaders [representatives of the five patriarchates]. He was entrusted with the imperial heraldship over that holy assembly (τὸ κατὰ τὴν ἱερὰν ἐκείνην σύνοδον ἐγχειρισθεὶς ἐπιφώνημα) by virtue of which he delivered the purity of the faith as a message to all; he cried out and made plain the ancient representation and worship of the holy images as if speaking from a place commanding a wide view; thereby he became the colleague of the holy assembly even before [he donned] the sacred garment.

If these words are impressive, they certainly are not distinguished by clarity. What was the βασιλικὸν ἐπιφώνημα which was entrusted to Nicephorus? One senses that these words hide a *terminus technicus* for an imperial function which Ignatius' puristic pen refused to name.

2. The second text, the *Vita Tarasii* by the same author, is even less clear than the first. There Ignatius remarks:

Tarasius arrived [at Nicaea] bringing along with him select and distinguished men of the apostolic sees [the names follow of the representatives], bringing furthermore several officials distinguished for their piety and intellectual graces, among whom there was Nicephorus, who was at that time serving the imperial secrets [i.e. he was *a secretis*].

3. In the Acts of the Council of Nicaea Nicephorus is indeed mentioned as Νικηφόρος ὁ εὐκλεέστατος βασιλικὸς ἀσηκρῆτις.[1] This mention occurs during the second meeting of the Council, at which Nicephorus read a Greek translation of a letter from Pope Hadrian to Constantine and Irene. Nowhere else does Nicephorus' name appear in the Acts.

The minutes of a second session begin with the announcement that a βασιλικὸς ἄνθρωπος is waiting at the door and that he is escorting a repentant Iconoclast Gregory, bishop of Neocaesarea. At the invitation of the president Tarasius, ὁ λαμπρότατος

---

[1] Mansi, xii. 1055A. Visser, *Nikephoros*, 53, overlooked this passage. He also suggests, on the basis of *Vita Nicephori*, p. 147, that shortly after the Council Nicephorus composed a poem against Iconoclasm. This is possible but not certain. The passage may refer to a simple declaration of orthodoxy made by Nicephorus.

μανδάτωρ enters and states that at the request of the Emperor he has taken Gregory to the Council. There follows a preliminary examination of Gregory's case, and after this the affair is postponed until the next meeting. Leontius the Imperial Secretary reminds the Council that a letter of Pope Hadrian is to be read. Thereupon Nicephorus proceeds to read the papal letter. In view of this sequence of events it is a natural inference that the unnamed βασιλικὸς μανδάτωρ[1] attending the second meeting is identical with the Imperial Secretary Nicephorus whose presence is recorded. This assumption is strengthened by the fact that, according to Ignatius, Nicephorus was entrusted with the βασιλικὸν ἐπιφώνημα. The noun ἐπιφώνημα is not frequent in Byzantine literature[2] but ἐπιφωνήτης occurs in the sense of town-crier[3] and ἐπιφώνησις in that of acclamation.[4] Ignatius' words therefore might well be a paraphrase of the term βασιλικὸς μανδάτωρ used in the Acts. If this hypothesis is correct, it would indicate that in 787 Nicephorus enjoyed the confidence of Irene and the Patriarch to a high degree. The case of Gregory of Neocaesarea was perhaps the most delicate procedural issue which the Council was expected to handle. It was bound to encounter violent feelings on the part of the monks and threatened to endanger the policy of ecclesiastical unity and reconciliation in which Irene and Tarasius were interested. The Empress and the Patriarch must have felt that young Nicephorus, who was then not even thirty years old, approved of their policy and could be trusted. The role assigned to him at the Council must have made it clear to the participants that the young courtier was destined to play a prominent part in the affairs of state.

4. *Retirement*

After the Council of Nicaea Nicephorus remained for some time in the imperial service. Later, as he writes in his *Epistula*

---

[1] On the office of βασιλικὸς μανδάτωρ cf. Bury, *Imp. Adm. Syst.* 113.

[2] In *Vita Nicephori*, p. 194: ἱμειρόμενοι . . . εἰσδέξασθαι τὸ παρὰ τῆς ἐκείνου γλώσσης ἡδυεπὲς ἐπιφώνημα it has the meaning of 'address'. In Mansi, xiii. 459D: καὶ [προ]καθεσθέντων ἁπάντων ἡμῶν κεφαλὴν ἐποιησάμεθα Χριστόν· ἔκειτο γὰρ ἐν ἁγίῳ θρόνῳ τὸ ἅγιον εὐαγγέλιον ἐπιφωνοῦν πᾶσιν ἡμῖν τοῖς συνελθοῦσιν ἱερουργοῖς ἀνδράσι· κρίμα δίκαιον κρίνατε, the verb ἐπιφωνεῖν signifies 'to proclaim'.

[3] Passion of St. Heliconis, *AA. SS. Maii*, vi. 741E. I owe this passage to A. Tougard, *Excerpta Bollandiana* (Paris, 1874), 131, who translates *praeco*.

[4] C. E. Zachariä von Lingenthal, *Ius Graeco-Romanum* (Leipzig, 1857), iii. 233.

ad Leonem, he felt that if he wished to obtain salvation he had to retire from the turmoil of life in Constantinople.[1] Accordingly he established himself on a mountain not far from the Propontis.[2] There he lived in the expectation that some day he might become a monk.[3]

The *Vita* follows the account of the *Epistula* closely, adding a few points here and there. According to the former Nicephorus crossed the Bosporus in complete poverty and settled on a steep hill. The hagiographer takes delight in describing the barrenness of the place: it was rough, dry, and the overhanging part of the mountain (τὸ πρανές) deprived it even of the blessings of rain. A kind of grotto then must have been the scene of Nicephorus' ascetic life. Ignatius dispenses with further description of the locality: 'he who wishes [to do so] can go there and get acquainted with the locality rather than with [my] speech'. The changes which Nicephorus achieved, it is said, will astound any one who visits the place. Through his activity his place of exile was adorned with the shrines of holy martyrs and their images. It was 'fattened' by cisterns which communicated by means of a system of 'hollows'.[4]

After these transformations his refuge seemed fit for a monastery and Nicephorus founded one. There he and his monks devoted themselves to prayers, religious hymns, ascetic exercises, and also to the reading of sacred and secular writings.[5]

These two reports show a Nicephorus who has retired from the world. It would appear from certain comparisons in the *Life*[6] and from the tone of the passage that Nicephorus donned the monastic habit himself. Such an assumption would be erroneous; for Ignatius tells us that Nicephorus became a monk only shortly before his accession to the Patriarchate and the same may be inferred from Theophanes.[7] Although the hagiographer makes so

---

[1] *P.G.* c. 173 sq.

[2] Ibid. 176A: ἐσχατίαν γοῦν τινα καταλαμβάνω καὶ ἀκρώρειαν, τραχεῖάν τε οὖσαν καὶ δυσπρόσοδον· σταδίοις οὗτος [?] ὀλίγοις περὶ τὴν Προπόντιον χώραν τοῦ βασιλείου διειργομένην (διειργεμένην) ἄστεως. The text is hopeless.

[3] Ibid.: ὡς ἄρα εἰ δυναίμην τοῦ μονήρους βίου ἐφαπτόμενος.

[4] *Vita Nicephori*, 148: (the place was) διὰ σηράγγων ὑποτρεχόντων δεξαμένας ἐκ δεξαμενῶν ἀλληλούχῳ δαψιλείᾳ πιαινόμενος.

[5] Presumably this was the monastery τῶν Ἀγαθοῦ mentioned later in the *Vita*, 201, or possibly the monastery of St. Theodore (ibid.).

[6] Ibid. 147: ἐπί τινα λοφίαν ἀντικρὺ τοῦ Θρακικοῦ Βοσπόρου μεταναστεύει οὐδὲν πλέον τῆς Ἡλίου μηλωτῆς, τῆς ἀκτησίας φημί, πρὸς τὸν ὅμοιον ἐπιφερόμενος Κάρμηλον.

[7] Ibid. 157: τὸ μὲν σχῆμα τοῦ λαϊκοῦ πρὸς τὴν τοῦ μονήρους μεταμεῖψαι ἀγγελοειδῆ

much of the poverty which Nicephorus 'brought' ($\epsilon\pi\iota\phi\epsilon\rho\delta\mu\epsilon\nu\sigma s$) to his refuge, this does not exclude his having left property at Constantinople. In fact, the foundation of a monastery would imply that he disposed of considerable means.[1] Furthermore, Nicephorus was later appointed again to an important position at Constantinople, namely to the directorship of the greatest metropolitan poorhouse.[2] Thus we can look through the curtain of holiness with which Nicephorus himself and the hagiographer have surrounded the events: Nicephorus' departure was not a flight into monastic life, but either a retreat which was meant to be temporary, or the consequence of political disgrace.[3] The reasons for it are not quite clear. Certainly it was not connected in any direct way with the Moechian controversy of 795; for if at that time Nicephorus had given up or lost his office, this would have been mentioned when the Moechian controversy was revived in 806. It is more likely that it was the blinding of Constantine VI and the return of Irene to power in 797 that forced Nicephorus into retirement. If this is true, Nicephorus would have gone into exile at the very moment when his great contemporary Theodore of Studios was allowed by Irene to return to Constantinople. It would indeed explain a great deal about the future relations of Nicephorus and Theodore if in the nineties of the eighth century the former was a partisan of Constantine VI and the latter of his mother Irene.

The 'emperors' forced Nicephorus to accept the directorship of the largest poorhouse at Constantinople.[4] This, it is explained, meant that by means of this 'partial stewardship' he was entrusted with the direction of the entire Church. Consequently, Nicephorus held an important office which was ecclesiastical in character. Which office precisely did he hold? One might think of

$\pi o\lambda\iota\tau\epsilon ia\nu$ $\tau\delta\nu$ $\beta a\sigma\iota\lambda\epsilon a$ $\epsilon\vartheta\vartheta\vartheta s$ $\pi a\rho\eta\tau\eta\sigma a\tau o$. When Theophanes, p. 481, mentions the opposition of Plato and Theodore of Studios to Nicephorus' elevation to the see of Constantinople, he defends Nicephorus by stating that many others had become bishops after having been laymen.

[1] Eugène Marin, *Les Moines de Constantinople* (Paris, 1897), 47.

[2] See below, p. 64. Positions concerned with social work were semi-ecclesiastical in character.

[3] Cf. Michael Psellos' stay on Mt. Olympos.

[4] *Vita Nicephori*, 152: $\tau o\hat{v}$ $\mu\epsilon\gamma i\sigma\tau o\nu$ $\pi\tau\omega\chi\epsilon iou$ $\tau\hat{\omega}\nu$ $\kappa a\tau\dot{a}$ $\tau\dot{\eta}\nu$ $\beta a\sigma\iota\lambda i\delta a$ $\epsilon\pi\iota\tau\rho o\pi\epsilon\hat{\upsilon}\epsilon\iota\nu$ $\pi\rho o\tau\rho o\pi\hat{\eta}$ $\beta\iota a i\alpha$ $\tau\hat{\omega}\nu$ $\kappa\rho a\tau o\hat{\upsilon}\nu\tau\omega\nu$ $\dot{\eta}$ $\chi\dot{a}\rho\iota s$ $\dot{\eta}\xi i\omega\sigma\epsilon$. Cf. R. Janin, *La Géographie ecclésiastique de l'empire byzantin*, première partie: Le Siège de Constantinople, etc., tome iii: 'Les Églises et les monastères' (Paris, 1953), 581 f.

the Great Orphanage of Constantinople and its head, the ὀρφανο-
τρόφος,[1] but an orphanage is different from a poorhouse. It is
probable that the Patriarch Tarasius played some part in this
appointment of his former subordinate.[2] It would perhaps be most
natural to think of Nicephorus' return to Constantinople as
having occurred after Irene's overthrow by the Emperor Nicephorus I in 802.

It was while he was holding this semi-ecclesiastical position
that Nicephorus was appointed Patriarch of Constantinople.

[1] On this office cf. Bury *Imp. Adm. Syst.* 103. On public charity in general cf.
G. Schlumberger, 'Monuments numismatiques et sphragistiques du moyen-âge
byzantin', *Revue archéologique*, xl (1880), 193–212; idem, *Sigillographie*, 377–81.

[2] On Tarasius' interest in public charity cf. A. Vogt, 'S. Théophylacte de Nico-
médie', *Analecta Bollandiana*, l (1932), 69 sq.

IV

NICEPHORUS, PATRIARCH OF CONSTANTINOPLE[1]

1. *The Appointment*

ON 18 February 806 the Patriarch Tarasius died[2] after he had occupied the patriarchal see of Constantinople for more than twenty years. The *Vita Tarasii* has it that not only all Constantinople, but also the Emperor Nicephorus lamented his death.[3]

The appointment of a new patriarch of Constantinople normally proceeded in two steps. The first was the actual election (ψηφο-φορία); the second, the liturgical ordination or investiture (χειρο-τονία) of the candidate.[4] Between these two there was often an intermediate stage, since the ordination had to occur on a Sunday or holiday; it was during this interval that the Emperor might intervene—quite uncanonically but most efficiently.

The *locus classicus* for these proceedings is a passage from the *Book of Ceremonies* by Constantine Porphyrogennetus.[5] This chapter describes the election of an unknown Patriarch and sub-

---

[1] The sources for the Patriarchate of Nicephorus flow much more abundantly than those for either his youth or his exile. His own works, except for the *Epistula ad Leonem*, are not revealing from the point of view of ecclesiastical history. But the chroniclers Theophanes and George Syncellus, the *Scriptor Incertus de Leone Armeno*, the Letters of Theodore of Studios, a number of Saints' Lives, and the *Epistula ad Theophilum*—all contribute to our knowledge of Nicephorus' patriarchate. Finally, the *Vita Nicephori* continues to be of value for the period.

[2] Theophanes, 481.

[3] Ignatius Diaconus, *Vitae Tarasii*, 420 (ed. Heikel).

[4] N. Cotlarciuc's 'Die Besetzungsweise des (schismatischen) Patriarchalstuhles von Konstantinopel', *Archiv für katholisches Kirchenrecht*, lxxxiii (1903), 3–40, is of little use. P. P. Sokolov's *Izbranie patriarkhov v Vizantii s poloviny IX do poloviny XV vieka* (St. Petersburg, 1907/14) (see *B.Z.* xvii (1908), 267) was not available, but may be largely identical with H. I. Sokolov, 'Izbranie arkhiereev v Vizantii IX–XVv.', *V.V.* xxii (1915–16), 193–252, esp. 196. See also the brief summaries by Louis Bréhier, 'L'Investiture des patriarches de Constantinople au moyen âge', *Studi e Testi*, cxxiii (Miscellanea G. Mercati, iii) (1946), 368–72, and *Institutions*, 477–82. There is an interesting account of patriarchal elections in modern times by K. Lübeck, 'Die Patriarchenwahl in der griechisch-melkitischen Kirche', *Theologie und Glaube*, vi (1914), 730–40.

[5] ii. 14, ed. I. I. Reiske, *C.S.H.B.* ix. 564 sq.

sequently the 'ordination of the Patriarch Theophylactus in
A.D. 933.[1] It may be summarized as follows. After the death of
a Patriarch the Emperor requests the metropolitan bishops to
nominate three candidates. The metropolitan bishops assemble
at St. Sophia and submit three names to the Emperor. Thereupon the Emperor summons them to the palace. There he either
approves of one of the three nominees or else he says: 'I want So-
and-So to become Patriarch' (ἐγὼ τὸν ὁ δεῖνα θέλω γενέσθαι), and
the bishops assent. There follows an assembly of Senate and
clergy in the Magnaura where the new Patriarch is solemnly
proclaimed by the Emperor and finally escorted to the patriarchal
palace (πατριαρχεῖον). The ordination follows on a subsequent
Sunday or holiday.

From this account it is clear that, at least in A.D. 933, only the
metropolitan bishops took part in the election; the role of the lay
element in episcopal elections had been on the decline for a long
time[2] and even ordinary bishops had no vote in this matter.
Undoubtedly the most astonishing feature of the text is the
intervention of the Emperor; he could simply brush aside any of
the three candidates nominated by the metropolitan bishops and
appoint instead his own candidate. It need not be supposed that
an emperor always acted in this way. This would depend on the
balance of forces between Church and State at any given time,
and in 933 the imperial appointee was the Emperor's own son.
But such an attitude on the part of the Emperor, it would seem,
was not extraordinary.

There is an abundance of information on all the stages of
Nicephorus' elevation to the patriarchal see. In the course of the
ψηφοφορία the Emperor made a thorough inquiry. 'He declared
to all priests, monks and the senators whom he considered distinguished and outstanding' that he would accept the choice of
the majority as inspired by God.[3] This would imply that in 806

---

[1] This was proved conclusively by G. Ostrogorsky and E. Stein, 'Die Krönungsurkunden des Zeremonienbuches etc.', *Byzantion*, vii (1932), 185–237, esp. 187–90,
but only for the second part of the chapter: 'Kap. 14 des zweiten Buches besteht
offensichtlich aus zwei heterogenen Teilen, die ganz mechanisch und recht unge-
schickt miteinander verknüpft sind.' The compiler connected two ceremonies which
organically belong together: part 1 is concerned with the ψηφοφορία, part 2
with the χειροτονία. It is correct, however, that part 1 is not concerned with the
events of the year 933.

[2] Jules Pargoire, *L'Église byzantine de 527 à 847* (Paris, 1905), 57.

[3] Ignatius Diaconus, *Vita Nicephori*, 153 sq.

not only the metropolitan bishops but other members of the clergy, of the monastic order, and even distinguished laymen were consulted in the matter of the election.[1] Apparently, however, the electors could not agree; each of them voted (ἐψηφολόγει) for his own candidate.[2] From the preliminary inquiries made by the Emperor Nicephorus in preparation for the formal ψηφοφορία a valuable document is preserved in the correspondence of Theodore of Studios.[3] The abbot wrote to the Emperor Nicephorus, who had asked for his opinion, that he did not know an appropriate candidate, but added that the new patriarch should have risen gradually in the hierarchy, that he should be a bishop, abbot, stylite, recluse, or cleric. He adds that the patriarch should be able to help those who are in temptation.

Theodore's uncle Plato also was consulted, not only by distinguished clerics but also by the Emperors themselves. His answer is not preserved, but there remains an interesting though intentionally vague indication in the *Laudatio Platonis* by Theodore of Studios.[4] According to this account later critics of Plato said that he either should have claimed ignorance of who was a proper candidate, as his nephew Theodore actually did, or that he should have left the ψήφισμα to his inquirers. Plato did not act in this way but named a candidate. The clerics who had inquired endorsed (βεβαιοῦν) Plato's proposal, but the Emperor Nicephorus 'shook it off rolling the votes as if in a game of dice'. On this subject Plato even had a conversation with an influential relative of the Emperor who was a monk.

From these texts it has been inferred that Plato had suggested his nephew Theodore for the patriarchate, and that the latter, though holding himself ready, had had the stylite Symeon in mind as an alternative candidate.[5] These and similar inferences may be correct;[6] they certainly cannot be proved. At any rate it is clear that the Studites did not nominate Nicephorus and refused to consider a layman.

---

[1] See, however, Pargoire, *Église byzantine*, 57: 'Toutefois, la part du peuple dans cet acte [i.e. elections of bishops] tend à se restreindre.'

[2] *Vita Nicephori*, 154; Theodorus Studita, *Laudatio Platonis*, 34 (*P.G.* xcix. 837B): τὰ ψηφίσματα ἐπὶ πολλοὺς οἱ πολλοί, ὡς ἕκαστος εἶχεν κατὰ φιλίαν ἢ ἀλήθειαν.

[3] i. 16 (*P.G.* xcix. 960A–961A).

[4] Ch. 34 (*P.G.* xcix 837B).

[5] G. A. Schneider, *Der hl. Theodor von Studion, etc.*, Kirchengeschichtliche Studien v. 3 (Münster i. W., 1900), 27.

[6] Alice Gardner, *Theodore of Studium*, &c. (London, 1905), 112 sq.

Since the persons consulted could not agree, it is natural that the selection devolved upon the Emperor. Possibly it had been known before that he had a candidate of his own; in this case the stalemate may have been due to a desire not to interfere with the Emperor's choice and represents a diplomatic yielding to political pressure. However that may be, it is doubtful whether an emperor like Nicephorus would have hesitated to overrule even the unanimous vote of the assembled clergy. Like his successor Romanus Lekapenus more than a hundred years later, he made the appointment himself: his nominee was his namesake Nicephorus who was at that time head of a poorhouse at Constantinople and residing outside the city.[1] The imperial appointment was ratified by the formal vote of the clergy.

Good fortune has preserved not only a fairly clear account of the following events in the *Vita*, but as a valuable supplement an interesting notice in a catalogue of the Patriarchs of Constantinople. The relevant part of this document seems to have been written shortly after A.D. 909.[2]

Reluctantly Nicephorus followed the imperial messengers back to the city, and it was only after long hesitation that he acceded to the Emperor's demand.[3] The next step was that Nicephorus made his profession as a monk on 5 April. Here is a slight disagreement in our sources: the *Vita* represents this step as a special favour which Nicephorus asked of the Emperor, the *Catalogus* says that he was ordered to do so.[4] The tradition less favourable to Nicephorus, that is to say, the account given by the *Catalogus*, seems more plausible inasmuch as it was in the Emperor's interest to make a conciliatory gesture to the monks. The ceremony was performed in the monastery of SS. Sergius and Bacchus

---

[1] According to the *Vita*, 154 he had to be persuaded by messengers to come to Constantinople. I suppose that in good episcopal style Nicephorus had fled the honour which was to be bestowed upon him and had hidden outside Constantinople, as most bishops did at the time of their election (*nolo episcopari*).

[2] Ed. F. Fischer, *De patriarcharum Constantinopolitanorum Catalogis et de chronologia octo primorum patriarcharum*, Commentationes Philologae Jenenses iii (1884), 282–94. On Nicephorus see p. 291. On the date of the passage cf. p. 278.

[3] I do not take the speeches which Ignatius puts into the mouth of the Emperor and his appointee (154–7) as historical evidence. They would, however, support the tradition that Nicephorus hesitated to accept the office.

[4] *Vita*, 157: τὸ μὲν σχῆμα τοῦ λαϊκοῦ πρὸς τὴν τοῦ μονήρους μεταμεῖψαι ἀγγελοειδῆ πολιτείαν τὸν βασιλέα εὐθὺς παρῃτήσατο. *Catalogue*: προτραπεὶς ᾑρετίσατο τὸ μοναδικὸν ἀμφιάσασθαι σχῆμα.

founded by Justinian I in the quarter of Hormisdas.¹ This was
the second largest monastery at Constantinople and was chosen
because the monastery of Studios, for obvious reasons, was not a
suitable place for the ceremony. The *Vita* states that Stauracius,
son and co-emperor of Nicephorus I, gathered (ὑποδέχεσθαι) the
hair which fell from the novice's head when he was tonsured.²
Accordingly Stauracius was acting as 'sponsor' (ἀνάδοχος), just
as Michael I Rangabe acted as 'sponsor' a few years later when
Nicetas the Patrician became a monk.³

On 9 April Nicephorus was taken to the patriarchal palace and
was ordained deacon. On Good Friday, 10 April, he became
presbyter. The final ceremony took place on Easter Sunday in the
presence of the Emperors at Hagia Sophia. The consecration was
performed by Nicholas archbishop of Caesarea in Cappadocia,
Leo metropolitan Bishop of Heraclea in Thrace, and Thomas
archbishop of Thessalonica. As is well known, the custom of three
bishops ordaining a new bishop goes back to the first of the
Apostolic Canons. It was also an old privilege of the metropolitan
bishops of Heraclea to participate in the consecration, since at an
earlier date the bishop of Constantinople had been the suffragan
of this bishop.⁴ Finally it can be seen that Nicephorus' election
was open to the same criticism (he had been a layman and had
been ordained *per saltum*) as Tarasius' had been a generation
earlier and as that of Photius was to be fifty years later.⁵

The *Vita* adds one peculiar detail to the reports about the
ceremony: before the actual ordination took place the patriarch-
elect deposited a profession of faith, which he had composed
previously, on the altar.⁶ This act was a substitute for the προσ-
φωνητικὸς λόγος which the patriarchs of earlier centuries had
delivered orally on the day of their consecration.⁷ Such docu-

¹ Marin, *Moines*, 20 and passim.
² p. 157: (the Emperor Nicephorus) τὰ τῆς ἱερᾶς ἐκείνης κεφαλῆς ἀποκάρματα
ταῖς τοῦ υἱοῦ καὶ συμβασιλέως χερσὶν . . . ὑποδεχθῆναι σοφῶς ἐδικαίωσεν.
³ *AA. SS. Octobris*, iii. 448 F. On the ἀνάδοχος cf. Jules Pargoire, 'Saint Théophane le chronographe et ses rapports avec Saint Théodore Studite', *V.V.* ix (1902),
31–102, esp. 56–61. On monastic initiation see Marin, *Moines*, 107–18.
⁴ Cotlarciuc, *Besetzungsweise*, passim.
⁵ Bury, *East. Rom. Emp.* 190.
⁶ Grumel, *Regestes*, no. 374. Visser, *Nikephoros*, 56, erroneously calls the document
'die von ihm verfaßte Streitschrift gegen die Ikonoklasten'.
⁷ Fragments of a document of this kind are preserved from the sixth century,
Grumel, *Regestes*, no. 228. Note that the *Vita Nicephori*, p. 157, mentions a previous
reading (προσφωνεῖν) of the document to the clergy of St. Sophia.

ments had been signed by the patriarchs Anastasius (730–54) and Paul IV (780–4) under iconoclastic emperors, and they continued to be drawn up throughout the ninth century.[1]

Thus the Patriarch Nicephorus owed his appointment primarily to the secular power, and it was to be expected that this fact would determine the relations between the Patriarch and Emperor as long as they were in office. The Patriarch badly needed the imperial backing, for the Studites had been opposing his appointment vigorously on the ground that the candidate was a layman. The Emperor even thought of banishing their leaders and breaking up the monastery.[2] But on second thoughts he merely imprisoned Plato and Theodore for twenty-four days until the Patriarch was consecrated.[3]

From a short-term point of view the appointment of Nicephorus by the Emperor might have seemed a wise step. It could be foreseen that the new Patriarch would depend on imperial support and that the gulf which separated secular and monastic clergy and which had in fact been deepened by this appointment would prevent any unified opposition on the part of the Church. From the point of view of long-range policy, however, it was hardly in the true interest of the secular authorities to create friction within the Church. The discord between the two groups weakened not only the Church but also the state, and when Byzantium had recovered from internal strife after the restoration of orthodoxy, it had lost some of its most valuable possessions to the Infidels and had weakened its bonds with the West. There can be little doubt that in 806 the Emperor could have found a more appropriate candidate, a bishop or even an abbot, who would have been equally amenable to the will of the Emperor and would have disarmed Studite opposition.

It is difficult to say what must have been the new Patriarch's own expectations as to his new responsibilities. The tradition of his family, his education, as well as his experience in the imperial administration certainly qualified him for the administrative and academic aspects of his high office. His retirement from the world and his monastic foundation had revealed ascetic traits in his

---

[1] Examples: Grumel, *Regestes*, 343 (Anastasius), 348 (Paul IV), 414 (Methodius), 456 (Photius).
[2] Theophanes, 481.
[3] Theodorus Studita, *Laudatio Platonis*, ch. 35 (*P.G.* xcix. 838D).

character, on the strength of which he may have hoped to overcome the enmity of the Studites. His appointment of Theodore's brother Joseph to the archbishopric of Thessalonica and the affair of the monastery Τὰ Δαλμάτου make it probable that he planned, in the course of time, to win the monks over to his side. If these were his hopes, they were soon dashed by issues which the emperors were to raise: the restoration of the deposed priest Joseph ὁ μοιχοζεύκτης who had performed the marriage ceremony for Constantine VI and Theodote, and also by the new outbreak of Iconoclasm under Leo V. These two events were to make the patriarchate of Nicephorus one of the stormiest in the history of this venerable see.

2. *General Political and Ecclesiastical Activity of Nicephorus*

It has been said that the Patriarch of Constantinople was the Emperor's 'minister of the department of religion'.[1] This is true, but it meant two things. The first is that, to a certain extent, the Church was only a department of the state. The second, which has often been overlooked, is that the Patriarch of Constantinople was a member of the 'Council of Ministers'. His voice was heard, his opinion was heeded not only on religious matters but also on questions of general policy. In brief, in addition to the 'internal position' of the Patriarch as head of the Church he held an 'external position' with regard to the state which was by no means insignificant.[2]

It is not easy to get an accurate idea of the personality of the Emperor Nicephorus I. The judgement of historians with respect to this ruler has been led astray by the fact that our only contemporary Greek source, the chronicler Theophanes, evidently had personal reasons to be dissatisfied with this prince.[3] When describing the reaction of the population to Nicephorus' successful plot (803) Theophanes remarks:

[1] J. B. Bury, *The Constitution of the Later Roman Empire* (Cambridge, 1910), 32.
[2] A. Albertoni, *Per una esposizione del diritto bizantino con riguardo all' Italia* (Imola, 1927), 109.
[3] G. Ostrogorsky, 'Theophanes', *R.E.* B, x. 2128; G. Cassimatis, 'La Dixième "Vexation" de l'Empereur Nicéphore', *Byzantion*, vii (1932), 149, believes that the moderate attitude of the Emperor Nicephorus towards the images displeased Theophanes. P. Charanis, 'Nicephorus I, the savior of Greece from the Slavs', *Byzantina Metabyzantina*, i. 1 (1946), 75–92, argues that the Emperor Nicephorus I rescued Greece from the Slavic invaders.

The entire population of the city assembled, and everybody was irked at the events, and cursed him who crowned him [Tarasius], and the man who was crowned [the Emperor Nicephorus], and those who rejoiced along with them. And those who led a respectable and reasonable life were amazed at the divine judgment. . . . Others were as if distracted in mind at what had happened and believed they were dreaming and not perceiving that matters had come to pass. . . . Others again—and they belonged to those who are well capable of foreseeing [the future]—gave praise to past prosperity, and bewailed the misfortune which was to come out of the usurpation; [this was the opinion] particularly of all those who had had previous experience of the evil mind of the usurper.[1]

Again, when Bardanes Turcus rebelled against the Emperor (A.D. 803), and when subsequently the latter took an oath to execute the murderers of the rebel, Theophanes observed:

He Nicephorus always acted with ostentation (κατ' ἐπίδειξιν) and did nothing according to God; for along with his other transgressions he also had this outstanding intellectual characteristic by which he had deceived many even before he became Emperor.[2]

Theophanes then is strongly biased against the Emperor Nicephorus and it may be supposed that he was one of those who had 'had previous experience of the evil mind' of the cunning Minister of Finance. A passage from the Syriac chronicler Michael may indicate that Theophanes stood alone with this judgement: 'Un des écrivains chalcédoniens accuse ce Nicéphorus de beaucoup de choses.'[3] Under these circumstances it is regrettable that later chronicles based their account on Theophanes.[4]

Theophanes' judgement can be controlled with the help of other sources. Not only do Syriac sources speak very highly of the military exploits of the Emperor Nicephorus,[5] there are also hagiographic texts which praise other qualities of the Emperor. The *Vita Nicetae* written by Theosterictus in the third decade of the ninth century calls him ἅμα καὶ τὴν ὀρθοδοξίαν ὁ εὐσεβέστατος

---

[1] Theophanes, 476 sq.
[2] Theophanes, 480.
[3] Ed. J. B. Chabot, *Chronique de Michel le Syrien etc.* iii. 1 (Paris, 1905), 16.
[4] Cf. the texts quoted by Cassimatis, 'La Dixième Vexation', 151 sq., note 1.
[5] J. B. Chabot, *Chronique de Michel le Syrien*, iii. 1. 16: 'dans l'empire des Romains, depuis que les Taiyayê avaient commencé à régner, personne (ne s'était montré) aussi courageux et aussi brillant que lui à la guerre.' Cf. also Bar Hebraeus, translated by E. A. W. Budge (Oxford, 1932), i. 121.

καὶ φιλόπτωχος καὶ φιλομόναχος.[1] The *Vita Georgii episcopi Amastridos* reports that the Emperor preferred the company of the Saint to the imperial diadem.[2] The *Vita Nicephori*[3] calls him 'most astute' (ἀγχινούστατος), the *Vita Tarasii*[4] τῆς ἀλουργίδος πιστῶς διεξάγων τὸ τίμιον, the *Vita Theophanis* by Methodius contains a dithyramb on the Emperor in which all conceivable virtues are attributed to him.[5] None of these sources is contemporary with the Emperor Nicephorus but all of them were written within the first three decades after his death. Thus, if the sources are weighed, it must be admitted that among his contemporaries Nicephorus had the reputation of being not only an extremely able general and administrator but also an orthodox Christian.

It is not astonishing to find that under an emperor such as Nicephorus I his patriarchal homonym had little influence on political affairs. In his letter to Pope Leo III, written in 811, Nicephorus the patriarch apologized for not having sent the customary letter of enthronement earlier. He asks the Pope to understand that this was not due to negligence, but 'the authority's [i.e. the Emperor's] harsh and implacable mind was in the ascendant and was able to hinder us from doing what we deemed best'.[6] In a letter to an abbot Symeon, written in 808/9, Theodore of Studios mentioned that the Emperors Nicephorus and Stauracius were on a campaign; the Patriarch Nicephorus, he continued, 'neither sends word nor is willing to receive a message—in all [respects] he is Caesar's steward' (μήτε λόγον διαπέμψαντα, μήτε ἐθέλοντα ἀκοὴν παραδέξασθαι, ταμιευόμενον πάντα Καίσαρι).[7]

---

[1] This text (*AA. SS. Aprilis*, i, col. xxix), as well as a similar one (*Epistula ad Theophilum, P.G.* xcv. 365C) is quoted by Bury, *East. Rom. Emp.* 8, n. 3, and Cassimatis, 'La Dixième Vexation', 150 sq., n. 3.

[2] Ch. 35, ed. Vasil'evski, *Trudy*, iii. 54.   [3] Ed. de Boor, 153.

[4] Ed. Heikel, 420. In the *index nominum* the editor erroneously interprets this as referring to the *Patriarch* Nicephorus.

[5] V. V. Latyshev, *Methodii Patriarchae Constantinopolitani Vita S. Theophanis Confessoris etc.*, Mémoires de l'Académie des Sciences de Russie, VIIIᵉ série, Classe Hist.-Phil. xiii. 4 (1918), 26.

[6] Nicephorus, *Epistula ad Leonem, P.G.* c. 197A: ἐξουσίας γνώμη σκληρά τε καὶ ἀμείλικτος ἐπρυτάνευσε κωλύειν ἡμᾶς τοῖς δεδογμένοις χρῆσθαι δυναμένη.

[7] Theodorus Studita, *Epistulae*, i. 26 *P.G.* xcix. 992 D). There are two indications which may help to date the letter: (1) the Emperors are on a campaign; (2) Theodore is not yet exiled (the exile was decreed in January 809, Theophanes, 484), but the affair of Joseph of Kathara had begun. It is hard to identify this particular campaign. The Emperor Nicephorus left Constantinople to fight against the Bulgarians in 806/7 (Theophanes, 482) and again around Easter 809 (ibid., p. 495); he left for a campaign against the Arabs for the last time in 806/7 (E. W.

There is one political event, however, which cannot have failed to implicate the Patriarch. In February 808 a rebellion was planned. The rebels intended to crown the quaestor and patrician Arsaber.[1] Among the conspirators there were not only prominent laymen, but 'also holy bishops, monks, and men of the Great Church, the synkellos and the sakellarios and the chartophylax'. Unfortunately Theophanes must have had his reasons for omitting names. Of the officials mentioned the *synkellos* was appointed by the Emperor, a liaison officer between the Emperor and the Patriarch.[2] The *sakellarios* was in charge of monastic discipline, and the *chartophylax* was the head of the patriarchal chancery.[3] All three officials were in the immediate entourage of the Patriarch. Still there can be no doubt that the Patriarch himself remained loyal to his master; otherwise the latter would not have hesitated to make him share the fate of the conspirators.

Nicephorus' position with regard to the secular power changed markedly after the Emperor Nicephorus had fallen in a battle against the Bulgarians on 26 July 811. The death of a Byzantine patriarch often served to strengthen the position of an emperor: the new patriarch would be his appointee and even if he did not have to sign written promises of loyalty, &c., the Emperor frequently would act more boldly under the new patriarch than under the old. The affair of Joseph of Kathara, to be discussed presently, will illustrate this point. If these considerations are true, the reverse should be true also. The death of an emperor relieved the Patriarch from many checks and restraints, particu-

Brooks, 'Byzantines and Arabs in the time of the early Abbasids', *English Historical Review*, xv (1900), 746 sq.). But the year 806/7 is impossible since Theodore says (*Epistulae*, i. 25, *P.G.* xcix. 989D) that he kept quiet for two years after the restoration of Joseph. The only solution is to suppose that the sources omitted a campaign in which the Emperor took part.

[1] Theophanes, 483. Cf. Bury, *Eastern Roman Empire*, 14; N. Adontz, 'Role of the Armenians in Byzantine Science', *Armenian Quarterly*, iii (1950), 55–73, esp. 66.

[2] Bury, *Imperial Administrative System*, 116 sq.: Bréhier, *Institutions*, 499 f. The study of B. K. Stephanides, 'Οἱ σύγκελλοι ἐν τῷ διοικετικῷ συστήματι τοῦ Οἰκουμενικοῦ Πατριαρχείου', 'Ο Νέος Ποίμην, ii (1920), 481–93 was not available. Sometimes more than one synkellos was attached to the Patriarch, cf. Dvornik, *Les Légendes*, 60.

[3] On the *chartophylax* cf. E. Beurlier, 'Le Chartophylax de la Grande Église de Constantinople', *Comptes rendus du IIIᵉ Congrès scientifique international des Catholiques à Bruxelles*, Cinquième Section, 1895, 252–66; L. Clugnet, 'Les Offices et les dignités ecclésiastiques dans l'église grecque', *Revue de l'Orient chrétien*, iii (1898), 148 sq.; Dvornik, *Les Légendes*, 52–66; Bréhier, *Institutions*, 501–3. On the *sakellarios* cf. Clugnet, *Offices*, 146 sq.; Bréhier, *Institutions*, 501.

larly if that emperor had nominated him; in fact, the new emperor would depend on the Patriarch for his coronation. It can hardly surprise then that after the death of the Emperor Nicephorus, the Patriarch's political stature at Constantinople increased considerably.

This natural development was accentuated by the situation at the court. The heir to the throne, Stauracius, was seriously wounded in the battle and was to survive for a few months only. He escaped to Adrianople and delivered a speech to the survivors in which he criticized his father. From the very first, however, there was a group of courtiers who preferred Nicephorus' son-in-law, Michael Rangabe, to Stauracius. But since there remained some hope that Stauracius would recover, he was proclaimed Emperor at Adrianople. He was taken to Constantinople where the Patriarch Nicephorus is said to have advised him to reconcile himself to God and to 'comfort those who had been wronged by his father'. Stauracius after some hesitation declared that he could not give more than three talents for this purpose.[1]

This is not the place to deal with the intrigues staged around the dying emperor.[2] When in September 811 it became clear that Stauracius wished to leave the Empire to his wife Theophano of Athens, the Patriarch Nicephorus joined forces with the group which favoured Michael Rangabe. On 1 October 811 Michael was proclaimed Emperor. Meanwhile Stauracius donned the monastic garb as an indication that he was abdicating. On several occasions he summoned the Patriarch who finally arrived together with Michael and Procopia, sister of Stauracius and wife of Michael. Theophanes' account gives a vague impression of a pitiful scene. Nicephorus, Michael, and Procopia claimed that their action was prompted not by treachery but by his (Stauracius') moribund condition. It is quite natural that Stauracius, arrayed in monkish garb, did not accept these apologies but replied to the Patriarch enigmatically: 'You will find no better friend than me.'[3] On the same day Nicephorus crowned Michael

---

[1] Theophanes, 492.

[2] See Bury, *Eastern Roman Empire*, 18–20, to be corrected by the important article of G. I. Bratianu, 'Empire et démocracie à Byzance', *B.Z.* xxxvii (1937), 86–111 (*Études byzantines*, 95–124).

[3] Theophanes, 493: φίλον αὐτοῦ κρείττονα οὐχ εὑρήσεις. Bury, *Eastern Roman Empire*, 20, n. 2, believes that this mistake (αὐτοῦ for ἐμοῦ) is due to the fact that 'the last pages of his chronography were insufficiently revised by the author'.

Rangabe at St. Sophia. Finally, on 12 October, Nicephorus crowned the Empress Procopia and on 25 December the coronation of Michael's son Theophylactus was performed. Before the ceremony, however, the Patriarch had required, and obtained, a written affirmation of orthodoxy. In it Michael had promised that he would not defile his hands with Christian blood and that he would not issue orders concerning any member of the monastic or secular clergy.[1]

It has been stated that 'in matters that touched the Church the pliant Emperor was obedient to the counsels of the Patriarch'.[2] Others have assumed that 'it was to the Studites that he chiefly deferred'.[3] In fact whenever there was disagreement between the Studites and the Patriarch, Michael followed the advice of the monks. The decisions reached in the affair of Joseph of Kathara, on the problem of the Paulicians, on the re-establishment of peaceful relations with the West, and on the Bulgarian war, will be dealt with later and will illustrate these general remarks. For the moment some minor problems of Church discipline which the Patriarch had to face will be discussed.

The first is that of the so-called 'double monasteries'. 'Double monasteries' were combinations of a monastery with a nunnery separated in space but under the direction of the same person. The best example is that of τὰ Μαντινέου, mentioned in the *Synaxarium Constantinopolitanum*[4] and in the Georgian translation of the *Life of St. Romanos*.[5] At the time of Constantine V Copronymus, St. Anthusa had founded a convent on an island in a lake and a monastery on the shores of the lake. The two communities were wisely separated by the waves.[6] The dangers of this type of

[1] Bury, *Eastern Roman Empire*, 39 sq. I am accepting the conjecture τυποῦσθαι, instead of τύπτεσθαι; cf. Dölger, *Regesten*, no. 384.

[2] Bury, *Eastern Roman Empire*, 26.

[3] Gardner, *Theodore*, 131; Bréhier, *Vie et mort de Byzance*, 100 f.

[4] cols. 848–52. Another example may be found in Theodorus Studita, *Epistulae*, ii. 182 (*P.G.* xcix. 1562 sq.). Unfortunately, the letter cannot be dated, except that it must precede the measure of the Patriarch Nicephorus mentioned below in the text.

[5] P. Peeters, 'S. Romain le néomartyr (†1 mai 780) d'après un document géorgien', *Analecta Bollandiana*, xxx (1911), 393–427. On 'double monasteries' cf. J. Pargoire, 'Les Monastères doubles chez les Byzantins', *E.O.* ix (1906), 21–25; H. Leclercq and J. Pargoire, 'Monastère double', *D.A.C.L.* xi. 2182–7 (these authors did not know the article of P. Peeters).

[6] Peeters, *S. Romain*, 409 sq.: 'Est autem Mantineon lacus, in quo medio locus est siccus, ubi aedificatum fuit monasterium sanctarum virginum; itemque in

monastic settlement were obvious, in spite of the waves. So the Seventh Ecumenical Council had forbidden the foundation of new double monasteries and had reaffirmed strict rules for those which were already in existence. The Patriarch Nicephorus took the final step: he suppressed all double monasteries.[1] This is the last heard of 'double monasteries' under the jurisdiction of the Patriarch of Constantinople.

An incident touching Church discipline occurred when the Governor of one of the Tauric climata, that is the Toparch of Gotthia in the Crimea, planned to divorce his wife and marry another woman.[2] The Patriarch wrote him a letter in which he gave him advice and threatened him with penalties if he should not change his mind. Unfortunately, the Toparch was not much impressed by Nicephorus' letter. Theodore of Studios, in a letter written in A.D. 808, speaks of the divorce as of a *fait accompli*.[3] Since Nicephorus' letter must have preceded that of Theodore, Nicephorus' letter was written between 806 and 808.[4]

Nicephorus' influence on affairs of state seems to have decreased when Leo V the Armenian (813–20) overthrew Michael I and was proclaimed Emperor by the army. In marked contrast with his weak predecessor, Leo was a competent ruler who asked for nobody's advice, least of all for that of the clergy. Yet Nicephorus had played a considerable role at the time of Leo's accession to the throne. Pleased with the role of kingmaker, which he had assumed after the death of the Emperor Nicephorus, he had once again shown his initiative. Michael I had fled to Constantinople

litore huius lacus monasterium alterum aedificatum est, quod incolunt sancti patres etc.'.

[1] Grumel, *Regestes*, nos. 385 and 386. Pargoire, *E.O.* ix. 24, had given as the date 'vers 810'. Grumel thinks of 811/14. This date is based exclusively on the order of events in the *Vita Nicephori*. This sequence, however, is not always chronological. Such inferences, therefore, are dangerous.

[2] *Vita Nicephori*, 160. On this passage see A. A. Vasiliev, *The Goths in the Crimea* (Cambridge, Mass., 1936), 105 sq. The passage has been overlooked by P. Grumel in his *Regestes*.

[3] *Epistulae*, i. 31 (*P.G.* xcix. 1013A). In this letter Theodore tells us that the ruler of Lombardy likewise divorced his wife. This seems to refer to the divorce of Duke Grimoald of Benevent from Euanthia, sister of Mary of Amnia (M. H. Fourmy and M. Leroy, 'La Vie de S. Philarète', *Byzantion*, ix (1934), 85–167, esp. 104–9).

[4] The apologetic purpose of this incident in the *Vita Nicephori* was emphasized by Ernst von Dobschütz, 'Methodius und die Studiten', *B.Z.* xviii (1909), 55, n. 3. On the strength of Nicephorus' courageous attitude towards the Gothic Toparch, Ignatius felt justified in omitting the record of his less upright behaviour in the affair of Joseph of Kathara.

after he had been defeated by the Bulgarians at Versinicia. He returned to Constantinople on 24 June and immediately expressed the desire to abdicate and appoint a successor.[1] The Patriarch Nicephorus backed his plan because he believed that in this way the lives of the Emperor and his children would be spared. But as was the case in 811, there was another faction led by the Empress Procopia, Theoctistus, and Stephanos. Leo the Armenian wrote a letter to the Patriarch Nicephorus in which he asserted his orthodoxy and expressed his desire 'to seize the power with his [Nicephorus'] prayer and assent'.[2] The standing of the Patriarch could not be illustrated more clearly than by this episode.

What answer the Patriarch gave is not known, but in view of his earlier attitude it can hardly have been negative. On 11 July Michael, Procopia, and their children had themselves tonsured, and on the next day Leo was solemnly crowned by the Patriarch on the ambon of St. Sophia. Before the coronation Nicephorus had asked for a formal statement of orthodoxy, but Leo had given him only vague promises.[3] At the coronation, according to the *Vita Nicephori*,[4] the Patriarch when placing the crown on the head of Leo had the impression that he was touching 'thorns and burrs' and even felt a pain.[5]

Of the events of the year 813 there is a curious and confused report in a letter of Pope Leo III to Charlemagne dated 25 November 813.[6] As far as I can see, it has not yet been used by Byzantinists.[7] According to the Pope, there landed a vessel with several *Greci homines* on board. One of them told the Pope that when Leo (who apparently had already been proclaimed by the troops) was campaigning against the Bulgarians, Procopia, wife of Michael, had tried to persuade a patrician named Constantine

---

[1] Theophanes, 502.

[2] Ibid.: αἰτῶν μετὰ τῆς εὐχῆς καὶ ἐπινεύσεως αὐτοῦ τοῦ κράτους ἐπιλαβέσθαι.

[3] On the various accounts of this incident cf. Bury, *Eastern Roman Empire*, 56 sq.

[4] p. 164.

[5] The coronation of Leo V may be referred to in the *Book of Ceremonies*, i. 38 (first part). G. Ostrogorsky and E. Stein, 'Krönungsurkunden', *Byzantion*, vii (1932), 190–4, proved that this part of the chapter referred to the coronation of Michael I, Leo V, or Michael II, and inclined towards the last event. Dölger, *B.Z.* xxxvi (1936), 150, has given reasons for his belief that this is an account of the coronation of Leo V.

[6] *M.G.H.*, *Epistolae Karolini Aevi*, vol. v, no. 8, 99 sq.

[7] Cf., however, M. Amari, *Storia dei Musulmani di Sicilia*, ed. 2 (Catania, 1933), i. 352, note.

to marry her and to become Emperor in Michael's stead. Constantine agreed and bribed many adherents with a treasure which had been hidden by the late Emperor Nicephorus. He entered the imperial palace, summoned the Patriarch Nicephorus, and asked to be crowned. Nicephorus refused and was slain by Constantine. Leo's wife and one little son were likewise killed. When Leo heard this, he complained bitterly to the patricians and optimates that they had made him Emperor. On their advice he took 15,000 choice troops and entered Constantinople by stratagem. His troops slaughtered 16,000 men and women. Leo, pitying his countrymen, offered to fight a duel against Constantine in which he killed him. He also killed a patrician Theodore and all other partisans of Constantine. Procopia was put away in a particularly cruel manner. After having arranged affairs of state Leo returned to the Bulgarian campaign. So far the report of the Byzantine traveller. Later the Pope had talked to a messenger of Gregory patrician of Sicily (*unum hominem Gregorii patricii*) who said that neither the Patriarch Nicephorus nor the wife of Leo nor her son had been killed, and that Procopia had slain only a small daughter of Leo.

Before examining the content of these reports it should be noted that this is more than a traveller's tale. The messenger of the Governor of Sicily evidently had heard of something similar; he denied certain details, but he did not deny the main facts themselves. And Sicily certainly was in close contact with Constantinople.

The situation described evidently followed the battle of Versinicia. Leo is campaigning against the Bulgarians and has been proclaimed Emperor by the troops. Procopia is at Constantinople. Not a word is said about Michael. It may be supposed that the report deals with that intermediary period when Michael was still Emperor, but when it was clear to everybody that something had to be done. It is known from another source that Procopia was *de facto* ruler of Byzantium.[1] She hated Leo's wife, and when she learned of Michael's decision to abdicate in favour of Leo, her first idea was that Barca—as she called her—would place the *modiolon* on her head.[2] In view of these facts it is not impossible that Procopia had indeed designs of her own when it became clear

---

[1] *Scriptor Incertus de Leone Armeno, P.G.* cviii. 1012A.
[2] Theophanes Continuatus, 9 (*P.G.* cix. 32c).

that her husband Michael was doomed. She might have wanted
to make it plain to the rebel Leo that his family was in her hands;
perhaps she actually had one daughter of his murdered. Whatever her further plans might have been, it is clear from the silence
of the sources that she did not carry them out. The rest of the
report cannot be verified; in particular nothing is known about
the patrician Constantine to whom Procopia supposedly promised her hand and the Empire, or of the slaughter of Procopia.

Orthodox sources have heaped all possible injuries on Leo V
the Armenian because of his iconoclastic policy. Still Theophanes,
who finished his Chronicle in 814 at the latest[1], makes no re-
servations when he reports that Michael believed Leo to be
'pious and very manly and made in all respects for seizing the
Empire'.[2] Soon, it is true, Theophanes changed his opinion at
least so far as the Emperor's piety is concerned; for Genesius
knew of a lost poem by Theophanes in which he blamed Leo for
having been lured into Iconoclasm by Theodotus Cassiteras and
an anonymous monk.[3] Genesius praised Leo's statesmanship[4]
and quoted the favourable opinion of a man who certainly
would have been excused if he had been less impartial, namely
that of the Patriarch Nicephorus who said after Leo's death:
'The Roman state has lost a great though impious provider.'[5]

3. *Secular and Monastic Clergy*

Nicephorus' activities as Patriarch of Constantinople cannot
be understood apart from the important struggle between secular
and regular clergy. The origins of this conflict in the eighth
century must be sketched briefly in order to clarify the problems
faced by the Patriarch.

Rivalry between these two groups of the clergy was natural
and traditional in view of their different aims. The iconoclastic
persecutions of Constantine V transformed this rivalry into un-

[1] Ostrogorsky, 'Theophanes', *R.E.* A, x. 2129.

[2] Theophanes, 502.

[3] Genesius, 15 (*P.G.* cix. 1008A): ὡς καὶ παρὰ τοῦ μακαρίτου Θεοφάνους καὶ
ὁμολογητοῦ ταῦτα δι' ἐμμέτρου ποιήσεως ἐστηλιτεύετο. The name of the monk was
not Antonius as Bury, *Eastern Roman Empire*, 59, thinks. Theodotus merely calls
him 'a second Antonius the Great' (1005B), thereby comparing him to the famous
Egyptian saint.

[4] Genesius, 17 (*P.G.* cix. 1009C).   [5] Ibid.

disguised hostility.[1] At the Seventh Ecumenical Council of Nicaea
it had made itself felt with special force on the intricate problem
of the *lapsi* who had embraced Iconoclasm in one form or another.
The secular clergy, led by Tarasius and evidently reflecting the
policy of the court, were in favour of leniency. The monks directed
by Sabas of Studios, were more rigorous, insisted on the punishment of the ringleaders, and tried to wreck the conciliatory
policy of Tarasius.[2] In the end the monks compromised in the
interest of ecclesiastical unity, but it is clear that the unity
achieved at the Council was artificial. The fifth canon issued by
the Council decreed that a bishop who had performed ordinations
for money was to be deposed. Soon after the Council Tarasius
at the request of the Empress Irene declared that the 'Simoniacs'
would be restored after one year of penance. Sabas and his
followers objected, and the Patriarch yielded: he denied having
ever granted penance to the Simoniacs and declared that he
would not enter into communion either with those who had
ordained for money or with those who had been ordained in this
way. But the Empress objected. On 6 January 788, at the festival
of Theophany, again under pressure from Irene, Tarasius held
communion publicly with the Simoniacs who had completed their
year of penance. He made it clear, however, that in the future
Simoniac ordinations would not be permitted. When Irene was
deposed in 790, Tarasius reversed his earlier decision and declared
that he had not granted penance and would not hold communion

---

[1] Above, p. 14.

[2] The first two sessions of the Council were taken up altogether with the question of ten bishops who had been prominent among the Iconoclasts, see esp. Mansi,
xii. 1002–23. The attitude of the monks at the Council was later characterized in
a letter of Theodore of Studios, *Epistulae*, i. 38 (*P.G.* xcix. 1044A) : ['Sabas of Studios
and Theoctistus of Symboli] insisted that bishops returning from the iconoclastic
heresy should not be admitted to their sees, but not with regard to all of them, but
(only) the prominent ones and the originators of the heresy, according to the word
of St. Athanasius [his letter to Rufinianus, *P.G.* xxvi. 1180 sq., which played a
prominent role at the Council, cf. Mansi, xii. 1023E ff.]. That was not unreasonable.
But since the contemporary council [i.e. of 787] decided that all should be admitted
on the precedent of the fourth council they agreed; for the matter was not an
offence against essentials.' One wonders whether the tone of Tarasius' remark
(Mansi, xii. 1118) : ἐπαινοῦμεν ὑμᾶς ὡς ζηλωτὰς τῶν κανονικῶν καὶ εὐαγγελικῶν
διατάξεων revealed impatience or irony. The Sabas group even hesitated to recognize ordinations which directly or indirectly proceeded from the three iconoclastic successors of the Patriarch Germanos (Mansi, xii. 1047B–1050D; Theodorus
Studita, *Epistulae*, i. 53, *P.G.* xcix. 1104C). This attitude threatened most members
of the Council.

with a person whom he knew to be a Simoniac. He wrote a number of letters directed against simony past and future. In one of them it is said expressly that the accusations of simony were made by the monks and that they threatened the majority of bishops. The Simoniac affair thus was the sequel to the monastic attack on the secular clergy at the Seventh Council. At the Council the monks had been handicapped by the slogan of *homonoia*, unity, a common front against Iconoclasm. After Iconoclasm had been condemned, they renewed their attack against the episcopal majority. Tarasius had to yield: after some hesitation he refused to reinstate Simoniacs provided that the accusation was proved. But proof was difficult and the measures against Simoniacs, therefore, could be restricted to those few bishops who had openly boasted of having bought their see. The victory in principle fell to the Studites, but their general attack on the secular clergy failed to attain its real purpose. Few bishops could have lost their sees, and the monks must have felt dissatisfied with this result of their campaign.[1]

The two parties were to clash again in the Moechian Controversy. In A.D. 781 the young Emperor Constantine VI, then only a child, had been betrothed by his mother to Rotrud, or Erythro, daughter of Charlemagne. But in 787 and 788 Irene took sides with Charles's enemies, the Beneventans, and consequently the betrothal between the Byzantine prince and his romantic *princesse lointaine* was broken off. The Empress forced Constantine to marry Maria of Amnia, granddaughter of St. Philaretus, of whose life and family there is a vivid picture by his grandson Nicetas. In A.D. 795 Constantine divorced Maria, and in September of the same year he married a lady-in-waiting

---

[1] Chronology: V. Grumel, *Regestes*, no. 360. The obligation which is due to Grumel for elucidating not only the chronology but also many other details of Church history can hardly be over-emphasized—particularly for a period when the main source are the Letters of Theodore of Studios with their confusing wealth of historical information. The passage quoted above (p. 14) from the *Adversus Constantinum Caballinum* proves that the question of the simoniac bishops was debated even prior to the Council of Nicaea. Canon 5 of Nicaea Council: Mansi, xiii. 421 ff. Main source for Simoniac episode: Theodorus Studita, *Epistulae*, i. 38 (*P.G.* xcix. 1041B sqq.) and 53 (ibid. 1101C ff.). On this matter compare furthermore Ignatius Diaconus, *Vita Tarasii*, 406. Cf. Grumel, *Regestes*, no. 361. Tarasius' retractation: Theodorus Studita, op. cit. i. 38 (*P.G.* xcix. 1045A). Tarasius' letters on simony: Grumel, *Regestes*, nos. 363–6. Mansi, xiii. 474B: οἱ πλείονες τῶν ἐπισκόπων χρήμασιν ὠνήσαντο τὴν ἱερωσύνην. Tarasius' proviso, Mansi, xiii. 475B: ἐλεγχθεὶς ἐπὶ χρήμασι τὴν χειροτονίαν ἢ δοὺς ἢ λαβών.

(κουβικουλαρέα) of the Empress called Theodote. Tarasius apparently refused to perform the ceremony, but it was held against him by his opponents that he continued in communion with the Emperor, that he allowed an unnamed catechist (κατηχητής) to tonsure Maria, and Joseph abbot of τὰ Καθαρά to perform the ceremony.[1]

This second marriage brought Constantine and Tarasius into conflict with Plato of Saccudion and his nephew St. Theodore who were relatives of the new Empress Theodote. At this time Plato was living at Saccudion as a simple monk and Theodore had become abbot. Only two of Theodore's letters seem to belong to this early period. Their tone is quiet. He protests his loyalty to Constantine and to all his (Theodore's) relatives. He is still mentioning the Emperor and praying for him; he is still trying to prevent the adulterous wedding. In the second letter he claims the right of criticizing the Patriarch even where matters of faith are not involved. The Studites were exiled. Once again they were in opposition to the Patriarch, who headed the party of moderates. But this time the lines were not drawn as clearly as during the days of Iconoclasm. Among those who sided with the Patriarch are found prominent members of the monastic clergy, like Theophanes, the abbot τοῦ μεγάλου Ἀγροῦ (the chronicler), Joseph abbot of τὰ Καθαρά who had married Constantine and Theodote, and it would seem that very few people indeed sided openly with the monks of Saccudion. On the other hand, even members of the secular clergy respected the courageous attitude of the monks, as for instance the archbishop of Thessalonica who received the exiles kindly.[2]

[1] On the Moechian Controversy see the summary by Robert Devreesse, 'Une Lettre de S. Théodore Studite relative au synode mœchien (809)', *Analecta Bollandiana*, lxviii (1950), 44–57, esp. 48–52. On Constantine VI's betrothal to Rotrud see Theophanes, 455, 463, also A. Kleinclausz, *Charlemagne* (Paris, 1934), 124 f., 127. Life of St. Philaretus: M.-H. Fourmy and M. Leroy, 'La Vie de S. Philarète', *Byzantion*, ix (1934), 85–170. On Constantine's wedding to Theodote see Theophanes, 470; Theodorus Studita, *Epistulae*, i. 28 (*P.G.* xcix. 1000A). Later it was said in defence of Tarasius that Constantine threatened to revive Iconoclasm unless the Patriarch acquiesced to his demand: *Narratio de sanctis patriarchis Tarasio et Nicephoro*, *P.G.* xcix. 1852D.

[2] On Theodore of Studios see Jules Pargoire, 'Saint Théophane le chronographe et ses rapports avec Saint Théodore Studite', *V.V.* ix (1902), 85–88; A. Gardner, *Theodore of Studion, His Life and Times* (London, 1905). The two letters from the early period: i. 4 and 5 (*P.G.* xcix. 919D–926D). The mention of Theodore's affection for his relatives obviously refers to Theodote who was his second cousin; it

On 15 August 797 Constantine VI was blinded by his mother Irene, who thereby recovered the throne. The exiles were recalled. It was probably soon after their return that they persuaded Tarasius to excommunicate and depose Joseph. But Plato and Theodore were not yet satisfied. The 'zealots' strove utterly to humiliate their opponents. Tarasius had to offer his formal apologies to Plato and to invite him to make peace. Probably Tarasius did not do so without some bitterness. For the time being peace was re-established in the Church: Joseph, τὸ σκάνδαλον, was removed. The Empress Irene was orthodox and proved a benefactress to Plato and Theodore: in A.D. 799 they were installed in the monastery of Studios at Constantinople and in the following years they seem to have profited greatly from Irene's tax abatements (A.D. 801). The ex-Emperor Constantine VI died before A.D. 805. There remained the memory of almost fifty years of rancorous feud between secular and monastic clergy. Iconoclasm, Simoniac controversy, and Moechian affair had been but episodes in this long-drawn struggle; the last scene was the personal humiliation of the Byzantine Patriarch.[1]

One of the first acts of the new Patriarch Nicephorus revealed his conciliatory attitude towards the monks. He summoned Theodore of Studios to take part in the election of an abbot at the Constantinopolitan monastery τὰ Δαλμάτου.[2] It is not easy to see why the abbot of Studios should have been invited to participate

would be inconceivable after the second outbreak of the Moechian Controversy. Exile: *Epistulae*, i. 1 (ibid. 903–8) and i. 3 (ibid. 913–20: itinerary of exiles). Theodorus Studita, *Laudatio Platonis*, 26 (ibid. 829B): πάντων σχεδὸν συνελθόντων τῇ παρανομίᾳ μόνος, ὡς εἰπεῖν, οὗτος (Plato of Saccudion) σὺν τοῖς ἑαυτοῦ παισὶν, εἶτ' οὖν φοιτηταῖς ἀκλόνητος διαμένων. The Emperor Constantine VI issued a decree (omitted in Dölger's *Regesten*) to the effect that the exiles should not be received anywhere. This decree was adhered to by most of the abbots, and few were those who dared give lodgings to them, *Laudatio Platonis*, 27 (ibid. 829D). Archbishop of Thessalonica: *Epistulae*, i. 3 (ibid. 917D).

[1] Recall of exiles: Theodorus Studita, *Laudatio Funebris in Matrem Suam*, 10 (*P.G.* xcix. 897A). Joseph deposed: *Epistulae*, i. 28 (ibid. 1000A); i. 30 (ibid. 1008A); *Laudatio Platonis*, 31 (ibid. 833C); Grumel, *Regestes*, no. 369. Irene's tax abatements: *Epistulae*, i. 7 (ibid. 929 ff.), cf. above, p. 21). Death of Constantine VI: E. W. Brooks, 'On the Date of the Death of Constantine the Son of Irene', *B.Z.* ix (1900), 654–7.

[2] Theodorus Studita, *Magna Catechesis*, ii, no. 89, 277–80, ed. A. Papadopoulos-Kerameus (Mrs. N. Scheffer, of Dumbarton Oaks, kindly located this rare publication in Makarius, *Velikiia Minei Chetii*, 11 November, fasc. 7, prilozhenie, St. Petersburg, 1904, which Dumbarton Oaks owns). Cf. Grumel, *Regestes*, no. 375. On the monastery Τὰ Δαλμάτου see Janin, *Constantinople byzantine*, 311 f.

in the election of an abbot at the monastery of Dalmatos. Normally an abbot was elected by the majority of the monks of the monastery in question.[1] However, abbots of the monastery of Dalmatos were often exarchs or 'inspectors' of the Byzantine monasteries although this dignity was not reserved to them.[2] The man who was elected at this particular moment, Hilarion, was not only an ordinary abbot but an archimandrite and most likely he was the exarch mentioned in two letters of Theodore of Studios.[3] It is not impossible, therefore, that special rules applied to the abbot of the monastery of Dalmatos. It would be interesting to know whether the invitation sent to Theodore by the Patriarch Nicephorus was meant as a friendly gesture of reconciliation or whether it was merely a matter of routine.

Relations which had been friendly or at least correct at first soon took a turn for the worse. It will be remembered that in 797 Tarasius had excommunicated the priest Joseph who had performed the wedding of the Emperor Constantine VI and Theodote. In 806 the Emperor Nicephorus asked the new Patriarch Nicephorus to restore Joseph. This gave rise to a continuation of the Moechian controversy. This time, however, the issue was quite different. The 'adulterer' Constantine VI was dead and his dynasty had lost the throne. With Constantine VI and his house there disappeared the personal motives that had initiated the conflict, and it is most puzzling why the Emperor Nicephorus should have reopened this most delicate issue. It was once again Joseph of Kathara who gave rise to this new controversy. As time went on it assumed an aspect of political principle, but in the beginning it centred around the status of Joseph in the hierarchy. What circumstances persuaded the Emperor Nicephorus to insist on the reinstatement of this man? He knew undoubtedly that such a measure would meet with the most stubborn resistance on the

---

[1] Marin, *Moines*, 90; Bréhier, *Institutions*, 534.

[2] Marin, *Moines*, 168–73.

[3] An unedited biography of Hilarion, by a monk Sabas, exists in an interesting palimpsest, the *Vat. Gr.* 984 (cf. Ehrhard, *Überlieferung und Bestand*, i. 650). A short notice is contained in the *Synaxarium Constantinopolitanum*, 731–4. Theodore of Studios addressed to him the *Epistula* 19, ed. J. Cozza-Luzi, *N.P.B.* viii. 18. He was praised each year in the liturgical commemoration of the restoration of orthodoxy, see F. Uspenski, *Sinodik v nedeliu pravoslaviia* (Odessa, 1893), 11. On the title of archimandrite cf. Marin, *Moines*, 85–89. Mention of exarch: no. 140, ed. Cozza-Luzi *N.P.B.* viii. 125, and no. 205, ibid., p. 177. Cf. J. Pargoire, 'Saint Théophane etc.', *V.V.* ix (1902), 84 f., accepted by Bury, *Eastern Roman Empire*, 73.

part of the Studites. After all they had suffered once because of the adulterous union, and they were not likely to give in at this time.

In answer to this question Bury has advanced a curious theory. According to him, 'the circumstances furnished Nicephorus [the Emperor] with a pretext for reopening a question which involved an important constitutional principle. . . . Soon after the accession of the new Patriarch, Nicephorus proceeded to procure definite affirmation of the superiority of the Emperor to canonical law.'[1] Thus in this view the Emperor Nicephorus had reopened the controversy because he wanted to test the principle: *princeps legibus solutus*. This theory does credit to the great constitutionalist that Bury was, and it is certain that as the controversy dragged on it became a struggle between Church and State. But if one remembers the conciliatory attitude of the Emperor Nicephorus in other respects, it becomes extremely unlikely that he should have asserted an abstract constitutional principle in this abrupt and dangerous way.

Fortunately, there is more than these general considerations to refute Bury's theory. There are two texts which indicate why the Emperor was anxious to have Joseph reinstated. The first is contained in a *Vita* of Theodore of Studios written by the monk Michael. Here we read that Satan suggested to the Emperor the reinstatement of Joseph 'for having been instrumental for peace, [Satan] says, and for thinking of the [public] weal'.[2] Thus Satan thought that Joseph had brought about peace, and Satan must have known why. What peace? With the Arabs? With the Bulgarians? With the Pope? Here a second text proves helpful.

It is a passage from the *Synodicum Vetus*, a compilation written during the Patriarchate of Photius. It runs as follows:

After the Christ-loving Nicephorus had taken over the Empire from Irene the pious-minded, there appeared a rebel against the Emperor, Turkos, the *strategos* and patrician, who claimed to side with the Empress Irene. But God scattered his assault without bloodshed through the mediation of Joseph the Presbyter and *oeconomus* of the Great Church of Constantinople ('Ιωσὴφ . . . μεσιτεύσαντος). For this reason the thrice-blessed Patriarch Nicephorus, who succeeded Saint Tarasius, assembled a sacred and holy local synod at Byzantium

---

[1] Bury, *Eastern Roman Empire*, 34. Cf. Visser, *Nikephoros*, 60: the purpose was to provoke the monastic party and to extirpate it.

[2] Cf. xxv (*P.G.* xcix. 265D): ὡς παραίτιον γεγονότα εἰρήνης, φησί, καὶ τοῦ λυσιτελοῦντος φροντίσαντα.

with the support of the Emperor; and by way of dispensation (οἰκο-
νομικῶς) he restored to the presbyterate Joseph who had been deposed
by the late Tarasius because of the adulterous union of the Emperor
Constantine, son of Irene.[1]

Thus Joseph had done valuable service in bringing to terms the
dangerous rebel Bardanes Turcus in 803.[2] If he was instrumental
in liquidating this rebellion without bloodshed, it is easy to see
that the Emperor Nicephorus was in a receptive mood for the
inspiration of Satan: he owed it to Joseph that the Empire had
been spared a civil war. It is significant that the Emperor waited
for three years, until the death of Tarasius, before he carried out
his design; Tarasius could not be expected to make a third shift
with respect to Joseph. Thus Joseph's reinstatement was due to
the services which he had rendered to the Crown. The Emperor
Nicephorus wanted to pay a debt of gratitude which he had contracted during the dangerous revolt of Bardanes Turcus.

It was probably in 806 that Joseph was restored to the priesthood.[3] This was done by a synod of fifteen bishops.[4] For two years

---

[1] *Syndicon Vetus*, ed. J. A. Fabricius and G. C. Harles, *Bibliotheca Graeca*, editio
nova (Hamburg, 1809), xii. 415.

[2] On the revolt of Bardanes Turcus see Bury, *Eastern Roman Empire*, 10–14.
I have no doubt that the following passage refers to the revolt of Bardanes Turcus.
Iohannes Venetus, *Cronaca Veneziana*, ed. G. Monticolo, Fonti per la Storia d'Italia
IX (1890), 100: 'Nicyforus imperiale fastigium adeptus est; quem quidem tirran-
nus, Turchis nomine, magna expedicione stipatus conatus est ad prelium pro-
vocare; sed augustus cum sui imperii pene omnia loca contra tyrrannum tueretur,
tantumodo solum Tarsaticum destruere potuit. Postmodum vero predictus tir-
rannus paenitens quod contra imperiale numen aliquod nefas peregisset, devotus et
cernuus suam adinvenit gratiam.' The editor, *ad locum*, and Bury, *Eastern Roman
Empire*, 329, n. 1, identify the place with Tersatto on the Croatian coast, the latter
believing that we are dealing with some local rebellion. But the date, the considerable scope of the campaign, and the end of the tyrant make it certain that Bardanes
Turcus is meant; the sources often call him Τοῦρκος alone (cf., for example, *Acta
Graeca Davidis, Symeonis et Georgii Mitylenae in insula Lesbo*, ed. H. Delehaye, *Analecta
Bollandiana*, xviii (1889), 232, and the above passage from the *Synodicon*). On the
other hand, it would be quite contradictory to the other sources to say that Bardanes Turcus 'destroyed' (the text is corrupt at this place) only one place in
Dalmatia. I propose therefore with some hesitation to identify the *solum Tarsaticum*
of Johannes Venetus with the *regio Tarsia* on the east bank of the River Sangarius
(see Ramsay, *Asia Minor*, 191) near the city of Nicomedia which was the goal of his
march (Theophanes Continuatus, col. 21C). See furthermore on the sources of
Iohannes Venetus, G. Monticolo, 'I manoscritti e le fonti della Cronaca del Diacono
Giovanni', *Bullettino dell' Istituto Storico Italiano*, ix (1890), 37–328, esp. 152, and
below, pp. 107 f., n. 3.

[3] Grumel, *Regestes*, no. 377.

[4] Theodorus Studita, *Epistulae*, i. 24 (*P.G.* xcix. 985B).

the Studites did not react; later they called this attitude of theirs
οἰκονομία.[1] Joseph, brother of Theodore of Studios, even accepted the archbishopric of Thessalonica during these years—an
appointment which was certainly meant by the government as a
conciliatory gesture towards the Studites.[2] At a later date Joseph
of Thessalonica was asked by the monk Symeon why he had
accepted this dignity after the restoration of Joseph the oeconomus. Joseph of Thessalonica replied that he had indeed hesitated
to accept.[3] He had yielded finally to the urgent requests of the
Thessalonicans who knew him from his first exile and of the
emperors because he had thought of the following possibilities:
(1) he did not need to compromise himself with respect to Joseph
since his enthronement ʹ(χειροτονία) would be performed by
bishops of the dioceses of Thessalonica; (2) in the future he would
be far from Constantinople where Joseph, τὸ σκάνδαλον, was
officiating, and even if he should travel to Constantinople, he
would find means to avoid him; and (3) a death might occur and
the σκάνδαλον might be removed. And indeed up to the fateful
interview with the Logothete of the Course this plan had worked
satisfactorily. During all this time he had felt convinced that the
emperors knew his attitude. The Patriarch certainly knew it, for
Joseph had written to him in this sense at the time of his appointment. This letter explains better than any other document the
Studite attitude. They avoided liturgical communion with
all those who held communion with Joseph the oeconomus,
especially with the Patriarch Nicephorus, but otherwise
they were completely loyal to the Emperor and Patriarch and
prayed for them in their liturgy.[4] Theodore held that the right
and duty of criticism belonged to bishops only, and that for
a monk like himself it was sufficient to abstain from communion.[5]

So far, then, both parties had been careful to avoid an open
conflict. It is clear that the Studites believed that this precarious
situation could be prolonged *ad infinitum* or at least until the

[1] Ibid. i. 21 (972C); i. 24 (984A); i. 30 (1005D).
[2] Ch. van de Vorst, 'La Translation de S. Théodore Studite et de S. Joseph de
Thessalonique', *Analecta Bollandiana*, xxxii (1913), 39 sq.
[3] Theodorus Studita, *Epistulae*, i. 23 (*P.G.* xcix. 981A sq.). The true writer of the
letter is Joseph of Thessalonica.
[4] Cf., for example, i. 21 (972A), 22 (973B), 25 (989B).
[5] i. 25 (989D).

moment when Joseph of Kathara would die. The motives which lay behind the actions of Emperor and Patriarch are less clear, but it may be supposed that they too would not have been displeased if Joseph, the stumbling-block, were removed. But Joseph was stubborn, and matters came to a head in 808.

When it became known in that year that the Emperor was leaving for a campaign, Theodore of Studios wrote and asked for an audience; it was not granted.[1] Joseph of Thessalonica was not even allowed to take part in the ceremonial departure from Constantinople.[2] The Studites understood which way the wind was blowing. They continued to write apologetic letters to a monk Symeon, a relative of the Emperor, but he gave evasive answers and was a pliant tool in the hands of his master.[3] As long as the Emperor was absent, the Patriarch Nicephorus 'neither sent word nor was prepared to receive a message—in all he is Caesar's steward'.[4]

The Studite position was that Joseph by marrying Constantine VI and Theodote and by not obtaining a reinstatement within a year from his deposition had violated two ecclesiastical canons.[5] It had been claimed by Stephanus, an imperial secretary, that the Patriarch should not be criticized by anybody except in matters of faith. Theodore, on the contrary, now held that this might be done by those 'who excel over the others in knowledge and understanding'[6] and he considered himself as belonging to this category. He would be satisfied if only Joseph might be prevented from exercising the functions of the priesthood. He would not, he writes in a letter to the powerful magister Theoctistus, object to Joseph remaining oeconomus; if such a concession should be impossible, the Emperors should at least permit the Studites not to enter into communion with him. Even Joseph of Kathara would be praised and pitied if he made this concession.[7]

---

[1] *Epistulae*, i. 26 (993A). On the date of this campaign see above, pp. 73 f., n. 7.

[2] Ibid. i. 23 (980D).

[3] Ibid. i. 26 (993A): (the monk Symeon continues) ἐκεῖνα φρονῶν καὶ ζητῶν ἃ ἐφετὰ πάντως τοῖς κρατοῦσιν.

[4] Ibid. (992D): μήτε λόγον διαπέμψαντα, μήτε ἐθέλοντα ἀκοὴν παραδέξασθαι, ταμιευόμενον πάντα Καίσαρι.

[5] They are quoted in *Epistulae*, i. 21 (972A), 22 (977A).   [6] i. 5 (924).

[7] *Epistulae*, I. 24 (984A sq.): 'Let him who has been deposed cease officiating as a priest, and we shall immediately hold communion with the saintly Patriarch . . .; or if this is unacceptable, we shall withdraw in the same way as before and leave it to the Lord to exact punishment on this count.'

Theodore goes on to say that he went to the limit of permissible
οἰκονομία, any further step in this direction would no longer be
οἰκονομία but breaking the law (παρανομία) and a transgression
of the divine canons. The following passage of the same letter is
worthy of being translated in full:

It is not permissible, indeed, that either our own church, or any
other, does anything against the established laws or canons. For if that
were granted—vain would be the Gospel, futile the canons. And
everybody will be, during the period of his own archbishopric, a new
Evangelist, another Apostle, another lawgiver since he is allowed to
act as he pleases together with his associates. But this is impossible, for
we have a command from the Apostle himself which says that if anybody decrees or orders us to act contrary to tradition, or contrary to
the canons of the ecumenical or local councils [which met] at various
times he shall be not acceptable (ἀπαράδεκτος) and he shall not be
considered among the Saints (ἐν κλήρῳ ἁγίων), and we omit to cite the
words of ill boding (τὸ δύσφημον) which he himself [the Apostle]
spoke.[1]

In a passage like this, which is directed against the bishops as
the dispensers of οἰκονομία, there is nothing left of a conciliatory
policy. Theodore does not attack the living rulers, but he does
not hesitate to express his indignation with the 'adulterer', Constantine VI. To the monk Symeon Theodore writes that the fact
that the adulterer was an emperor does not make any difference,
'for the laws of God hold sway over everybody' according to the
Scriptures.[2] And in the same letter he declares that by reciting
the wedding prayer over Constantine and Theodote, Joseph
opposed Christ Himself who condemned adultery.[3] He informs the
Patriarch Nicephorus that nobody is fully orthodox unless he has
the right faith and obeys the sacred canons.[4]

It was probably after the return of the Emperor that Joseph
of Thessalonica had his fateful interview with the Logothete of
the Course.[5] The circumstances surrounding the interview are not

---

[1] *Epistulae*, i. 22 (984B and 985D sq.), i. 24 (984A). On the magister Theoktistos
cf. Bury, *Eastern Roman Empire*, 5, 16.

[2] *Epistulae*, i. 22 (976B).

[3] *Epistulae*, i. 22 (973C), cf. also i. 31 (1012C). In both letters the wording of the
prayer is quoted—an interesting piece of liturgical information.

[4] i. 25 (989A).

[5] On this office cf. Bury, *Imperial Administrative System*, 91–93; Dölger, *Beiträge
zur Geschichte der byzantinischen Finanzverwaltung &c.*, Byzantinisches Archiv ix
(Leipzig and Berlin, 1927), 22 f., and 'Der Kodikellos des Christodulos von Paler-

known. It is certain, however, that the Logothete asked Joseph of Thessalonica: 'For what reason did you not hold communion with us and the Patriarch up to the present time after so many festivals have passed? State the reason freely!' Joseph answered: 'I have no grudge against our pious Emperors nor against the Patriarch, but against the oeconomus [i.e. Joseph of Kathara] who wedded the adulterer, etc.' Thereupon the Logothete replied: 'Our pious Emperors have no need for you, neither at Thessalonica nor elsewhere.'[1]

The course of events makes it clear that it was the Emperor who was responsible for the final clash. The Studites had been anxious to preserve peace. The Patriarch had taken no initiative. The constant emphasis of the Studites that their opposition was not directed against Emperor or Patriarch but only against Joseph of Kathara showed what the real difficulty was. The Emperor considered the Studite resistance disloyal and was determined to break it. It may be that the rebellion of Arsaber made plain to the Emperor the danger of the Studites' passive resistance. Many monks and clerics had participated in the plot, and although there is not the slightest indication that the Studites were implicated, it showed clearly the potential dangers of an ecclesiastical opposition. It is quite certain, at any rate, that the affair of Joseph of Kathara, which had been reopened to reward a loyal servant of the Crown, had now become a political issue. It was a test case for the domination of the State, between the Emperor and the Patriarch on the one side, and the Studite monks on the other.

Of the subsequent events there is again a lively account in a letter of Theodore of Studios.[2] The monastery was occupied by soldiers. The bishops of Nicaea and Chrysopolis arrived and

---

mo', *Archiv für Urkundenforschung*, xi (1930), 1–65, esp. 53 f.: 'Insbesondere erscheint er [i.e. the Logothete of the Course] schon in der Mitte des 9. Jh. als der Überbringer aller Anträge an den Kaiser, als der vortragende Rat des Kaisers'; Dvornik, *Légendes*, 35 sq.; Bréhier, *Institutions*, 301–3. I have not been able to identify this person.

[1] *Epistulae*, i. 31 (1009B) written only 13 days after the event. Is it mere coincidence that the words of the Logothete of the Course (οἱ εὐσεβεῖς ἡμῶν βασιλεῖς χρείαν σου οὐκ ἔχουσιν) agree literally with the words of Leo V to the Patriarch Nicephorus in 815, according to the *Vita Nicetae* by Theosterictus, *AA. SS. Aprilis*, I. xxx B: οὐ γὰρ ἔχει σου χρείαν ἡ Ἐκκλησία. Or was it perhaps the formula of deposition?

[2] *Epistulae*, i. 48 (1069–84). Cf. Grumel, *Regestes*, no. 378.

pleaded with Theodore and Plato to hold communion with
Joseph of Kathara, on the grounds that he had been ordered by
Tarasius to perform the marriage. Later on the Studites had
sundry interviews with the monk Symeon, who was a relative of
the Emperor. Finally, in January 809, they were brought before
a synod of many bishops, which assembled in the presence of three
high secular dignitaries. There Theodore was insulted by some
bishops who shouted: 'You do not know what nonsense you talk
nor what you say.' Theodore shouted back: 'The Forerunner is
falling (πίπτει), the Gospel is brought to naught, [this] is not dispensation (οἰκονομία).'[1] They answered: 'It is. And thus the
Saints practised dispensation, and so did the blessed predecessor
[Tarasius].' And Theodore adds that when he called Joseph of
Kathara μοιχοζεύκτης 'they gnashed their teeth as though to gulp
[them] down' (διεπρίοντο τοὺς ὀδόντας τοῦ οἰονεὶ ῥοφῆσαι). All those
who refused to hold communion with Joseph of Kathara were
anathematized. To make it quite clear, however, that the restoration of Joseph of Kathara did not imply a recognition of the
adulterous marriage of Constantine VI, the Emperors Nicephorus
and Stauracius decided about the same time that the adulterous
union with Theodote should be severed posthumously, and that
only Constantine's marriage to Mary of Amnia was valid; also
that Theodote's child should not inherit from Constantine. All
this was in accordance with Roman Law, as Theodore of Studios
had been pleased to hear from the mouth of the Emperor.[2]
Theodore and Joseph of Thessalonica were deposed, Plato and
many other abbots and monks were exiled.[3] Apart from Joseph
of Thessalonica, who was a special case, only two bishops seem

---

[1] A reference to John the Baptist's attitude towards Herod is frequent in the
Letters with respect to the adultery of Constantine, cf., for example, i. 5 (924D), i.
22 (976B), i. 31 (1012C), ii. 218 (1657A), &c.

[2] *Epistulae*, i. 31 (*P.G.* xcix. 1012B): ἀλλ' αὖθις εὐδόκησεν ἀποδοκιμασθῆναι τὴν
ἐπιχαρμονὴν τῶν μοιχοζευκτῶν καὶ μοιχοφίλων Ναζιραίων, διὰ τῆς τῶν εὐσεβῶν ἡμῶν
βασιλέων δικαιοκρισίας ἀποδωσάντων, μετὰ τὸν θάνατον, τὸν μοιχὸν τῇ νομίμῳ αὐτοῦ
γαμετῇ, ἀποκαλεσάντων δὲ τὴν μαχλῶσαν μοιχαλίδα καὶ τὸ μοιχογέννητον τέκνον ἐασάν-
των ἄκληρον, ὡς ἀθέμιτον καὶ ἀνομώτατον, ὡς ἐν ἐπηκόῳ μοι τὸ τίμιον αὐτῶν στόμα
λελάληκε κατὰ τοὺς Ῥωμαϊκοὺς νόμους. On Theodore's letter cf. E. W. Brooks, 'On
the Date of the Death of Constantine the Son of Irene', *B.Z.* ix (1900), esp. 654–5.
This letter was written only 13 days after Theodore of Studios had been tried by the
synod. I assume, though I cannot offer conclusive evidence, that the above decision
was taken about the same time. This is what the context of the letter would
suggest.

[3] See the enumeration *Epistulae*, i. 48 (1072B sqq.). Grumel, *Regestes*, 379–81.

to have sided with Theodore.[1] All his ecclesiastical opponents, on the other hand, were bishops, those of Nicomedia, of Nicaea, of Chrysopolis, and the others who participated in the synod which anathematized and condemned him.

The sufferings of Theodore during this second exile are of no concern here. What matters primarily is the development of his attitude. If before he had shown restraint and moderation, all that is gone now. Previously Theodore had declared that Joseph had acted contrary to the precepts of Christ and the canons.[2] Now he says clearly that his opponents are heretics.[3] If the Studites are called schismatics, they retort by saying that the Patriarch Nicephorus and his followers are creating a schism.[4] In a letter to a devout orthodox adherent, the abbot Theophilus, Theodore repeats that Joseph of Kathara and all those who hold communion with him are heretics. After the heresy had come to the fore in the synod at which he (Theodore) and many others were anathematized, the Patriarch and the Emperor should not even be mentioned in the liturgy. It is the task of the monk not to tolerate the slightest infringement of the gospel.[5] There are two letters by Theodore addressed to Pope Leo III in the affair of Joseph of Kathara which offer a good summary of the arguments used by the two parties.[6] Theodore's opponents characterize their attitude as οἰκονομία. They decree that the divine laws do not hold sway over the emperors and they claim that each 'hierarch' has the power of suspending the divine canons.[7] Against this, Theodore maintains that the synod which anathematized him and his partisans violated the gospel of which Pope Leo is the guardian. This point is supported by numerous quotations from the Bible.

[1] Ibid. One is anonymous (ἅμα ἐπισκόπῳ, 1072c), the other is Bishop Leo nicknamed ὁ Βαλελάδης, persecuted at Cherson (1072D).

[2] In *Epistulae*, i. 28 (1001A) he especially reminds a monk Basil of the canons with a reference to Basil's former 'teacher' Sabas of Studion. Cf. furthermore on the canons, i. 30 (1005D).

[3] i. 48 (1069 sqq.).

[4] i. 30 (1008C).

[5] i. 39 (1048 sqq.). Cf. 1049D: ἔργον δὲ μοναχοῦ μηδὲ τὸ τυχὸν ἀνέχεσθαι καινοτομεῖσθαι τὸ Εὐαγγέλιον.

[6] i. 33 and 34 (1017–28). See also the Epistle to the Lavra of St. Sabas in Palestine edited by R. Devreesse, 'Une Lettre de S. Théodore Studite relative au synode mœchien', *Analecta Bollandiana*, lxviii (1950), 44–57.

[7] *Epistulae*, i. 33 (1017D sqq.): οἰκονομίαν οὖν τὴν ζευξιμοιχείαν δογματίζουσιν · ἐπὶ τῶν βασιλέων τοὺς θείους νόμους μὴ κρατεῖν διορίζονται . . . ἕκαστον τῶν ἱεραρχῶν ἐξουσιάζειν ἐν τοῖς θείοις κανόσι παρὰ τὰ ἐν αὐτοῖς κεκανονισμένα ἀποφαίνονται.

There is no special gospel for emperors[1] and one single violation
invalidates the entire gospel. The synod held by his opponents
is void since even an orthodox council cannot be convened without the consent of the Pope. It is all the more advisable that the
Pope assemble an orthodox synod in which he would denounce
the heretical decision of the Synod of Constantinople.[2]

On the basis of these letters, and of others written to the Pope
during the second period of Iconoclasm, it has been asserted that
Theodore was in the East the most energetic advocate of the
prerogatives of the Holy See. It should be noted, however, that in
all these letters the Studite asks the Pope for help, and it has been
overlooked that there exists a letter which is written in a very
different mood.

What do we care whether the Pope acts in one way or another? You
have to admit that he has been caught in his own nets as the proverb
goes. For by saying that he was not concerned about the manifest sins
of the priest [Joseph of Kathara], he jeered and abused not some little
priest but the head of the Church [Jesus Christ] so much that we felt
ashamed even when we heard of it. If this is true, alas for the hierarchy!
But please, let us move our tongue discreetly against the heads [of the
Church] and let us not denounce them so bitterly.[3]

The last sentence of the quotation shows Theodore's feeling
that he had gone rather far. Still this valuable passage shows that
in Theodore's eyes the Pope was not beyond criticism. He felt
himself deserted by the entire hierarchy, by the Pope, by the
Patriarch, by the bishops, let alone the secular power. Hardly
anybody dared to espouse his cause openly, not even the monks.
Even Joseph of Thessalonica had had some hesitations whether
his brother Theodore was not going too far.[4] On the other hand,
it is known from Theodore himself that the Emperors were
anxious not to exile and imprison too many persons.[5] The attitude

---

[1] Ibid. i. 34, 1024D: καὶ ποῦ τὸ τῶν βασιλέων Εὐαγγέλιον;

[2] Ibid. i. 33, 1020C: ὑπὸ τῆς θείας πρωταρχίας σου ἔννομον κροτηθῆναι σύνοδον ὡς
ἂν τὸ ὀρθόδοξον τῆς Ἐκκλησίας δόγμα τὸ αἱρετικὸν ἀποκρούσηται.

[3] *Epistulae*, i. 28 (the relevant passage will be found 1001A). The expression
ἐν τοῖς οἰκείοις ἑάλω πτεροῖς is found again in *Epistulae*, ii. 162 (1513): τοῖς οἰκείοις
ἑάλως πτεροῖς. But in this latter passage it is said to be borrowed from a secular
writer not from a proverb (ὥς πού τις ἔφη τῶν ἔξω).

[4] I infer this point from Joseph's three theses which Theodore quotes *Epistulae*, i.
43 (1065C sq.).

[5] *Epistulae*, i. 39 (1045D): (Theodore feels certain that the addressee, the abbot

of the Patriarch Nicephorus towards Theodore is well illustrated by an episode which must relate to the beginning of Theodore's exile.[1] Theodore's jailer (φυλακίτης) had journeyed to Constantinople with a message from his prisoner to the Patriarch Nicephorus which contained the following phrases: 'We wished we had you here for our assistance.' The messenger returned with the following reply for his prisoner: 'You left and established yourself there. I envy you.' When Theodore heard this, he laughed. The appropriate answer would have been, he writes to his brother: 'If he envies me, let him come out himself.' But there is no need to follow Theodore in imagining that the Patriarch's message was sheer hypocrisy. If anything, it confirms the assumption that in the affair of Joseph of Kathara the Patriarch Nicephorus did not act of his own free will but that he was obeying orders. Quite possibly he really envied the abbot Theodore who could afford to act with complete disregard of political considerations.

There was indeed much to be said, in this struggle, for the attitude taken by Pope Leo III, the Patriarch Nicephorus, perhaps even by the Emperor Nicephorus. In the eyes of Theodore any mistake was apt to look like heresy. The fact that Joseph of Kathara had recited the wedding prayer for Constantine VI and Theodote was a sin against Christ and the Gospel. Not even ten years of retirement on the part of Joseph, not even distinguished services in the interest of Emperor and Empire, not even the expressed wish of the Emperor and the obedience of the clergy could bend Theodore's strictness. The Emperor could hardly continue to ignore the passive resistance of the Studites. The struggle which had started over the restoration of Joseph of Kathara came to be one which involved the relations between Church and State, between Pope and Patriarch, between secular clergy and the monastic party. In the last respect it is noteworthy that the affair of Joseph of Kathara involved the same principle which had been at issue in the treatment of the *lapsi* at the Seventh Council of Nicaea, in the Simoniac affair, and in the

Theophilus, would gladly have suffered persecution) κᾶν οὐκ ἐβουλήθησαν οἱ κρατοῦντες, φειδοῖ τοῦ μὴ πολλοὺς ἐξορίζειν καὶ καθείργειν.

[1] Ibid. i. 43 (1068c): ῾ο φυλακίτης μου ἐξελθὼν ἤγαγέ μοι προσκύνησιν ἐκ τοῦ Πατριάρχου λέγοντος ὅτι ὁ Θεὸς συγχωρήσει σοι· τοῦ, ηὐχόμεθα ἔχειν σε ὧδε εἰς βοήθειαν ἡμῶν· 'Εξῆλθες καὶ ἐκάθισας αὐτόθε καὶ ὅτι φθονῶ σε. Καὶ ἀκούσας ἐγέλασα. Οὐ γὰρ ἦν χρεία τέως ἀποκριθῆναί με· ἢ μόνον· ὅτι ἐὰν φθονῇ, ἐξέλθῃ κἀκεῖνος.

Moechian controversy. It was again a case of οἰκονομία against ἀκρίβεια. Once again one party was anxious to fulfil the wishes of the Emperor. Once again the Studites insisted on the canons, watched the attitude of Rome, and glorified the function of the monastic order. It is no mere coincidence that during the affair of Joseph of Kathara the opponents of Sabas, Plato, and Theodore referred again to those former controversies, and that Theodore had to defend himself and his predecessors in his letters.[1] This continuity did not go unnoticed by Theodore's contemporaries. It was rumoured in 808/9 that were Joseph of Kathara deprived of priestly rank, Theodore would proceed to accuse the Patriarch Nicephorus and even Tarasius of having held communion with him.[2] Theodore, it is true, solemnly disclaimed any such intention, but the very accusation proves how closely the past was connected with the present in the eyes of Theodore's contemporaries.

On the basis of a passage in Theophanes it is usually asserted that the Studites were recalled from exile under Michael I (811–13).[3] Strictly speaking this is incorrect, for Theodore himself says in one of his letters that they returned during the reign of Nicephorus I.[4] The aged Plato had fallen seriously ill in his prison and therefore the Emperor Nicephorus had him brought to Byzantium.[5] The context suggests that the Emperor even planned to restore Plato and Theodore to their monastery, but that death prevented him from carrying out this intention. Since the *Laudatio Platonis* was written in 814, there is no reason to disbelieve the

---

[1] Above all, *Epistulae*, i. 38.

[2] *Epistulae*, i. 32 (1015B).

[3] Theophanes, 494 (A.M. 6304 = last months of A.D. 811): (Michael) καὶ Θεόδωρον, τὸν ἡγούμενον τῶν Στουδίου, καὶ Πλάτωνα καὶ 'Ιωσήφ, ἀρχιεπίσκοπον Θεσσαλονίκης, ἀδελφὸν Θεοδώρου, ἐν φυλακαῖς πικραῖς συνεχομένους, μετὰ καὶ τῶν προὐχόντων τῆς κατ' αὐτοὺς μονῆς ἔσπευδεν ἐνωθῆναι, ὃ καὶ πεποίηκεν. Cf. Bury, *Eastern Roman Empire*, 41, who mentions in his account of the ecclesiastical policy of Michael I: 'the Studites were recalled from exile.'

[4] *Epistulae*, ii. 109 (1369B): ὑποστροφὴ τῆς ἐξορίας ἐπὶ τοῦ Νικηφόρου.

[5] Theodorus Studita, *Laudatio Platonis*, 39 (*P.G.* xcix. 841D): ἐπειδὴ δὲ ἐκ τῆς τοιαύτης καθείρξεως νοσηλεύεσθαι αὐτὸν ἐπιθανάτιον ἀκήκοεν ὁ Καῖσαρ [Nicephorus], μετάγει ἐν τῷ Βυζαντίῳ μαλαχθεὶς τὴν ἀτεράμονα καρδίαν καὶ ἐνεγκὼν παρασκευάζεται ἐπανορθοῦν δῆθεν τὸ κακῶς γεγενημένον. ἀλλ' ἐπειδὴ οὐκ ἀπὸ ὀρθῆς γνώμης ὁ σκόπος, οὐδὲ εἰς πέρας ἄγει τὴν πρόθεσιν. (The Emperor is killed on his Bulgarian campaign), τὸν δὲ (Plato) σὺν ἡμῖν (Theodore), ῥοπὴ τῶν τηνικαῦτα εὐσεβῶς βασιλευσάντων (Michael I and his son Theophylactus) εἰς τὴν οἰκείαν πάλιν ποίμνην ἀποκαταστήσασα, ὁμολογητὴν ἑαυτοῖς ἀναδείκνυσιν. See also the *Vitae* (*P.G.* xcix. 272B and 164B).

combined evidence of the letter and of the *Laudatio*. An explanation for this act of leniency, however, is hard to find.

The official reconciliation between secular and monastic clergies took place under Michael I Rangabe. From Theophanes it would seem that neither party was much inclined towards concessions and that it required repeated attempts of the Emperor Michael (πολλά τε τὸν ἁγιώτατον πατριάρχην καὶ τοὺς δυναμένους συντρέχειν τῇ κοινῇ εἰρήνῃ παρακαλῶν οὐκ ἐπαύετο) to bring them together.[1] Pope Leo III likewise admonished both parties to settle their differences.[2] Joseph of Kathara was deposed once more and the Patriarch Nicephorus had to apologize for his attitude in the affair of Joseph of Kathara.[3] He declared that 'all that happened was caused by the oppression (ἐπήρεια) of the late Emperor (Nicephorus)'.[4] Theodore, on the other hand, exhorted his fellow-sufferers to accept this reconciliation. To Antonius, abbot of St. Peter, who had been exiled to Amorium,[5] he wrote:

And since . . . with the approval of God, so extremely good, he through whom the discord in our church began [Joseph of Kathara] was removed, peace has been proclaimed, with the approval, authority, and kindness, I may add also, the exhortations of our victorious and Christ-loving Emperors, and with the collaboration and apology (ἀπολογία) of our most holy Patriarch—for this is how we have to call him henceforth.[6]

Theodore even had to defend himself against one of his followers, Gregory, who, more radical than the Studite abbot, objected to the *rapprochement*. Gregory demanded the deposition of the Patriarch because of his conduct during the Moechian Controversy even after the fresh outbreak of Iconoclasm under Leo V. Theodore represented to Gregory what would be the consequences of Gregory's demands: Nicephorus would have to be deposed by an iconoclastic emperor and it would look as if the monks had allied themselves with the Iconoclasts.[7]

---

[1] Theophanes, 494.
[2] The texts are quoted by Grumel, *Regestes*, no. 387, particularly *P.G.* xcix. 273A. Grumel, *Regestes*, no. 382, second critical note, believes that the ambassadors of 811 (below, p. 108) asked Pope Leo III to intervene in the affair of Joseph. This is very likely indeed if it be understood that it was *not* the Patriarch Nicephorus who made this request, but either the Emperor or the Studites.
[3] Grumel, *Regestes*, nos. 387, 388.
[4] Theodorus Studita, *Laudatio Platonis*, 40 (*P.G.* xcix. 844B).
[5] *Epistulae*, i. 48 (1072C *in fine*).   [6] Ibid. i. 56 (1112A sq.).
[7] Theodorus Studita, *Epistulae*, ed. Cozza-Luzi, no. 190, 162 ff.

In 1930 there came to light an important literary monument from the second stage of the Moechian Controversy: large sections of an anonymous commentary on the Gospel of St. John.[1] The name of the author is not preserved, but the editor proved conclusively that the commentary originated among the monks of Studios between 809 and 811. As the work proceeds, the unknown author abandons more and more his exegetical purpose and pays increasing attention to the theological problems raised by the Moechian Controversy. He cautiously refrains from mentioning names or referring to specific events, but on the basis of the exhaustive investigations by the *editor princeps* the author's hints and allusions can be applied safely to this conflict.

The title of the fifth λόγος is characteristic. This section is directed 'against the bishops who are indifferent and violate the divine laws and rules concerning adultery and falsify truth and justice'.[2] The author considers those who knowingly violate those divine commandments worse than Infidels and heretics.[3] On the contrary, those who suffer in defence of these divine commandments, i.e. the Studites, deserve the reward of the martyrs.[4] He feels particularly angry with those members of the clergy who yield to the pressure of the Emperors, who tolerate violations of divine laws and canons in order to preserve the peace of the Church. They rationalize their cowardice claiming that resistance is legitimate only in matters of faith, not in matters of practical ethics.[5] No Christian may hold communion with the

---

[1] It was edited from the manuscript, London, British Museum Add. 39605 (early tenth century), by Karl Hansmann, *Ein neuentdeckter Kommentar zum Johannes-Evangelium*, Forschungen zur christlichen Literatur und Dogmengeschichte xvi. 4–5 (Paderborn, 1930). See also Werner Jaeger, 'Der neuentdeckte Kommentar zum Johannes-Evangelium und Dionysios Areopagites', *Sitzungsberichte der Preußischen Akademie der Wissenschaften*, 1930, 569–94. The name of the author was erased from the lemma. He himself tells us that he wrote another work entitled Θεογνωσία and a scholiast adds that he wrote this last work ἐν Χερσῶνι.

[2] p. 174: . . . κατὰ τῶν ἀδιαφορούντων ἐπισκόπων καὶ τοὺς θείους νόμους καὶ γνώμονας παραβαινόντων καὶ παραχαραττόντων τὴν ἀλήθειαν καὶ τὴν δικαιοσύνην.

[3] Violators of divine commandments worse than Infidels: v, § 60, p. 192. Worse than heretics: vii, § 149, p. 278.

[4] v, §§ 62, 193, and frequently.

[5] Yielding of clergy to political pressure condemned v, § 66, p. 194; &c. Divine laws and constitutions must not be violated even to preserve ecclesiastical peace (διὰ τὸ καλὸν μάλιστα τῆς εἰρήνης καὶ τῆς πρὸς ἀλλήλους ἀγάπης), vii, § 65, p. 254. Truth and justice must be mentioned not only in doctrine but also in actions: vii, §§ 59 ff., p. 252; vii, §§ 113 f., p. 267 *passim* (this is one of the central tenets of the commentary).

violators of the divine laws and canons, and the Studite attitude in this respect is entirely justified.[1] In general the commentator agrees in all respects with the Studites' position, except that unlike Theodore, he does not call his opponents heretics.[2]

Theodore never allowed his distrust of the Patriarch to die completely. A decision of the permanent synod of Constantinople declared that Paulicians[3] and Athinganoi[4] were to be executed. Thereupon the Patriarch Nicephorus drew up a report for the benefit of the Emperor, which is unfortunately lost. In it he explained at great length the teaching of Jews, Phrygians, and Paulicians, criticized them, and asked the Emperor to pronounce the death penalty against them.[5] The Emperor followed his advice and issued a πρόσταγμα to execute Paulicians and Athinganoi.[6] There followed indeed a number of executions, particularly in the Armeniac theme, before Theodore of Studios intervened.[7] He claimed that there was always a chance of conversion and that no priest has the right to condemn to death the impious.[8] Michael followed the new advice given to him and abstained from continuing to carry out the death penalty against these heretics.

The zealous Studites saw religious aspects even in matters which moderns would term political. Towards the end of the year 812 Krum, the powerful Khan of the Bulgarians, was threatening Mesembria.[9] Krum proposed the renewal of a peace treaty which stipulated among other things that both sides should extradite refugees from the other side even if they had plotted

---

[1] No communion (κοινωνία) with the violators: vii, §§ 111 f., pp. 266 f.

[2] Moechians not heretics: Hansmann, pp. 70, 77 ff.

[3] On the Paulicians cf. K. Ter Mkrttschian, *Die Paulikianer im byzantinischen Kaiserreiche etc.* (Leipzig, 1893); F. C. Conybeare, *The Key of Truth. A Manual of the Paulician Church of Armenia* (Oxford, 1898). Recently much light has been shed on the history of the Paulicians by the researches of Henri Grégoire, whose publications on this subject are most conveniently listed in *Annuaire de l'Institut de Philologie et d'Histoire orientales et slaves*, x, 1950 (*Mélanges Henri Grégoire II*), p. L.

[4] On the Athinganoi see J. Starr, 'An Eastern Christian sect: the Athinganoi', *Harvard Theological Review*, xxix (1936), 93–106.

[5] On the whole problem see the excellent remarks of Grumel, *Regestes*, nos. 383 and 384. Cf. also Bury, *Eastern Roman Empire*, 40.

[6] Theophanes, 495; Petrus Siculus, *Historia Manichaeorum*, 41 (*P.G.* civ. 1301A).

[7] Theophanes speaks only of certain κακότροποι σύμβουλοι of the Emperor. But a letter of Theodore of Studios (no. 23, ed. Cozza-Luzzi, *N.P.B.* viii. 21) makes it clear that the Studites are meant.

[8] Theophanes, 495: μὴ ἐξεῖναι ἱερεῦσιν ἀποφαίνεσθαι κατὰ ἀσεβῶν θάνατον.

[9] For the following account see Theophanes, 497 sq. and the comments of Bury, *Eastern Roman Empire*, 347–9.

against their rulers.[1] On two occasions the Emperor Michael
summoned his chief advisers to confer about the peace proposals
and both times the opinion prevailed that the offer was unacceptable, on account of the refugee clause. The Emperor
Michael, the Patriarch Nicephorus, the metropolitan bishops
of Nicaea and Cyzicus were all for acceptance. But they were
opposed by several unnamed persons and by Theodore of Studios.
This party quoted the saying of the Lord: 'him who cometh
unto Me I shall in no wise cast out' (Joh. vi. 37). Theophanes,
who took sides with the advocates of peace and criticized the war
party bitterly, admitted that there were a few Bulgarian refugees
in the Empire. He pointed out, on the other hand, that first of
all by refusing the peace terms the Empire was betraying certain
persons held captive at the Bulgarian court (τοὺς ἔσω τῆς αὐλῆς).
It was also abandoning the parts of Thrace which were being
overrun by the Bulgarians; after all, the inhabitants of Thrace
were Byzantines, one's own countrymen (οἰκεῖοι), whereas the
refugees were Bulgarians.[2]

This was the last battle fought by the protagonists of the two
parties, the secular clergy and the monastic group. The fight had
been going on for half a century, almost without interruption,
and feelings had been embittered by exiles. Great sufferings were
meted out to the monks by their opponents when they were
allied with the government, and when the monks had the upper
hand personal humiliations had been imposed upon two successive patriarchs. The lines were no longer as clearly drawn as at the
time of the outbreak of this struggle, and a process of disintegra-
tion within the monastic party had been gathering momentum
for some time. Monks had been won over to the party of the
secular clergy by obtaining episcopal sees. Others hoped to
become bishops. The reverse was less frequent; only a few clerics
sided with the monks in these various controversies. The attitude
of Theodore of Studios with respect to the Paulicians and
Bulgarian refugees happened to coincide with the precepts of

---

[1] Theophanes, 497: τοὺς πρόσφυγας ἑκατέρων ἀποστρέφεσθαι πρὸς ἑκάτερον, κἂν
τύχωσιν ἐπιβουλεύοντες ταῖς ἀρχαῖς. It would seem that as a rule the Byzantines
applied the principle of modern international law that nobody should be extradited
to a foreign government for political action against his government.

[2] Theophanes, 498: τὴν τῶν πλειόνων μᾶλλον καὶ ὁμοφύλων σωτηρίαν ἐχρῆν
πραγματεύσασθαι. Ibid.: ἀλλὰ καὶ ὁ περὶ τοὺς οἰκείους ἀπρονοήτως διακείμενος τὴν
πίστιν κατὰ Παῦλον ἤρνηται καὶ χείρων ἀπίστου κρίνεται.

humanity, but in all probability considerations of this kind did not count for much with Theodore. It is a safe guess that the refugees from Bulgaria had been baptized, otherwise Theodore would hardly have given them much thought.[1] Considerations of policy or expediency were unknown to him; compromise was impossible. He heeded nothing but what he believed to be the precepts of religion.

Nicephorus the Patriarch was of a different stamp. He had been brought up in a family of civil servants and had been a member of the civil service himself. For him the restoration of a priest who had been punished for an action which lay many years back was not a matter important enough to invite the risk of conflict with the Emperor. He believed that he served both his religion and his state by making collaboration between secular and ecclesiastical authorities possible. Time and again his attempts were counteracted by the monastic party and its head, Theodore of Studios. The result was that when the secular power under Leo V the Armenian began a new attack on the Church, the latter was divided: there was no common front, no recognized head; petty strife and rivalry were to weaken the orthodox ranks for many years to come. Before studying this new wave of Iconoclasm, the development of relations with the West and Nicephorus' part in them have to be analysed.

4. *Relations with the West*

In his relation with the Papacy Nicephorus fell heir to a tradition of misunderstandings and disagreements. In the eighth century Byzantine relations with the West, both political and ecclesiastical, had taken an alarming turn for the worse. It is difficult to say whether the reasons for the rift lay primarily in the traditional differences between Eastern and Western Christianity or in political and ecclesiastical events. On the issue of religious images East and West had felt very differently for centuries. The Greek Church, unlike the Western, emphasized salvation from death at the expense of salvation from sin. Consequently Eastern

---

[1] There was at least one Bulgarian among the Studite monks, the martyr Thaddeus. Theodore calls him Σκύθης (*Sermones Parvae Catecheseos*, ed. Cozza-Luzi, *N.P.B.* ix. 1 (Rome, 1888), 71, cf. also 129: ἐκ Σκυθικοῦ γένους, and this term ordinarily designates the Bulgarians, cf. *Epistulae*, ii. 155 (*P.G.* xcix. 1485ʙ).

Christians welcomed especially all those aspects of the liturgy which guaranteed or depicted immortality and life after death. They had the same sacraments as the Occidentals, but for them the sacraments themselves were only part of a liturgy which in its entirety and as a unit, as performed in the church building adorned by religious images and by priests clad in embroidered robes, gave a foretaste of eternal bliss. In this context the religious images had become objects of personal devotion and their usefulness as anagogical devices had been sanctioned officially by Eastern theologians at least as early as the sixth century. In Eastern theology also the theory of the icons had become an aspect of christological doctrine; and as sensible symbols of a suprasensible reality, of the Kingdom of God, they were competing with the sacraments. Their importance for uneducated and learned Easterners alike had manifested itself not only in the devotion of their advocates but perhaps even more clearly in the passionate hatred of their enemies.

In Western religiosity the fear of sin overshadowed that of death. Salvation was consequently equated with liberation from sin and could be found, at least partially, in an earthly life of faith, hope, and charity. Religious images therefore were less important than in the East and did not ever rival the sacraments. No theology of images was elaborated in the West, and the images rarely provoked such animosities as in the East. Western theologians authorized them as instruments of religious education and as such they were honoured, and few Occidentals ever understood the theoretical issues involved in the Eastern Controversy.[1]

Relations between Byzantium and the Holy See had been strained since the days of the Emperor Leo III. Even before he issued his iconoclastic edict, this emperor had decreed fiscal measures for Sicily, Calabria, and possibly Crete which were considered oppressive. He had also confiscated the revenue of the

---

[1] On religious images in the West see Louis Bréhier, *La Querelle des images* (Paris, 1904), 57–62; E. J. Martin, *A History of the Iconoclastic Controversy* (London, 1930), 222–73. The chief differences between Greek and Western Christianity are worked out in an extraordinarily suggestive essay by Adolf Harnack, 'Der Geist der morgenländischen Kirche im Unterschied von der abendländischen', *Sitzungsberichte der Kgl. Preußischen Akademie der Wissenschaften*, 1913, 157–83. This essay has, so far as I know, not found the attention which it deserves, probably because it was published on the eve of World War I. Above I have paraphrased the relevant parts.

patrimonia Petri in these regions amounting to three and a half talents of gold. Then came the iconoclastic edict of Leo III. The Emperor and Pope Gregory II had a lively correspondence on the subject of images. In 731 Pope Gregory III assembled a council of Italian bishops at Rome where all Iconoclasts were excommunicated and each successive pope tried to obtain the restoration of image-worship in the East.[1]

In spite of this dispute over image-worship, the popes remained loyal to their political masters at Constantinople until the pontificate of Stephen II (752/7), even during the dark days of the Italian Revolution. Under this pope, however, a number of fateful and irreversible steps were taken. When Italy was in danger of becoming unified under Lombard rule and the Pope of becoming a Lombard bishop, the Papacy had set out on its fateful pro-Frankish policy. It would seem that the first steps in this direction were taken with the full approval of Byzantium. Closely connected with this first point was a second, the creation of the Papal State. In 751 Ravenna had been occupied by the Lombards and Rome herself had been in great danger of being seized by them. When in 756 the Franks defeated the Lombards, Ravenna was turned over to the Pope instead of to the Emperor. The Pope was willing to recognize the Emperor's overlordship over both Ravenna and Rome, but he claimed the immediate administration (*dicio*) of these cities for himself. The Emperor's answer to the papal secession was the transfer of Eastern Illyricum, Sicily, and Calabria from the ecclesiastical jurisdiction of the Pope to that of the Patriarch of Constantinople. Taken together the papal measures all but annihilated Byzantine control in Italy (except for the south) and made the Pope appear in Byzantine eyes as a 'Frankish bishop'.[2]

---

[1] The chronology of this period of tension between Byzantium and the Holy See has been clarified recently in an important study by V. Grumel, 'L'Annexion de l'Illyricum Oriental, de la Sicile et de la Calabre au patriarcat de Constantinople', *Recherches de Science Religieuse*, xl (1952, Mélanges Jules Lebreton II), 191–200. He has corrected the muddled and biased account of Theophanes in the light of the *Liber Pontificalis*. In particular he has shown that the fiscal measures and the confiscations of the *patrimonia Petri* preceded the iconoclastic edict of Leo and consequently cannot have possibly been meant as a punitive measure for the pope's resistance to Iconoclasm. On the correspondence between Gregory II and Leo III see the bibliographical data, Ostrogorsky 99 n. 5. On later papal attempts to have image-worship restored in the East: *Epistulae Hadriani*, Mansi, xii. 1059E.

[2] On the correct date of the ecclesiastical transfer see Grumel's article quoted in n. 1.

Both with regard to political and ecclesiastical relations a considerable *détente* occurred in the eighties of the eighth century. Charlemagne's daughter Rotrud was engaged to the young Emperor Constantine VI, the son of Irene. It was probably in 781 that Pope Hadrian I reopened negotiations with Constantinople with a view to restore image-worship. The most interesting part of Hadrian's letter to Irene (784) is that which was not read at the Council and where among other things Hadrian reminded the court of Constantinople that the victories of Charlemagne were due to his obedience to the Holy See.[1] Yet when the betrothal of Rotrud to Constantine VI was broken off, the Papacy committed itself definitely, after some hesitation, to the Frankish policy. Pope Leo III sent Charles the banner (*vexillum*) of the city of Rome immediately after his election and thereby declared him to be the secular ruler of the new Papal State. He took refuge with the Franks when Roman factions plotted against his life in 799. He did not object to his being tried by a secular court presided over by Charles and cleared himself from the accusation raised by his opponents by an oath. Finally at St. Peter's in Rome, on Christmas Day 800, Charles was recognized by acclamation to be what he had been in fact for some time: Emperor or Emperor of the Romans.[2]

Meanwhile there had also been friction in the ecclesiastical sphere. The Council of 787 had restored image-worship, but the question whether this Council was ever accepted by the Pope is difficult. In A.D. 791 Pope Hadrian wrote to Charlemagne: 'Et ideo ipsam suscepimus synodum', but adds: 'nos vero ad huc pro eadem synodo nullum responsum usque actenus eidem imperatori reddidimus, metuentes, ne ad eorum reverterentur errorem.' It seems that this *suscipere* on the side of the Pope was less than a confirmation, it was merely a *de facto* acknowledgement, and the fact of this acknowledgement was not communicated to Constantinople. When Pope Hadrian realized that the *Horos* of Nicaea did not meet with the approval of his Frankish protector, he agreed to send his representatives to the Council of Frankfurt (794) which condemned the Council of Nicaea. The Pope was in

[1] Mansi xii, 1055–76.

[2] Bibliography on the events at St. Peter on Christmas Day 800 in P. E. Schramm, 'Die Anerkennung Karls des Großen als Kaiser', *Historische Zeitschrift*, clxxii (1951), 449–515, esp. note 1. See also below, pp. 105 ff. In the text I have followed the results of Schramm's excellent article.

a difficult situation, for he had been represented on both councils. Hadrian found a curious way out: the conditions which he had laid down prior to the Council of Nicaea had included the restoration of the revenues from the *patrimonia* and the lost ecclesiastical provinces, and since the conditions had not been accepted, he was prepared to declare the Emperor a heretic. Under these circumstances it is understandable that at Byzantium in the beginning of the ninth century the impression prevailed that the Pope had not recognized the Seventh Council as ecumenical. A letter of Theodore of Studios, which has generally been overlooked, written after 806, declared:

> Rome, however, ... did not recognize the council itself as universal but as local and as correcting the private error of people here (τὸ ἴδιον πτῶμα τῶν τῇδε). The representatives of the Romans were sent here not on account of the council but for some other business. For this reason they were even deposed (καθῃρέθησαν) after they had returned, it is said, although they claimed that they had been forced.

From this letter it would seem that the Papacy carried out the intentions outlined in the *Epistula Hadriani*: it considered the Council of Nicaea a mere local council. By doing this the Pope recognized the local validity of its decisions, but deprived them of any effectiveness outside the patriarchate of Constantinople. It was only late in the ninth century that the Papacy recognized the Council of Nicaea as the Seventh Ecumenical Council.[1]

In the year 806 when Nicephorus became Patriarch of Constantinople the Byzantine Empire was at war with Charlemagne. The cause of this war was the coronation of Charlemagne in 800, and its battlefield was Venetia. Under normal conditions a newly

---

[1] Pope Hadrian's letter to Charlemagne: *M.G.H., Epistulae*, v. 56 f. On the meaning of *suscepimus synodum* cf. F. X. Funk, 'Die päpstliche Bestätigung der acht ersten allgemeinen Synoden', *Kirchengeschichtliche Abhandlungen und Untersuchungen* (Paderborn, 1897), i. 115 ff., and J. Forget, 'Conciles', *D.T.C.* iii. 1, col. 663. H. Barion, 'Der kirchenrechtliche Charakter des Konzils von Frankfurt 794', *Zeitschrift der Savignystiftung für Rechtsgeschichte, Kanonistische Abteilung*, xix (1930), 139–70, has shown that in the eyes of Charlemagne too the Council of Frankfurt was a local, not an ecumenical, council. Theodorus Studita, *Epistulae*, i. 38 (*P.G.* xcix. 1044c). The Papacy recognized the Council as ecumenical under Michael II only, cf. ibid. ii. 127 (1412c). Recognition of Council of Nicaea by Papacy as ecumenical: G. Lähr, 'Die Briefe und Prologe des Bibliothekars Anastasius', *Neues Archiv für ältere deutsche Geschichtskunde*, xlvii (1928), 429–32; Dvorník, *Les Légendes*, 306 sq.; H. Stern, 'Les Représentation des conciles dans l'église de la Nativité à Bethléem', *Byzantion*, xiii (1938), 453–5.

elected Patriarch, with the collaboration of the synod which
presided over the election, would have written soon after his
investiture letters of enthronement (τὰ συνοδικά) to the Pope and
to the three other Patriarchs.[1] In this case this was done only
much later, in 811, and Nicephorus himself gave the reasons for
this delay at the end of a letter of that year:[2]

Let nobody be astonished, or accuse our reputation (τῆς ἡμετέρας
ὑπολήψεως) if we presented ourselves (ἀπηντήκαμεν) on so late an
occasion with these remarks. Let it rather be known to your brotherly
self beloved by God that authority's harsh and implacable mind was in
the ascendant and was able to hinder us from doing what we deemed
best but that priestly custom has not been neglected nor fallen in
desuetude, nor did we become, out of some kind of carelessness, dis-
dainers of what is fitting and behoves men of the clergy. And may
your holy soul grant pardon, should it intend to blame me for slow-
ness; for it, too, has experienced that it is not easy to oppose the powers
that be (πρὸς δυναστείας ἀντιφέρεσθαι), which are carried away by
their own wishes and strive to fulfil their desires. For he who hindered
us saw fit to put forward even to us a specious pretext because of the
ceremony of the anointment,[3] and he murmured and was sorely irked
that you broke with the Church. For this reason because you also
suffered coercion in these matters, you can be indulgent (δύνασθε
συγγνώμονες ἔσεσθαι) towards those who unwillingly came into a
similar situation. And for these reasons, I believe, no further comments

---

[1] On these 'synodal letters' cf. L. Bréhier, 'Normal Relations between Rome
and the Churches of the East before the schism of the eleventh century', *The
Constructive Quarterly*, iv (1916), 645 sq., and *Institutions*, 455.

[2] Nicephorus, *Epistulae ad Leonem*, P.G. c. 196D–197C. On the date of this letter
see Theophanes, 494: during the last month of A.D. 811; Grumel, *Regestes*, no. 382.
A Latin translation was published by C. Baronius, *Annales Ecclesiastici* (Lucca,
1743), xiii. 476 ff. from a Verdun manuscript Baronius attributes this trans-
lation, which is superior to the modern translation printed in Migne, to Anastasius
Bibliothecarius. According to the Catalogue (*Catalogue Général des Manuscrits des
Bibliothèques Publiques des Départements etc.*, Quarto series (Paris, 1879), v. 423–536)
Verdun had in 1879 only two manuscripts (lectionaries) which had once belonged
to the Cathedral (nos. 104 and 118). In view of the facts set forth on p. 422 of the
Catalogue it is probable that the manuscript may be found in a Prussian collection
—if indeed it has not perished.

[3] *P.G.* c. 197A: ἐδόκει γὰρ τῷ εἴργοντι καὶ ἀφορμὴν εὐπρόσωπον προβάλλεσθαι ἐφ᾽
ἡμῖν τῶν ἐπιτελεσθέντων τοῦ χρίσματος ἕνεκεν, καὶ ὡς ὑμεῖς τῆς Ἐκκλησίας ἑαυτοὺς
ἀπερρήξατε διεθρύλλει καὶ ἐχαλέπαινε. The Latin translation published by Baronius
has: 'visum est enim ei, qui prohibebat, occasionem speciosam obiicere pro nobis,
ea, quae propter unctionem regis sunt facta, et quod vosmetipsos ab Ecclesia ex-
pulistis, exterrebat, et turbabat.' I have rendered τὰ ἐπιτελεσθέντα with 'ceremony'
as in Nicephorus' works the verb ἐπιτελεῖν normally refers to an ecclesiastical
ceremony, see, for example, *Antirrheticus*, iii. 7 (*P.G.* c. 388A) and 78 (ibid. 520A).

on the apology are needed; rather what is now being done and ac-
complished here will be summed up for you in suitable guise and will
bear us witness. Once the lock is broken, and the door opened, the
stumbling-blocks are lifted from our path, the latter has become all
smooth, solitary (ἀποστιβής, corruption?), and even, and the grievance
is gone for all time; there the stumbling-blocks are out of the way, gone
is the oppression (τὰ τῆς ἐπηρείας), the hindrances from that quarter
are undone, and the light of freedom has been shown forth to the
Church. For this reason it was possible to complete and fulfil the re-
quirements of love and of prevailing hierarchical custom.

This passage has been quoted in full because it shows two
things. The first is (and this is the only inference which Nicephorus himself wanted to be drawn from it) that it was the Emperor Nicephorus who hindered the Patriarch from communicating with the Pope.[1] The second point of interest in this passage
is the mention of the 'pretext' put forward by the Emperor
Nicephorus: 'the ceremony of the anointment'. What was this
'anointment' which, according to the Patriarch, the Emperor
Nicephorus considered so serious a matter that he prevented his
Patriarch from communicating with Pope Leo III and that he
accused the Pope of having created a schism? There can be only
one answer to this question: the 'imperial coronation' of Charlemagne at St. Peter's on Christmas Day 800. It is true, of course,
only Charlemagne's son Charles was anointed on that day,[2] and
this anointment cannot possibly have provoked so strong a reaction on the part of the Emperor Nicephorus. Theophanes makes
it clear, however, that because both father and son had the same
name, it was thought—wrongly—at Byzantium that on Christmas
800 Charlemagne himself had been anointed Emperor at St.
Peter's.[3] Thus Nicephorus' letter is one of our earliest sources—

---

[1] This point is confirmed by Theophanes, 494.

[2] *Liber Pontificalis, Vita Leonis III,* § xxiv (vol. ii, p. 7, ed. L. Duchesne): 'Ilico
sanctissimus antistes et pontifex unxit oleo sancto Karolo, excellentissimo filio eius,
rege, in ipso die Natalis domini nostri Iesu Christi', cf. P. E. Schramm, 'Die
Anerkennung Karls des Großen als Kaiser', *Historische Zeitschrift,* clxxii (1951),
449–515, esp. 486.

[3] Theophanes, 472 sq.: ὁ δὲ (Pope Leo III) τὸν Κάρουλον ἀμειβόμενος ἔστεψεν
αὐτὸν εἰς βασιλέα Ῥωμαίων ἐν τῷ ναῷ τοῦ ἁγίου ἀποστόλου Πέτρου, χρίσας ἐλαίῳ
ἀπὸ κεφαλῆς ἕως ποδῶν. E. Amann, *L'époque carolingienne,* in Fliche and Martin,
Histoire de l'Église, vi. 161, n. 3, explains this error by a confusion of Charlemagne
with his oldest son called Charles. In this same note Amann remarks that no
occidental writer speaks of an anointment of Charlemagne. See, however, Iohannes
Venetus, *Cronaca Veneziana,* ed. G. Monticolo, *Fonti per la Storia d'Italia,* ix (1890),

and one completely neglected by students of the Carolingian Age[1]—for the imperial coronation of Charlemagne. On the famous and difficult question whether the initiative was Charlemagne's or Leo's,[2] it takes the position that the coronation was imposed by Charlemagne on the Pope. But this is less decisive than might seem at first sight. It proves no more than that this was the view officially taken at Constantinople in 811. If at that time the Byzantine Patriarch wished to renew ecclesiastical relations with the Papacy, he was compelled, to save face, to put this interpretation on the events of Christmas 800.

This synodal letter of the year 811 was taken to Rome by an embassy, the main purpose of which was to communicate with Charlemagne. In the meantime the Franks won a valuable pledge, Venetia.[3] Furthermore, the Emperor Nicephorus was hard pressed by his Bulgarian neighbours.[4] Thus negotiations with the Franks, which had been interrupted since the accession of the Emperor Nicephorus, were resumed. In these negotiations the Byzantine Emperor could offer to recognize Charlemagne's coronation. Charlemagne, on the other hand, had conquered Venice, Istria, and certain cities in Dalmatia and was consequently in a strong bargaining position. Thus in 810 Nicephorus dispatched the *spatharius* Arsaphius to Pippin, King of Italy, and since the latter had died before the negotiator arrived, Charlemagne summoned him to Aix.[5] In a letter of 811 Charlemagne expresses his satisfaction at the arrival of a Byzantine ambassador for whom he had been waiting for so many years.[6] Venetia was

---

100: *ab apostolico coronatus et unctus est in imperatore.* This makes it very likely that Iohannes Venetus is using a Byzantine source. See above, p. 87, n. 2.

[1] The sources are conveniently collected by Heinz Dannenbauer, *Die Quellen zur Geschichte der Kaiserkrönung Karls des Großen*, Kleine Texte für Vorlesungen und Übungen, herausgegeben von Hans Lietzmann, no. 161 (Berlin, 1931). Nicephorus' *Epistula* is not mentioned. Visser, *Nikephoros*, 58 and 63, understood the reference to the coronation of Charlemagne but did not elaborate.

[2] See K. Heldmann, *Das Kaisertum Karls des Großen. Theorien und Wirklichkeit*, Weimar, 1928.

[3] L. H. Hartmann, *Geschichte Italiens im Mittelalter*, 4 vols. (Leipzig und Gotha, 1897–1915), iii. 55–62; Bury, *Eastern Roman Empire*, 324.

[4] Bury, *Eastern Roman Empire*, 340–2.

[5] *M.G.H., Epistulae Karolini Aevi*, ii. 546 sq.

[6] Ibid. 547: '. . . veluti in specula positi, longa fuimus expectatione suspensi . . . . Iamque ut se habet humanae mentis infirmitas, pro spe disperatio cordi nostro incipiebat oboriri . . .. Idcirco audito adventu memorati legati dilectionis tuae, Arsafii gloriosi spatarii, magnopere gavisi sumus.'

immediately handed over to the Byzantines[1] and a Frankish
embassy sent to Constantinople. There Michael I Rangabe had
succeeded Nicephorus and Stauracius. The new Emperor was
even more anxious than his father-in-law had been to make peace
with the West: not only did he send a new embassy composed of
Michael, metropolitan of Synnada, and the two *protospatharioi*
Theognostos and Arsaphius,[2] but he was also planning for the
marriage of his son Theophylactus, probably to some Frankish
princess.[3] At Aix the imperial ambassadors were received by
Charlemagne with great pomp. In a solemn church service they
received from him a copy of the peace treaty and acclaimed him,
at last, in Greek as Emperor and Basileus.[4] Charlemagne's
territorial concessions and the significance of his recognition as
Emperor are not germane to this context.[5]

It was this same embassy which transmitted to Pope Leo III
the synodal letter of the Patriarch Nicephorus on their return
from Aix.[6] At Rome in St. Peter the Pope repeated the ceremony

---

[1] Bury, *Eastern Roman Empire*, 325.   [2] Dölger, *Regesten*, no. 385.

[3] Theophanes, 494: ἀπέστειλε δὲ καὶ πρὸς Κάρουλον, βασιλέα τῶν Φράγγων, περὶ
εἰρήνης καὶ συναλλαγῆς εἰς Θεοφύλακτον, τὸν υἱὸν αὐτοῦ . . ..

[4] *Annales Regni Francorum*, edd. G. H. Pertz and F. Kurze (Hannover, 1895),
anno 812, p. 136: '[The Byzantine ambassadors] scriptum pacti ab eo in ecclesia
suscipientes more suo, id est Greca lingua, laudes ei dixerunt, imperatorem eum et
basileum appellantes.' Cf. also a letter of Charlemagne, *M.G.H.*, *Epistulae Karolini
Aevi*, ii. 555 f.

[5] However, I wish to mention one point. E. Stein, 'Zum mittelalterlichen Titel
"Kaiser der Römer" ', *Forschungen und Fortschritte*, vi (1930), 182–3, had shown that
Michael I was the first Byzantine emperor to call himself on his coins βασιλεὺς
'Ρωμαίων (instead of the simple βασιλεύς) and had considered it a consequence of
the recognition of Charlemagne in 812. Stein's thesis could be maintained in its
essentials even against a series of new discoveries (cf. *Byzantion*, x (1935), 723;
ibid. xi (1936), 482; *Orientalia Christiana Periodica*, xiii (1947) (*Miscellanea Guillaume
de Jerphanion I*), 380, but see *B.Z.* xxxvii (1937), 578 sq. To his arguments I can add
an important passage from an Arab historian which to a certain extent confirms
Stein's results. Masudi, *Le Livre de l'avertissement et de la revision*, translated by B.
Carra de Vaux (Paris, 1896), 229, when mentioning the Emperor Nicephorus,
writes: 'Les empereurs écrivaient en tête de leurs actes: D'un tel, empereur des
Chrétiens. Nicéphore [sc. the Emperor Nicephorus I] changea la formule et se
contenta d'écrire: empereur des Roumis. Cela est inexact, dit-il, je ne suis pas
empereur des Chrétiens, je suis empereur des Roumis, et les princes ne doivent dire
que ce qui est juste.' See also Bréhier, *Institutions*, 51 f. Stein's thesis, therefore, would
seem correct, with the modifications proposed by Franz Dölger, *B.Z.* xxxvii (1937),
579, to the effect that the title was used occasionally before 812, 'daß sie [the
Byzantines] ihn jedoch mit größerer Konsequenz und demonstrativer Bewußtheit
erst nach 812 stärker betont und bis zum Ende des Reichs beibehalten haben'.
See also Franz Dölger, *B.Z.* xlv (1952), 189 f.

[6] Grumel, *Regestes*, no. 382 (with important notes).

which had been performed by Charlemagne in the court chapel at Aix: the Pope handed over to them the same copy of the Peace Treaty.[1] These events—the same embassy sent to Charlemagne and Leo, and confirmation by the Pope of the Peace Treaty between the two Augusti—show clearly, as may be said with slight exaggeration, that at Byzantium the Pope was looked upon as the 'Frankish Patriarch'. As such he was suspect at Constantinople: 'If you are the friend of a Frank [the reason is that] you are not his neighbour' was a Greek proverb.[2] In the relations with the West the Patriarch Nicephorus had not shown the slightest initiative but had adopted the policy of his imperial masters. 'What do we care whether the Pope acts in one way or another?' Theodore of Studios exclaimed in an unguarded moment. The Patriarch Nicephorus did not think very differently.

[1] *Annales Regni Francorum*, loc. cit.: 'Et revertendo Romam venientes in basilica Sancti Petri apostoli eundem pacti seu foederis libellum a Leone papa denuo susceperunt.'

[2] Einhard, *Vita Karoli Magni Imperatoris*, 16, ed. L. Halphen (Paris, 1923), 50: Τὸν Φράγκον φίλον ἔχεις, γείτονα οὐκ ἔχεις.

V

THE NEW OUTBREAK OF ICONOCLASM

1. Social Composition of the Iconoclastic Party

THE return to image-worship in 787 had been due not to a serious weakening of the Iconoclastic party but to a number of fortuitous circumstances. The events of the ensuing three decades show that the forces of Iconoclasm were by no means exhausted. In A.D. 791, that is fourteen years after the Council of Nicaea, Pope Hadrian was still afraid of a recurrence of Iconoclasm.[1] In 797 the Emperor Constantine VI threatened the Patriarch Tarasius that unless the latter agreed to his divorce he would revert to the iconoclastic policy of his dynasty. Under the Emperor Nicephorus the Iconoclasts may have enjoyed some degree of imperial favour; for according to a chronicle which is, it is true, extremely hostile to the Emperor, the latter favoured a certain 'pseudo-hermit' Nicolaos who was residing at Hexakionion and his iconoclastic adherents. The chronicler adds that this made the Patriarch Nicephorus grieve.[2] The threat of Iconoclasm was still hovering over the Church and gave every emperor a means of exerting pressure on the Patriarch. It is not surprising that during the reign of Michael I Rangabe, Nikolaos of Hexakionion was forced to make a public recantation of his heretical views and that one of Nikolaos' adherents, who had scraped an image of the Theotokos, had his tongue cut off.[3]

A significant incident took place about June 813. At that time the Emperor Michael and the army were encamped near Versinicia, a few days before their terrible defeat by the Bulgarians. As often in times of crisis the population of Constantinople and the Patriarch Nicephorus prayed in the church of the Holy Apostles and implored God's protection for the coming battle.[4] In this church were buried, in the 'Heroon of Justinian', the bodies of many emperors and among them that of Constantine V

---

[1] *M.G.H., Epistolae Karolini Aevi*, iii. 56 f. (Ch. IV, p. 104, above.)

[2] Theophanes, 488 sq. The quarter of Hexakionion ('Εξακιόνιον) was situated on the seventh hill of the city, between the walls of Constantine and Theodosius, in the south-west; see Janin, *Constantinople byzantine*, 327 f.   [3] Theophanes, 496 sq.

[4] For the following account see Theophanes, 501.

Copronymus.[1] While the crowd was praying, several Iconoclasts without being noticed pried open the door which led to
the tombs and devised a plan so that it would open suddenly with
a great noise as if by a miracle. When this happened the congregation was taken aback. The ringleaders rushed through the
door to the tomb of Constantine V who had been so successful
against the Bulgarians. 'Arise', they cried, 'and help the ruined
State!' The rumour was spread that Constantine would ride on
horseback and fight the Bulgarians. Ultimately the Iconoclasts
were arrested by the City Prefect ($\xi\pi a\rho\chi os\ \tau\hat{\eta}s\ \pi\delta\lambda\epsilon\omega s$)[2] and confessed their trickery. They were punished (here the reading is
not quite certain) and afterwards marched in a public procession
through the streets of Constantinople. The chronicler proceeds
to give the reason for this measure: 'For thus had the inventor of
wickedness, the Devil, trained the soldiery that they did not blame
their own sins but the orthodox faith inherited from our fathers
and the sacred garb of the monks.'[3] And a little later the chronicler
remarks that these men praised Constantine the Judaizer as
prophet and conqueror.[4]

The incident throws light on the conditions of the masses
shortly before the new outbreak of Iconoclasm. Evidently the
'soldiery' in the capital was still iconoclastic, and Irene's change
of the garrison in 786 had altered the picture for a brief time only.
It shows, furthermore, the growth of legend around Constantine
Copronymus: in a period of constant invasions and defeats at the
hands of the Bulgarians it was natural that their great conqueror
became an epic hero of almost superhuman stature.[5] Thus the

[1] Constantine Porphyrogennetos, *Book of Ceremonies*, ii. 42 (*C.S.H.B.* xi. 645).

[2] On this important official see Bury, *Imp. Adm. Syst.* 69 sq. Cf., furthermore,
F. Uspenski, 'Konstantinopolskii Eparkh', *Izvestija Russkago Arkheologicheskago In-
stituta*, iv. 2 (1899), 79–104; A. Stöckle, *Spätrömische und byzantinische Zünfte*, &c.,
Klio, Beiheft ix (Leipzig, 1911), 74–78; Bréhier, *Institutions*, 187–92.

[3] Theophanes, 501: $o\dot{v}s$ [i.e. the perpetrators of the crime in the Church of the
Holy Apostles] . . . $\pi o\mu\pi\hat{\eta}\ \delta\eta\mu o\sigma\dot{\iota}a\ \pi a\rho\dot{\epsilon}\pi\epsilon\mu\psi\epsilon\nu$ [i.e. $\dot{o}\ \tau\hat{\eta}s\ \pi\delta\lambda\epsilon\omega s\ \xi\pi a\rho\chi os$] $\dot{a}\nu a\beta o\hat{\omega}\nu$-
$\tau a s\ \tau\hat{\eta}s\ \tau\iota\mu\omega\rho\dot{\iota}a s\ \tau\dot{\eta}\nu\ \pi\rho\delta\phi a\sigma\iota\nu\ \cdot\ o\ddot{v}\tau\omega\ \gamma\dot{a}\rho\ \dot{o}\ \tau\hat{\eta}s\ \kappa a\kappa\dot{\iota}a s\ \epsilon\dot{v}\rho\dot{\epsilon}\tau\eta s\ \delta\iota\dot{a}\beta o\lambda os\ \tau o\dot{v}s\ \sigma\tau\rho a\tau\epsilon\upsilon o$-
$\mu\dot{\epsilon}\nu o\upsilon s\ \xi\xi\epsilon\pi a\dot{\iota}\delta\epsilon\upsilon\sigma\epsilon\nu\ \dot{\omega}s\ \mu\dot{\eta}\ a\dot{\iota}\tau\iota\hat{a}\sigma\theta a\iota\ \tau\dot{a}s\ \dot{\epsilon}a\upsilon\tau\hat{\omega}\nu\ \dot{a}\mu a\rho\tau\dot{\iota}a s\ \dot{a}\lambda\lambda\dot{a}\ \tau\dot{\eta}\nu\ \dot{o}\rho\theta\delta\delta o\xi o\nu\ \kappa a\dot{\iota}$
$\pi a\tau\rho o\pi a\rho\dot{a}\delta o\tau o\nu\ \pi\dot{\iota}\sigma\tau\iota\nu\ \kappa a\dot{\iota}\ \tau\dot{o}\ \tau\hat{\omega}\nu\ \mu o\nu a\sigma\tau\hat{\omega}\nu\ \dot{\iota}\epsilon\rho\dot{o}\nu\ \sigma\chi\hat{\eta}\mu a$. I have deliberately chosen
the vague term 'soldiery' to render the Greek $\tau o\dot{v}s\ \sigma\tau\rho a\tau\epsilon\upsilon o\mu\dot{\epsilon}\nu o\upsilon s$.

[4] Ibid.: $K\omega\nu\sigma\tau a\nu\tau\hat{\iota}\nu o\nu\ \tau\dot{o}\nu\ '\Iota o\upsilon\delta a\iota\delta\phi\rho o\nu a\ \mu a\kappa a\rho\dot{\iota}\zeta o\nu\tau\epsilon s\ \dot{\omega}s\ \pi\rho o\phi\dot{\eta}\tau\eta\nu\ \kappa a\dot{\iota}\ \nu\iota\kappa\dot{\eta}\tau\eta\nu$.

[5] On the growth of this legend see A. Lombard, *Constantin V, Empereur des
Romains*, &c. (Paris, 1902), 10–21; N. Adontz, 'Les Légendes de Maurice et de
Constantin V empereurs de Byzance', *Melanges Bidez: Annuaire de l'Institut de
Philologie et d'Histoire Orientales*, ii (1934), 1–12; R. Goossens, 'A propos de la
légende de Constantin V', *Annuaire*, &c. iii (1935), 157–60.

'soldiery' now is willing to believe in a miracle performed by the resurrected Constantine. In the minds of the 'soldiery' the defeats of the present were a divine visitation for having given up the iconoclastic policy of the hero of the past. So powerful was this current of public opinion that the City Prefect thought it necessary to show by public demonstration the human agents behind the events at the church of the Holy Apostles.[1]

According to the chronicler the City Prefect did this because the 'soldiery' (οἱ στρατευόμενοι)[2] all blamed image-worship and the monks for the desperate military situation. Obviously the 'soldiery' who were to be impressed by the public demonstration were present at Constantinople. Yet it is known that the bulk of the army and of the garrison (τὰ βασιλικὰ τάγματα) in particular, were at that time at Versinicia.[3] This is suggested not only by a text of *Theophanes Continuatus* but also by the fact that the City Prefect was handling the matter: for the City Prefect, together with the *praepositus* and the *magister*, were the temporary rulers of the state whenever the Emperor was away on a campaign.[4] Evidently the troops lying at Versinicia, the θέματα and τάγματα, were not the ones for whose benefit the City Prefect paraded the culprits of the incident at the Holy Apostles through the streets of Constantinople. This seems to suggest that there were troops still at Constantinople who had not joined the rest of the army.

Here two lengthy but thus far barely noticed texts deserve to be examined.[5] Neglected because they are hidden away in a theological context, these passages occur in a treatise written by

---

[1] One look at the ground-plan of the church of the Holy Apostles (see A. Heisenberg, *Grabeskirche und Apostelkirche* &c. ii (Leipzig, 1908, 113) makes it clear that it was very easy indeed to work unnoticed at the door of the Heroon of Justinian (which lay east of the northern part of the cross-aisle) while a service was being conducted in the church.

[2] Text: see p. 112, n. 3, above.

[3] *Theophanes Continuatus*, P.G. cix. 29A. It is possible that Michael I had left part of the garrison at Constantinople to police and defend the city. This was pointed out to me by Professor Theodor Mommsen, of Cornell University, with whom I discussed briefly the material presented in this section.

[4] Uspenski, *Konstantinopolskii Eparkh*, 81.

[5] Nicephorus, *Apologeticus Maior*, 5–9 (*P.G.* c. 544B–556D), and *Antirrheticus*, iii. 62 (ibid. 488A–492B). The only writer who used these passages is Lombard, *Constantin*, esp. 94 sqq., but he very naturally referred only to those parts which relate to the period of Constantine V and ignored their bearing on the period of Leo the Armenian.

the Patriarch Nicephorus between the years 818 and 820, which I propose to call *Apologeticus atque Antirrhetici* (see below, pp. 167–73). At the beginning of this work, Nicephorus describes the peaceful condition of the Church after the Seventh Ecumenical Council. This blissful situation was disturbed, he continues, by a group of men whom he characterizes in general terms: perpetrators of wicked deeds became monks or invaded the clergy. They were worldly people and had said: 'Even if we have to sell our souls, we shall revel freely in the Palace.' Greedy for dainty food, and living only for their stomachs, they are now fed at the public expense. They are violating the profession of faith which they signed at the time of their ordination and do not respect the *Definition* of the Seventh Council of Nicaea. For these reasons they have been ousted from the priesthood by the synod. They now hold assemblies in the palace. It is probable that this invective is aimed primarily at the Committee appointed by the Emperor Leo V to prepare the Council of St. Sophia (below, p. 126) and at any other members of the clergy whom they may have won over to their views at an early stage. The description of their life of luxury in the imperial palace agrees even in wording with that given in the *Vita Nicephori* of the orgies of that Committee.[1] Their deposition by a synod is borne out by Nicephorus' biographer.[2] The beginning of the passage would thus characterize the ecclesiastical leadership of the iconoclastic movement.

From the leaders Nicephorus passes on to the rank and file. Both at the beginning and at the end of this work Nicephorus describes the social strata which favoured Iconoclasm.

Already they have attached to themselves as colleagues and supporters of their teaching the dignitaries from among the circus factions in the *demes*, as was fitting for this disorderly crew. . . . As is usual in such cases of disorder and confusion, even a part of the Church is being corrupted, namely those who were convicted and ousted for canonical accusations and charges, to make their sin sinful in the extreme. Neither are the leaders of the theatrical spectacles and of the stage, whom we are accustomed to call mimes in vernacular speech, left out of this venerable assembly. They even invited some of the traders, men from the street corners and the brothels, to lend a hand in their undertakings, and in starting riots they assemble the whole crowd of beggars, the rabble and the vulgar. But what adorns

---

[1] Cf. *P.G.* c. 545A with Ignatius, *Vita Nicephori*, 165 (de Boor).
[2] Ignatius, *Vita Nicephori*, 195 f. Cf. Grumel, *Regestes*, no. 400.

their array most of all is a numerous part of the men formerly enlisted in the garrison troops. Some of these were discharged from the armed forces as having passed and being beyond the age limit, others were discovered to be guilty of certain misdeeds and shameful acts. The majority of these adhere because of their very brutish and stupid disposition which they had had even at the time when they had been recruited, to that ancient and impious doctrine [Iconoclasm], and they are more attached to it than to anything else. After these men had been deprived of the imperial doles which furnished them with their livelihood together with the military equipment, they reached the limit of poverty and want of necessities, so that they are begging publicly from the passers-by: they are supplying themselves with their food by collecting contributions, peering about for drinking bouts and gatherings, where they flutter about as if on wings in order to alleviate from this source their destitution and distress. All these are, as we know, accustomed to yearn for the worse, they hate the established order at all times and rejoice at new situations and strive after revolutions in the hope that such disturbances and disorders may supply their wants and needs.[1]

At the end of the *Apologeticus atque Antirrhetici* the author repeats this description in almost identical terms. Of this second passage only those parts which contain additional information need to be paraphrased. The dismissed soldiers who make up the majority of the Iconoclasts have been ousted from the military registers (τῶν καταλόγων ἐξώσθησαν τῶν στρατιωτικῶν). They are satisfied only if their bellies and bodies have their fill of food and pleasure and blame the Christian faith for their lack of many necessities. They pride themselves on adhering to the faith of Mamonas [Constantine Copronymos]. They claim that during his reign prosperity and plenty prevailed, that grain and the other necessities of life were cheap.[2]

These passages call for several comments:

1. It need hardly be emphasized that they reflect the ideas of an ardent opponent of Iconoclasm. Still the *facts* mentioned may be trusted. Indeed the data themselves, as distinguished from the interpretation offered by Nicephorus, contain nothing particularly unfavourable to the Iconoclasts, provided only that their social status and the misfortunes described by him were undeserved. In these sections Nicephorus indicates the real enemy.

[1] Nicephorus, *Apologeticus*, 9 (*P.G.* c. 556).
[2] Nicephorus, *Antirrheticus*, iii. 63 f. (*P.G.* c. 492c and 493a).

It is Constantine Copronymus and his legend on the one hand, and certain dismissed soldiers, on the other.

2. The passages are enigmatic indeed. They seek to describe the social group or groups which followed the iconoclastic leadership. The first group are οἱ ἐκ τῶν ἐν τοῖς δήμοις χρωμάτων τῆς ἱππικῆς ἁμίλλης προὔχοντες, that is literally 'the dignitaries from among the parties of the horse race in the *demes*'. This can be understood with the help of the extensive literature on the *demes* and circus factions at Byzantium.[1] The political rivalry between the circus parties, which had been so prominent in the annals of the sixth and earlier centuries, had come to an end in the seventh century.[2] During the reign of the Heraclian dynasty a reform seems to have taken place which 'nationalized' the management of the Hippodrome and made the circus parties executive organs of the government. They retained, however, a hierarchy of their own and were represented in the individual *demes* by the γειτονιάρχαι and possibly by other officials such as πρωτεῖα, *chartularii*, and notaries.[3] It was these that Nicephorus must have had in mind and who were, according to him, infected with Iconoclasm.

3. It is no surprise to find, among the Iconoclasts, mimes, traders, and other members of the lower strata of the population. Nicephorus' indications are too vague to determine the various groups more accurately.

4. By far the most interesting and puzzling information concerns the military section of the Iconoclasts. This information is too specific to assume that Nicephorus invented it.

(*a*) Soldiers dismissed either for faults or because they have reached the age limit constitute, Nicephorus says, the vast majority of the Iconoclasts; these ex-soldiers are very numerous (μέρος οὐκ εὐαρίθμητον) and extremely poor. The difficulty with

---

[1] *P.G.* c. 556A. The earlier literature is listed in A. P. D'iakonov's article, 'Vizantiiskie dimy i faktsii (τὰ μέρη) v V–VII vv.', *Vizantiiskii Sbornik* (Moscow and Leningrad, 1945), 144–227. Add the important paper of F. Dvornik, 'The Circus Parties in Byzantium', *Byzantina-Metabyzantina*, i. 1 (1946), 119–33; Bréhier, *Institutions*, 195–202; *Civilisation byzantine*, 93–104. According to D'iakonov, a distinction should be made between *demes* and circus factions: the latter were the famous four parties of the Hippodrome while the *demes* were synonymous with the smallest topographical subdivisions of Constantinople, the γειτονίαι or τοποθεσίαι. (D'iakonov's article deserves a translation into a more accessible language.)

[2] D'iakonov, *Vizantiiskie Dimy*, 227; Dvornik, *Circus Parties*, 130–3.

[3] D'iakonov, *Vizantiiskie Dimy*, 160, 185, *passim*. See Constantine Porphyrogenetos, *Book of Ceremonies*, ii. 63 (55), ed. A. Vogt, ii. 75–78 and *passim*.

this passage lies in Nicephorus' vivid references to their poverty. Now *a priori* it is quite unthinkable that any government at any time did not take care of discharged professional soldiers. Such a neglect would invite disaster and would be explicable only under very exceptional circumstances. The organization of the themes in the Byzantine Empire had been accompanied by the creation of a national peasant army.[1] Just as late antiquity had seen the Roman army transformed into fortified peasant settlements distributed over the various frontiers of the Empire (*limitanei*),[2] so the emperors of the seventh century had assigned farms (στρατιωτικὰ κτήματα) to their soldiers. The owners of these farms were liable to military service and this obligation was hereditary. A Byzantine soldier, therefore, was taken care of during his old age: he retired to his farm and cultivated his fields. In spite of the attractions of Constantinople it is very unlikely that any large number of regular veterans would have preferred a life of misery in the capital to that of a soldier-farmer in the provinces. These regular veterans could not have been meant by Theophanes' στρατευόμενοι.

(*b*) It is known from Theophanes that the Emperor Nicephorus had enlisted 'the poor' (οἱ πτωχοί) in the army. This was the second of the famous ten κακώσεις of this emperor mentioned by Theophanes,[3] and it served a threefold purpose.[4]

First, the regular army had proved unreliable in the revolt of

[1] On the connexions between the creation of the themes and the peasants' army cf. L. M. Hartmann, *Untersuchungen zur Geschichte der byzantinischen Verwaltung in Italien (540–750)* (Leipzig, 1889), 71; E. Stein, *Studien zur Geschichte des byzantinischen Reiches vornehmlich unter den Kaisern Justinus II und Tiberius Constantinus* (Stuttgart, 1919), 132–5; F. Uspenski, *Voennoe ustroistvo*, 198 sq. and *passim*. On the origin of the themes see, apart from the important works of Stein and Uspenski, H. Gelzer, *Die Genesis der byzantinischen Themenverfassung*, Abhandlungen der Kgl. Sächsischen Gesellschaft der Wissenschaften XVIII. 5 (Leipzig, 1899); Ch. Diehl, 'L'Origine du régime des thèmes dans l'Empire byzantin', *Études byzantines*, 276–92; Iu. Kulakovskii, *Istorija Vizantii* (Kiev, 1915), iii. 387–431; Bréhier, *Institutions*, 355–66.

[2] M. Rostovtzeff, *Gesellschaft und Wirtschaft im römischen Kaiserreich* (Leipzig, no date), ii. 136 sq., 211; E. Stein, *Geschichte des spätrömischen Reiches* (Vienna, 1928), i. 90, 189, 363. For a comparison of the *limitanei* of late antiquity with the military lands of the Middle Ages see Hartmann, *Untersuchungen*, 71; Stein, *Geschichte des spätrömischen Reiches*, i. 90.

[3] Theophanes, 486: προσέταξε στρατεύεσθαι πτωχοὺς καὶ ἐξοπλίζεσθαι παρὰ τῶν ὁμοχώρων, παρέχοντας καὶ ἀνὰ ὀκτωκαίδεκα ἡμίσους νομισμάτων τῷ δημοσίῳ, καὶ ἀλληλεγγύως τὰ δημόσια.

[4] On the following see the interesting remarks of G. I. Bratianu, *Études byzantines*, 197 sq.

Bardanes Turcus. During the last thirty years the Garrison of Constantinople, the τάγματα,[1] had generally played very much the same role as the Pretorian Guards had at Rome: during this entire period the τάγματα had been a constant source of disturbance.[2] The enlistment of 'the poor' was designed to find politically reliable recruits for the army.

Secondly, the Emperor was straining the military resources of the Empire to the utmost against the Bulgarian danger. For this purpose he was drawing on the civilian population by a process which was not very different from the conscription of the population (δημότευσις) of earlier times.[3]

Thirdly, the enlistment of the 'poor' created a new source of revenue for the Treasury. If interpreted correctly,[4] this second κάκωσις meant that the 'neighbours' (ὁμόχωροι) were responsible not only for the taxes of the new recruits by way of the ancient ἐπιβολή, but also for an additional 18½ nomismata for the equipment of each recruit.

Thus the Emperor Nicephorus increased his army by an act of conscription. The Byzantine term for such an act was στρατεύειν, and the recruits brought into the army in this fashion were called οἱ στρατευόμενοι or conscripts.[5] One of the Saints' Lives of the period contains an account which illustrates this process from the point of view of the individual recruit. The *Life of St. Philaretus*, written in all probability under Michael II, tells of a military

[1] On the τάγματα as garrison cf. Uspenski, *Voennoe Ustroistvo*, 155–8; Bury, *Imp. Adm. Syst.* 47.

[2] This point has not been brought out by historians. Here are a few examples from Theophanes. The garrison had prevented the Ecumenical Council from meeting at the church of the Holy Apostles in 786 (Theophanes, 461). It had played a sinister role in the fall of Constantine VI in 796 (Theophanes, 471). It had helped the Emperor Nicephorus to obtain the throne in 802 (Theophanes, 476); but it had also plotted against him in 806/7 when he was on a campaign against the Bulgarians (Theophanes, 482).

[3] G. Manoljović, 'Le Peuple de Constantinople', *Byzantion*, xi (1936), 625–34.

[4] H. Monnier, 'Études de droit byzantin', *Nouvelle revue historique de droit français et étranger*, xix (1895), 90–100; F. Dölger, *Beiträge zur Geschichte der byzantinischen Finanzverwaltung besonders des 10. und 11. Jahrhunderts*, Byzantinisches Archiv, Heft 9 (Leipzig and Berlin, 1927), 129 and *B.Z.* xxxvi (1936), 158. Dölger believes, however, that the 'neighbours' had to furnish equipment and 18½ nomismata and taxes. I think that the 18½ nomismata were a substitute for, not an addition to, the equipment.

[5] Theophanes uses the term στρατεύειν frequently in the sense of *milites conscribere*, see de Boor's index. D'iakonov, *Vizantiiskie Dimy*, 163 f., states that the verb στρατεύειν referred to the privilege and duty of carrying arms.

conscription held in Paphlagonia in 782 or shortly thereafter. Recruiting officers appeared in the Saint's village of Amnia and registered the soldiers 'so that they would bear arms against the Arabs' (ἵνα στρατεύσωνται κατὰ τῶν 'Ισμαηλιτῶν). Each soldier was to supply a pair of horses and a carriage. In Philaretus' village there was a poor (πτωχός) soldier Musulios who possessed only one horse with a carriage. The recruiting officer threatened him with dire penalties unless he brought a second horse. He finally borrowed one from the over-generous Saint, and determined to flee as soon as the mustering was over, apparently in order to evade military service.[1] There probably were not many villages with men like St. Philaretus, but otherwise the incident reveals a situation that must have been typical: a sudden conscription of farmers because of the danger of an Arab attack; the desperate poverty of some owners of military land, and their determination to evade the draft by flight. It was presumably from among poor farmers like Musulios that the Emperor Nicephorus conscripted his soldiers a generation later.

This new measure was taken not only on paper, it was carried into effect when the Emperor Nicephorus started on his fateful campaign against the Bulgarians in 811. 'He assembled the troops not only from Thrace but also those of the peratic themes, and along with the troops many blaspheming poor men equipped at private expense with slings and sticks'.[2] The equipment of these 'poor men' was deplorable,[3] and their morale cannot have been better.

The morale of these 'soldiers' must have deteriorated further after the disaster which concluded Nicephorus' campaign. It

---

[1] M. H. Fourmy and M. Leroy, 'La Vie de S. Philarète', *Byzantion*, ix (1934), 85–167, esp. 125 ff. On the date of the incident see Louis Bréhier, 'Les Populations rurales au ixᵉ siècle' &c., *Byzantion*, i (1924), 177–90, esp. 187 f. It is not impossible that Philaretus' horse represented his share in the equipment of Musulios.

[2] Theophanes 490: ἐπισυνάξας δὲ τὰ στρατεύματα οὐ μόνον ἐκ Θρᾴκης ἀλλὰ καὶ τῶν περατικῶν θεμάτων, πένητάς τε πολλοὺς ἰδίοις ὀψωνίοις σφενδόναις καὶ ῥάβδοις ὡπλισμένους, βλασφημοῦντας ἅμα τοῖς στρατεύμασι. A newly recovered fragment of the *Scriptor Incertus de Leone Armeno* (H. Grégoire, 'Un Nouveau Fragment du Scriptor Incertus de Leone Armeno', *Byzantion*, xi (1936), 422) informs us that all the *tagmata* including the newly formed Hikanatoi formed part of the expedition.

[3] If the above translation of ἰδίοις ὀψωνίοις ('at private expense') is correct, the 'neighbours' had satisfied only the letter of the second κάκωσις. If, however, it should be translated 'at their own expense', this would show that the second κάκωσις could not be enforced against the 'neighbours'.

would seem that Stauracius was afraid of an uprising of this 'people in arms', the δημοκρατία, during his short reign.[1] Michael I Rangabe tried to reconcile all parts of the population by his lavishness, and among the beneficiaries the sources tell of 'soldiery and beggars, both those in the imperial city and in the themes'.[2] Yet though Theophanes knows of a special appropriation of five talents of gold for the widows of the troops from the themata who had been killed on Nicephorus' Bulgarian campaign,[3] no specific sum is mentioned for the widows of the 'soldiery' and 'beggars'. Michael I Rangabe is known to have levied fresh conscripts to replace the casualties suffered on Nicephorus' Bulgarian expedition, and new recruits took part in the assembly for the campaign of 813.[4]

(c) Curiously enough the *Scriptor Incertus* does not mention the garrison of Constantinople among the troops assembled by Michael I Rangabe for his Bulgarian campaign. Still, the garrison troops certainly participated in the campaign. If in fact they had stayed at Constantinople, no author, however biased in favour of Leo the Armenian, could have reported the tradition that they betrayed Michael I at Versinicia. Yet such a tradition is reported by the Continuators of Theophanes.[5] This difficulty is solved if one assumes that Michael's new recruits came to constitute the garrison of Constantinople and that the *Scriptor Incertus* means the garrison troops when he speaks of new recruits. The passage from the *Scriptor Incertus* presents a further puzzle. According to it the new recruits replaced the casualties of Nicephorus' campaign. Yet it is known from Theophanes that some of the 'soldiery' had remained at Constantinople during the campaign of Versinicia. It is probable that the new recruits of Michael I replaced the casualties of the earlier campaign and that other recruits were assigned to the garrison as a substitute for soldiers discharged

---

[1] G. I. Bratianu, *Études byzantines*, 95–124.

[2] Theophanes, 494: πάντας δὲ τοὺς πατρικίους καὶ συγκλητικούς, ἀρχιερεῖς τε καὶ ἱερεῖς καὶ μοναχούς, στρατευομένους τε καὶ πτωχούς, τούς τε κατὰ τὴν βασιλίδα πόλιν καὶ ἐν τοῖς θέμασι κατεπλούτισεν.

[3] Ibid.: τῶν δὲ ἀναιρεθέντων ἐν Βουλγαρίᾳ θεματικῶν στρατιωτῶν ταῖς γυναιξὶ ε΄ τάλαντα χρυσίου ἐδωρήσατο.

[4] *Scriptor Incertus de Leone Armeno*, P.G. cviii. 1012C: συνήγαγεν πάντα τὰ θέματα, στρατεύσας καὶ ἄλλους πολλοὺς ἀντὶ τῶν ἀπολειφθέντων ἐν τῷ πολέμῳ, καὶ τοὺς φυλάσσοντας τὰς κλεισούρας τῆς Συρίας συναθροίσας, Λυκάονας καὶ Κιλίκας καὶ Ἰσαύρους καὶ Καππαδόκας καὶ Γαλάτας, καὶ πάντας παραλαβὼν ἐξῆλθεν . . ..

[5] *Theophanes Continuatus*, I, 6 (*P.G.* cix. 29A).

previously because according to Nicephorus they had reached the age limit or committed crimes. Yet is it really conceivable that these discharged soldiers formed 'a *numerous* part of the men who formerly served in the garrison troops' (μέρος οὐκ εὐαρίθμητον τῶν ἐν στρατιωτικοῖς τάγμασι τελούντων ποτέ) and at the same time were as destitute as Nicephorus describes them? There can be no question that normally discharged veterans were provided for by the government. The exceptional condition of the discharged garrison troops is explicable only if it is assumed that under the Emperor Michael I Rangabe there had taken place a punitive mass discharge of garrison troops. Technically this discharge might well have been based on regulations defining the military age limit or on more or less trumped-up charges against individual soldiers.[1] The real motive must have been different. Louis Bréhier has pointed out that during the reign of the devout Michael I Rangabe the Studite reform party ruled the Empire and tried 'to establish the universal authority of Christian ethics'.[2] This objective of the Studites manifested itself in the recognition of Charlemagne, in the second excommunication of Joseph of Kathara, and in the abortive peace negotiations with the Bulgarian ruler Krum reported by Theophanes.[3] Is it not likely that under a régime such as that of Michael I Rangabe soldiers from the garrison troops were dismissed *because of their iconoclastic leanings* and replaced by new recruits? This is the only hypothesis which seems to explain the data furnished by the various sources. If it is correct, then the policy which dictated it was unbelievably short-sighted. The Empress Irene had used a similar expedient in 786 but at that time most of the discharged soldiers owned land to which they could retire. Not so the veterans of Nicephorus' campaign, most of whom seem to have been recruited from the 'poor men' or 'beggars'. These men had no place to which to go after their dismissal. Even if they had come originally from farms, their lands had been assigned in the meantime to their neighbours

---

[1] Nicephorus does not state that the reaching of the age limit or the commission of crimes were the exclusive reasons for their discharge. He merely says that 'some' (οἱ μέν) were discharged for the former reasons, others (οἱ δέ) for the latter. This does not exclude the possibility that a third category was discharged for an altogether different reason.

[2] *Vie et mort de Byzance*, 100–2.

[3] Theophanes, 497 f. Bréhier, *Vie et mort de Byzance*, 101, speaks appropriately of the Crown Council assembled by Michael to consider Krum's proposals as 'un véritable conseil de conscience'.

who had payed their taxes. Thus it is very understandable
that they should have stayed at Constantinople hoping to find
occasional employment or to be taken care of by the various
charitable institutions in the city or at least to get free meals once
in a while. Small wonder, therefore, that, according to Nicephorus, these men were obstinate Iconoclasts and intent on
'innovation'. Their unprovided dismissal was an act of political
folly, but one that would be in keeping with the general Studite
position towards the affairs of State. The price for this mistaken
policy was to be paid not only by the Studite party but also by
the moderates headed by the Patriarch Nicephorus and by the
cause of orthodoxy as such.

4. Nicephorus reports that prior to their dismissal the soldiers
had received both arms and food ἐκ τῶν βασιλικῶν σιτηρεσίων.[1]
Whereas from the fourth century on, the *annona* had been replaced more and more by money-payments,[2] the seventh century,
in this as in many other respects, seems to have been marked by
a return to the barter system. The *Liber viarum et regnorum* of the
Arabic geographer Ibn Khurdadhba[3] states that the Byzantine
State levied a tithe on the grain crops of the Empire and stored it in
granaries for the use of the armies.[4] It is also correct that, as
Nicephorus says, soldiers received their arms from public store-
houses or arsenals. At Byzantium all private production of arms

---

[1] The term σιτηρέσιον originally means 'provision-money'. Plutarch used it as
the equivalent of the Roman *frumentatio*, i.e. the allowance of grain given to poorer
citizens (Liddell and Scott, s.v.). Reiske (Commentary on Constantine Porphyrogennetus, *De ceremoniis*, *C.S.H.B.* x. 347) remarks: 'Est annona seu stipendium militi
annuatim, aut per tempus quaternosve annos dari solitum, prout imperii constitu-
tio ferret, alias *roga*. Patet ex Cedreno, 797 A. 10 et Io. Scylitz., 823 C. 5, ubi τὸ
ὀψωνικόν commestus, res victuales, ad victum facientes, opponuntur τῷ σιτηρεσίῳ
stipendio nummis constanti.' In the ninth century, however, it is certain that the
σιτηρέσιον did not mean 'provision-money'.

[2] R. Große, *Römische Militärgeschichte von Gallienus bis zum Beginn der byzantinischen
Themenverfassung* (Berlin, 1920), 245 sq.; G. Ostrogorsky, 'Löhne und Preise in
Byzanz', *B.Z.* xxxii (1932), 303.

[3] The work was written between 844 and 849, see C. Brockelmann, *Geschichte der
arabischen Literatur*, i (Weimar, 1898), 225. The present text represents an edition of
the year 885–6 (ibid., Erster Supplementband, Leiden, 1937, 404).

[4] M. J. de Goeje, *Bibliotheca Geographorum Arabicorum* (Leiden, 1889), vi. 83:
'L'impôt foncier (kharaj) dans l'Empire Romain est établi par un cadastre régulier;
et se paye selon le tarif de 3 denares pour deux cents modii dont chacun contient
trois makkouk. La dîme ('ushr) prélevée en nature sur les céréales est entreposée
dans les greniers pour l'approvisionnement de l'armée.' I suppose that this tithe
was the συνώνη or *coemptio*, on which E. Stein, *Vierteljahrschrift für Sozial- und
Wirtschaftsgeschichte*, xxx (1928), 160, and his references should be consulted.

was forbidden, and though private individuals may have paid for the arms, the arms themselves could be obtained from no other source than the public arsenals.[1]

5. The final point in the analysis of the two passages from Nicephorus has now been reached. The Patriarch speaks of the importance of the legend of Constantine and of the fact that under Constantine Copronymus grain had been very cheap at Byzantium. There can be no doubt that the legend of Constantine V had a great influence on the second outbreak of Iconoclasm, particularly on Leo V.[2] But the Patriarch Nicephorus is more concerned with its impact on the population. People remembered the long rule, the prosperity and the victories of the Emperor and believed that all this had changed because Byzantium had abandoned his religious ideas. Particularly interesting are the data about general prosperity and the cheapness of grain.[3] The grain supply of Constantinople must have become a most difficult problem after the Arab conquest of Egypt. It is not known how it was solved at the time. As to the period under discussion the *Kitab Al 'Uyun* reveals that at some time between 716/18 and the first half of the ninth century the grain supply of Constantinople which had come formerly from 'outlying and exposed lands of the Romans' began to come 'from the places nearest to them', probably from Thrace.[4] If this information is read against the

[1] D'iakonov, *Vizantiiskie Dimy*, 163 f.

[2] Bury, *Eastern Roman Empire*, 58.

[3] The cheapness of grain at Constantinople under Constantine is confirmed by Nicephorus, *Breviarium*, 76 (60 modioi of wheat or 70 modioi of barley for 1 nomisma); Theophanes, 443. Cf. G. Ostrogorsky, 'Löhne und Preise', *B.Z.* xxxii (1932), 320, n. 3.

[4] Translated by E. W. Brooks, 'The Campaign of 716–718 from Arabic sources', *Journal of Hellenic Studies*, xix (1899), 23 : 'And when Maslama had encamped at Kustantiniyya [Constantinople], he blockaded the inhabitants and attacked them with siege-engines; and he collected together the provender and the corn, and they were conveyed to him from the outlying and exposed lands of the Romans, and they came to him in waggons, until that which was brought to him became like mountains, and these stores abounded in his camp; and he excluded the inhabitants of Kustantiniyya from all gainful occupation by land and sea. And the district of Marakiya [Thrace] was at that time waste, having been laid waste in that civil war; but at the present time it is well peopled. And this was in their time one of the greatest weaknesses of Al Kustantiniyya. If an army went at the present time to Al Kustantiniyya, when it was in need of provisions, and there was no importation of corn, their provender-dealers would bring them more than they wanted from places nearest to them.' The *Kitab Al 'Uyun* was written in the eleventh century but according to Tabarī the above passage was taken over either from Al Waqidī (797–845) or al Madā'inī (753–849), cf. Brooks, p. 19. On Al Wakidi see

passages from Nicephorus and Theophanes on the cheapness of grain at Constantinople under Constantine V, it becomes clear that either Leo III or his son Constantine must have been responsible for the change. Nothing indeed is more plausible than that Leo III or Constantine, after the experience of the siege of 716/18, took measures to prevent a recurrence of the blockade. Perhaps the mass transplantations of colonists to Thrace under the Isaurian dynasty were prompted by the desire to recolonize this region and render it capable of supplying the city with grain. The reduction of the cost of transportation would explain the low price. It may be that an additional reason was that from time immemorial the *coemptiones* of grain were done at prices which lay considerably lower than the 'just price'.[1] It does seem that Constantine made the city population prosperous at the expense of the peasants.[2]

If grain had become so cheap under Constantine, why had the price under Leo V gone up sufficiently high to make the city population unruly? The reason is very simple. In the years preceding the new outbreak of Iconoclasm the military situation had deteriorated markedly. In particular the Bulgarians were constantly plundering Thrace, the new granary of Byzantium. One need merely read Theophanes' reports of these raids to understand the rise in the price of grain.

So much for Nicephorus' remarks on the composition of the iconoclastic party. And what of Theophanes' description of the events of 813? Who were the iconoclastic 'soldiery', it may again be asked, who were present at Constantinople while the regular army was fighting at Versinicia? With the help of the passages from Nicephorus the question is easy to answer: they were in part at least conscripts who had mostly been drafted into the garrison troops under the Emperor Nicephorus and discharged by Michael

---

Brockelmann, *Geschichte*, i. 135, and Erster Supplementband, 207 f. On Al Madā'inī see Brockelmann, i. 140 sq. and Suppl., 214 sq. With all due caution I suggest that Al Waqīdī is the more likely source: he was a grain-dealer (i. 135) and wrote a work entitled 'k. ta'm annabi, über die Anweisungen von Datteln und Getreide in Haibar' (*Suppl.* 208). On the siege of 716–18 see M. Canard, 'Les Expéditions des Arabes contre Constantinople dans l'histoire et dans la légende', *Journal Asiatique*, ccviii (1926), 80–94. G. I. Bratianu's 'Études sur l'approvisionnement de Constantinople et le monopole du blé à l'époque byzantine et ottomane', *Études byzantines*, 129–81 is quite insufficient for the ninth century.

[1] Hartmann, *Untersuchungen*, 79.
[2] Lombard, *Constantin V*, 99 sq.

Rangabe, presumably because of their iconoclastic leanings. Representatives of the *demes*, small craftsmen, dismissed and impoverished veterans, discontented with their present poverty, with the desperate military and economic condition of the Empire, and inspired by the memory of the great Isaurian emperors who had saved the State from similar ruin—this was indeed a favourable medium for the spread of a religious doctrine which was connected in the minds of all with the names of these emperors.

The revolutionary character of the ensuing campaign against the images is best indicated in an incidental reference by which the Patriarch Nicephorus seems to conjure up the memory of a specific popular outbreak which he himself had witnessed. After reporting 'Epiphanides' contention that painters were representing archangels with bones and sinews', he continues:

From this we learn that his present disciples, out of the same rudeness, call out with unruliness and unseemliness: 'Let the bones of the icons be exhumed!' (ἀνασκαφῇ τὰ ὀστέα τῶν εἰκόνων), for this ` is literally (ἐπὶ λέξεως) what they uttered.[1]

In the Byzantine tradition the phrase ἀνασκάπτειν τὰ ὀστέα had the definite flavour of popular revolution. For example, with the popular shout: 'Let the bones of Justinian be exhumed!' the revolution against Justinian II had begun in 695. The curious cry reported by Nicephorus shows that the phrase had lost its precise meaning,[2] but it also proves that the iconoclastic campaign was assuming the character of a popular revolution against the images.

2. *Preliminaries*

The events which marked this second outbreak of Iconoclasm have often been told.[3] What needs to be mentioned here is only what is indispensable to a proper understanding of the activity of the Patriarch Nicephorus. The Bulgarian danger had been averted

---

[1] *Contra Eusebium et Epiphanidem*, ed. Pitra, iv. 306.

[2] de Boor, in his index to Theophanes (s.v., vol. ii. 729) remarks: ἀνασκαφῇ τὰ ὀστέα τῶν εἰκόνων 'proiciantur ossa e tumulo, frequens inter vociferationes plebis seditiosae convicium . . . unde ἀνασκάπτειν τινά dicitur vulgus turbulentum depositionem imperatoris patriarchae cet. flagitans'.

[3] K. Schwarzlose, *Der Bilderstreit* (Gotha, 1890), 71 sq.; Bréhier, *Querelle*, 30–34; Bury, *Eastern Roman Empire*, 56–76; Martin, *History*, 160–83.

by the death of Krum which occurred before the walls of Constantinople on 14 April 814. Leo seized the very next opportunity to initiate an iconoclastic programme.[1] There is the report of an eyewitness, Theosterictus; his *Vita Nicetae Mediciensis* was written at some time between 829 and 840.[2] Theosterictus was staying at Constantinople when his hero Nicetas was being installed as abbot of Medikion by the Patriarch Nicephorus. At that time unknown persons 'began to whisper the impious and hateful dogmas against the venerable images'.[3] The Emperor Leo appointed a committee to which he assigned the function of laying the theological foundations for his iconoclastic programme. The task before the Committee was to compile an iconoclastic *florilegium*, i.e. a collection of excerpts from authoritative writings which would support the iconoclastic contentions.[4] According to a contemporary source, the Committee based its work on the *florilegium* contained in the *Acta* of the Iconoclastic Council of Hiereia (754).[5] The members of this Committee took up residence and met in the imperial palace.[6] They were thus working in the immediate vicinity and, presumably, in personal contact with their imperial master.

It seems, however, that Leo, in selecting the personnel of his committee, took another precaution to insure that its labours would result in a product agreeable to himself. The Emperor was himself of Armenian descent, and the Armenian personal names in his own as well as in his wife's family make it certain that he still felt close to the country of his origin.[7] Leo's committee con-

---

[1] Καὶ λοιπὸν μετὰ ταῦτα λαβὼν εὐκαιρίαν ἤρξατο πορθεῖν τὴν ᾿Εκκλησίαν, says the *Scriptor Incertus de Leone Armeno*, P.G. cviii. 1024C.

[2] *AA. SS. Aprilis*, I. 253. *Terminus post quem*: the death of the Patriarch Nicephorus in 829 (App. col. xxx C); *terminus ante*: death of the deposed and exiled ex-Emperor Michael I Rangabe in 840; he is still alive at the time of the writing (col. xxix A), but died in 840, according to *Theophanes Continuatus*, P.G. cix. 333.

[3] Ibid., App. col. xxvii C: (Nicetas was ordained) δι᾽ ἐπιθέσεως τῶν χειρῶν τοῦ ἐν ἁγίοις Νικηφόρου, τοῦ τότε τὸν πατριαρχικὸν Κωνσταντινουπόλεως κατέχοντος θρόνον. ῎Ετι δὲ ὄντων ἡμῶν εἰς τὸ Βυζάντιον, ἤρξαντο ψιθυρίζεσθαι τὰ ἀσεβῆ καὶ θεοστυγῆ κατὰ τῶν σεβασμίων εἰκόνων δόγματα.

[4] Ibid., App. col. xxix A.

[5] *Scriptor Incertus de Leone Armeno*, P.G. cviii. 1025A: οὐδὲν εὕρισκον οἱ ἄφρονες ὧνπερ αὐτοὶ κακούργως ἐπεζήτουν, ἕως οὗ μετὰ χεῖρας ἔλαβον τὸ συνοδικὸν Κωνσταντίνου τοῦ ᾿Ισαύρου τοῦ καὶ Καβαλλίνου.

[6] Ignatius, *Vita Nicephori*, 165, ed. de Boor.

[7] Leo V's Armenian origin has been doubted by J. B. Bury, *History of the Eastern Roman Empire* (London, 1912), 43; Louis Bréhier, *Vie et mort de Byzance* (Paris, 1947), speaks of him as 'appartenant à une famille d'origine mésopotamienne'. Jos.

sisted of six persons: two members of the Senate, Iohannes Spektas and Eutychianus, the Lector (ἀναγνώστης) John the Grammarian, the bishop Antonius of Sylaeum, and the monks Leontius and Zosimas.[1] Of these the most energetic member, John the Grammarian, was an Armenian like Leo himself.[2] In addition one other member was an Armenian and was called or nicknamed Hamazasp.[3] Thus in a committee of six appointed by an emperor of Armenian origin the most active member, John the Grammarian, and at least one other member were Armenians.

It is questionable whether the *florilegium* compiled by the imperial committee is preserved. It will be seen later that it was read at the first meeting of the Council of St. Sophia and that to the *Definition* of this same Council there was attached a *florilegium* of patristic quotations. It is difficult, however, to say with assurance whether or not these two *florilegia* were identical in all details. It is noteworthy that the first iconoclastic Council of Hiereia (754) asserted its independence from the Emperor by

Markwart, *Südarmenien und die Tigrisquellen*, &c. (Vienna, 1930), 210–12, n. 3, and N. Adontz, 'Sur l'origine de Léon V, empereur de Byzance', *Armeniaca*, ii (1927), 1–10, have shown, apparently independently of each other, that the story of Leo's 'Assyrian' or 'Mesopotamian' connexions is based ultimately on an extract from a lost work of Nicephorus (see below, pp. 179 f.) cited by Georgios Monachos (ed. de Boor, ii. 780 ff.). Here Nicephorus asserts Leo's Armenian descent but traces his Armenian family to the Assyrian king Sennacherib. Adontz has destroyed conclusively any doubts concerning the Armenian descent of Leo V, which is supported by a great number of Armenian names in Leo's family (Adontz, p. 9) as well as by all the Byzantine sources (except those that misunderstood Nicephorus). The connexion with the Armenian princely family of the Arzrunis, however, which is clearly implied by Georgios Monachos, may well be legendary and is not proved by Georgios' assertion (against Adontz, p. 9). It may be mentioned in passing that an echo of Nicephorus' story occurs in the *Synodicum Vetus* written at the time of Photius where Leo V is called ὁ Συραρμέλιος (=Συραρμένιος), Fabricius, xii. 215.

[1] Theosterictus, *Vita Nicetae*, *AA. SS. Aprilis*, i, App. col. xxix A sq.: εἶτα ἐζήτει [Leo V] συμμύστας καὶ διδασκάλους τοῦ κακοῦ· εὗρεν δὲ ὀλίγους τῆς συγκλήτου, Ἰωάννην τὸν καλούμενον Σπέκταν καὶ Εὐτιχιανόν. ἐζήτει δὲ καὶ ἐκ τοῦ ἱερατικοῦ τάγματος· περινοστήσας δὲ ὁ ταῦτα ὑποσπείρας αὐτῷ διάβολος τὸ Βυζάντιον εὗρεν Ἰωάννην τὸν ἐπίκλην Γραμματικὸν τὸν νέον Τέρτυλον (sic, cf. Acts xxiv) . . . εἶχεν μὲν συνέργους ἐκ μὲν τῶν ὑπὸ θρόνον Ἀντώνιον τὸν τοῦ Συλαίου, ἐκ δὲ τοῦ μοναχικοῦ καταλόγου Λεόντιόν τινα καὶ Ζωσιμᾶν. . . . Eutychianus is almost certainly identical with the iconoclastic πρωτοασηκρῆτις mentioned by Ignatius, *Vita Nicephori*, pp. 189 f. (de Boor), cf. Grumel, *Regestes*, no. 397. Antonius of Sylaeum became Patriarch in 821.

[2] On John the Grammarian see Note F, pp. 235 f.

[3] This I infer from Ignatius, *Vita Nicephori*, 208 (de Boor), who continues, after the account of Leo's murder, as follows: πῶς οἱ ἀπὸ κοιλίας φωνοῦντες Γραμματικοὶ . . . τὴν κατά σου [Leo V] τοῦ ξίφους βολὴν μαντικῶς οὐ προέβλεψαν; πῶς οἱ Σπέκται καὶ Ἀμαζάσπαι, τὰ τῆς σῆς ἀπειλῆς ἀκροθίνια, τὴν νῦν ὁρωμένην ἀσχήμονα θέαν καὶ τῶν ὑφαίμων ὠτειλῶν τὰ αἴσχη παρέβλεψαν (for παρέβλαψαν);

omitting from its own *florilegium* some of the patristic passages compiled under the Emperor's supervision and by adding new quotations.[1] There is some reason to believe that a similar relationship
obtained between the *florilegium* compiled by Leo's Committee
and the one appended by the Council of St. Sophia to its
Definition.[2] Thus the *florilegium* attached to the *Definition* issued by
the Council of St. Sophia represents, perhaps with some additions
or omissions, the labours of the committee appointed by Leo V in
814. Nicephorus states that the committee brought together 'no
more' quotations than had been collected by Constantine V,[3] and
the *Scriptor Incertus de Leo Armeno* also affirms its dependence on
this Emperor's compilations.[4]

Around December 814 Leo took the first open step towards
Iconoclasm. He summoned the Patriarch Nicephorus to the
palace and said to him: 'The people take offence at the images.
They say: 'We are wrong in worshipping them, and because of
this the barbarians defeat us. Make a small concession, exercise
dispensation (οἰκονομία) towards the people, let us take away those
images which are hanging low.'[5] The Patriarch Nicephorus remained firm and refused to enter into any kind of theological discussion with the members of the iconoclastic committee. Later on
several prominent bishops and abbots had discussions with the
Emperor and answered his questions.[6]

---

[1] Ostrogorsky, *Studien*, 13 f., n. 4, with the corrections made below, p. 175, n. 1.
Nicephorus, *Refutatio et Eversio*, fol. 291ʳ reports that at the Council of Hiereia Constantine V wanted to delete certain quotations from the *florilegium* compiled by the
Council but was dissuaded from doing so by the most prominent number of the
clergy (ὁ κατὰ τὴν ἱερωσύνην ἐπὶ κακῷ τῷ ἑαυτοῦ τὸ τηνικαῦτα προὔχων), i.e. presumably by Theodosius of Ephesus who presided over the Council.

[2] This hypothesis would explain why certain quotations of the *florilegium* have
no connexion with its central thesis (below, pp. 139 f., n. 5). The reason would be that
they were added by the Council of St. Sophia to the original *florilegium* prepared by
the Committee.

[3] *Antirrheticus*, i. 2 (*P.G.* c. 208D–209A); *Refutatio et Eversio*, 236ʳ: ... συγκομίζουσι
χρήσεις ἀχρήστους ... ἤνυσαν δὲ πλέον οὐδὲν ὧν ὁ τῆς ἀποστασίας ἡγεμὼν Μαμωνᾶς
Κωνσταντῖνος παρὰ τῶν ἀγόντων μυούμενος ἀκόσμως τε καὶ ἐκθέσμως ἠθροικὼς
συνέθεικε.

[4] *Scriptor Incertus de Leone Armeno*, *P.G.* cviii. 1025B.

[5] On the interpretation of this passage see the views of Martin, *History*, 31, 165,
and L. Bréhier, 'Sur un texte relatif au début de la querelle iconoclaste', *E.O.*
xxxvii (1938), 19. It may be granted to Bréhier that the texts speak of a complete
removal of those portable icons which were hanging low, not of hanging them higher
on the wall. Undoubtedly this was considered only a temporary compromise on the
part of the Emperor. Cf. further Grumel, *Regestes*, no. 390.

[6] *Scriptor Incertus*, 1028D.

The chronology of the subsequent developments is involved, but the following is the probable order of events.[1] The Patriarch held an all-night vigil at which a great number of clerics, monks, and laymen participated. There the Patriarch besought[1] God to bring to naught the designs of the Emperor. This meeting enraged the Emperor. Upon his orders soldiers stoned and insulted the image of Christ above the Chalke Gate. Then the Emperor intervened and said to the people (ὁ λαός): 'Let us tear down from there the image lest the army (ὁ στρατός) dishonour it.' Clearly the Emperor was satisfied even with an ill-disguised pretext for taking down the image, and it is hardly correct to say that 'the Emperor still worked for a policy of moderation', and 'gives the impression of trying to preserve the peace'.[2]

On the day before Christmas 814 a great number of bishops and monks assembled in the Patriarchal Palace, among them Euthymius, archbishop of Sardis, Aemilianus of Cyzicus, Joseph of Thessalonica, Eudoxius of Amorion, Michael of Synnada, and Theophylactus of Nicomedia.[3] The Patriarch had the *florilegium* of iconoclastic quotations read to the assembly and commented on each passage.[4] At the end Patriarch and clerics rejected the quotations. Nicephorus declared that the orthodox formed the majority.[5] All the members of the assembly signed a promise never to separate and to endure death rather than to yield to Iconoclasm.[6] At daybreak on Christmas Day the Patriarch and his congregation were summoned to the palace. At first Nicephorus alone was admitted to the presence of the Emperor. The *Vita Nicephori* inserts what purports to be an account of this interview.[7] In reality it is a regular theological treatise on image-worship in the form of questions and answers. The Emperor brings

---

[1] In the main I am following the chronology established by Grumel, *Regestes*, nos. 390 sqq. Against Grumel I maintain, however, that in view of *Scriptor Incertus*, 1029, one has to assume *two* all-night vigils, one preceding the incident at the Chalke and one following it.

[2] Martin, *History*, 166.

[3] *Scriptor Incertus*, col. 1029C; *Vita Theophylacti Nicomediae*, ed. A. Vogt, *Analecta Bollandiana*, l (1932), 77 sq.

[4] The *florilegium* read was in all probability that prepared by the Imperial Committee. The oral comments of Nicephorus are the nucleus of his *Refutatio et Eversio*, a work which constituted a refutation of the Definition and *florilegium* of the iconoclastic Council of 815 (see below, pp. 180–2).

[5] Ibid.: πλείους γὰρ αὐτῶν ἐσμεν.

[6] Grumel, *Regestes*, no. 391.

[7] pp. 167 ff. (de Boor).

up the right questions at the right time, the answers of the Patriarch take up most of the space, and at the end the Emperor can do no more than refer Nicephorus to the theologians on his iconoclastic committee. The discussion certainly did not produce any results, and it may have been in the interest of both parties to forget the details. One source reports that the Patriarch offered his resignation in case the Emperor had any personal grievances against him and implored his imperial master not to violate the faith.[1]

At the end of this interview both parties brought in reinforcements: the Patriarch his faithful clergy who had been waiting in the antechamber, the Emperor the high dignitaries of his court, girt with their swords. It was a scene which stimulated the curiosity of contemporaries, the open clash between Church and State, surrounded by the pomp and glitter of ceremony and sumptuousness. The sources agree with respect to what was said, they differ only with regard to the person who did the speaking.[2]

The vivid account in the *Vita Nicetae*—a source which it is difficult to procure—is worth translating in full:

And the most holy Nicephorus says to those advanced in prominence: [here follows a theological argument]. . . . To this the Emperor replies nothing, but says to the Fathers: 'Behold, Fathers, I too am of your opinion.' He took out the *enkolpion* which he was wearing and while worshipping it hypocritically he said: 'As you see I do not disagree with you at all. But there have arisen some men who have different teachings and who say that their teachings are correct. Now let them come before you and let the matter be discussed between you.

---

[1] *Scriptor Incertus*, col. 1032A.

[2] Apart from the *Vita Nicephori*, 187, there is the report of Theosterictus in the *Vita Nicetae*, App. cols. xxix sq., and an unedited *Life of Euthymius Bishop of Sardis* by a monk Metrophanes. It is contained in two manuscripts: (1) *Cod. Mon.* 88 of the Theological School of Chalki, ninth to tenth centuries, fols. 226^v–251^v, see A. Ehrhard, *Überlieferung und Bestand*, i. 509–12 with further references, and (2) *Cod. Bodl. Laud.* 69, eleventh century, fols. 306^v–324, of which the end is missing, see Ehrhard, *Überlieferung und Bestand*, i. 516–18. I inspected the latter manuscript briefly at Oxford on 3 August 1939. A comparison of the above passages of the *Vita Nicetae* with the *Vita Nicephori* shows either that the latter is based on the former or that they both go back to a common source. In any case the *Vita Nicetae* contains much more detail and is much livelier though less polished than the *Vita Nicephori*. For this reason I am not following Bury, *Eastern Roman Empire*, 65, who based his account of the interview on the *Vita Nicephori*, but prefer the corresponding passage of the *Vita Nicetae*.

And if they persuade you that they are right, do not prevent what is right. But if they are persuaded by you that their teachings are innovations, let them stop their evil teaching and let orthodoxy rule as before. For even if I had been criticized for some minor matter, I should not have remained silent. How could I remain silent concerning a Church inquiry?' Aemilianus bishop of Cyzicus said: 'If as you said this is a Church inquiry, oh Emperor, let it be inquired into in the Church as is the custom, for from old and from the beginning Church inquiries are inquired into in Church, and not in the Imperial Palace.' 'But I too,' says the Emperor, 'am a son of the Church, and as a mediator ($\mu\epsilon\sigma\acute{\iota}\tau\eta s$) I shall listen to both parties and after a comparison of the two I shall determine the truth.' To this there answered Michael, bishop of Synnada, 'If you are a mediator, why do you not do the job of a mediator? [I say this] because the one side you shelter in the Palace and even assemble and encourage, even giving them permission to teach their impious doctrines; whereas the other side does not dare to utter a sound even on the streets and crouches down everywhere before your decrees. This is characteristic not of mediation but of dictation ($\tau\nu\rho\alpha\nu\nu\acute{\iota}s$).' 'Not at all,' said the Emperor, 'but as I said before I hold the same views as you. However, if I am criticized I cannot pass it over in silence. We know why you are unwilling to talk to them, it is your being at a loss and the fact that you have no evidence in support of your assertions.' Thereupon Theophylactus, bishop of Nicomedia, said: 'First of all our evidence is Christ . . ., then there are innumerable pieces of evidence in support of this, and we are not at a loss as you suspect, but there are no ears to listen, and we should not be very useful if we stated our case, for we are waging war against the government ($\tau\grave{o}$ $\kappa\rho\acute{a}\tau os$).' Thereupon Peter, bishop of Nicaea, said: 'How can you ask us to talk with them? Behold you are fighting on their side. Don't you know that even if you introduced the so-called Manichaeans and protected them, they will overpower us because they are supported by you, etc.' Thereupon Euthymius, bishop of Sardis, also spoke: [He sets forth some of the traditional arguments for image-worship.] The Emperor, being shrewd, so far had pretended to be forbearing. Theodore, the zealous ($\theta\epsilon\rho\mu\acute{o}s$) teacher of the Church, abbot of Studios, answered: 'Do not undo the status of the Church, for the Apostle spoke thus: "And he gave some apostles, and some prophets, and some evangelists, and some pastors and teachers, for the perfecting of the saints" (Eph. iv. 11), but he did not speak of Emperors. To you, Emperor, has been entrusted the political system and the army. Take care of them, and leave the Church to its shepherds and teachers according to the Apostle. If you do not agree to this—even if an angel from Heaven should give us a message about a deviation from our faith we shall not listen to him, and certainly not to you.'[1]

From this account two facts emerge. Firstly, the Patriarch Nicephorus this time sided with the monks. Secondly, the struggle had from the very beginning the character of a conflict between Church and State, which the Moechian Affair had assumed only in its final stage. Again, the Emperor was invoking οἰκονομία, and once more the opposition was fond of expressing the view that the Emperor was outside, and even subject to, the Church. This was an argument which had been advanced by John of Damascus,[2] but the latter had been beyond the reach of the Byzantine Emperor. It took almost a century before a man was found who dared to voice the sentiments of the Damascene in the presence of the Emperor and of his court.

Once the open breach had been made events moved rapidly. On the Feast of Epiphany (τὰ Φῶτα), i.e. on 6 January 815, Leo omitted the customary act of image-worship. Furthermore, the Emperor won over many clerics by flatteries and promises. Almost all those who had signed the declaration of loyalty at the patriarchal palace went over to the enemy.[3] The Emperor, the *Vita Nicephori* says, was trying to isolate the Patriarch.[4] The latter was still trying to avert disaster. He wrote to the Empress asking her to use her influence on her husband in favour of image-worship.[5] Another letter went to an imperial treasurer (ὁ τηνικαῦτα

---

[1] The account of the (unpublished) *Vita Euthymii* by Metrophanes (see preceding note) is similar. In it the Patriarch Nicephorus is more prominent than in the *Vita Nicetae* but not quite as important as in the *Vita Nicephori*. The Emperor Leo declares openly that he will persecute all obstinate Iconophiles. The final point in the interview is again reserved for Theodore of Studios. He quotes Ephesians iv. 11 and then continues: ὦ βασιλεῦ, ἔθετο ὁ Θεὸς τῇ Ἐκκλησίᾳ πρῶτον ἀποστόλους, δεύτερον προφήτας, τρίτον διδασκάλους, βασιλέα οὐκ ἔθετο· ἀμέλει τοῖς συνεμπίπτουσι ταύτῃ πράγμασί τε καὶ δόγμασι οὐδαμῶς παρατίθεσθαι οὔτε μὴν τούτοις οἷς ὁ παμβασιλεὺς καὶ τῶν ὅλων Θεὸς ἔθετο εἰσηγητικῶς πως συνάπτεσθαί σου τὸ κράτος, ἀλλ᾽ ἔπεσθαι τῷ κατὰ πνεῦμα πατρί σου καὶ διδασκάλῳ τῆς Ἐκκλησίας καὶ μεγάλῳ φωστῆρι τῆς οἰκουμένης, τῇ ὁσίᾳ χειρὶ τὸν μεγαλώνυμον ἀρχιερέα ὑπαινιξάμενος.

[2] *Oratio II adversus eos qui sacras imagines abiciunt*, ch. 12 (*P.G.* xciv. 1296c sqq.).

[3] *Scriptor Incertus de Leone Armeno*, 1032c: σχεδὸν πάντες ἐστράφησαν εἰς τὸ ἐναντίον.

[4] *Vita Nicephori*, 189.

[5] Grumel, *Regestes*, no. 395. The Empress's name is given as Theodosia, daughter of the quaestor and patrician Arsaber (cf., for example, Genesios, 21. 8, ed. Bonn; Theophanes Continuatus, 35, ed. Bonn), but Procopia, wife of Michael I, calls her Barca (Genesios, p. 6. 14; Theophanes Continuatus, p. 18. 15). Since there are indications that Leo's marriage with Theodosia was considered by some as illegal (Genesios, p. 20. 20 and Symeon Magister, p. 610. 3)—Michael the Amorian was

τῶν δημοσιῶν χρημάτων ταμίας) conveying the same sense.¹ Finally
Nicephorus addressed himself to an arch-iconoclast, the *protoasecre-
tis* Eutychianus, probably identical with the Eutychianus who was
a member of the imperial committee, threatening him with terrible
punishments if he did not revert to orthodoxy.² The Emperor, his
mind made up, continued his iconoclastic policy. He sent some of
the bishops who had joined the Iconoclasts to the patriarchal palace
with the request that the Patriarch either consent to the removal
of low-hanging icons (τὰ χαμηλά) or leave the patriarchal palace.³
The Patriarch remained firm. Thereupon the Emperor tried once
more to obtain the resignation of the Patriarch. He sent the
Patriarch a message which ran: 'Resign, for the Church has no
need of you.' The written answer of the Patriarch was worded as
follows: 'Oh Emperor, I shall not descend in this casual way,
for I gave you no reason to depose me. If, however, I am forced
because of my orthodoxy, or piety, either by yourself or by one
of your imperial officers—send him and I shall descend.'⁴

The Emperor had made up his mind. He appointed Thomas,
who was of patrician rank and who had held the consulship twice
(he was δισύπατος) to be λογοθέτης and σκευοφύλαξ of the Church.⁵

accused of having given expression to such a thought—there is a possibility that
Leo, after he had ascended the throne, saw fit to repudiate his first wife Barca and
to marry the noble lady Theodosia. Her father is perhaps identical with the Arsaber
who had rebelled under the Emperor Nicephorus (above, p. 74). After the murder
of Leo, Theodore of Studios addressed to Leo's widow Theodosia his *Epistulae*, ii.
204 (*P.G.* xcix. 1620 sqq.).

¹ Grumel, *Regestes*, no. 396; Bury, *Eastern Roman Empire*, 66, understands this
person to be the General Logothete. But in view of F. Dölger, *Beiträge zur Geschichte
der byzantinischen Finanzverwaltung &c.*, Byzantinisches Archiv Heft 9 (Leipzig and
Berlin, 1927), 25, and the frequent use of the title in the *Breviarium* of Nicephorus
(see de Boor's index, s. v. ταμίας), it seems preferable to assume that he was ὁ ἐπὶ
τοῦ σακελλίου.

² Grumel, *Regestes*, no. 397. Bury, *Eastern Roman Empire*, 517, suggests we identify
this Eutychianus with the Eutychianus mentioned by the *Vita Nicetae* (App. col.
xxix A) as a member of the iconoclastic committee (above, p. 127, n. 1).

³ *Scriptor Incertus*, col. 1032C: μικρὸν σύνελθε ἡμῖν ἵνα περιέλωμεν πάντα τὰ
χαμηλά. ἐπεὶ εἰ οὐ βούλει, γνῶθι ὅτι οὕτως οὐ παραχωροῦμεν αὐτόθι σε εἶναι.

⁴ *Vita Nicetae*, col. xxx B. Cf. Grumel, *Regestes*, no. 399.

⁵ *Vita Nicephori*, 190: ἐγχειρίζει γοῦν τὰ τοῦ λόγου τῆς ἐκκλησίας καὶ τὰ τῶν ἱερῶν
σκευῶν ἀναθήματα ἀνδρὶ τὴν τοῦ πατρικίου ἀξίαν διέποντι. The name is given by the
Scriptor Incertus, col. 1033B. On the Μέγας Σκευοφύλαξ see L. Clugnet, 'Les Offices
et les dignités ecclésiastiques dans l'église grecque', *Revue de l'Orient chrétien*, iii
(1898), 147 sq. and 262 sq.; Bréhier, *Institutions*, 501. On the Λογοθέτης see Clugnet,
pp. 262 f. Evidently both offices could be held by a layman appointed by the Emperor.
The unusual mention of two dignities (ἀπὸ δισυπατῶν and πατρίκιος) is explained
by Justinian's *Novella*, 80, which grants consuls the precedence over ordinary

The duties of the latter office included the care of the images, and presumably this was the reason for the appointment.

The strain and excitement of these events had been too much for the Patriarch. He fell seriously ill. He had to stay in bed and the doctor even declared his condition to be hopeless. The Emperor thought that death might save him the trouble of removing the Patriarch.[1] But the crisis passed and the patient recovered. When he was still convalescent, the Emperor dispatched the *spatharios* Theophanes, a brother of the Empress, to the Patriarch and once again requested him to hold a disputation with the Iconoclasts. The Patriarch answered that he would agree only if the persecution were stopped immediately and both parties were put on an equal footing.[2]

At this time Nicephorus must have been completely isolated. Part of his clergy had been exiled or imprisoned, others had joined the Iconoclasts. The latter were even calling together the σύνοδος ἐνδημοῦσα, the permanent assembly of bishops present in the capital, and took a decision concerning the Patriarch which unfortunately is not preserved.[3] Nicephorus' attitude was judged unsatisfactory. The members of the synod wrote him a letter in which he was summoned to appear before them. This letter was delivered at the patriarchal palace by a group of bishops and clerics escorted by a mob. Nicephorus did not want to receive the delegation, but he was forced to do so by Thomas the Patrician.[4] The delegates read the synodal letter to the Patriarch. It claimed that Nicephorus had been charged with crimes; what these were is not mentioned in the sources. He could avoid punishment only if he accepted Iconoclasm.[5] The Patriarch replied that he could be judged only by his peers, by the Pope or one of the other patriarchs. He added that by assembling at Constantinople against his will the bishops had violated a canon which he read to them.[6] It is not impossible that he even deposed the

patricians. This Thomas may be identical with a correspondent of Theodore of Studios, *Epistulae*, i. 12 (*P.G.* xcix. 949c ff., written probably under the Emperor Nicephorus, Bury, *Imp. Adm. Syst.* 27).

[1] *Vita Nicephori*, 190; *Scriptor Incertus*, col. 1032D.   [2] *Vita Nicephori*, 191.
[3] Ibid. 192: τὰ . . . τῇ ἐνδημούσῃ συνόδῳ κεκριμένα.   [4] Ibid. 193.
[5] Ibid. 193 sq.
[6] See J. Luczak, *La Résidence des évêques dans la législation canonique*, Thèse Strasbourg (Paris, 1931), 42–51. The canons in question are collected in Vl. Beneshevich, *Iohannis Scholastici Synagoga L Titulorum*, Abhandlungen der Bayerischen Akademie der Wissenschaften, Phil.-Hist. Klasse, N.F., xiv (1937), 73–76.

bishops and clerics who formed part of the delegation.[1] Thereupon the delegation left while the mob shouted and cursed the
Patriarchs Germanos, Tarasios, and Nicephorus.[2] It may have
been on this occasion or soon afterwards that Nicephorus heard
the masses shout: 'Let the bones of the icons be exhumed!'
(above, p. 125, n. 2). The Iconoclasts even attempted murder,
but it failed.[3] They removed the name of the Patriarch from
the diptychs.[4] At last the Patriarch gave in. He wrote a letter to the
Emperor in which he resigned because he did not wish that the
Emperor should commit further sins and acts of persecution.[5]
On the first day of Lent, 815, the sick hierarch made his last visit
to St. Sophia where he took leave of his congregation. 'My
children,' were his last words, 'I dismiss you as Christians.'[6] Then
he was taken on a litter to the Milion, where he was left for half
an hour so that soldiers might come and slay him. It may be, one
source has it,[7] that the soldiers were fast asleep—it was after
midnight—or it may be that this story is fictitious. The fact remains that the dethroned Patriarch was soon taken to the Acro-
polis, the present Seraglio Point, put into a small boat, and carried
across the Bosporus to Chrysopolis. He never again set foot within
the city walls of Constantinople.

The storm of Iconoclasm had found the Patriarch a courageous
and independent member of the Church. It is impossible to
assume that in this crisis he had been the tool of the Studites or of
any other group or person. It had been the policy of the Emperor
to isolate Nicephorus: the bishops and abbots had either joined
the Iconoclasts or were imprisoned or exiled. During the last
weeks the Patriarch had lived like a prisoner in his own palace;
nobody had had access to him. No matter how remote the theological subtleties of Iconoclasm appear to modern eyes, it is hard
to deny the Patriarch the admiration which political and religious courage merit. Unlike Theodore of Studios he was ready
for concessions, but where he believed the principles of his faith
to be involved, he was prepared to resist and to suffer the consequences. This he did.

---

[1] Grumel, *Regestes*, no. 400.
[2] *Vita Nicephori*, 196; *Scriptor Incertus*, col. 1033.
[3] *Vita Nicephori*, 197.   [4] Ibid.
[5] Ibid. 197 sq.
[6] *Vita Nicetae*, col. xxx: τέκνια, Χριστιανοὺς ὑμᾶς ἀφίω.
[7] *Scriptor Incertus*, col. 1033C.

VI

HERETICAL COUNCIL, PERSECUTION, AND EXILE

INFORMATION about the years which Nicephorus spent in exile is scanty. From the letters of Theodore of Studios and from various Saints' Lives there emerges a fairly accurate picture of the course of political events and of the persecution, but next to nothing is known about the ex-Patriarch's personal affairs. Before the latter can be examined a general survey of the major events will have to be presented.

One of the first acts of the Emperor Leo was to fill the vacant patriarchal see of Constantinople. On the morning after the deposition of Nicephorus, Leo assembled a *silention*[1] at which he declared that Nicephorus had resigned because he was unwilling to renounce image-worship. The Emperor tried to have John the Grammarian elected, but the patricians objected that he was too young and of an undistinguished family. Leo thereupon chose Theodotus, son of the patrician Michael Melissenos. His mother had been a sister of Eudoxia, third wife of Constantine V Copronymus,[2] and his father had been appointed general of the Anatolic theme in 765/6.[3] Theodotus himself held the rank of a *spatharokandidatos*[4] and was recommended not only by his blue blood and the iconoclastic record of his family, but also, as the *Scriptor Incertus* grudgingly admits, by the gentleness of his manners and by the reputation of virtue which he enjoyed.[5]

---

[1] The following account is based on the *Scriptor Incertus de Leone Armeno*, P.G. cviii. 1033 sqq.

[2] I infer this from ibid. 1036A: Θεοδότον υἱὸν Μιχαὴλ πατρικίου τοῦ Μελισινοῦ συγγάμβρου ὄντος Κωνσταντίνου τοῦ βασιλέως τοῦ Καβαλλίνου κατὰ τὴν τρίτην αὐτοῦ γυναῖκα.

[3] Theophanes, 440. On the identity of Michael Melissenos with the patrician Michael who founded the monastery of the Theotokos τὰ Ψιχᾶ under Irene see P. van den Ven, 'La Vie grecque de Saint Jean le Psichaite', *Le Muséon*, N.S., iii (1902), 110.

[4] The *Vita Nicetae* by Theosterictus calls him an ἀπὸ σπαθαρίων (*AA. SS. Aprilis*, i, p. xxx c).

[5] *Scriptor Incertus*, 1036A: πρᾶος ἦν καὶ ἐφαίνετο τοῖς ἀνθρώποις ἐνάρετος. The *Vita Ioannicii* by Sabas, *AA. SS. Novembris*, ii. 348B, states that he was a native of Nacoleia.

1. *The Iconoclastic Council of St. Sophia* (815)

Immediately after Easter, 815, a council assembled at Constantinople in St. Sophia. It was presided over by the new Patriarch Theodotus and the Emperor was represented by his son Symbatios, also called Constantine.[1] The number of the participants is unknown. It consisted of the original Iconoclasts among the bishops and of those bishops and abbots whom the Emperor had won over to the iconoclastic cause. The council met in three sessions. During the first the iconoclastic *florilegium* compiled by the Imperial Committee was read and the members affirmed their acceptance of the iconoclastic Council of 754.[2] On the following day they began the discussion of the dogmatic issue and afterwards a number of orthodox bishops, among them John Bishop of Sardis, were brought before the Council.[3] First the bishops had to wait outside like prisoners. Then an attempt was made in open council to win them over to Iconoclasm by threats, but they remained firm. Thereupon the iconoclastic bishops' demonstration of the intensity of their religious beliefs took violent form. They smote their orthodox colleagues to the ground and called upon bystanders to trample upon them.[4] Subsequently the Iconophiles were asked to withdraw from the church and as they left each member of the *ecclesia militans* either struck or spat at them. After thus exhibiting the most shameful behaviour, the members of the Council felt that it was time for luncheon. They acclaimed the Emperors in the customary way, anathematized the image-worshippers, and adjourned the Council. A *Horos* was prepared and the Emperor was persuaded to sign it. This was done at the third solemn meeting of the Council under the presidency of the Emperor after the *Horos* had been read and approved by the majority of the assembly.

This *Horos*, together with the patristic *florilegium* attached to it, has been reconstructed in its entirety from the *Refutatio et Eversio*

---

[1] *Scriptor Incertus*, 1036B.

[2] above, p. 127. This seems to be the meaning of *Vita Nicephori*, 202: πάσας τὰς προμελετηθείσας ἀνοήτως παραγραφὰς καὶ περικοπὰς προσεμέσαντες.

[3] For the following account see *Vita Nicephori*, 204 (de Boor). I infer the presence of John of Sardis from Theodorus Studita, *Epistulae*, no. 85, ed. Cozza-Luzi, 74, addressed to John of Sardis. Theodore remarks: μακάριος εἶ διὰ Κύριον ἐμπαιχθεὶς καὶ κονδυλισθεὶς ὑπὸ τῶν ἀσεβῶν ἔμπροσθεν τοῦ καϊαφαϊκοῦ συνεδρίου.

[4] *Vita Nicephori*, 204. Cf. Theosterictus, *Vita Nicetae*, col. XXX D.

of the Patriarch Nicephorus.[1] The meaning of this document is understood best by a comparison with the corresponding Dogmatic Definition issued by the iconoclastic Council of Hiereia–Blachernae (754). The earlier council had rejected religious images on three grounds. They were said to be idols in the sense that their worshippers substituted worship of created things for the worship of the Creator ('argument from idol worship'). Icons of Christ in particular violated christological doctrine inasmuch as they either separated Christ's human nature from His divinity or confused the two natures ('argument from christology').[2] Finally, the Council of Hiereia–Blachernae had used a third line of reasoning which is of considerable importance in the present context and will be referred to henceforth as 'argument from holiness'. According to the Council paganism with its practice of making and worshipping images was the source of Christian image worship. Since it had no hope for a resurrection from the dead 'it thought up a toy [the making and worship of idols] worthy of itself in order jestingly to present what was absent as if it were present' [i.e. the dead as if they were alive]. The Christian Church rejects this because 'the Saints . . . enjoy eternal life with God'. It is blasphemy against God to attempt to portray the Saints 'by means of an art which is dead, hateful, and never life-giving'. These remarks mean that the bestowal of true life (ζωή) is God's prerogative, that the portrayal of a dead person constitutes an attempt to make him 'live' again and is consequently an encroachment upon God's domain. The artist offends likewise against the Theotokos or the Saints whom he wishes to portray, 'for it is not permissible for Christians who possess the expectation of the resurrection . . . to insult by means of inglorious and dead matter the Saints who will be made bright in such glory'.[3] The Council clearly implies that the artistic portrait of a Saint can do no more than portray the Saint's mortal body and can hope to represent neither his soul nor his incorruptible and glorified body after the resurrection. Artistic portraits consequently 'insult' the essential holiness of the Saint, to be revealed (rather than brought about) by the future resurrection. Such in brief are the arguments against Christian images as presented in the 'Doctrine' of the Iconoclastic Council of Hiereia–Blachernae. It can be shown the biblico-patristic *florilegium* and the anathemas of this

e Note G, p. 237.   [2] See Note H, p. 237.   [3] See Note I, pp. 237f.

Council are closely related to the 'Doctrine' and justify or proclaim the three arguments summarized above.[1] Most of the
biblical and patristic quotations supporting the argument from
holiness, as well as the corresponding anathemas, object to pictorial images and exalt in their stead the role of the inner man (the
heart or the soul) as the proper instrument of worship. If, however,
these passages are read against the background of the 'Doctrine',
it becomes clear that they are nothing but positive formulations
of the (negative) argument from holiness. The positive doctrine
was indeed expressed in these passages, yet the character of these
quotations as authoritative support for the 'Doctrine' shows that
the emphasis lay on condemning the icon for offending against
the concept of holiness rather than on any positive definition of
true holiness. In other words the argument from holiness as proclaimed by the Council of Hiereia–Blachernae was a new version
of the old view of the image as essence.[2]

Of the three arguments advanced by the Council of Hiereia–
Blachernae, the later Council of St. Sophia (815) dropped the
first, on the reasoning that there was a distinction between
degrees of evil as well as between good and evil. The argument
from Christology and perhaps that from holiness were proclaimed
in vague terms by the Dogmatic Definition of the Council of St.
Sophia.[3] The argument from holiness does play, however, a
major role in the patristic *florilegium* issued by the Council of St.
Sophia. This is immediately clear in the case of those patristic
quotations which had already been cited at Hiereia–Blachernae.[4]
To a greater or lesser extent this is also true, however, for most of
the 'new passages', i.e. the patristic fragments quoted at St.
Sophia and not previously cited at St. Sophia.[5] The Council of

[1] See Note J, p. 238.   [2] See Note K, p. 238.   [3] See Note L, pp. 238f.
[4] In my earlier article (*Dumbarton Oaks Papers*, p. 54, n. 20) I called them 'old
passages'. I remark in passing that I am now able to identify the fragment from
John Chrysostom's *On the Gaoler* (frg. 28); it is printed in *P.G.* lv. 521 among the
dubia.
[5] I discuss the 'new passages' in the order of their closeness to the argument
from holiness and shall speak of passages 'from' Gregory Nazianzen or 'from'
Epiphanius without meaning to prejudice the question of their genuineness. The
citation from John Chrysostom's *On Abraham* (frg. 27), like the Doctrine, rejects
images as outside (i.e. pagan) proofs of the Christian faith. The long excerpt from
Epiphanius' Κατὰ τῶν ἐπιτηδευόντων κτλ. also agrees with the 'Doctrine' in speaking of images as insults to the Saints and in contrasting the glory of the resurrection
with the inglorious and dead matter of the image (frg. 30B). The quotation from
Basil of Seleucia denies that artistic images honour the Saint represented on them

Hiereia–Blachernae, then, proclaimed the arguments from christology and from holiness. It based the former on established christological positions and the latter on the accepted views of the resurrection. Both arguments reappear in the Dogmatic Definition and *florilegium* of St. Sophia, but the theological foundations insisted upon in 754 (views as to Christ's two natures and as to the resurrection of the dead) are dispensed with by the later Council.

The argument from holiness must indeed have seemed familiar to the men charged with preparing the Council of St. Sophia. The *florilegium* in which the argument from holiness plays an important part was compiled by an *ad hoc* committee of six members appointed by an emperor of Armenian origin and staffed with at least two other Armenians.[1] In Armenia there had been active, down to the eve of the Iconoclastic Controversy in the Byzantine Empire, an ascetic sect that had objected to religious images as being unlawful rivals of the Christian ascetic. Underlying this objection was the 'essential concept of the image'. Now the argument from holiness likewise was based on the essential concept of the image.[2] 'Pictorial images are not holy, only the Christian ascetic is holy' had been the thesis of the Armenian Iconoclasts. 'Pictorial images are not holy, they do not reveal the true glory of sanctity' was the doctrine emphasized in the patristic *florilegium* of St. Sophia. Armenian Iconoclasm started from the same premise as the argument from sanctity and it is therefore no coincidence that this argument appealed to and was elaborated by a committee dominated by Armenian thinking and religiosity.

2. *The Persecution of the Iconophiles*

Bury has reviewed the individual cases of persecution and from his conclusions it would appear that the persecution was violent

and connects them with paganism (frg. 21), and the citation from Basil the Great has a similar meaning (frg. 23). In the 'new passages' the argument from holiness is even extended to cover both images of Christ and the Saints (frgs. 30B, 30D) or even images of Christ only (frgs. 18, 19, 26). The fragment from Gregory of Nyssa (frg. 24) makes no mention of pictorial images, but stresses the glory of Christ the Word and was clearly introduced to show up the presumption of the artist claiming to represent Him. Three quotations (frgs. 17, 29, and 30D) can hardly be connected with the argument from holiness.

[1] On Armenian influence upon the Imperial Committee see pp. 126 f. above.
[2] On the Armenian sect of Iconoclasts see pp. 42 f. above.

enough although it seldom involved the death of the persecuted.[1]
The Emperor and the Patriarch Theodotus tried every means in
their power to win over the orthodox. The image-worshippers
were not asked to reject or insult the images, but only to hold
communion with the Patriarch Theodotus. A good many abbots
obeyed. Theosterictus' *Vita Nicetae* has preserved an interesting
description of such an act of communion.[2] It took place in a
chapel (τὰ 'Εὐκτήρια) which was adorned with images as before
(ἱστορισμένα δὲ ἦν ὡς τὸ πρότερον). The abbots took the Eucharist
from the hand of the Patriarch Theodotus who said: 'Anathema
to those who do not adore the images of Christ.' Even John the
Grammarian, the arch-Iconoclast, assured Makarios, abbot of
Pelekete, that both he (John) and the Emperor were honouring
the images.[3] These incidents date probably from the earliest
period of the persecution when the Emperor did not yet dare to
reveal the full scope of the attack.

Even later Leo attempted to win over the orthodox by various
means including promises and bribes, as in the cases of Theophanes of Sigriane, John of Psicha, and Macarius of Pelekete.[4]
It is understandable that Iconoclasm was most violent in and
around Constantinople. In an interesting letter Theodore of
Studios complained:

Almost every soul yielded and gave his signature to the impious.
Few offer resistance, and they are tested by misfortune as in fire.
Among the bishops there backslid he of Smyrna and he of Cherson;
among the abbots he of Chrysopolis, he of Dios, he of Chora, and
almost all those in the city. By the grace of Christ those of Bithynia hold
firm. . . . Of the lay order nobody holds his ground except Pexi-
menites, and he has been beaten and exiled; among the clerics the
admirable Gregory who is nicknamed Kentrokukuros; and from
among the abbesses six at the most, and they are guarded in nun-
neries.[5]

And in another letter the emphasis is almost identical: 'Almost

---

[1] Bury, *East. Rom. Emp.* 71–76.

[2] *Vita Nicetae*, col. xxxi A.

[3] Sabas, *Vita Macarii, Analecta Bollandiana*, xvi (1897), 155: ἐκ τῶν παρ᾽ ἐμοῦ
(John the Grammarian) κειμένων εἰκόνων . . . ἃς ἔνδον κατέχων ὁμοίως κρατοῦντι
τὴν πρὸς αὐτὰς τιμὴν ἀποδίδωμι.

[4] Methodius, *Vita Theophanis*, 29 (bottom); *Vita Ioannis Psichaitae*, 116; Sabas,
Vita Macarii, 154.

[5] Theodorus Studita, *Epistulae*, ed. Cozza-Luzi, no. 41, p. 34.

all monks and abbots at Byzantium were captured.'[1] No doubt in their hearts many laymen and clerics sided with the image-worshippers. Openly, however, in Constantinople only these very few dared to profess image-worship.

It is almost a dogma among students of Byzantine history that the new outbreak was confined, and remained confined, to Constantinople. 'Throughout the second period of Iconoclasm', says Bury, 'in Greece and the islands and on the coasts of Asia Minor, image-worship flourished without let or hindrance, and the bishops and monks were unaffected by the decrees of Leo V.'[2] Martin remarks of the same period: 'All the records go to show that active measures were confined to Constantinople itself.'[3] Yet closer examination of the evidence shows that the persecution spread over the entire Empire.

In the Letters of Theodore of Studios it is said that Peter bishop of Nicaea,[4] the bishop of Demetrias in Thessaly,[5] the archbishops of Smyrna in Lydia and of Cherson in Crimea,[6] of Laodicea in Phrygia[7] and of Chios[8] (to quote the unambiguous cases only)— all held communion with the Iconoclasts at some time or other. Some of these bishops, such as Peter of Nicaea, may have repented later and others may have held communion with the Iconoclasts without being converted to their views. Still there is irrefutable evidence for active Iconoclasm outside of Constantinople. Leo Archbishop of Mitylene on the island of Lesbos was an active Iconoclast: at his instigation the Emperor forced the Stylite Symeon to descend from his pillar.[9] The bishop of one of the cities belonging to the Isaurian Decapolis was found hiding in the mountains by Gregory the Decapolite; he had lost his see

[1] Theodorus Studita, *Epistulae*, ed. Cozza-Luzi, no. 165, p. 144.

[2] Bury, *East. Rom. Emp.* 141. This statement occurs in Bury's treatment of the persecution under Theophilus, but as it stands it refers to the whole of the second period of Iconoclasm. A. A. Vasiliev, *Histoire de l'Empire byzantin* (Paris, 1932), i. 377 sq., reports the opinion of Bury without clarifying his own position.

[3] Martin, *History*, 174.

[4] See J. Pargoire, 'Saints iconophiles', *E.O.* iv (1901), 350–4.

[5] Theodorus Studita, *Epistulae*, ii. 20 (*P.G.* xcix. 1177c), and no. 104, ed. Cozza-Luzi, p. 91.

[6] Theodorus Studita, *Epistulae*, no. 41, ed. Cozza-Luzi, 34 (translated above, p. 141).

[7] Ibid. ii. 89 (*P.G.* xcix. 1337A) and ii. 11 (1149c).

[8] Ibid. ii. 183 (1564D).

[9] *Acta Graeca SS. Davidis, Symeonis et Georgii Mitylenae in insula Lesbo*, ed. I. van den Gheyn, *Analecta Bollandiana*, xviii (1899), 227 sq.

as a consequence of Iconoclasm.[1] An order of the Emperor to refuse lodging to iconophile fugitives was observed on the island of Prokonesos in the Propontis.[2] The bishop of Otranto ('Υδροῦς) in southern Italy was an Iconoclast and tried to prevent communication between the orthodox in the Byzantine Empire and Rome.[3]

Other texts show that these were not isolated cases. Theodore of Studios, in a letter to Pope Paschal, described the violence of the Iconoclasts. 'The venerable images of our Saviour and God . . . have been insulted, annihilated, not only in the imperial city, but also in every region and township.'[4] Nicephorus remarks in the *Apologeticus Maior*: 'They are anxious, not that one, or two, or three, but that every person under the Roman scepter should take into his soul the decay of their ruinous words.'[5] The *Vita Methodii* comments that Iconoclasm 'seized upon the inhabited world inasmuch as it was subject to the imperial city'.[6] The *Oratio de Exilio Nicephori* by the presbyter Theophanes mentions that while the iconoclastic Patriarchs Theodotus, Antonios, and Ioannes sat on the patriarchal throne at Constantinople, 'thoughtless and unworthy priests and abbots of similar views were established over the churches in the other parishes and cities'.[7] Furthermore, if Iconoclasm was limited to Constantinople and its surroundings, why did the persecuted hide 'in deserts and mountains and caves and holes',[8] why was Rome full of Byzantine refugees if it would have sufficed, according to Bury or Martin, to proceed to 'Greece or the islands or the coasts of Asia Minor' in order to be safe? Why did the Iconophiles have their new presbyters ordained at Rome, at Naples, in 'Longibardia', in Sicily, if an orthodox ordination could have been obtained so much more closely at hand?[9] All this shows that at least under Leo V Iconoclasm held

---

[1] *Vita Gregorii Decapolitae*, ed. Fr. Dvornik, 48.   [2] Ibid. 54.

[3] Ibid. 58, see the comments of Dvornik, 41.

[4] Theodorus Studita, *Epistulae*, ii. 12 (1152D): οὐ μόνον ἐν τῇ βασιλευούσῃ πόλει, ἀλλὰ γὰρ καὶ κατὰ πᾶσαν χώραν καὶ πολίχνην. Cf. ii. 14 (1157B): destruction of images ἐκ πάσης πόλεως καὶ χώρας τῆς ὑπὸ χεῖρα.

[5] Ch. 9 (*P.G.* c. 560A).

[6] *Vita Methodii*, P.G. c. 1248A: τὴν οἰκουμένην κατέλαβεν, ὅση ὑπὸ τὴν βασιλίδα.

[7] Theophilos Ioannu, *Mnemeia Hagiologika* (Venice, 1884), 120: ἔν τε ταῖς ἄλλαις παροικίαις καὶ πόλεσι τοῦ ὁμοίου φρονήματος ἱερεῖς καὶ καθηγεμόνες ἀλόγιστοι καὶ τοῦ μηδενὸς ἄξιοι ταῖς Ἐκκλησίαις καθειστήκασιν.

[8] Theodorus Studita, *Epistulae*, ii. 14 (1157D): ἕτεροι ἐν ἐρημίαις καὶ ὄρεσι καὶ σπηλαίοις καὶ ταῖς ὀπαῖς τῆς γῆς ἐνδιαιτώμενοι.

[9] Ibid. ii. 215 (1645C sq.).

sway as far as the arm of the Emperor and the Patriarch could reach. It may have been more violent and energetic at the centre of the government, it may have reached outlying districts later than those around the capital; the fact remains that it is found all over the Empire.

While during the first period of Iconoclasm the monasteries had been the centres of resistance and nearly all the bishops sided with the Iconoclasts, the picture in the ninth century was entirely different. A good many monasteries are now iconoclastic. Perhaps it was during the reign of Leo V that the famous rural churches of southern Cappadocia came under iconoclastic influence.[1] The abbot of a monastery in the Isaurian Decapolis is a violent Iconoclast.[2] There is the letter of Theodore of Studios already quoted, according to which not only an abbot at Chrysopolis, but also at Constantinople those of Dios, Chora, 'and almost all those in the city' hold communion with the Iconoclasts. On Mt. Olympus a good many hermits and monks seem to have gone over to the camp of the enemy.[3] In a letter to Joseph of Thessalonica, Theodore complains that Joseph abbot of Kathara, those of Photeinudion, Heracleia, Medikion, Mylion, Hypolichnion, Gulaion, and Phlubution have joined the Iconoclasts,[4] and in another passage he adds the abbot of Eukairia to the black list.[5]

On the other hand, during this second period of Iconoclasm, many members of the hierarchy are among the confessors. Apart from the Patriarch Nicephorus, Joseph of Thessalonica, Peter of Nicaea, Antonius of Dyrrhachium, Michael of Synnada, and Euthymios of Sardis are well known among the orthodox correspondents of Theodore of Studios, and others could easily be added. On various occasions Theodore confirms the fact that there are bishops among the confessors and abbots among the Iconoclasts.[6]

This difference from the first period of Iconoclasm can be attributed to the policies of Leo IV the Khazar. He was the first iconoclastic emperor to appoint bishops from among the monks. From that moment on, the episcopal *omophorion* and the monastic *schema* were no longer mutually exclusive. Even monks and

---

[1] See Note M.
[2] *Vita Gregorii Decapolitae*, 48 sq.
[3] Dvornik, *Légendes*, 119–21.
[4] Theodorus Studita, *Epistulae*, ii. 9 (*P.G.* xcix. 1140B).
[5] Ibid. ii. 35 (1209C).
[6] A good example will be found in *Epistulae*, ii. 14 (1157C, D).

abbots now had something to lose in resisting the imperial wishes:
the chance of becoming a bishop. The events of the second decade
of the ninth century proved that the policy of Leo the Khazar had
been satanically wise.

Historians of the second period of Iconoclasm often quote those
letters of Theodore of Studios which describe the rigours of persecution in apocalyptic language. In fact the Studites had only
one martyr, St. Thaddeus.[1] Still, a great number of Studite
monks suffered privations and exile. There is some interesting information about a certain Arkadios, a monk of noble Asiatic
extraction, who was not a Studite. Theodore, who addresses one
of his letters to him, mentions that he had been led before the
Emperors whom he resisted courageously. In consequence he was
flogged, exiled, and flogged again. When all this proved to be of
no avail, he was condemned to forced labour as a weaver in the
imperial household.[2] Theodore asks him not to marvel at his fate,
'for such things happen to the Saints'.

It is certain that Theodore and his fellow-sufferers could have
avoided most of their afflictions if they had agreed to lie low. A
number of prominent abbots signed a written promise 'neither to
assemble nor to teach', and it does not seem that they suffered
further hardships.[3] Theodore disapproved vehemently of their
attitude. According to him it was the duty of everybody,
whether high or low in the hierarchy, to proclaim the cause of
orthodoxy.[4] From the very beginning it was Theodore's activity
as a religious propagandist which most irked the Emperor. In one
of his letters Theodore wrote to Naucratius:

There appeared an imperial messenger who announced to us what
had been asked, in other words what had been commanded by the
Emperor. It was this: 'If you find that he taught anybody, or if he
says: "I can teach," administer to him a hundred lashes.' The man
spoke those words respectfully, apologized to me for his speech.
I answered him: 'Here where I have been banished I have none to
converse with except perhaps the birds', etc.[5]

[1] Chr. van de Vorst, 'S. Thaddée Studite', *Analecta Bollandiana*, xxxi (1912),
157–60.
[2] Theodorus Studita, *Epistulae*, ii. 46 (*P.G.* xcix. 1249c sqq.): τοῖς ἱστουργοῖς σε
συνηρίθμησαν ὡς βασιλικὸν οἰκέτην.
[3] Theodorus Studita, *Epistulae*, ii. 2 (*P.G.* xcix. 1120B); no. 278, ed. Cozza-
Luzi, 223.
[4] *Epistulae*, ii. 38 (*P.G.* xcix. 1232); no. 278, ed. Cozza-Luzi, 223.
[5] Ibid., no. 35, ed. Cozza-Luzi, 28.

To Theodore, however, the birds did not suffice. In another letter to Naucratius Theodore wrote:

It is not fitting to keep silence for fear of the rulers when it is necessary to speak, for it is said: 'his soul which is lifted up is not upright in him' (Hab. ii. 2). This the Emperor opposes and orders not to teach nor to speak at all. But although we are sinners, we know that we are disciples of those who say: 'Whether it be right in the sight of God to hearken unto you more than unto God, judge ye.' We cannot but proclaim what we learned or know.[1]

It is clear that matters could have been arranged if Theodore had kept silence. But this was the last thing that he would do.

One of the most striking features of Theodore's letters is his relations with the Pope and the countries under Moslem rule. van de Vorst's study of the history of Theodore's correspondence with the Papacy has rendered its retelling unnecessary here.[2] One point should, however, be noted. Nowhere is the real purpose of Theodore's intervention with the Pope revealed more clearly than in a letter to Basil, an archimandrite at Rome. There Theodore expressed the hope that 'through the mediation and God-given authority of the holder of the first throne [Pope Paschal] help might be given by a *démarche* of the ruler of your part of the inhabited world [the Emperor Lewis the Pious]'.[3] He thus not only knew perfectly well what the political situation in the West was, but even did not hesitate to provoke an interference by the Western Emperor in Eastern affairs. This step had an exact parallel in a letter of Michael II a few years later when the Emperor tried to bring pressure to bear on the Pope through the mediation of Lewis.[4]

Less known are Theodore's relations with Egypt, Syria, and Palestine. Identical letters were sent from his place of exile to the 'Papa' of Alexandria and the Patriarch of Antioch, still others to the Laura of St. Sabas, the monastery of St. Theodosius, and the Laura of St. Chariton, not to speak of other letters to various intermediaries in foreign countries and to Theodore's

[1] *Epistulae*, ii. 38 (*P.G.* xcix. 1232), no. 48, p. 41.
[2] Chr. van de Vorst, 'Les Relations de S. Théodore Studite avec Rome', *Analecta Bollandiana*, xxxii (1913), 439–47.
[3] Theodorus Studita, *Epistulae*, no. 192, ed. Cozza-Luzi, 165: ῥοπῇ τοῦ κρατοῦντος τῆς καθ᾽ ὑμᾶς οἰκουμένης τὴν ἐπικουρίαν διὰ τῆς τοῦ πρωτοθρόνου μεσιτείας καὶ θεοδωρήτου ἐξουσίας γενέσθαι.
[4] *M.G.H.*, *Legum Sectio* iii, Concilia, ii, pt. 2, 475–80.

own couriers.[1] In these letters Theodore described the effects of Iconoclasm: the orthodox are surrounded by informers; every object adorned with religious images is destroyed; the children are brought up in the iconoclastic doctrine; liturgical poetry where images are mentioned is replaced by iconoclastic verses. Theodore acquainted his correspondents with the iconoclastic tenets and his own refutations and asked them to assist the Iconophiles at least with their prayers. The Arabs, he believed, were more respectful of Christ than the Iconoclasts. Of Theodore's foreign correspondents all but one answered and encouraged the Iconophiles.[2]

The situation of the Iconophiles changed when Leo V was murdered and Michael II ascended the throne. There is a letter of Theodore in which he rejoiced over the murder, although he was still uncertain whether the new ruler would restore image-worship.[3] As soon as Michael's indifferent policy towards religious images became known, Theodore resorted to the formula: 'The winter is over, but spring has not arrived yet.'[4] During the first years of his rule, Michael was concerned mainly with the dangerous rebellion of Thomas the Slavonian (821–3) and with his Moslem allies.[5] The rebel tried to win the support of the image-worshippers, but Michael anticipated this by recalling the exiles who were allowed to reside in the neighbourhood of Constantinople. The Emperor tried to arrange for a conference between Iconoclasts and Iconophiles, but the orthodox did not abandon their point of view that discussion with heretics was out of the question.[6]

3. *The Patriarch Nicephorus in Exile*

Nicephorus' first place of exile was the monastery τὰ Ἀγαθοῦ, north of Chrysopolis, which he may have built himself.[7] There

---

[1] Theodorus Studita, *Epistulae*, ii. 15 and 16.

[2] Ibid. 121 (*P.G.* xcix. 1396c sq.).

[3] Ibid. 73 (*P.G.* xcix. 1305 sq.).

[4] Ibid. 121 (1397B); cf. also 79 (1320A) and *passim*.

[5] See A. A. Vasiliev, *Byzance et les Arabes* (Bruxelles, 1935), i. 22–49; Bury, *East. Rom. Emp.* 84–110 and 462–4.

[6] On these negotiations and their chronology cf. Bury, *East. Rom. Emp.* 113–16, and Vasiliev, op. cit. 34 sq.

[7] *Vita Nicephori*, 201. On the doubtful location of the monastery τὰ Ἀγαθοῦ, see J. Pargoire, 'A propos de Boradion', *B.Z.* xii (1903), 476; R. Janin, 'L'Église byzantine

he stayed only a short time before being moved to another of his monastic foundations, the monastery of the martyr Theodore.[1] This transfer from τὰ Ἀγαθοῦ to the monastery of St. Theodore was ordered by the Emperor himself who had dispatched his young nephew Bardas for this purpose. When Bardas arrived at τὰ Ἀγαθοῦ, he asked his escort to bring Nicephorus into his presence. He remained seated when the aged Patriarch entered. Thereupon Nicephorus said: 'Fair Bardas, learn by the misfortune of others to meet your own.' This prophecy, Nicephorus' biographer notes, was fulfilled a little less than four years later—a fact which may be tested by anybody who meets the man and beholds his pitiful appearance (τὸ πονηρὸν τῶν ὄψεων).[2] It has been suggested that Bardas might be identified with a kinsman of Leo called Bardas who died at Smyrna in 819/20.[3] This identification, however, is doubtful since the Bardas of the *Vita Nicephori* was still alive when this text was written, that is after 828: one could meet him and behold his pitiful demeanour. More probably the Bardas of the *Vita Nicephori* was mutilated, as so many members of Leo's family were in 820 when Leo was succeeded by Michael II.

Nicephorus seems to have remained at the monastery of St. Theodore until his death. Of his exile not much is known. The *Vita Nicephori* in particular gives very little information about this period. When, in one of his letters addressed to the Emperor Basil I, Photius complained that he was not allowed to have his books or to receive sufficient food, he argued that even the Iconoclast Leo V allowed that much to Nicephorus.[4] It may be supposed that Nicephorus tasted all the bitterness of exile, although concrete information is missing. Not many of the friends of the good days can have stood by him in the spring of 815. Otherwise it is hardly understandable why his biographer was unable to gather more information about the exile of his hero.

What were Nicephorus' relations with the Studites? Theodore

sur les rives du Bosphore (Côte asiatique)', *Revue des études byzantines*, xii (1954), 69–99, esp. 91 f.: '. . . sur le rivage, quelque part au nord de Chrysopolis . . .'.

[1] On the location cf. Pargoire, loc. cit. 476 sq.; Janin, loc. cit. 96 ff. It is not impossible that either the monastery τὰ Ἀγαθοῦ or that of St. Theodore is identical with that which Nicephorus founded before he became Patriarch (above, p. 62).

[2] *Vita Nicephori*, 201.

[3] Bury, *East. Rom. Emp.* 72.

[4] Photius, *Epistulae*, i. 16 (*P.G.* cii. 768ʙ).

had been exiled from Constantinople shortly after Nicephorus, but apparently he was not fully informed of the latter's attitude. He must have known of Nicephorus' abdication, for the Emperor had made it public in a *silention* on the day after Nicephorus' departure. Thus Theodore declared, in a letter addressed in the name of all the abbots to the Council of 815, that he would not enter into a discussion with the heretics against the will of his bishop, the Patriarch Nicephorus.[1] Theodore even wrote to the ex-Patriarch, and Nicephorus answered in a letter full of humility towards the valiant abbot, but neither Theodore's letter nor Nicephorus' dealt with questions of practical policy.[2] It is clear, however, that Theodore was informed of Nicephorus' courageous attitude in 815 only two years later: for it was as late as A.D. 817 that Theodore wrote to his brother Joseph: 'Our true Patriarch also confesses the truth as I learned by the mouth of a man who heard it from him and praised the resistance which he then showed.'[3] Accordingly in another letter to his brother (which dates probably from the earliest period of persecution) he re-marked that he, as archbishop of Thessalonica, surpassed all other members of the hierarchy 'except the one who lives in hiding', that is Nicephorus.[4] It is quite unlikely that the Emperor could have prevented Nicephorus from communicating with Theodore if Nicephorus had been anxious to do so. Theodore had an elaborate system of correspondence which enabled him to reach even the Pope and the Oriental Patriarchs. It may be remembered that Leo had asked the orthodox abbots, and Theo-dore in particular, to keep silence, not to assemble and not to teach. Now it is probable that a similar request was presented to Nicephorus who, unlike Thodore, complied with it. The fact is

[1] Theodorus Studita, *Epistulae*, ii. 1 (*P.G.* xcix. 1116c).
[2] Theodorus Studita, *Epistulae*, ii. 18 (1173B). In this letter Theodore praises Nicephorus and compares the latter's sufferings with those of Christ. The tone of Nicephorus' reply may be gathered from Theodorus Studita, *Epistulae*, ii. 79 (1317B sqq.). He had called himself the spiritual son of Theodore and a sinner, had praised Theodore and encouraged him to continue his fight.
[3] Ibid. 31 (1204B): καὶ αὐτὸς ὁ ἀληθινὸς ἡμῶν πατριάρχης ὁμολογῶν ἐστι τὴν ἀλήθειαν, ὡς ἔμαθον ἐκ στόματος τοῦ παρ' αὐτοῦ ἀκηκοότος καὶ ἐπαινοῦντος τὴν τότε ἔνστασιν. The letter was written in or after 817, since in it Theodore informed his brother of the death of St. Theophanes which occurred in 817 (cf. Chr. van de Vorst, 'En quelle année mourut S. Théophane le Chronographe?', *Analecta Bollandiana*, xxxi (1912), 148–56.
[4] Theodorus Studita, *Epistulae*, ii. 9 (1140C): τῶν ἁπάντων εἰ ὑπερέχων τῇ κεφαλίδι τῆς ἱερωσύνης πλὴν τοῦ ἑνὸς ἐν παραβύστῳ κειμένου.

that when in 816/17 Theodore and four other orthodox abbots appealed to Pope Paschal for help, they mentioned expressly that Nicephorus was prevented from writing.[1] It would seem that the ex-Patriarch pointedly refrained from interfering in ecclesiastical matters.

Nicephorus kept aloof to such a degree that Theodore, in his first letter to Michael II after the latter's accession, ignored him. He said that the Church of Constantinople had separated itself from the *four* patriarchs. He admonished the Emperor to work for a reconciliation with Rome and the other three patriarchs, but not a word was said about Nicephorus and the possibilities of his restoration.[2]

Nicephorus himself, however, had not given up the hope of playing once more a role in the religious policy of the Empire. The *Vita Nicephori* speaks of a (lost) letter which Nicephorus wrote to Michael II.[3] In this letter he reminded the Emperor of his miraculous escape from death and set forth the orthodox dogma. Michael's answer was that Nicephorus could recover his patriarchal office if he agreed not to disturb the present condition of the Church and to observe complete silence about the problem of images.[4] Nicephorus did not accept this offer.[5]

As far as the relations between Theodore of Studios and Nicephorus are concerned it is obvious that in his correspondence Theodore was formally correct. In a letter to Thomas Patriarch of Jerusalem he refused to accept the praise which Thomas had bestowed on him and remarked that by right it belonged to Nicephorus.[6] On his death-bed the Studite asked his disciples 'to give the greeting of respect and reverence to the archpriest and the other fathers, hierarchs, and priests of the Church', etc. It is probable that 'the archpriest' he spoke of was Nicephorus.[7]

---

[1] Theodorus Studita, *Epistulae*, ii. 12 (1152C): τῆς κεφαλῆς ἡμῶν εἰργομένης.
[2] Ibid. 74 (1308D sqq.).
[3] *Vita Nicephori*, p. 209 (de Boor).
[4] Ibid., p. 210 (de Boor). Cf. Bury, *East. Rom. Emp.* 113.
[5] For Michael II's religious policy see Bury, *East. Rom. Emp.* 110–19.
[6] Theodorus Studita, *Epistulae*, ii. 121 (1396C).
[7] Naucratius, *Encyclica de obitu Sancti Theodori Studitae*, *P.G.* xcix. 1844B: τῷ δεσπότῃ ἡμῶν τῷ ἀρχιερεῖ τὸν δι' αἰδοῦς καὶ τιμῆς ἀσπασμὸν ἐξ ἐμοῦ ἀπονείματε· τοῖς λοιποῖς Πατράσιν, ἱεράρχαις τε καὶ ἱερεῦσιν τοῖς Χριστοῦ . . .. One may doubt whether Nicephorus or Joseph of Thessalonica are meant by the words ὁ δεσπότης ἡμῶν ὁ ἀρχιερεύς. I favour Nicephorus because he is often called by Theodore ὁ ἀρχιερεύς (ii. 18, 1173C: ἀρχιερατικὰς ὑπηρεσίας); ii. 86, 1329D; 1332A; etc.) whereas Joseph is constantly referred to as ὁ ἀρχιεπίσκοπος (no. 35, p. 28, ed. Cozza-

For Theodore, Nicephorus was the only true and legitimate Patriarch of Constantinople and the iconoclastic patriarchs were usurpers.

On the other hand former frictions were not forgotten, even during the exile. Nowhere in his correspondence did Theodore press strongly for Nicephorus' restoration. Although he often declared emphatically that questions of Church policy were to be decided by the Patriarch, Theodore had no difficulty in finding reasons for exceptions to this principle. Furthermore, Theodore sometimes suggested an intervention by Rome where one might have expected more stress to be laid on the position of the Patriarch. In a letter addressed to the Emperor Michael in the name of all the abbots Theodore justified his refusal to take part in a disputation with the iconoclastic theologians, and continued:

If, however, your divine magnaminity doubts or disbelieves that some point could be settled piously by the archpriest [i.e. Nicephorus], let your great and divinely supported hand . . . give orders that the elucidation be laid down from the Older Rome as was received from old and from the very beginning by patristic tradition.[1]

The style of this sentence revealed Theodore's true feelings towards Nicephorus: Nicephorus was mentioned only in a subordinate clause which expressed doubt as to his authority in matters of faith. A similar attitude is found in a letter of Theodore to Leo the *sakellarios*. Here Theodore set down his suggestions for the restoration of ecclesiastical peace:

The heterodox are to keep out of the churches of God and Nicephorus the holy Patriarch is to recover his own throne. When he assembles his fellow-sufferers—unless it be possible that representatives of the other patriarchs be present, which is possible if the Emperor should desire the presence of him of the Occident [the Pope] to whom belongs the power of assembling an ecumenical council—then peace might be established. . . . If however, this is not acceptable to the Emperor, and if, as he says, Nicephorus the *prohedros* has been turned aside from the truth along with us, then both parties must send

Luzi; no. 62, p. 51; etc.). It is unknown whether Joseph of Thessalonica was present when his brother Theodore died, see Ch. van de Vorst, 'La Translation de S. Théodore Studite' &c., *A.B.* xxxii (1913), 46.

[1] Theodorus Studita, *Epistulae*, ii. 86 (*P.G.* xcix. 1332A).

messengers to him of Rome and should thence receive the certitude of faith.[1]

Theodore recognized the authority of the Patriarch. Yet if one reads between the lines, it seems that Theodore suspects that the Emperor might lack confidence in a decision made by Nicephorus. It would seem that Theodore's famous 'Roman proclivities'[2] are connected with his deep-rooted mistrust of Nicephorus, a mistrust which had been nurtured over many decades of strife between secular and monastic clergy.

This personal animosity between Nicephorus and Theodore, as well as the old opposition between the two groups of the clergy, threatened to flare up once more during the years of persecution. The causes for this last duel are not easy to grasp. In ecclesiastical discipline contact with an Iconoclast constituted a lapse into heresy. There were subtle distinctions, as for instance that between eating and drinking with a heretic.[3] Like other tyrannical régimes before and after, the Iconoclasts made it their policy to win over their opponents by wringing from them a gradated series of concessions, beginning with a harmless act of everyday life and ending in ecclesiastical communion. Thus the transition from indifferent gestures of human behaviour to 'sin' was almost imperceptible. Since not infrequently the Iconoclasts used force and torture in order to break the resistance of the Iconophiles, it can be easily understood that many were 'converted' to Iconoclasm more or less against their will. Hence the phenomenon that almost from the first day of persecution there were clerics, monks, and laymen who regretted their 'fall' and wished to return to image-worship.[4] As repentant sinners they had to obtain pardon from an orthodox bishop. Now the orthodox church was living in hiding, its bishops were scattered over the world. There was no recognized authority, and the *lapsi* accordingly often confessed to monks. It was precisely during these years that the sacrament

---

[1] Theodorus Studita, *Epistulae*, ii. 129 (1420A).

[2] The term is used by Bury, *East. Rom. Emp.* 115.

[3] Theodore, for example, calls it 'dispensation' to greet a heretic and to drink with him, whereas to eat with him would be sin, *Epistulae*, ii. 63 (1281D sq.).

[4] A Photian homily to which F. Dvornik, 'The Patriarch Photius and Iconoclasm', *Dumbarton Oaks Papers*, vii (1953), 87 f., called attention renders it probable that at this time John the Grammarian and other iconoclastic leaders were refused a pardon by Nicephorus.

of penance (τὸ ἐπιτίμιον) gradually passed from the hands of the secular clergy into those of the monks (πνευματικοὶ πατέρες).[1]

What was Theodore's attitude with respect to the *lapsi*? He considered himself in a position of authority only for Studite monks. With respect to them he took it upon himself to determine the character of the penance. For everybody else the final decision had to be reserved for the Patriarch Nicephorus and a synod to be held after the restoration of orthodoxy.[2] Since, however, it was uncertain when this time would come, it was a practical necessity to take provisional measures. These, Theodore held, could be taken by any priest (and here it should be remembered that many abbots were priests like Theodore himself)—but not, as he constantly repeated, 'by way of an authoritative decision, but by way of advice'.[3]

Theodore was not the only cleric to whom the *lapsi* resorted. As a matter of fact the practice of confession gave rise to schisms among the image-worshippers. The practice of penance was attacked by various conservative ecclesiastics. They claimed that in many cases the repentance was not sincere, that members of the clergy tried to attract as many *lapsi* as possible and refused to recognize the penance administered by their colleagues.[4] Theodore rejected these accusations, but they do not sound like inventions.

Theodore's critics attempted to sow discord between him and Nicephorus. In a letter to Peter of Nicaea Theodore stated that his opponents had called the Studites schismatics with respect to the problem of penance. Furthermore, they again referred to the earlier opposition of the Studites to the Patriarch Tarasius and to the Studite refusal to recognize the Council of Nicaea as ecumenical rather than local. Theodore, who wished to discredit these accusations, visited Nicephorus immediately after his own return from exile in 821 when he was staying at Chalcedon. Nicephorus,

---

[1] On this development see J. Pargoire, *L'Église byzantine*, 347–50; E. Vacandard, 'Confession du Iᵉʳ au XIIIᵉ siècle', *D.T.C.* iii. 1, 861–74; Tixeront, *Histoire des dogmes*, iii. 252–60; M. Jugie, 'La Pénitence dans l'église grecque après le schisme', *D.T.C.* xii. 1, 1127–38. From this point of view the Letters of Theodore the Studite deserve detailed study.

[2] See, for example, *Epistulae*, ii. 11 (1148c); ii. 152 (1473A).

[3] Ibid. 40 (1240c): οὐχ ὁριστικῶς, ἀλλ' . . . συμβουλευτικῶς; ii. 49 (1260B): οὐ νομοθετικῶς . . ., ἀλλὰ συμβουλευτικῶς; ii. 152 (1473A): οὐχ ὁριστικῶς, ἀλλὰ συμβουλευτικῶς.

[4] Ibid. 162 (1512D and 1513A sqq.).

Theodore writes, received him with great condescension and did not even mention the problem of penance. Theodore made it a point, however, to clarify his own position towards Tarasius and the Council of Nicaea at the first opportunity.[1] From Theodore's account it would seem that Nicephorus was polite and respectful, but that he refrained from discussing controversial matters with his hot-tempered opponent. Even later Theodore emphasized on various occasions that Nicephorus either approved, or at least did not disapprove, of his attitude with respect to penance.[2] One cannot be certain, however, that Nicephorus participated in the 'synods' which the orthodox assembled at various times on this and other matters.[3]

What lay behind the accusations of schism levelled against the Studites? To Theodore they appeared to be iconoclastic attempts at separating Nicephorus from the Studites and at winning over the former to the moderate Iconoclasm of Michael II. This may be inferred from the fact that Theodore contemptuously calls the slanderers 'the agents of peace'.[4] Both Nicephorus and Theodore were careful not to fulfil the hopes which the Iconoclasts put on their old enmity. 'Concord', the old slogan of the secular clergy, was now adopted even by the Studites. The quarrels concerning the Council of Nicaea and the Adulterous Wedding were forgotten. Wrote Theodore:

These things ... should not be inquired into and torn open now, for it causes turmoil and brings no profit to the Church of God, rather strife of words and offence. One party wrote in this sense, the other in another, and both believed to possess the truth. You know, triply beloved, that this notorious event came to pass many years ago and became known in East and West; neither party can annul what it did or wrote. Now is the time for concord, now is the time for mutual suffering. If the surviving writings meet with the approval of posterity, they are worthy of praise; if they do not, the opposite holds true. This statement is to be believed, and we do not wish to say anything else about this subject, not now and not later.[5]

It is regrettable that Theodore arrived at this conciliatory attitude only after both he and his opponents had gone through the terrors

---

[1] *Epistulae*, ii. 127 (1412).
[2] Ibid. 139 (1444B); 152 (1473C); 154 (1480A); 203 (1617C).
[3] Ibid. 86 (1329C); 139 (1444A); 211 (1636D).
[4] Ibid. 127 (1412B).   [5] Ibid. 127 (1412C).

of persecution and when the shadow of death was soon to be cast upon them both.

Like the date of Nicephorus' birth the date of his death is known only from the *Synaxarium Constantinopolitanum*.[1] According to this text he died after thirteen years of exile, i.e. in A.D. 828. The *Vita Nicephori* adds that his death took place at Easter, that is, on 5 April.[2] The prospects for a restoration of image-worship were poor and the iconoclastic tendencies of Theophilus, the heir-designate to the throne of Michael the Amorian, cannot have failed to worry the aged prelate. It was indeed a benign act of providence which spared him the spectacle of a recrudescence of persecution far more cruel and determined than that of the preceding reign.

[1] *Synax. Const.* 725. 12: ὁ δὲ μακάριος οὗτος χρονίαις ταλαιπωρίαις καταπονηθεὶς ἑβδομηκοστόν ποτε χρόνον πληρώσας εἰς χεῖρας Θεοῦ τὸ πνεῦμα παρέθετο, ἐννέα μὲν ἐν τῇ ἀρχιερωσύνῃ διατελέσας χρόνους, τρεισκαιδέκα δὲ ἐν τῇ ἐξορίᾳ.

[2] *Vita Nicephori*, 213: ἐν ᾗ τῶν πρωτοτόκων ἐν οὐρανοῖς ἀπογεγραμμένων ἡ ἐκκλησία μετ' ἤχου χορεύουσα πανηγυρίζει ἑορτὴν τὴν μακραίωνα, i.e. Passover = Easter.

VII

SURVEY AND CHRONOLOGY OF
NICEPHORUS' LITERARY LEGACY[1]

As Nicephorus' life was darkened by tragic conflicts, so an
unfriendly fate presided over his literary legacy. While the
manuscript tradition of his contemporaries Theodore of
Studios and Theophanes is rich and extensive, presumably because
their works were tended with care and affection in their respective monasteries, the same cannot be said of the Patriarch. It is
true that a two-volume edition of his works was made shortly
after Nicephorus' death.[2] This edition, however, did not include
Nicephorus' historical works; neither they nor his theological
works were used to any large extent. However, Ignatius Diaconus
and Georgius Monachus read at least some of them. Of the
Breviarium there are two manuscripts representing two different
versions, of the *Apologeticus atque Antirrhetici* four codices, of the
Refutatio et Eversio two. Furthermore, by the tenth century at the
latest, Theodorus Graptos was credited with the authorship of
some of Nicephorus' works. Nor is this all. When Nicephorus'
writings were edited in modern times, they were scattered over a
number of volumes some of which are hard to procure. It was
even more disastrous that, as will be shown, well-meaning but
misguided editors arranged some of Nicephorus' works so con-
fusingly that they defy understanding. Finally, Nicephorus' most
important and most mature work, the *Refutatio et Eversio*, still
awaits its *editio princeps*.

[1] I do not propose to discuss either the *Book of Dreams* attributed to the Patriarch
Nicephorus in one manuscript (see F. Drexl, 'Das Traumbuch des Patriarchen
Nikephoros', *Festgabe Albert Ehrhard*, Bonn und Leipzig, 1922, 94–118) or the variety
of ecclesiastical canons attributed to him (see Grumel *Regestes*, nos. 403 ff.), because of the extremely doubtful authorship of both. Neither shall I pay attention
to the Χρονογραφικὸν Σύντομον (ed. de Boor, 80–135), which can be discussed
profitably only in connexion with other similar lists of dates.
[2] R. P. Blake, 'Note sur l'activité littéraire de Nicéphore Ier Patriarche de
Constantinople', *Byzantion*, xiv (1939), 14. P. Maas, 'Die ikonoklastische Episode
in dem Brief des Epiphanios an Johannes', *B.Z.* xxx (1929–30), 279, proves the
existence of a ninth-century archetype for the two manuscripts of the *Refutatio et
Eversio*.

The present chapter does not pretend to exhaust the rich content of the Patriarch's literary legacy. It aims at surveying Nicephorus' literary activity, characterizing his various works, explaining their structure and establishing as reliable a chronology as possible. The next chapter will attempt to define the Patriarch's place in the development of iconophile theory. It should, however, be emphasized that the works of the Patriarch will require the labours of theologians in order to elucidate his doctrine fully, especially his teachings on problems other than image-worship.[1] This book is meant merely to lay the foundations for such a study.

1. *Historical Works*

Among students of medieval history Nicephorus' reputation rests primarily on his historical works, more particularly on his 'Ιστορία Σύντομος or *Breviarium*. As it is a most important source for the period which it covers (the years 602–769, from the murder of the Emperor Maurice to the marriage of Leo the Khazar to Irene), it merits full treatment as to purpose, sources, date, credibility, and similar inquiries. Here, however, only a few questions raised by it will be discussed.

The *Breviarium* is preserved in two manuscripts, which represent two different versions: the 'London Version' appears in the British Museum Add. MS. 19390 and the 'Vatican Version' in the *Vaticanus Graecus* 977. Both begin with the murder of Maurice in 602, in fact with the words: Μετὰ τὴν τοῦ Μαυρικίου τοῦ βασιλέως ἀναίρεσιν . . .. This is not a natural beginning for a history or chronicle written in the eighth century—a more obvious starting-point would have been the accession of Heraclius. If an historian of the eighth century began his account of the seventh century with the murder of Maurice, he must have had special reasons. He must have intended to continue a narrative which happened to end at that point. The only source which meets this specification is the *Histories* of Theophylactus Simocatta who in his last chapters (viii. 11–15) related the murder of Maurice. In fact, in the *Vaticanus Graecus* 977 the *Histories* of Theophylactus immediately precede the *Breviarium*.[2] A connexion

---

[1] See now the two sections of A. J. Visser, *Nikephoros und der Bilderstreit* (Haag, 1952), 97–108, on Nicephorus' doctrine of the Church and on his christology.
[2] De Boor, in his edition of Nicephorus' *Breviarium* (*Nicephori . . . Opuscula*

between the two works is further supported by Photius' *Biblio-théké* (written before 857). There the *Histories* of Theophylactus appear as no. 65 and the *Breviarium* as no. 66. Perhaps Photius had been reading one manuscript which contained both works and which was to become the archetype of the *Vat. gr.* 977. It would seem, then, that Nicephorus wrote his *Breviarium* as a continuation of Theophylactus' *Histories*. If this hypothesis proves correct, it would suggest two corollaries. In the first place, it would mean that, in historiography as in other fields, the continuity of tradition was interrupted for several generations by the Arab invasions. Secondly, it would show that an author of the eighth century who set out to continue the *Histories* of Theophylactus was (or felt) unable to write a history in the proper sense, as Theophylactus had done, but was satisfied with a chronicle in its stead.

The Vatican Version differs in two ways from the London Version. First of all, the latter ends in 713 while the Vatican Version, as was said above, continues to 769. Secondly, the Vatican Version is a stylistic revision of the London Version.[1]

Nicephorus' *Breviarium* is the subject of an important publication written by K. N. Uspenskii more than thirty years before its publication in Soviet Russia.[2] It was known for a long time that for the period of the Emperors Leo III and Constantine V the chroniclers Nicephorus and Theophanes used the same source.[3] Uspenskii tried to characterize this common source and arrived at the conclusion that it was an iconoclastic work written during the reign of Constantine V. According to him this iconoclastic source was excerpted and rewritten, in the second decade of the ninth century, by the two iconophile chroniclers, Nicephorus and Theophanes, who attempted, each in his own way, to undo its iconoclastic bias. Where the source would speak of military vic-

Historica, Leipzig, 1880, p. iv), considers the connexion of Theophylactus' *Histories* with Nicephorus' *Breviarium* to be the result of an accident. The considerations given in the text will help to invalidate this view. One is reminded of the relationship between Thucydides' *Histories* and Xenophon's *Hellenic History*. The latter work was a continuation of the former and in several manuscripts the two works appear together.   [1] See Note N, p. 239 f.

[2] K. N. Uspenskii, 'Ocherki po istorii ikonoborcheskogo dvizheniia v vizantiiskoi imperii v VIII–IX vv. Feofan i ego Khronografiia', *V.V.*, N.S., iii (1950), 399–438 and iv (1951), 211–62.

[3] Karl Krumbacher, *Geschichte der byzantinischen Litteratur*, 343, 350. Gyula Moravcsik, *Byzantino-Turcica*, i (Budapest, 1942), 279, 333.

tories of the iconoclastic emperors over a foreign enemy, the chronicler would minimize or deny them. Where the common source exalted the prosperity of the Empire under Leo III and Constantine V, the later writers would again present the same data in a light less favourable to these emperors. If any other achievements of Leo and Constantine were mentioned, they would deal with the events in the light of their theological bias. Finally, the later chroniclers condemned the religious views of the iconoclastic emperors.

Indeed there can be no doubt that Theophanes and Nicephorus used the same source in compiling their chronicles and there is no need to labour the point here. However, against Uspenskii's theory of an iconoclastic source, it can be shown to be at least very probable that the common basis of Theophanes' *Chronicle* and Nicephorus' *Breviarium* was a (lost) iconophile chronicle written after the death of Constantine V (775). It condemned many specific acts of the iconoclastic emperors, but did not omit or belittle some of their military and other achievements. Indeed this source can be traced not only in the chronicles of Nicephorus and Theophanes but also in the former's *Third Antirrheticus*.[1] Perhaps the most instructive passage where all three sources (Theophanes, *Breviarium*, *Third Antirrheticus*) clearly depend upon the same lost chronicler deals with Constantine V's fiscal oppression of the farmers (see p. 160).

The unflattering comparison with King Midas which occurs in all three passages must have been part of the common source. Consequently this source must have been critical of Constantine's economic policy which, according to the *Breviarium*, enriched the city population at the expense of the farmers. Indeed the verbal agreement in the three passages concerns not only the facts mentioned (the hoarding of the gold, the cheapness of agricultural produce) but extends to the condemnation of imperial policy (Constantine's lust for gold, his fiscal oppression).[2]

[1] On this work see below, p. 170. This third witness to the lost source is often ignored. It shows striking agreements with the two chronicles, especially in its description of the Great Plague (A.D. 747).

[2] Uspenskii, 'Ocherki' &c., *V.V.*, N.S., iv (1951), 233 f., discusses the agreement between Theophanes and Nicephorus' *Breviarium* in their accounts of Constantine's economic policy. He fails to point out, however, the decisive feature: the agreement is not restricted to the facts but extends to the unfavourable evaluation of the Emperor. Once this is granted, Uspenskii's theory of an iconoclastic source collapses.

Nicephorus, *Breviarium*, p. 76 de Boor A.D. 766–7	Theophanes, p. 443 de Boor A.D. 767–8	Nicephorus, *Third Antirrheticus*, ch. 75 (*P.G.* c. 513D)
φιλόχρυσος δὲ ὢν ὁ μισόχριστος νέος Μίδας Κωνσταντῖνος ἀναδείκνυται καὶ τὸν χρυσὸν ἅπαντα ἀποθησαυρίζει. ἐν οἷς συνέβαινεν ἐν ταῖς τῶν φόρων πράξεσι τῶν φορολογουμένων βιαζομένων εὐώνως τὰ τῆς γῆς καρπήματα καὶ γεννήματα διαπιπράσκεσθαι... ὅπερ τοῖς μὲν ἀνοήτοις εὐφορία τε γῆς καὶ πραγμάτων εὐθηνία ἐνομίζετο, τοῖς δὲ εὖ φρονοῦσι τυραννίδος καὶ φιλοχρηματίας ἔργον καὶ ἀπανθρωπίας νόσος ἐκρίνετο.	ἐποίησε δὲ εὐθηνῆσαι τὰ εἴδη ἐν τῇ πόλει τῷ χρόνῳ τούτῳ. νέος γὰρ Μίδας γενόμενος τὸν χρυσὸν ἀπεθησαύρισε καὶ τοὺς γεωργοὺς ἐγύμνωσεν, καὶ διὰ τὴν τῶν φόρων ἀπαίτησιν ἠναγκάζοντο οἱ ἄνθρωποι τὰς τοῦ Θεοῦ χορηγίας εὐώνως πιπράσκειν.	ὁ μισοχριστότατος καὶ φιλοχρυσότατος τύραννος, τὸ τοῦ χρυσοῦ ἀνδράποδον, ὁ τὸν Λύδιον ἐκεῖνον τῇ φιλοχρύσῳ μανίᾳ ὑπερβαλόμενος... συχναῖς καὶ ἐτησίοις προσθήκαις τῶν τελεσμάτων τοὺς τῆς γεωργίας ἅπαντας πιέζων καὶ ἀποθλίβων παρανομότατα...

Furthermore, Nicephorus himself hints, in the same part of the *Third Antirrheticus* which shows such striking resemblances to Theophanes and the *Breviarium*, that he used an iconophile source for the reign of Constantine V. He prefaced his account of the Great Plague of A.D. 747 and of the divine visitations that befell the people under this emperor with the remarks: 'Exceedingly shocked at the number and size of the misfortunes, some of those then present acting opportunely and appropriately saw fit to record for posterity also the types of evils then experienced as follows . . . .'[1] Thus the informant used by Nicephorus was 'exceedingly shocked' at the misfortunes that occurred under this emperor, especially at the Great Plague. It is unlikely that the Patriarch used more than one source for the reign of Constantine in a treatise which was theological rather than historical in nature. It may therefore be assumed that the same source contained not only the account of the Great Plague but also the unfavourable appraisal of Constantine's economic and fiscal policy which reappears in all three sources.

The iconophile character of the source may further be demonstrated from another passage in the *Breviarium* found at the end of the account of the Plague. There Nicephorus says:

This [the Plague] was judged by those who could think correctly to have befallen [the Empire] by an act of divine wrath when he who then ruled godlessly and impiously [Constantine V] and all those who agreed with his lawless mind had dared to lay hands on the holy images as an act of insult against Christ's Church.[2]

The *Third Antirrheticus* shows that Nicephorus knew of a written historical work whose author had been 'exceedingly shocked' by the disasters under Constantine V, especially the Great Plague and had described them in writing. On the other hand, Nicephorus

---

[1] Nicephorus, *Third Antirrheticus*, 65 (*P.G.* c. 496A): . . . ὧν τῷ πλήθει καὶ τῷ μεγέθει τῶν συμφορῶν ὑπερεκπληττόμενοι τῶν τότε παρόντων τινές, εὐκαίρως καὶ εἰς δέον χρώμενοι, ἱστορίᾳ παραδοῦναι ἄξιον ᾠήθησαν καὶ τὰ εἴδη τῶν κακῶν εἰς πεῖραν ἀγόμενα τοιαῦτα . . . . The following account of the Great Plague shows many literal agreements with that in Theophanes, on the one hand, and with that in the *Breviarium* on the other. One wonders whether the words quoted at the beginning of this note do not introduce a more or less literal quotation from the lost source (note the τοιαῦτα at the end).

[2] Nicephorus, *Breviarium*, 64 (de Boor): ταῦτα ἐκρίνετο τοῖς ὀρθὰ φρονεῖν εἰδόσιν ἐκ θείας ἐπισκήπτειν ὀργῆς ἡνίκα ὁ τότε ἀθέως καὶ δυσσεβῶς κρατῶν καὶ ὅσοι αὐτῷ συνῆνουν τῷ ἀθέσμῳ φρονήματι τὰς χεῖρας ἐπαφεῖναι κατὰ τῶν ἁγίων ἀπεικονισμάτων εἰς ὕβριν τῆς τοῦ Χριστοῦ ἐκκλησίας τετολμήκασιν.

says in the *Breviarium* that the Great Plague 'was judged by those who could think correctly to have befallen [the Empire]' as an act of divine wrath. Who was it who pronounced this 'judgement'? The chances are overwhelming that the same lost chronicler who had been 'exceedingly shocked' at the disasters proceeded to inquire into their causes and thus arrived at his verdict so unfavourable to Constantine V.[1] The *historia calamitatum* was therefore in all probability an iconophile source,[2] a chronicle written by an iconophile monk.[3]

The last-quoted passage permits the assertion that Nicephorus' *Breviarium* was written after the death of Constantine V (cf. ὁ τότε . . . κρατῶν) in 775. On the other hand, it is impossible to say how soon after Constantine's death it was completed. On general grounds it is unlikely that Nicephorus should have devoted himself to the writing of a chronicle after 806 when weightier matters and greater responsibilities required his attention. Ehrhard's proposal to assign the *Breviarium* to the period of Nicephorus' attendance at court, i.e. to the period between 775 and 797 is plausible.[4] It may perhaps have been written before 787 as its author shows no knowledge of the official restoration of image-worship.

2. *Theological Works—Survey*

Nicephorus' literary production was interrupted by his career in the Imperial Secretariate, his retirement, his administration of the poorhouse, and finally by his tenure of the patriarchal office. When he turned again to literature, his interests had changed from history to theology.

---

[1] The only alternative would be to assume that Nicephorus is referring, in the last passage, to *oral* utterances made in iconophile circles at the time of the Plague (ἐκρίνετο), which occurred before Nicephorus was born. Is it really conceivable that the lost informant who was sufficiently 'shocked' by the disasters to record and describe them, should have refrained from inquiring into the causes?

[2] It is clear, on the other hand, that the source did not always allow its theological bias to affect its concern for truth. Otherwise the relative restraint and objectivity of the *Breviarium* (p. 159 above) would be inexplicable.

[3] See Note O, pp. 240f.

[4] A. Ehrhard, 'Nicephorus', Wetzer und Welte, *Kirchenlexikon*, ix. 256. He adds the further reason that Nicephorus' relative moderation towards the iconoclastic emperors in the *Breviarium* would be inconceivable after he became Patriarch. Uspenskii's incidental remark (p. 421) according to which the *Breviarium* was composed in the second decade of the ninth century is unsubstantiated and unlikely.

1. The earliest work written by Nicephorus after the interruption of his literary activity, his Letter to Pope Leo III (*P.G.* c. 169–200), cannot be called theological in any strict sense. The date of the letter is given by Theophanes (p. 494) as the year 811/ 12. It is a delayed letter of enthronement (τὰ συνοδικά) and is therefore a chancery document rather than a literary work. Nicephorus carefully avoids the title of οἰκουμενικὸς πατριάρχης which had antagonized Pope Hadrian in an earlier generation. Modestly Nicephorus styles himself ἐπίσκοπος Κωνσταντινουπόλεως. After the customary formulas of Christian humility Nicephorus gives brief indications of his antecedents, his position at the court, and his retreat from Constantinople. The Emperor Nicephorus I, the entire Church, and the Senate forced him, he says, to accept the patriarchal dignity. There follows a long Creed and, finally, the already quoted apology.[1]

2. The Letter to Pope Leo had been a document of State. The earliest theological work of the Patriarch Nicephorus, the *Apologeticus Minor*, is entitled in the manuscripts: τοῦ ὁσίου πατρὸς ἡμῶν Νικηφόρου πατριάρχου Κωνσταντινουπόλεως Ἀπολογήτικος πρὸς τὴν καθολικὴν ἐκκλησίαν περὶ τοῦ κατὰ τῶν σεπτῶν εἰκόνων πάλιν νέου σχίσματος (*P.G.* c. 833–50).

It was named *Apologeticus Minor* by its first editor, A. Mai, to distinguish it from a much lengthier (and later) *Apologeticus Maior*. The *Apologeticus Minor* is a more or less official document issued by Nicephorus in his capacity as Patriarch of Constantinople.

The reason for its compilation is indicated in the beginning: several members of the clergy had separated themselves from the Church. The Patriarch proceeds to give a short history of the image-problem down to the second Council of Nicaea (chs. 2–5). The mention of certain quotations which are stated by the Iconoclasts to come from Epiphanius (ch. 4) deserves particular notice. In the past all those who were ordained priests after the Seventh Council had to state their acceptance of the *Horos* of Nicaea and those who now are separating themselves from the Church are subject to the anathemas pronounced at Nicaea. No cleric, therefore, should enter into discussion with them, in particular since, in accordance with the canons of the Church, they are deposed from the priesthood for holding illegal assemblies

[1] Above, pp. 106 f.

(παρασυναγωγαί) and for trying to influence the Emperor (ch. 6). If the new schismatics claim that they have worshipped idols up to the present, they ought to do penance. No inquiry can be permitted on the image-problem since it has been settled by an ecumenical council (ch. 8). The impious views of Constantine Copronymus should not be discussed by any member of the clergy.

Of the quotations contained in his unholy writings, those that are heretical should be rejected out of hand, those that were interpreted by him in an impious sense should be declared unavailing and useless, but if on the basis of his quotations there were found certain synodal books (τινὰ βιβλία πρακτικά) pronouncing on the images, the Church may accept and explain them to satisfy our most pious Emperor (τὸν εὐσεβέστατον βασιλέα ἡμῶν).[1]

If that should prove insufficient, an ecumenical council must be called (ch. 9). There follows an inquiry into the validity of the canons of the Sixth Council (chs. 9–10) and into certain heretical quotations, in particular from Eusebius, and finally once again the statement that if the present schism does not cease an ecumenical council will have to meet.

The date of this work has been given by Mai and Ehrhard as 813 because in one passage it is said that the canons of the Trullanum (692) have been valid ὑπὲρ τὰ ἑκατὸν εἴκοσι ἔτη, 'more than 120 years'. The Emperor is still referred to as 'most pious', so that it must be written prior to December 814 when the incident at the Chalke Gate revealed the imperial intentions.[2] Perhaps it would be preferable to think of it as written in 814. In 813 the Patriarch Nicephorus can hardly have had any knowledge of 'illegal assemblies'.

The document does honour to the ecclesiastical statesman who

---

[1] The 'synodal books' concerned with the images which might be found on the basis of Constantine V's *florilegium* can only be the records of the Council of Hiereia (754). One thinks immediately of the *Scriptor Incertus de Leone Armeno* (text above, p. 126, n. 5) who asserted that the Imperial Committee appointed by Leo V in 814 (above, pp. 126 ff.) based its *florilegium* on that of the Council of Hiereia. The passage is interesting inasmuch as it may help to date the *Apologeticus Minor*. It presupposes that the new schismatics were studying carefully the writings of Constantine V and were searching the libraries. This points to the year 814 when the Imperial Committee, of which John the Grammarian was the most prominent member, was compiling a new *florilegium* in support of Iconoclasm (above, pp. 126 ff.).

[2] Above, p. 129.

is its author. He clings to the principle that matters which are settled by an ecumenical council cannot be taken up again, and that no cleric will be entitled to discuss the writings of a layman like Constantine. But he himself shows the Emperor and his advisers a way to overcome this difficulty: a new discussion may be engaged on the basis of new evidence—probably a reference to the Acts of the Council of Hiereia (754)—which the quotations of Constantine may help to uncover. Thus the *Apologeticus Minor* still breathes the spirit of compromise which marked the entire patriarchate of Nicephorus.

3. Another work of Nicephorus is printed by J. B. Pitra, *Spicilegium Solesmense*, i. 302–35, under the title: Ἐπίκρισις ἤτοι διασάφησις τῶν οὐκ εὐαγῶς ἐκληφθεισῶν κατὰ τῶν ἱερῶν εἰκόνων χρήσεων, γενομένη παρὰ τῶν προεστώτων τοῦ ὀρθοῦ τῆς Ἐκκλησίας δόγματος.

In the introduction to this work (which for the sake of brevity will be called here *De Magnete*), Nicephorus declares that the Bible has imposed the duty upon orthodox Christians to examine carefully any doctrine which claims to be inspired. At the present time certain men who are contentious (τὸ φίλερι . . . τοῦ φρονήματος νοσοῦντες) and politically ambitious (πρὸς ἓν μόνον βλέπουσιν ὡς ἂν τιμὴν ἑαυτοῖς ἐκ φιλαρχίας περιποιήσοιντο) are misleading many people. They have published certain quotations, but the compiler, whose identity Nicephorus does not seem to know (ὅστις ποτὲ εἴη ὁ ταῦτα ἀναλεξάμενος), has failed to make available the entire text from which the excerpts were taken. In fact the papyrus document which they issued is the fragment of a fragment, not a quotation (οὐδὲν ἕτερον ἢ περικοπῆς περικοπὴν ἀλλ' οὐ χρῆσιν τὸν ἐκπεμφθέντα χάρτην εἰργάσατο). The excerpts call the work: τοῦ ἁγίου Μακαρίου, ἐκ τῆς τετάρτης βίβλου τῶν Ἀποκριτικῶν (ch. vi). It is only with great difficulty that Nicephorus has secured a very ancient (illuminated) manuscript of the work, and from it he has learned that by arbitrary additions and omissions the compiler has obscured completely the purpose of the work. The quotations were taken from the *Apocriticus* of Macarius Magnes.[1] This work contained the *quaestiones* of a pagan

---

[1] C. Blondel (ed.), *Macarii Magnetis quae supersunt* (Paris, 1876). The quotations discussed by Nicephorus may be found on pp. 199–214. English translation by T. W. Crafer, *The Apocriticus of Macarius Magnes* (London, 1919). On the author see G. Bardy, *D.T.C.* ix. 2, 1456–9 (with full bibliography). See also Giovanni

called Theosthenes and the *solutiones* proposed by Macarius. The pagan had argued a thesis traditional in anti-pagan Christian literature that the Christian doctrine of angels differed from pagan polytheism only in terminology. In the course of the treatise the pagan interlocutor quoted (ch. xxiii) from Matthew xxii. 29–30: 'You are wrong, because you do not understand the Scriptures nor the meaning. For after the resurrection there is no marrying or being married, but they live as angels do in heaven.' Macarius explained (chs. xxviii, xxxi, and xxxiii) that Christ called the resurrected dead 'angels' so that men would imitate the angels in their earthly lives, abstain from marrying, avoid the 'symbols of corruption', and ascend to heaven after their death, but would not form their [the angels'] images.

It was clearly because of the last clause that the passage had been referred to by the Iconoclasts of the ninth century. The passage as quoted equated the resurrected dead with the angels and interpreted the Gospel to mean that true Christian behaviour required the imitation of the angels, not their artistic representation. It will be realized that this interpretation is in entire harmony with the thought of the Council of St. Sophia (815) especially with the argument from holiness (p. 138 above). It is therefore safe to infer that the quotation from Macarius was considered at the time when John the Grammarian and his committee were preparing their iconoclastic *florilegium*, i.e. in the second half of the year of 814.[1] No searching for iconoclastic quotations had been done prior to the appointment of the Committee; and it is difficult to see why a passage so obviously suited to the views of the Committee should have been brought into play at any later time. These considerations date Nicephorus' *De Magnete* in the years 814–15. The wording of the title would indicate that the *De Magnete* is the work not of Nicephorus exclusively but of various orthodox persons. On the other hand it forms part of the *corpus Nicephorianum* and nothing in the style indicates that the Patriarch is not the author. Nicephorus seems

Mercati, 'Per l'apocritico di Macario Magnete. Una tavola dei capi dei libri I, II e III' *Studi e Testi*, xcv (1941), 49–76.

[1] On the 'argument from holiness' see above, p. 138. It is not known whether the Committee actually included the quotations from Macarius in its *florilegium*. It may have rejected them, perhaps under the influence of Nicephorus' *De Magnete*. If it ever appeared in the Committee's *florilegium*, it was eliminated later by the Council of St. Sophia.

to have written it as spokesman for the orthodox section of the hierarchy.

4. Another work by Nicephorus lacks a uniform title in the manuscripts, but it is proposed to call it here *Apologeticus atque Antirrhetici*. It consists (1) of the so-called *Apologeticus Maior* and (2) of three books of *Antirrhetici*. This is the order in which these works appear in all manuscripts,[1] and this is also the order which Banduri had planned for his edition. Cardinal Mai, who was the *editor princeps* of this work, writes in the preface to his edition: 'Editionis autem hunc ordinem tenui, ut primo tres Antirrheticos ponerem, quorum iucundiorem lectionem fore existimavi: deinde maiorem Apologeticum, cuius prolixitas et alta theologiae strues multo maius studiosorum otium requirit.'[2]

This is also Migne's arrangement. It is certainly true that the *Antirrhetici* make easier reading than the *Apologeticus*. None the less it would have been better if the learned cardinal had thought as Krumbacher did sixty years later when he discussed a similar argument in favour of beginning a new edition of Romanos with the famous 'Christmas Song': 'eine Ausgabe ist kein Kaufladen, in dem man die Prachtstücke zur Lockung des Publikums an den sichtbarsten Stellen etabliert.'[3] Mai has rendered his author a poor service, as any reader of his edition or of Migne's reprint will realize: his arrangement has made the development of the argument completely unintelligible and the reader of the three books of *Antirrhetici* marvels what the ultimate purpose of the work may have been.

To A. Ehrhard belongs the credit of having demonstrated the connexion between the two works and discovered the original sequence.[4] The correctness of Ehrhard's view, which is probable *a priori* from the manuscript tradition, will become evident by an analysis first of the *Apologeticus* and then of the three *Antirrhetici*.

[1] *Apologeticus Maior*: *P.G.* c. 533–831; *Antirrhetici*: ibid., 205–533. For the Paris manuscripts see R. P. Blake, *Activité littéraire de Nicéphore I*; for the *Vat. Gr.* 682, the letter of R. Devreesse mentioned ibid., p. 3, n. 5, and his description of the manuscript in the *Codices Vaticani Graeci*.

[2] See the reprint of his conspectus in *P.G.* c. 19 sqq.

[3] Mai's statement: *N.P.B.*, vol. v, p. v. K. Krumbacher, 'Miscellen zu Romanos', *Abhandlungen der Phil.-Hist. Kl. d. Kgl. Bayer. Akademie der Wissenschaften*, xxiv (1909), 109.

[4] A. Ehrhard, 'Nicephorus', Wetzer und Welte, *Kirchenlexikon*, 2nd ed. (Freiburg, 1893), ix. 253 f.; see also his remark in Krumbacher, *Geschichte*, 72.

The manuscript title of the *Apologeticus* seems to be: Λόγος ὑπὲρ τῆς ἀμωμήτου καὶ καθαρᾶς καὶ εἰλικρινοῦς ἡμῶν τῶν Χριστιανῶν πίστεως καὶ κατὰ τῶν δοξαζόντων εἰδώλοις προσκεκυνηκέναι. The contention of the Iconoclasts—'down to the times of Constantine (V Copronymus) we Christians have worshipped idols' (ch. 17, 577D)—forms the central topic of this part.[1]

In the introduction the author declares that he is embarking on a subject of immediate import. The Christian faith was built up from old through the Bible, the fathers, and the councils. Its blissful state was disturbed by false monks and priests who declared that they would sell their immortal souls to revel freely in the imperial palace. There they lived lavishly at the public expense. They polluted their priesthood and our faith, and re-fused to recognize the Seventh Council of Nicaea and its *Defini-tion*: for this reason a synod has rightly deposed them and they are now taking refuge in the palace (ch. 5). This disorderly crowd, this 'sanhedrin of Caiaphas' (ch. 7), consists of the rabble of the city (ch. 9),[2] but the worst is that they try to convert to their impiety 'every person under the Roman sceptre' (ch. 9 *in fine*).

Now the detractors of Christ add to their former impieties the thesis that Christ has assumed an uncircumscribable body. They try to prove it by taking it over ready-made from the inventor (εὑρέτης) of this apostasy [Constantine V Copronymus]. He lived during the first period of impiety, collected (συναγήγερκε) biblical and patristic passages which in reality referred to idols but which he applied to the holy images. He inspired Iconoclasm in its second phase while he himself started out from Arianism and Manicheanism (ch. 10). His *florilegium* is used by the Iconoclasts of our period who cannot add anything of their own. As far as the argument of idol-worship is concerned it can deceive nobody, but the 'Arian impiety', as compiled by him [Constantine], is pre-sented in such a subtle way that Nicephorus deems a discussion advisable (ch. 11).

Constantine V relied on the Arian Eusebius and on certain other patristic passages which he misunderstood. Nicephorus'

---

[1] This thesis of the ninth-century Iconoclasts had already been mentioned in the *Apologeticus Minor*, 8 (*P.G.* c. 844C): . . . ὁμολογοῦσιν εἰδωλολατρῆσαι πρὸ τοῦ παρόντος καιροῦ.

[2] Above, pp. 114 ff.

contemporary Iconoclasts are starting a terrible persecution. They work with threats and promises. The principal bishops and a few holders of less important sees remain firm, but the other bishops as well as the lower ranks of the clergy prefer to join the ranks of the Iconoclasts rather than lose their posts or their possessions (ch. 16). To the author the struggle against the Council of Hiereia (754) seems still to be at its height (ἀκμαῖος ἔτι). The assertion of that Council had been that down to the time of Constantine V 'we Christians have worshipped idols'.[1] All the rest of the *Apologeticus* is devoted to the refutation of this thesis taken in its most literal sense. First of all, the absurdity of the accusation is demonstrated by examining more closely its implications (18–33). In a second part (34–64), the Prophets are discussed in chronological order from the point of view of idol-worship: they all fought against idols, and to claim that the latter are still worshipped is to deny the Prophets and their work. In the third part (65–73), the author shows that images have been in use from the oldest times. Christ abolished the idols, and if the Iconoclasts are talking of idol-worship in our days, they imply that Christ either did not know how to destroy them, or did not wish or was unable to do so. All three alternatives are then duly refuted by the Patriarch. Thus, Nicephorus concludes, even from this angle, Iconoclasm is an attack on Christ because it denies His conquest of the idols.

To the *Apologeticus* Nicephorus appends a *florilegium* from the Bible and the Fathers of the Church which is designed to urge the Christian to rely on faith and not to follow the Iconoclasts into subtleties and questioning (*P.G.* c. 811–32).

The title of the *Antirrhetici* is: Ἀντίρρησις καὶ ἀνατροπὴ τῶν παρὰ τοῦ δυσσεβοῦς Μαμωνᾶ κατὰ τῆς σωτηρίου τοῦ Θεοῦ Λόγου σαρκώσεως ἀμαθῶς καὶ ἀθέως κενολογηθέντων ληρημάτων; and the *First Antirrheticus* is called Ἀντίρρησις πρώτη. It begins as follows:

Thus we have finished and completed the labour of our previous inquiries, for with the help of the Holy Scriptures our previous inquiry has shown the Christian religion to be free from the impiety of

---

[1] *Apologeticus Maior*, 33 (*P.G.* c. 613c): ... πρὸς δὲ καὶ Χριστιανῶν καταρραψῳδῆσαι ὅτι δὴ ὡς θεοῖς ταῖς ἱεραῖς προσῆλθον εἰκόσιν. This is the way in which the Council of St. Sophia (815) formulated the doctrine of the Council of Hiereia; see the *Definition* of St. Sophia, frg. 3 Ostrogorsky (= frg. 4 Alexander).

the idols. . . . Let us now strip and proceed to the second arena of the impiety, for, as we have said before, the enemies of truth are engaged on a twofold struggle against piety, etc. (*Prooemium.*)

Since their first argument has failed, the Iconoclasts now declare Christ to be ἀπερίγραπτος (uncircumscribable) (ch. 1). The iconoclastic leaders found this argument in the writings of Constantine [V Copronymus] whom they worship with divine honours (ch. 2). It would indeed be superfluous, even ridiculous, to refute a doctrine so obviously erroneous and self-contradictory, were it not for the fact that the followers of Constantine had already misled many of the simpler folk. First of all, Nicephorus proposes to examine the writings of Constantine: 'for it will be evident that once we overthrow the contrivances of him who initiated them, the evil devices of those who depended upon him for their initiation will be destroyed together with them' (ch. 7). He will argue against the inventor together with the followers (ch. 8). The entire remainder of this first *Antirrheticus* is devoted indeed to the christological argument against images of Christ as contained in one of the writings of Constantine; the latter is taken up sentence by sentence and refutation is attempted.

The structure of the *Second Antirrheticus*, entitled Ἀντίρρησις δευτέρα, is more complex. The *First Antirrheticus* had dealt with the first πεῦσις or inquiry of Constantine. In the beginning of the *Second Antirrheticus*, Nicephorus announces his intention to deal with the second πεῦσις. The first three chapters and part of the fourth (329–41A) simply continue the discussion of Constantine's christological argument. Chapters 4–10 deal with Constantine's ideas about images of the Virgin Mary, of the other Saints, and of angels, with a lengthy appendix discussing the difference between the terms γραπτός and περίγραπτος (chs. 11–19).

The *Third Antirrheticus*, entitled Ἀντίρρησις τρίτη, declares its main objective at the beginning: it is to answer the Iconoclasts' question what the scriptural basis for the painting and worship of images is. To answer this question Nicephorus first lists the reasons and authorities which support the images of Christ and their worship and formulates various iconoclastic theses in order to refute them (chs. 1–48). He then proceeds to the images of the Virgin Mary, of the Saints, and of the Angels (chs. 49–61). The last part of the work (chs. 62–84) is perhaps, of all of Nicephorus' works, the most interesting for the student of Byzantine history and historiography. It begins (chs. 62–63) with the data on the social composition of the iconoclastic party which have been analysed above.[1] The poverty of its members and their tendency to make the price-level the standard for their judgement on theological issues leads him to discuss the alleged prosperity of the reign of Constantine V (chs. 64–69). According to Nicephorus the reign of Constantine was not one of prosperity but of distress. Swineherds, shepherds, and cowherds were drafted into the army and used not against the foreign enemy but against the Iconophiles. Churches were defiled, monasteries turned into military barracks or even sold. Historians contemporary with the events have recorded, and eyewitnesses are still alive to tell of, the natural catastrophies that occurred during his reign, especially of plague (A.D. 747), earthquakes, and famine. During one famine, a measure of wheat sold for almost fifty gold pieces. When Irene expelled Constantine's iconoclastic soldiers from the city, most of them joined the ranks of the Manicheans, some of them were arrested and executed (ch. 68). Contrary to iconoclastic claims, Constantine was not given a long and happy life or victories over the barbarians. He died of a long and most painful disease, at the age of only fifty-seven years. His great 'victories' were all like the defeat at Anchialos where, according to the text, almost the entire Byzantine army was annihilated by the Bulgarians. Constantine's military successes were due exclusively to civil wars among the Bulgarians and Arabs (ch. 72). Compared with an Alexander, an Augustus, a Timotheus, or with the kings of the Old Testament, Constantine V was insignificant. The cheapness of food was achieved by the ruthless exaction of taxes from the rural population. Nicephorus says that he himself saw people hanged on high trees under Constantine V because they could not pay their taxes. While earlier emperors had strengthened the Church, Constantine waged war upon it and especially upon the monks. Nicephorus ends this part of his work with the account of the Jew Tessarakontapechys and the Khalif Yazid (ch. 84).[2] Unfortunately, the concluding *florilegium* of patristic texts was not printed by Mai together with the work which it was meant to accompany, but as a separate treatise by Pitra.[3] The quotations contained in the *florilegium* are arranged to illustrate the patristic

---

[1] Above, pp. 114 ff.   [2] Above, pp. 6 ff.
[3] *Spicilegium Solesmense*, i. 336–70.

teaching of the circumscript character of Jesus Christ, of His human nature and of His resurrected body.

This analysis makes it clear that the *Apologeticus Maior* and the two first *Antirrhetici* belong together. Ch. 10 of the *Apologeticus Maior* clearly foreshadows a discussion first of the accusation of idol-worship, and secondly of the christological argument as set forth by Constantine Copronymus. Furthermore, the introductory clauses of the *First Antirrheticus*, rendered in translation above, clearly refer back to the *Apologeticus Maior*. The plan of the work, therefore, is the following: the *Apologeticus Maior* was to deal with the problem of idol-worship while the two first *Antirrhetici* took up Constantine's christological argument. The first *Antirrheticus* was concerned with the first πεῦσις of his work on the image of Christ, and the second *Antirrheticus* with the second πεῦσις and with Constantine's views on images of the Virgin Mary and the Saints.

The connexion of the *Third Antirrheticus* with the *Apologeticus Maior* has been doubted. Banduri remarked about it: 'Antirrheticus non eodem tempore editus, quo reliqui; multa enim continet, in superioribus jam exposita.'[1] Ehrhard, who did not mention Banduri's view, took the *Third Antirrheticus* to form an organic whole with the *Apologeticus Maior* and the first two *Antirrhetici*.[2] Neither of these two authors gave specific reasons for this opinion. An attempt to supply them must be made.

It may be granted to Banduri, first of all, that the programmatic chapter 10 of the *Apologeticus Maior* does not mention the material covered by the *Third Antirrheticus*, i.e. the iconoclastic thesis that there was no scriptural authority for the painting and worship of images. Secondly, if the *Third Antirrheticus* is considered to form a whole with the *Apologeticus Maior* and the first two *Antirrhetici*, the entire work would contain a number of repetitions to which attention has been called by Banduri, in particular the long passages on the social structure of the iconoclastic party.

Against Banduri it can be said, however, that the *prooemium* of the *Third Antirrheticus* clearly assumes that the author has previously refuted certain theses of the Iconoclasts: it cannot possibly be an independent work. Secondly, repetitions, such as the passages on the social composition of the iconoclastic party,

[1] *P.G.* c. 25–26.　　　　　　　　　[2] *Kirchenlexikon*, ix. 253.

permit no other inference, except that this work did not receive a final polish. After all, the central topic of the *Third Antirrheticus* is the logical supplement to those dealt with in the other parts in the work. Ehrhard himself admits that it proceeds 'ohne ersichtliche Ordnung'. One may well suppose that after the completion of his *Apologeticus* and the two *Antirrhetici* it occurred to Nicephorus as an afterthought to discuss the scriptural evidence for image-worship. But some unforeseen event (the murder of Leo V ?) made him lay aside the work for more urgent tasks before it was put into final shape and before he had inserted this new topic in the programmatic chapter 10 of the *Apologeticus Maior*.[1]

5. Next in time is a work which in the manuscripts bears the title: Ἀντίρρησις καὶ ἀνασκευὴ τῶν Ἐυσεβίου καὶ Ἐπιφανίδου λόγων τῶν κατὰ τῆς τοῦ Σωτῆρος ἡμῶν Χριστοῦ σαρκώσεως ληρωδηθέντων. Neither Pitra nor Ehrhard has made it clear that this title covers two works printed separately by Pitra: (1) *Eusebii Caesariensis Refutatio, Spicilegium Solesmense*, i. 371–503, and (2) *Pseudo-Epiphanii sive Epiphanidis Confutatio*, ibid. iv. 292–380. They follow each other in this order in all the manuscripts in which they appear. Proof for the connexion between the two parts of the work will be found in the following analysis. The work will be referred to as *Contra Eusebium et Epiphanidem*.

In the *prooemium* Nicephorus remarks that in an earlier writing (ἐν τοῖς πρόσθεν ἡμῖν εἰρημένοις)[2] he had confuted the 'counter-theses' (ἀντιθέσεις) of Mamonas, i.e. of Constantine Copronymus, and of his followers. In the present work he proceeds to examine the quotations (χρήσεις) adduced by Mamonas. There follows a short inquiry into the motives and manifestations of Constantine's Iconoclasm (chs. ii to vi).[3] Chapter vii contains the

---

[1] There is one passage in the *Third Antirrheticus* which might be helpful to date it. In ch. 67 (*P.G.* c. 500C) when speaking of a serious famine under Constantine Copronymus Nicephorus remarks that 'it was not surpassed by the one which is beginning now' (τοῦ νῦν ἐντεῦθεν ἐναρξαμένου [λιμοῦ]). Unfortunately I have been unable to discover any other source for a famine under Leo V or Michael II. Probably it did not become very serious.

[2] Pitra seems to have considered this work a part of the *Antirrhetici* and accordingly published it under the Latin title *Sancti Nicephori Antirrheticus Liber Quartus* (Pitra, *Spicilegium Solesmense*, i. 371). Though there seems to be no manuscript authority for such a title, the underlying idea is not implausible.

[3] In ch. iii (p. 375) Nicephorus retells the story of the Jew Tessarakontapechys and the Khalif and mentions that he has dealt with it more elaborately in another work (ὧν πέρι ἐν φθάσασι πλατύτερον εἴρηται). He means the *Third Antirrheticus*, 84 (*P.G.* c. 528C–532), but it is interesting that in the later work a new feature of the

programme of the present work; of those who inspired the impious dogma he proposes to discuss

    (a) Eusebius of Caesarea,

    (b) Epiphanides,

    (c) Epiphanius, Archbishop of Cyprus, whom the adherents of Constantine V call their own,

    (d) certain further advocates of this doctrine, such as Leontius, Theodotus, Basil, and others who are referred to by the Iconoclasts of the present generation.

After preparing the reader for Eusebius' Arianism by selections from Eusebius' other works (ch. ix. 387–91), Nicephorus continues with an elaborate and detailed refutation of Eusebius' *Letter to the Empress Constantia* (chs. x–lxii). This refutation cannot be analysed here, although it shows Nicephorus' theological learning and polemical skill to better advantage than some of his other works, especially in his discussion of Eusebius' doctrine of the Incarnation. At the end of ch. lxii (p. 472) Nicephorus remarks: 'It may be time to turn to those other quotations which Mamonas produced and which belong to our God-inspired men so that we may see whether they are consonant with his teachers and that hence we may marvel at the understanding of him who collected them.' The first passage which Mamonas quoted in his *florilegium* immediately following the quotation from Eusebius (ἐπεὶ καὶ ἄγχιστά που παρ' αὐτῷ τοῖς παρ' 'Ευσεβίου τέτακται λόγοις) is from Gregory of Nyssa's *Funeral Oration on Basil* which is duly discussed (ch. lxiii).[1] After this Nicephorus returns to Eusebius[2] and demonstrates that Eusebius' doctrine of the Incarnation, as expressed in the *Letter to the Empress Constantia*, was not shared by those same fathers whom Constantine V himself had quoted in his *florilegium* (see Pitra, 477 and 480): St. John Chrysostom, Cyril of Alexandria, Athanasius, Gregory Nazianzen, Gregory of Nyssa, Amphilochius of Iconium, Methodius

---

story makes its first appearance: here Yazid is critically ill (ἐσχάτῃ νόσῳ τηνικαῦτα βληθέντα) when he comes under Jewish influence.

[1] Here Nicephorus mentions in passing (p. 476) that Constantine V's *florilegium* contained quotations from Athanasius' *Against the Idols*, Cyril's *Commentaries on the Prophet Isaiah*, and Nilus' *Letter to Olympiodorus*.

[2] The arrangement of the treatise is not clear to me at this point. Why does the author, after announcing his intention to discuss other quotations (p. 472) and actually beginning with one from Gregory of Nyssa (ch. lxiii), return to Eusebius (ch. lxiv)?

Myrensis.[1] Nicephorus appends some further authorities on orthodox christology (pp. 486–90) and defines his own views (pp.
490 f.). Next he takes up (chs. lxxx–lxxxvi. 491–503) another
quotation by Constantine: Eusebius' famous account of the
Image at Paneas (*Hist. Eccl.* vii. 18).[2] Nicephorus then announces
his intention to discuss further quotations presented (παράγειν) by
his opponents:

And thus let the views of Eusebius be refuted (πεφωράσθω). And
now that, with the sword of the Word and with the power of the
Spirit, we have cut the head off the fierce monster, we ought henceforth to put an end to our speech, even though it [the monster] may
skip along with its tail (παρασκαίρῃ τὸ οὐραῖον) feebly and weakly. Yet
lest it coil and roll itself up and seem to be somehow alive and create
difficulties for those who preside over the correct views, we shall select
some brief passages from the remaining unholy and monstrous compilations (συντάγματα) and shall triumph over their impious and vain
content. For they adduce even other quotations which they have
forged, for of some of them even unto this day the full and genuine
manuscripts have not ever been found even though those who preside
over the heresy have made a long search. . . .[3]

This difficult passage needs careful interpretation. The 'monster'

[1] Pitra, *Spicilegium Solesmense*, i. 477–86. Ostrogorsky's (*Studien*, pp. 13 f., n. 4)
data on the contents of Constantine's *florilegium* are not complete. It seems to have
contained a passage from Amphilochius of Iconium. Amphilochius is specifically
mentioned (p. 485) before Nicephorus makes the transition (p. 486) to authorities
not referred to by Constantine. Ostrogorsky also forgot Methodius Myrensis (p.
485).

[2] Constantine's reference to this passage seems to have been partly quotation,
partly paraphrase. Nicephorus (p. 492) notes that Constantine referred to the
Image of Paneas as a χαλκοῦν ζῴδιον, a bronze idol, where Eusebius himself spoke
of an ἀνδρίας, a statue. He adds that Constantine 'cut out' (ὑποτέμνειν) the end of
the quotation because it did not suit his purpose. Nicephorus' defence of the Image
of Paneas is interesting from several points of view. In the first place, he, unlike
some modern apologists, is not embarrassed by the admission that the Church had
taken over a pagan practice. Indeed he says quite categorically (p. 499): 'Among
the Christians even their (the pagans') shrines have been transformed into sacred
buildings, and in general things pagan (τὰ τῶν ἔξωθεν) are transferred and adapted
to our purposes, and things profane and impure have been changed into things
pure.' Secondly, to support this thesis he quotes at length from the Greek Acta of
St. Gregory the Illuminator, the Apostle of Armenia, who made this principle the
foundation of his missionary policy. This reference, incidentally, supplies a *terminus
ante quem* for the Greek text of Agathangelus (ed. P. de Lagarde, *Agathangelus*,
Abhandlungen der kgl. Gesellschaft der Wissenschaften zu Göttingen, xxv, 1899).

[3] Pitra, i. 503. The passage on the search for full manuscripts is probably a
reference to the activities of John the Grammarian's committee (above, pp. 126–
8).

of which it speaks is obviously Iconoclasm. The 'head' which has been 'cut off' seems to be either Constantine's entire *florilegium* which Nicephorus has refuted in the first part of the treatise or the quotation from Eusebius' *Letter to Constantia* contained therein. The further quotations which Nicephorus plans to collect are specifically said to come from other 'compilations' (συντάγματα), not from Constantine's *florilegium*. The identity of these 'compilations' and their author (or authors) are not revealed, but it is noteworthy that while the iconoclastic quotations discussed by Nicephorus in the first part of his treatise are all explicitly attributed to Constantine V's *florilegium*,[1] the passages now to be discussed are said to be 'adduced' not by one person but by several.[2]

The *Eusebii Caesariensis Refutatio*, as printed by Pitra, breaks off at this point, but it is clear from its last paragraph quoted above that the work does not end here. The *incipit* of the *Pseudo-Epiphanii sive Epiphanidis Confutatio* states expressly that it is the continuation : τῶν οὐ[3] παρενηνεγμένων ἡ μὲν ἐπιγραφὴ τὸν θεοφόρον ἡμῖν Ἐπιφάνιον, τὸν τῆς Κυπρίων ἐκκλησίας καθηγησάμενον, ἐμφανίζει . . . . Τὰ οὐ παρενηνεγμένα : those are clearly the other quotations which Nicephorus had promised to refute at the end of his *Eusebii Caesariensis Refutatio*.

In the first chapters (i–iii) Nicephorus asserts his thesis that the works quoted by the Iconoclasts as taken from Epiphanius are not genuine. He reports statements made in open synod by the Archbishop of Side (in Pamphylia) who was still alive at the time of Nicephorus' writings.[4] He had said that he had seen as a young

---

[1] Gregory of Nyssa: παρ' αὐτῷ (i, 472); Athanasius, Cyril, Nilus: ἐν πᾶσιν αὐτοῦ τοῖς . . . συγγράμμασιν (p. 476); see also p. 477 (τῶν Πατέρων αἱ φωναὶ οὓς συνηγόρους Εὐσεβίου ὁ Μαμωνᾶς συνεκάλεσε); Eusebius, *Hist. Eccl.* vii. 18: παράγει καὶ αὖθις τὸν Εὐσέβιον (p. 491).

[2] Epiphanius' Will: προτείνουσι (iv, p. 295); Gregory Nazianzen: παράγουσι (iv. 366); Basil of Seleucia: προάγουσι (iv. 369); Leontios: προκομίζουσιν (iv. 370); Amphilochius of Iconium and Theodotus of Galatia παραγάγοιεν (iv. 372). The only exception is Nilus' *Letter to Olympiodorus* where Nicephorus accuses one individual of having tampered with the wording: οὗτος τοίνυν τὰ μὲν ἐρωτηθέντα παρὰ τοῦ Ὀλυμπιοδώρου ὡς τοῦ Νείλου φωνὰς κακούργως παρέθετο, αὐτὴν δὲ τὴν γνώμην τοῦ Νείλου ἀπεκρύψατο (iv. 369), but there the subject is 'the forger' (ὁ νενοθευκώς, iv. 368).

[3] This is the reading of the *Paris. Gr.* 911, saec. x. The *Paris. Gr.* 1250, saec. xiii (xiv?) reads οὖν.

[4] A scholiast gives the Archbishop's name as Thomas, see Pitra, *Spicilegium Solesmense*, iv. 299 note and 301, note 2.

man a manuscript at Nacoleia in Phrygia in which a certain
'Ἐπιφανίδης had originally been named as the author and where
subsequently the letter δ had been erased. Nicephorus decides
henceforth to call the author of the quotations Epiphanides.[1]

Of the writings quoted, he discusses first of all the 'Will'
(ch. iv), secondly the 'dogmatic Epistle' (ch. v), thirdly a treatise
entitled: Κατὰ τῶν ἐπιτηδευόντων ποιεῖν εἰδωλικῷ θεσμῷ εἰκόνας
εἰς ἀφομοίωσιν τοῦ Χριστοῦ καὶ τῆς Θεοτόκου καὶ τῶν μαρτύρων,
ἔτι δὲ καὶ ἀγγέλων καὶ προφήτων (chs. vi.–xiii), and finally an
'Ἐπιστολὴ πρὸς Θεοδόσιον τὸν βασιλέα (chs. xiv–xxiii). As in the
case of Eusebius' *Letter to the Empress Constantia*, the details of Nicephorus' arguments against the quotations from Epiphanius cannot
be followed here Nicephorus, takes up in order quotations from
Gregory Nazianzen's "Ἔπη (ch. xxiv), from Nilus' *Letter to Olympiodorus* (ch. xxv), from unidentified works of Basil of Seleucia (ch.
xxvi), and of 'a certain Leontius' (ch. xxvii), from Amphilochius
of Iconium's *Enkomion on St. Basil*, and from a work of Theodotus of
Galatia (ch. xxviii). At the end of his treatise the Patriarch summarizes his arguments against the quotations attributed to Epiphanius and remarks that the person who collected the quotations
(ὁ συναγηγερκὼς τὰς χρήσεις) has found that his authorities contradict each other (ch. xxix, p. 375). The treatise concludes with a
small collection of heretical passages meant to demonstrate the
ignoble ancestry of the iconoclastic views.

It remains to define the purpose of the *Contra Eusebium et
Epiphanidem*. The Patriarch states at least part of his programme
at the beginning: it is to supplement his refutation of Constantine's ἀντιθέσεις as contained in the *Apologeticus atque Antirrhetici* by a criticism of Constantine's patristic *florilegium*. This
programme is completed at the end of the first part of the treatise.

---

[1] The authenticity of the passages attributed to Epiphanius is debated by
modern scholarship, see the bibliographical data *B. Z.* xxxi (1931) 389. The question
needs separate treatment. Here I note only (1) that Lequien (*P.G.* xciv. 1305, n. 14)
suggested that Philoxenus of Hierapolis was the author of the *Letter to Theodosius*,
(2) that the author of the Νουθεσία (cf. above, p. 11) considered the writings
attributed to Epiphanius to be fabrications of the Ναυατιανοί (ed. Melioranski,
p. xxvii), and (3) that the *Epistula ad Theophilum*, ed. L. Duchesne, *Roma e l'Oriente*,
v (1912–13), 354 f. names an author Epiphanides of Cyprus who was a Docete and
was exiled by Theodosius the Great. Lequien's suggestion agrees with what
Theodorus Lector tells us (above, p. 45, n. 1) about Philoxenus' Iconoclasm but
lacks evidence. The Novatianist hypothesis, which so far as I know has escaped the
attention of modern scholarship, perhaps deserves some consideration; it is too
surprising and specific to be ignored.

At this point, in the passage translated above (p. 176), the author enlarges the scope of his enterprise by including a refutation of select quotations contained in other (and unidentified) 'compilations' which he attributes not to one but several persons. Now all the quotations here discussed occur in the *florilegium* appended by the Council of St. Sophia to its *Definition*.[1] The 'compilations' which form the targets of Nicephorus' attack in the second part of the treatise are, therefore, either the *florilegium* of the Council of St. Sophia, or the *florilegium* compiled by the Imperial Committee on which the conciliar *florilegium* was based, or both.[2]

6. Another *opusculum* of Nicephorus is entitled: Κατὰ τῶν ἀσεβῶς τετολμηκότων εἴδωλον ὀνομάσαι τὸ θεῖον ὁμοίωμα, καὶ ὅτι δεῖ ἔπεσθαι ταῖς πατρικαῖς παραδόσεσιν, ἔτι δὲ καὶ τί ἔστι γραπτὸν καὶ περιγραπτόν, καὶ πῶς νοητέον τό Οὐ ποιήσεις πᾶν ὁμοίωμα, ἀνασκευή τε τῶν δυσσεβῶς εἰσληφθεισῶν πατρικῶν ῥήσεων παρὰ τῶν τῆς Ἐκκλησίας ἐχθρῶν. The *incipit* makes it clear that it is identical with a work which in the *Parisinus* 911 and the *Coislinianus* 93 appears under the title of Πρόλογος καὶ ἀνατροπὴ τῶν δι' ἐναντίας χρήσεων.[3] For the sake of brevity it will be referred to as the *Adversus Iconomachos*.

In the introduction the author contrasts orthodoxy with apostasy. He declares that the Enemy has attacked the Church in various ways, and he (Nicephorus) is going to refute this attack briefly as he has already done so more elaborately in another work. This he will do for the benefit of inquirers (τῶν αἰτησάντων χάριν, p. 238). The first iconoclastic accusation, that of idol-worship the Iconoclasts have withdrawn since they had become the laughing-stock even of children (i). Secondly, they have claimed that Christ is uncircumscribable (ἀπερίγραπτος) and unpaintable (ἄγραπτος), and by doing so they reveal themselves to be docetists (ii). Thirdly, they have referred to the second commandment, but they ignore what kind of likenesses Moses forbids, and that this prohibition is addressed to the Jews (iii).

---

[1] Of the quotations discussed in the second part of the *Contra Eusebium et Epiphanidem*, the following did not appear in the *florilegium* of the Council of Hiereia: Epiphanius (except for the *Will*); Nilus' *Letter to Olympiodorus*; Basil of Seleucia; Leontius.

[2] There are clear references in the *Contra Eusebium et Epiphanidem* to the Iconoclasts of the ninth century, see Pitra, i. 381: οἱ αὐτοῦ νῦν φοιτηταὶ γνήσιοι; i. 393: οἱ νῦν αὐτοῦ ἀναφανέντες φοιτηταί.

[3] Ed. J. B. Pitra, *Spicilegium Solesmense*, iv. 233–91. See Banduri, *P.G.* c. 31 and Blake, 'Activité littéraire', *Byzantion* xiv (1939) *e*, 9, 14.

Christians are no longer under the sway of the Law, but under the rule of grace since they have seen Christ (iv). Whereas the Law forbids images τῶν περικοσμίων, God Himself ordered the making of images τῶν ὑπερκοσμίων by ordering the golden cherubim made (v). They ask for written texts in favour of image-worship, but forget that nobody ever decrees what is already the universal custom (vi). Their question with regard to scriptural evidence is hardly worth a refutation (vii). Christians need no formal decrees or written evidence (viii). Next they used, first of all, certain Manichean and Arian quotations, but those even some of their own party rejected. Secondly, they availed themselves of quotations taken from the Church Fathers. 'Most of those we have examined more elaborately in another place and separately and have revealed more clearly the absurd deception, and we consider it superfluous and redundant to refute them in this work. It is time now to begin to speak, provided that God stretches out his hand, about certain other quotations which remain, and to demonstrate the meanness and falseness of those persons who in their villainy collected them' (ix). The first of these quotations is from John Chrysostom, which is scrutinized and found to be orthodox,[1] and the second to be examined is from Methodius 'of Myroi or Patara'.[2]

The *Adversus Iconomachos* is clearly a work written to satisfy certain iconophile inquirers. It is simple, brief, and direct, and perhaps the most readable of the Patriarch's theological works. Since it discusses two quotations from John Chrysostom and Methodius of which Nicephorus says that they formed part of Constantine V's *florilegium*,[3] this little treatise clearly popularizes and supplements the *Contra Eusebium et Epiphanidem*.

7. Mention should be made here of a lost work by Nicephorus, the title, nature, content, and date of which are most uncertain. The historian Genesius cites a dictum of the Patriarch Nicephorus about the Emperor Leo V: 'The Roman Empire has lost a great though impious provider.'[4] This saying occurs neither in the published works of the Patriarch, nor in the *Refutatio et*

---

[1] Chs. x–xviii. See *In Matthaeum Homilia*, xlix (*P.G.* lviii. 501).

[2] Chs. xix–xxiv. See *De Resurrectione*, ed. G. N. Bonwetsch (Leipzig, 1917), p. 257.

[3] *Contra Eusebium*, chs. lxi (pp. 477–9) and lxvi (pp. 481 f. and 485), see above, p. 174.

[4] Genesius, i. 17 (*P.G.* cix. 1009C): ἡ πολιτεία ʿΡωμαίων κἂν δυσσεβῆ ἀλλ' οὖν γε μέγαν προμηθευτὴν ἀπολώλεκεν.

Eversio. Indeed it might be considered an oral pronouncement made under the impact of the news of Leo's murder. However, the Chronicle of Georgios Monachos, which quotes elaborately and at length from the *First Antirrheticus* and from the *Vita Nicephori*, contains a long citation explicitly attributed to Nicephorus and dealing with the descent of Leo V and with his iconoclastic views.[1] Again, this quotation does not derive from any of the preserved works of Nicephorus, published or unpublished. On the other hand, this long passage which betrays both in content and in style unmistakably the characteristics of the author must derive from a carefully prepared work, perhaps from a homily. If the attribution of the quotations from Genesius and Georgius Monachos to the same lost work of Nicephorus is correct,[2] it must have been written after the murder of Leo V and combined an appraisal of this Emperor as a competent ruler with a passionate and venomous condemnation and refutation of his iconoclastic leanings.

8. The last of the preserved works of Nicephorus is the *Ἔλεγχος καὶ ἀνατροπὴ τοῦ ἀθέσμου καὶ ἀορίστου καὶ ὄντως ψευδωνύμου ὅρου τοῦ ἐκτεθέντος παρὰ τῶν ἀποστατησάντων τῆς καθολικῆς καὶ ἀποστολικῆς ἐκκλησίας καὶ ἀλλοτρίῳ προσθεμένων φρονήματι ἐπ' ἀναιρέσει τῆς τοῦ Θεοῦ Λόγου σωτηρίου οἰκονομίας.* This will be referred to as the *Refutatio et Eversio*. It is unpublished, except for the quotations from the *Horos* of 815 which it undertakes to refute and for certain minor passages. It is contained in two Paris manuscripts, namely (1) the *Parisinus Graecus* 1250, saec. xiii (xiv?) and (2) the *Coislinianus* 93, saec. xv (xii?).[3]

---

[1] Georgios Monachos, ed. de Boor, ii. 780. 15 ff. See the *testimonia* collected by de Boor for quotations from the published works of Nicephorus, and G. Moravcsik, *Byzantino-Turcica*, i (Budapest, 1942), 146–8. The precise extent of the quotation is difficult to define, but stylistic and other criteria would indicate that it goes to the end of the chapter on Leo V (p. 792). The work from which it was taken seems to have contained an account of Leo's murder which was used by Ignatius Diaconus (*Vita Nicephori*, 207. 30 ff., cf. Georgios Monachos, 788. 19 ff.). I have used the fragment (pp. 126 f., n. 7 above) in the discussion of Leo's Armenian descent.

[2] Both fragments deal with Leo V. The citation from Genesius clearly dates after 820. The excerpts in Georgios Monachos do not yield a precise date, but it is most unlikely that Nicephorus could have penned so venomous an attack during the lifetime of Leo V. Note also that Ignatius Diaconus inserts the quotation from this work (n. 1 above) immediately after his account of Leo's murder. It remains puzzling, however, how Nicephorus could have inserted a sentence as favourable to Leo V as that reported by Genesius in a framework so hostile to this Emperor.

[3] On the manuscript tradition see R. P. Blake, 'Note sur l'activité littéraire de

The treatise clearly falls into two parts. The first part (fols. 173–235) contains the refutation of the *Horos* of 815 and the second part is a criticism of the conciliar *florilegium*. Whereas the character of Part I has been known ever since Serruys's discovery, that of Part II has been ignored, except perhaps by Banduri. Yet there can be no doubt that it contains the *florilegium* of the Council of St. Sophia. The same 'they' who issued the *Horos* of 815 are responsible for the χρήσεις. These quotations are arranged in the same order in which they appeared in the Acts of the Council, and none of the iconoclastic quotations are omitted.[1]

Nicephorus' system of refuting the heretical *florilegium* is as follows. Wherever possible he undertakes to prove that the quotations do not actually belong to the Church Father to whom they are attributed. This proof is conducted in such a way that the iconoclastic quotation is confronted with undoubtedly genuine works of the Father in question and found to be inconsistent with this second text. Where this method of rebuttal is impossible, Nicephorus shows that although the quotation is genuine, it is not really directed against image-worship. This method makes the second part of the *Refutatio et Eversio* a long-drawn-out duel of quotations.

In this last great work of his the Patriarch Nicephorus draws on a wealth of sources. Foremost among them is Tarasius' *Refutation* of the *Definition* of Hiereia which is explicitly referred to only once or twice, but which seems to have been in Nicephorus' mind throughout the treatise.[2] He also incorporated into it excerpts from his earlier works, notably part of a *florilegium* originally appended to his *Third Antirrheticus* and part of his *Contra Eusebium et Epiphanidem*. Like his other theological works, the *Refutatio et Eversio* could hardly be addressed to the laity. Its

---

Nicéphore Ier Patriarche de Constantinople', *Byzantion*, xiv (1939), 1–15. I plan to edit the treatise as soon as possible. For the present a somewhat fuller analysis of its contents than that furnished by Banduri (reprinted in *P.G.* c. 31–35) must suffice. See Appendix.

[1] Fol. 236, verso, line 20, Nicephorus asks: πῶς οὖν καὶ πόθεν τῶν συμπεφορημένων τῶς ματαιοπονίας λόγων κατάρχονται οἱ τὸ πρὶν εἴδωλα κατονομάσαι τὰ ἅγια φεισάμενοι; and then remarks that the following quotation from the Apostolic Constitutions is the 'very first' (πρωτίστη). At the end of his discussion of each iconoclastic quotation, he usually remarks that there follows 'the next'. Cf. Nicephorus' remarks introducing each quotation, published in parentheses in my edition of the *Horos* of St. Sophia, *Dumbarton Oaks Papers*, vii (1953), 60–65.

[2] Above, pp. 20 f.

wealth of religious and patristic learning and its wearisome confrontation of iconoclastic and orthodox quotations could have had little appeal even to Byzantine laymen. In another work Nicephorus says himself that it is addressed to the clergy,[1] and one may suppose the same holds true for the present treatise. Only one of the works, the *Adversus Iconomachos*, professes to be written as an answer to a question from outsiders.[2] It is known from the *Letters* and *Catecheseis* of Theodore of Studios that the orthodox side never gave up the hope for the restoration of image-worship and for an orthodox council. Here we have an elaborate refutation of Iconoclasm from the pen of the orthodox Patriarch of Constantinople. What is more natural than to assume that with it Nicephorus meant to lay the foundation for the work of the future orthodox council which must have been the centre of all his hopes and thoughts?

3. *Nicephorus' Theological Works—Chronology*

The order in which Nicephorus' works were analysed in the preceding section was chronological. This sequence will now have to be justified. Absolute dates can be assigned only to the Epistle to Pope Leo III and to three of Nicephorus' theological works, and these must form the basis of any chronological system. The Epistle was written in 811/12. The next work to be composed was the *Apologeticus Minor*. Its date is determined not only by the remarks on the Trullanum (p. 164 above), but also by internal criteria. A new outbreak of Iconoclasm is envisaged, but the Emperor has not yet come out openly for the iconoclastic side and is still called εὐσεβής. This makes it certain that the *Apologeticus Minor* was written between 813 and 815, probably rather close to the latter date.

To the year 814 belongs the *De Magnete* since the point of the quotation here discussed is entirely in harmony with the views of the Imperial Committee which was preparing a patristic *florilegium* in favour of Iconoclasm in that year.[3]

---

[1] *Apologeticus Maior*, ch. 26 (*P.G.* c. 600C): ἐπειδὴ δὲ πρὸς ἱερεῖς ἡμῖν οὐκ οἶδα ὧντινων καὶ ὁποίους ὁ λόγος . . . .

[2] Pitra, *Spicilegium Solesmense*, iv. 238: περὶ ὧν καὶ ἐν ἑτέροις ἤδη πλατύτερον ἡμῖν διαπεπραγμάτευται, οὐδὲν δὲ χεῖρον ὀλίγα ἄττα καὶ ἐνταῦθα περὶ τῶν αὐτῶν διειληφέναι συνοπτικώτερον τῶν αἰτησάντων χάριν.

[3] Above, pp. 138 f., cf. 127 f.

The lost work (homily?) from which Georgios Monachos and Genesius have preserved fragments was almost certainly written after the murder of Leo V in 820.[1]

The same is true of the *Refutatio et Eversio*. At the beginning there is an allusion to the murder of Leo V: εἰς οἷον τέλος τὰ ἐπικεχειρημένα ἐκβέβηκε τὸ θυσιαστήριον μέγα κεκράξεται ὃ καὶ ζῶν κακῶς καθαιρῶν ἐβεβήλου καὶ ἀναιρούμενος ἐνδίκως τῷ λύθρῳ τῶν ἐναγῶν αἱμάτων πλέον ἔχρανε καὶ κατεμόλυνεν, ὄντως τὰ ἐπίχειρα τῆς εἰς Χριστὸν ὕβρεως δεξάμενος ὁ ἀλιτήριος.[2] Nicephorus clearly means the murder of Leo V on Christmas Day 820 in the palace chapel of St. Stephen.[3] Since Nicephorus died in 828, the *Refutatio et Eversio* was finished between 820 and 828.

To the other works of the Patriarch only relative dates can be assigned. First of all it may be stated that the *Contra Eusebium et Epiphanidem* preceded the *Refutatio et Eversio*. In the second part of the latter, where Nicephorus refutes the *florilegium* of quotations used by the Council of 815, he discusses in the last place those passages which according to the Iconoclasts were taken from Epiphanius. Nicephorus argues that they are spurious and remarks: ὡς δὲ πόρρω ταῦτα τῆς 'Επιφανίου δόξης κεῖται, ἤδη μὲν διὰ πλειόνων ἐπιχειρημάτων καὶ ἐν ἄλλοις ἡμῖν ἱκανῶς ἐπιδέδεικται, ἀλλ' οὖν κἀνταῦθα ἐν ἰδίῳ ἑκάστου λόγῳ συνοπτικώτερον εἰρήσεται.[4] This is clearly a reference to that part of the *Contra Eusebium et Epiphanidem* which refers to Epiphanius, and since it has been shown above that the two parts belong together, the *Contra Eusebium et Epiphanidem* precedes the *Refutatio et Eversio*.[5] On the other hand, the discussion, in the *Contra Eusebium et Epiphanidem*, of quotations from the *florilegium* of the Imperial Committee or from that of the Council of St. Sophia makes it clear that it was written later than 814/15. Since, in addition, the *Apologeticus atque Antirrhetici* preceded the *Contra Eusebium et Epiphanidem* and was written between 818 and 820, the *Contra Eusebium et Epiphanidem* must have been completed somewhat later than these dates.

The *Adversus Iconomachos* was written, as has been argued here, as a supplement to the therefore earlier *Contra Eusebium et Epi-*

---

[1] Above, p. 179.
[2] B, fol. 174ʳ, lines 5–10.
[3] There is another allusion to Leo's death in *Coisl.* 93, fol. 35ʳ.
[4] B, fol. 296ʳ, lines 2–6.
[5] Visser, *Nikephoros und der Bilderstreit*, 83, is therefore wrong in making the *Adversus Epiphanidem* follow the *Refutatio et Eversio*.

phanidem. As the author was aware that the contemporary Iconoclasts had withdrawn the accusation of idol-worship, it must have
been composed after the Council of St. Sophia (815).[1] Whether
it was written before, concurrently with, or after the *Refutatio
atque Eversio* is difficult to state with confidence, but it is so close
to the spirit of the *Contra Eusebium et Epiphanidem* that one would
hesitate to assign it to a date later than 820.

Still earlier than the *Contra Eusebium et Epiphanidem* (and therefore earlier also than the *Refutatio et Eversio*) is the *Apologeticus
atque Antirrhetici*. In the preface to the *Contra Eusebium et Epiphanidem* Nicephorus remarks that in a previous work he has refuted
the ἀντιθέσεις of Mamonas and that in the present work he is
going to refute the quotations set forth by Mamonas.[2] Now the
term ἀντιθέσεις is not regularly used by Nicephorus in the *Apologeticus et Antirrhetici* for the writings of Constantine,[3] but firstly no
uniform title is employed in any case, and secondly it is indeed an
accurate description. There is another passage dealing with the
Jew from Tiberias who persuaded the Khalif to destroy all
Christian images on which Nicephorus remarks: ὧν πέρι ἐν
φθάσασι πλατύτερον εἴρηται ὥστε δείκνυσθαι ἀληθῶς ἐξ ᾽Ιουδαίων
τε καὶ Σαρακηνῶν τὴν τοιαύτην ἠρτῆσθαι πλάνην.[4] This refers to the
last chapter of *Antirrheticus* where this story is related in great
detail.[5] A passage in the *Apologeticus Maior* itself leads to the same
conclusion. Here Nicephorus is speaking of quotations from
Eusebius which the Iconoclasts are producing: ὧν τὸ ληρῶδες καὶ
φαῦλον τῆς ἀπιστίας ἐν τοῖς μετέπειτα ἐξελέγξομεν, εἴπερ εὐδοκοίη
Θεὸς καὶ τῷ πόνῳ συνεφάπτηται καὶ συναίρηται.[6] Clearly Nicephorus was already envisaging a later work on the quotations
from Eusebius when he wrote the *Apologeticus Maior*.

Indeed, apart from the *Epistle to Leo*, the *Apologeticus Minor*, and
the *De Magnete*, the *Apologeticus atque Antirrhetici* is the *earliest* theological work of the Patriarch Nicephorus. In the *Apologeticus
atque Antirrhetici* will be found only such references which relate
to an earlier part of the same work,[7] but no references to the

---

[1] Pitra, iv. 241. [2] Pitra, i. 373.

[3] It occurs twice in the singular (*P.G.* c. 232B and c), but I doubt whether it is
meant to designate a particular statement of Constantine rather than the pair of
contraries ἔνυλος—ἄϋλος which Constantine mentions. [4] Pitra, i. 376.

[5] *Antirrheticus*, iii. 84 (*P.G.* c. 528c–534).

[6] *P.G.* c. 564c.

[7] Here are some examples of references to earlier parts of the *Apologeticus atque*

author's other writings.[1] By contrast, in all his other works
Nicephorus often mentions that he has dealt with a given topic
already in a previous work. The fact that the *Apologeticus atque
Antirrhetici* alone does not contain any such references renders it
likely that, with the exceptions noted above, this is his first
major work.

It is thus possible to establish a relative date for the *Apologeticus
atque Antirrhetici*, but there are difficulties about an absolute
date. Ehrhard, following Mai, attempted to find one. He wrote:
'Den Apologeticus Maior (einschließlich der LL. III Antirrhetici)
schrieb Nicephorus nach seiner eigenen Angabe ungefähr 30
Jahre nach der Synode vom Jahre 787, also um das Jahr 817, zu
welcher Zeit er schon im Exile weilte.'[2] This remark goes back
to a note by Mai on the following passage concerning the *Horos*
of Nicaea: ὁ παριππεύσας μικροῦ τριακοντούτης χρόνος συλλαβὼν
ἐβεβαίωσε.[3] On this passage Mai remarked: 'Nicaenum II generale
concilium anno DCCLXXXVII celebratum scimus. Ergo Nicephorus maiorem hunc apologeticum scribebat anno circiter
DCCCXVII, Leonis Armenii imperantis quinto.'

It is easy to see how Mai and Ehrhard arrived at their dating;
it is based on an incorrect interpretation of the text. If the passage
is read in its context,[4] it may mean merely that 'almost thirty
years' elapsed between the Council of Nicaea (787) and the
iconoclastic Council of 815: Nicephorus is explaining how during
this interval all priests confirmed the decision of Nicaea and how
the pious among the emperors and all the laymen accepted it.
This interpretation is made possible by merely reading the *Apolo-*

Antirrhetici: *P.G.* c. 208A (καθὰ δὴ καὶ πρότερον ἡμῖν ἐρρήθη) refers to ibid. 560B;
col. 260C (ἤδη πρόσθεν ἀρκούντως εἴρηται) refers to 549; 349B (καὶ εἴρηταί γε ἡμῖν ἐν
ἑτέροις πλατύτερον) refers to 768D sqq., &c. Other passages announce a later treatment of a problem within the same work, e.g. the promise given col. 213D (περὶ ὧν
εἰς ὕστερον διαληψόμεθα) is fulfilled 353C; that given col. 240D (ἐν τοῖς μετὰ ταῦτα
εἰρήσεται) refers to 137B sqq., &c.

[1] The passage *P.G.* c. 536B (οὐκοῦν οὐδὲ ἄλλοτε περὶ τῶν τοιούτων σιγήσαντες)
seems to refer to oral disputations rather than written pronouncements.

[2] *Kirchenlexikon*, ix. 253. See also G. Moravsik, *Byzantino-Turcica*, i. 279.

[3] *P.G.* c. 600A.

[4] *P.G.* c. 597D sq.: τοῦτο τὸ δόγμα καὶ οἱ μετὰ ταῦτα ἱερεῖς ἅπαντες ἅτε θεόφρονες
καὶ ὀρθοδοξίᾳ κεκοσμημένοι ἐπεσφράγισαν καὶ βασιλέων οἱ εὐσεβεῖς καὶ πιστοὶ
ἡρέτισαν καὶ ἠσπάσαντο καὶ ὁ σύμπας τῶν Χριστιανῶν λαὸς περιεπτύξατο καὶ ὁ παριππεύσας μικροῦ τριακοντούτης χρόνος συλλαβὼν ἐβεβαίωσε καὶ ἡμεῖς γε ὡς πλῆρες
εὐσεβείας ὑπάρχον ἀπεδεξάμεθα καὶ καθυπεγράψαμεν ἐξ οὗ τάς τε χειροτονίας καὶ
καθιδρύσεις ἐν τοῖς ἱερατικοῖς θρόνοις ἔχομεν.

geticus Maior. Possibility becomes a certainty, however, as soon as a parallel passage of the *Refutatio et Eversio* is considered. There Nicephorus declares likewise that 'almost thirty years' had elapsed since the Iconoclasts had been publicly denounced at the Council of Nicaea.[1] The *Refutatio et Eversio* is definitely written after 820, therefore 'the almost thirty years' can mean only the lapse of time between 787 and 815. In the light of this passage from the *Refutatio et Eversio* the above passage from the *Apologeticus* must be interpreted to refer to the same interval and accordingly has no bearing on the date of the work.

There is, however, in the *Apologeticus Maior*, another sentence which both Mai and Ehrhard seem to have overlooked. Here Nicephorus is speaking of Arius and the first Council of Nicaea. He writes: 'Five hundred years and slightly more ago that well-attended gathering assembled by God, I mean the holy Council of Nicaea, of the God-inspired and admirable men ... deposed and ousted the adherents of the Arian heresy from the Church, etc.'[2] The Council of Nicaea met in 325; a lapse of time of 500 years brings us to 825, and the remark 'and slightly more ago' seems to make it clear that we have to think of a somewhat later date rather than an earlier one. If this statement were true, the *Apologeticus atque Antirrhetici* would have been written between 825 and 828 since Nicephorus died in 828.

This indication, apparently so clear and definite, is misleading. The argument thus far has established that both this work and the *Contra Eusebium et Epiphanidem* precede the *Refutatio et Eversio*. It will be seen presently that all the other writings probably also preceded the *Refutatio et Eversio*. If these results are to be reconciled with an absolute date of the *Apologeticus atque Antirrhetici* in 825 or thereafter, Nicephorus would have written all his theological works in the short lapse of time between 825 and 828. This is extremely unlikely. The strongest argument against the late date of the *Apologeticus atque Antirrhetici* is its connexion with certain remarks in the *Apologeticus Minor*. It will be remembered that the writings of Constantine and their refutation had been in the centre of discussion in the *Apologeticus Minor*. Nicephorus had

---

[1] Fol. 293ᵛ, lines 28–30: τριάκοντα γάρ που σχεδὸν διαγεγόνασιν ἐνιαυτοὶ ἐξ οὗ ἡ πονηρὰ αὕτη ἐπίνοια, ἡ κατὰ τῶν ὀρθῶν λόγων ἐξευρεθεῖσα, πεφώραται δημοσιευομένη καὶ θριαμβευομένη.

[2] *P.G.* c. 564A.

forbidden members of the clergy to mention those writings, but had permitted an inquiry into Constantine's patristic quotations. It is precisely the writings of Constantine that form the topic of the *Apologeticus atque Antirrhetici*. It is true that Nicephorus is transgressing his own prohibition not to discuss the writings of Constantine V. It would seem, therefore, that after the *Apologeticus Minor* was completed the Patriarch realized that Constantine's writings were still a living force and required a rebuttal. So, for all these reasons, there can be no doubt that the *Apologeticus atque Antirrhetici* was written not too long after the Council of St. Sophia, certainly not after 825, as the above passage would seem to indicate.

But what is the explanation of the passage which states that Nicephorus is writing a little more than 500 years after the First Council of Nicaea? It is plain that in the Middle Ages a simple error of computation would cause no surprise. Fortunately, it can be shown that an error in chronology is more probable. The earlier redaction of the Χρονογραφικὸν Σύντομον, which is attributed by some of the manuscripts to Nicephorus, mentions in its list of emperors under Constantine the Great: τῷ ιβ' ἔτει τῆς αὐτοῦ βασιλείας ἡ πρώτη σύνοδος γέγονε τῶν τιη' πατέρων τῶν ἐν Νικαίᾳ, ἔτους τιη' ἀπὸ τῆς ἐνανθρωπήσεως τοῦ Κυρίου ἡμῶν Ἰησοῦ Χριστοῦ.[1] The year A.D. 318 is probably a confusion with the number of participants, but it shows that in the ninth century erroneous ideas existed about the date of the First Council of Nicaea. Thus no matter whether Nicephorus himself or another person is the author of the Χρονογραφικὸν Σύντομον, the passage of the *Apologeticus* concerning the lapse of time between that Council and the time of the writing may safely be disregarded.

The *Apologeticus atque Antirrhetici* was thus completed at some time after 818.[2] It remains puzzling why Nicephorus, three years after the Council of St. Sophia, should have written a work attacking the writings of Constantine V and why he should have taken the trouble of formulating various iconoclastic theses at a time when the official iconoclastic programme had been embodied in the *Definition* and *florilegium* of the Council of St. Sophia.[3]

---

[1] Ed. de Boor, pp. 95 f.

[2] One reason why the work cannot have been completed prior to 815 is the fact that the author describes the persecution of Iconophiles under Leo V; see *Apologeticus Maior*, 15 (*P.G.* c. 569A–C).

[3] *Apologeticus Maior*, 17 (*P.G.* c. 577D); 26 (601A); *Antirrheticus*, iii. 28 (420A); 34

It is difficult to imagine that Nicephorus, even in the strictest of exiles, should not have had access to the *Definition*. In fact it is likely that every attempt was made to acquaint him with this document in order that he might be induced to support it. It may be argued that he considered it more dangerous to attack the decision of a church council than to criticize Constantine V and Iconoclasm in general. Yet the *Apologeticus atque Antirrhetici* is so full of the most venomous attacks against the Iconoclasts of his own day that caution can hardly have played a role in Nicephorus' choice of a target. The only alternative seems to be that, in Nicephorus' opinion, a fundamental refutation of Iconoclasm was possible only if it were directed against the writings of Constantine V and against Iconoclasm in general. For Nicephorus, Iconoclasm seems to a large extent to have remained what it had been in the days of his early manhood: the particular brand of Iconoclasm inspired by Constantine V and refuted by Nicephorus' great predecessor, Tarasius.

The results of the foregoing inquiry can now be summarized:

Chronological Table[1]

811–12	*Epistle to Pope Leo III*
813–15	*Apologeticus Minor*
814	*De Magnete*
818–20	1. *Apologeticus atque Antirrhetici* 2. *Contra Eusebium et Epiphanidem* 3. *Adversus Iconomachos*
820–8	1. *Lost work on Leo V* 2. *Refutatio et Eversio*

(425D); 37 (436B); 38 (437B); 40 (445D); 41 (457B); 44 (464A); 50 (468D–469A); 54 (477C). In a footnote to the first of these passages Mai remarks that it occurred in the acclamations appended to the Council of 754. I have been unable to find this passage in the place indicated by Mai.

[1] What can now be recognized as the chronological order of Nicephorus' writings happily coincides by and large with the arrangement that Banduri had planned for his edition (see *P.G.* c. 17–38). Unless I am mistaken, he overlooked the *Apologeticus Minor* altogether and placed the *De Magnete* wrongly between the *Contra Eusebium et Epiphanidem* and the *Adversus Iconomachos*.

VIII

NICEPHORUS AND THE THEORY OF
RELIGIOUS IMAGES

AFTER completing the survey of Nicephorus' writings, it is important to define his position in the long development of theories concerning religious images. The history of this development is still unwritten. Scholars who have dealt with the theoretical side of Iconoclasm have either concentrated on one particular author or have given a composite picture of the theories during the 120 years of the Controversy. Yet unless one adheres to preconceived ideas concerning the rigidity and stagnation of Byzantine culture, it seems *a priori* unlikely that an author of the ninth century should have done nothing but repeat the views of John of Damascus, who lived roughly a century earlier.

Iconophile theory can be divided into three main periods. The first, which reaches down to the accession of Constantine V, may be called the traditional period. The arguments of Christian apologists for image-worship (John of Damascus, Germanos of Constantinople) largely repeat and adapt those used by pagan defenders of cult statues, with an admixture of points connected with christological doctrine. The second period of iconophile theory, beginning with the reign of Constantine V, may be called christological. During this time the traditional arguments are rehearsed again and again; but under the prodding of Constantine's famous christological dilemma iconophile theory focuses attention on the connexion between christology and image. At some time after the Seventh Ecumenical Council the need was felt to justify religious images and their worship in terms of the philosophy taught in the Byzantine schools; there is, therefore, a third, scholastic, period of iconophile theory.[1] The Patriarch Nicephorus reflected this new orientation although he was neither its originator nor perhaps its most effective representative.

In the scholastic period of iconophile theory Peripatetic

[1] The beginning of the new orientation will be dated more closely below (pp. 195-7).

philosophy, especially the Aristotelian logic as taught in the Byzantine schools, was applied to the theological problem of religious images and image-worship. This logic ought to be relatively well known, for its methods of instruction and its results have been made available in a monumental edition, the *Commentaria in Aristotelem Graeca*.[1] Yet this edition was conceived not from the point of view of the historian of medieval philosophy, but from that of the student of ancient learning. In the former respect the study of the Aristotelian tradition has hardly begun. Therefore, however desirable it would be to determine precisely the text-books or other works on Aristotelian philosophy used by the authors of the scholastic period, such a result cannot be expected in the present state of ignorance concerning the development of Byzantine philosophy. Only in very few cases will it be possible to locate the precise source used by a theologian of the ninth century for a particular argument. In most instances it will be necessary to proceed in a more haphazard way. Where the sources cannot be defined, parallels from the Aristotelian commentaries, from the *Dialectica* of John of Damascus, and from Aristotle will be noted to prove the scholastic nature of an argument. In other cases even this will be impossible and the scholastic character of a passage will be affirmed simply on grounds of terminology, style, and content.

How did the scholastic theory of images come into being? The Seventh Ecumenical Council had settled the question of religious images in favour of the image-worshippers, yet the resistance which the Empress Irene had to overcome in assembling the Council showed that the strength of the iconoclastic movement was far from spent. From the Council to the second outbreak of Iconoclasm the threat of a return to the religious views of the earlier iconoclastic dynasty determined relations between Church and State and placed into the hands of the emperor powerful instruments for bargaining; mere allusion to Iconoclasm sufficed to make the patriarch accede to any imperial requests, as was shown in the Moechian affair. The details of the development which the theories concerning religious images underwent between 787 and 815 cannot be studied, as few writings concerned with this issue and dating from these years are preserved. Yet

---

[1] 23 vols. (Berlin, 1882–1909).

the iconoclastic party had retained much driving power so that both sides must have continued to elaborate upon the existing arguments and added new ones as the opportunity presented itself. Now arguments of a specifically scholastic character, that is those based on the Aristotelian system and the later literature of commentaries, handbooks, &c., were conspicuously absent from the argumentation down to (and including) the Council of Nicaea.¹ Neither John of Damascus nor Germanos of Constantinople employed scholastic reasoning to defend Christian images; nor was there any trace of their opponents' applying such arguments to the image problem. This is all the more remarkable as the author of the *Fons Scientiae,* John of Damascus, supplied Eastern Christianity with the most popular handbook of Aristotelian Logic. Yet neither in his *De Imaginibus* nor in his summary of the image problem in the *Fons Scientiae* did he avail himself of his knowledge of Aristotelian philosophy to buttress his views about religious images.² The same negative result holds true for the fragmentary writings of Constantine V and for the *Horos* of the Council of 754. The proceedings of the Seventh Council again are limited to the traditional and christological lines of argumentation. This negative finding means that the scholastic theory of images emerged for the first time almost eighty years after the first outbreak of Iconoclasm.

It has long been recognized that during the second period of Iconoclasm, both in the works of Theodore of Studios and in those of Nicephorus, a great amount of Aristotelian material is directly applied to the image question.³ The dogmatic works of Theodore, especially his three *Antirrhetici,* may serve as an introduction to the Aristotelian argumentation of this period. To be sure, in these works all the arguments which had appeared during the preceding periods occur repeatedly. But it is the new method which characterizes this scholastic period of Iconoclasm, not the traditional and christological arguments.

Theodore's *First Antirrheticus* is cast in the form of an imaginary dialogue with an Iconoclast and deals with the problem of

¹ The following does not refer to Aristotelian arguments in general. All ecclesiastical writers, at least since Leontius of Byzantium, used them. What is of interest here is the application of such arguments to the image problem.

² Iohannes Damascenus, *Fons Scientiae,* iv. 16 (*P.G.* xciv. 1168–76).

³ Schwarzlose, *Bilderstreit,* 183; Ostrogorsky, *B.Z.* xxxi (1931), 391 (review of Martin).

whether or not Christ can be circumscribed.¹ Scholastic terminology occurs for the first time when the heretic denies that
there is a scriptural foundation for Christ's image. Theodore
replies that what is said of the archetype (τὸ ἀρχέτυπον) and the
cause (τὸ αἴτιον) holds for the derivative (τὸ παραγωγόν) and the
effect (τὸ αἰτιατόν). The only difference is that in the first case it
is meant properly (κυρίως) because it is said in the natural meaning (φύσει), while in the second case it is asserted improperly (οὐ
κυρίως) because it is used equivocally (ὁμωνύμως).² Somewhat
later the Iconoclast raises the question whether the image of
Christ is Christ or Christ's image. Theodore replies that although
from the point of view of essence, of shape and of truth the opposites—nature and convention (φύσις καὶ θέσις), archetype and
derivative, cause and effect, Christ and His image—are different,
the image is both 'Christ' and 'Christ's image' from the point of
view of resemblance; it is Christ equivocally (κατὰ τὸ ὁμώνυμον),
it is 'Christ's image' relatively (κατὰ τὸ πρός τι).³ These references
to equivocal concepts and to the fourth category of relation (τὰ
πρός τι) in their application to images, together with the connected
notions of correlatives (τὰ ἀντιστρέφοντα) and simultaneousness
(ἅμα τῇ φύσει εἶναι), are among the central arguments with
which both Theodore and Nicephorus operate.⁴ They will be
encountered again and again in the course of this chapter. Only
a few lines after the passage just discussed, Theodore avails himself of this same category to answer an iconoclastic question. The
name inscribed on the image, he explains, is, like any name, a
relative term (τὸ γὰρ ὄνομα ὀνομαζομένου ὄνομα) and image and
prototype ought to enjoy identical worship.⁵ Theodore determines the respective merits of representations of the Cross and of
Christ by pointing out that the degree of veneration of the results
is dependent on that of the causes, and that therefore the image
of Christ is more venerable than a representation of the Cross.⁶

The *Second Antirrheticus* deals with the question whether or not
the image of Christ should be worshipped. Here the orthodox
interlocutor continues to operate with the notions of pattern and

¹ *P.G.* xcix. 329A: ἤδη δὲ προβληθήσεται ὁ λόγος κατὰ ἀντίθεσιν τοῦ τε οἰκείου
δόγματος καὶ τοῦ ἀλλοτρίου.
² Ibid. 337A–D. On homonyms see Aristotle, *Cat.* 1 a 1.
³ *P.G.* xcix. 341B–D.
⁴ Aristotle, *Cat.* 6 a 37–8 b 24, 14 b 25–15 a 12.
⁵ *P.G.* xcix. 345A.   ⁶ Ibid. 345B.

derivative and states that whereas Christ Himself is called Christ univocally (συνωνύμως) or properly (κυρίως), His image is called 'Christ' equivocally (ὁμωνύμως) or improperly (οὐ κυρίως).[1] In order to prove that a representation of Christ is more venerable than one of the Cross, Theodore makes the Iconoclast admit (as he had already admitted in the *First Antirrheticus*) that the derivatives differ according to the difference of the prototypes.[2]

The *Third Antirrheticus* has a structure of its own. The author proclaims in the beginning: 'I shall use certain syllogisms for the subject of my discourse. They are not constructed according to the Aristotelian prescription or foolery but are based on simpler language, the power of truth.'[3] He expresses the hope that his labours will not be unprofitable to his readers. The learned will use them as a starting-point for more learned inquiries, while to the uninitiated they will serve as an introduction (στοιχείωσις). He then proceeds for the sake of greater clarity (τὸ εὐκρινές) to divide his study into four chapters (κεφάλαια), thereby assigning his treatise to its proper literary *genus*, that of κεφάλαια.[4]

The first chapter is devoted to the question whether Christ is circumscribable. The affirmative answer is supported by a great number of syllogistic ἐπιχειρήματα which follow one another for the most part under the heading ἄλλο. They are taken from the 'common notions' (κοιναὶ ἔννοιαι) of philosophy, from the Bible, and especially from christological doctrine. Some of them consist of an imaginary iconoclastic objection followed by Theodore's reply or by a *reductio ad absurdum*. Inasmuch as Theodore's christological views appear in the Aristotelian guise customary since the days of Leontius of Byzantium, the whole chapter abounds in Aristotelian terminology—yet without specific application to the problem of images. In the second chapter Theodore argues the thesis that there can be an artistic image of Christ in which He may be contemplated. The third is devoted to the demonstration that the worship of Christ and of His image are

---

[1] Ibid. 360D, cf. Aristotle, *Cat.* 1 a 1–12.
[2] *P.G.* xcix. 368B: οὐκ ἔστιν ἀμφιβάλλειν . . . ὅτι μὴ κατὰ τὴν διαφορὰν τῶν πρωτοτύπων καὶ τὰ παράγωγα διαλλάττει. . . .
[3] Ibid. 389A.
[4] Note the interesting discussion of this type of literature by O. Schissel, *B.Z.* xxxvii (1937), 113–17 (review of E. R. Dodds's edition of Proclus' *Elements of Theology*). The structure of Theodore's *Third Antirrheticus* seems to have been influenced by the *Thesaurus* of Cyril of Alexandria.

one and the same. Here the author develops a theory of the religious image which is once again heavily influenced by orthodox christology in its Aristotelian form. The prototype, according to Theodore, is different from the image in nature and essence, but is contained in the image 'according to the likeness of the hypostasis'. This formula is at the centre of Theodore's views on images, and, although fashioned after the orthodox doctrine of the Trinity, it is Theodore's own contribution to the question of images.[1] The thesis of the fourth chapter is similar to that of the third: Christ and His image have *one* likeness and *one* worship. The imaginary Iconoclast is made to object that since the original exists by nature (φύσει) and the image by convention (θέσει) and since therefore they do not exist simultaneously (ἅμα), they cannot receive the same worship.[2] Theodore replies that the image is potentially (δυνάμει) simultaneous with Christ. Images belong to the category of relatives (τῶν πρός τί ἐστιν) as the notions 'double' and 'half' do; therefore they come into existence together with the model, and model and image cancel each other.[3]

This scholastic trend, so conspicuous in the *Antirrhetici* of the Studite, is not absent from his other writings. In one of his letters to his disciple Naucratius he avails himself of the doctrine of the faculties of the soul to refute the iconoclastic claim that images are useless. One of these faculties, Theodore argues, is imagination (φαντασία) which may be called a kind of image (τις εἰκών) because both are representations (ἰνδάλματα). Now if the image, the more important of the two (εἰκών and φαντασία), were useless, so would the lesser one be (φαντασία). And if that were so, what would become of the other four faculties of the soul: perception, opinion, thought, and intelligence?[4]

---

[1] The credit for having called attention to this theory of Theodore belongs to G. B. Ladner, 'Origin and Significance of the Byzantine Iconoclastic Controversy', *Medieval Studies*, ii (1940), 127–49, esp. 144 f. See also *Epistulae*, ii. 65, 1288B; ii. 85, 1329; ii. 194, 1588D; *Epigram* no. 30, 1792B.

[2] *P.G.* xcix. 428D–429B. For τὰ ἅμα, see Aristotle, *Cat.* 14 b 25–15 a 12. This notion is further used by Theodore, *Epistulae*, ii. 21, 1184A.

[3] Cf. *P.G.* xcix. 429B–C with Aristotle, *Cat.* 7 b 15–23.

[4] *P.G.* xcix. 1220B–C: ἔπειτα καὶ ἡ μία τῶν πέντε τῆς ψυχῆς δυνάμεων ἡ φαντασία· φαντασία δὲ δόξειέ τις εἰκών· ἰνδάλματα γὰρ ἀμφότερα. οὐκ ἀνωφελὴς ἄρα ἡ εἰκὼν τῇ φαντασίᾳ ἐοικυῖα. εἰ δὲ ἀνωφελὴς ἡ προὔργιαιτέρα, πολλῷ οὖν μᾶλλον ἡ ὑφειμενεστέρα, μάτην συνυπάρχουσα τῇ φύσει· καὶ εἰ μάτην, καὶ αἱ σύστοιχοι αὐτῆς, αἴσθησις, δόξα, διάνοια, νοῦς. οὕτω φυσιολογῶν ὁ λόγος ἄνουν ὑπαγορεύει διὰ θεωρίας ἐπαγωγικωτέρας τὸν τῆς εἰκόνος ἤτοι φαντασίας ἐξουδενωτήν. Cf. Aristotle, *De Anima*, 428 a 1–4. In

These examples from the writings of Theodore may suffice to illustrate the scholastic material with which a writer of the second period of Iconoclasm could operate. This material can be traced in the last resort to Aristotle, yet it is probable that many authors of the ninth century knew his writings only as reflected in philosophical handbooks. Besides forming the proper background for a discussion of the scholastic element in Nicephorus, Theodore's writings also provide a *terminus ante quem* for the application of scholastic argumentation to religious images. As has been shown, this emerged later than the Seventh Council of Nicaea, but, it would seem, before Iconoclasm broke out again in A.D. 815. In fact there exists a letter of Theodore of Studios to John the Grammarian in which Theodore justifies the view of the relative worship of Christ's image in the same way as in the *Antirrhetici*. John had criticized an earlier letter of Theodore to his disciple Athanasius, in which Theodore had expounded the view, advanced by the Council of 787, that Christ's image demanded not adoration but relative worship. To John's objections (which are not preserved) Theodore replied:

Relation (σχέσις) belongs to the relative terms (τῶν πρός τί ἐστιν). They exist simultaneously and are correlatives as pattern and image are. The one could not exist without the presence of the other, as philosophers have said about simultaneous terms (τὰ ἅμα). I added in the previous letter to Athanasius [which the addressee had criticized] 'or equivocal' (ὁμωνυμική, i.e. equivocal *worship*). This word, too, has the same meaning; for 'name' is name of something named, so that even here we deal with relation. Furthermore, we are taught according to the definition of philosophy that things are said to be named 'equivocally' if, though they have a common name, the definition (λόγος τῆς οὐσίας) corresponding to the name differs for each, as in Christ himself and his portrait. . . .[1]

Parva Catechesis, no. 30 (ed. Auvray, p. 111) Theodore distinguishes three ψυχῆς δυνάμεις: λογιστικόν, θυμικόν, ἐπιθυμητικόν, cf. Plato, *Rep.* iv. 440E.

[1] Theodorus Studita, *Epistulae*, ii. 194 (*P.G.* xcix. 1588B–1592A, esp. 1589C). French translation of this letter by V. Grumel, 'Jean Grammaticos et saint Théodore Studite', *Échos d'Orient*, xxxvi (1937), 180–9, esp. 184–6, but the article does not stress the Aristotelian character of the terminology. On John the Grammarian see below, note F, p. 235. Theodore inserts the entire text of his previous letter, ibid. 1588D–1589B. In Migne it appears also as ii. 85, 1327D–1329B. The same letter had been criticized by 'one of our hierarchs', see ii. 161, 1501C–1504D. There is nothing to prove that John the Grammarian is identical with this 'hierarch', and similar criticisms were voiced somewhat later by one of Theodore's own disciples, ii. 151, 1469C–1472D.

Here is the terminology and argumentation which is by now familiar from Theodore's *Antirrhetici*. The last sentence of the excerpt is an almost literal quotation of the first sentence of the *Categories*. Also, Theodore is evidently pleased to use even Aristotle's example for things equivocal, that of man and his portrait, by applying it to Christ and His image.[1] Chronologically this letter is of great value as it speaks of Theodore's uncle, Plato, as living. The abbot Plato died on 4 April 814,[2] and the letter must have preceded that date. This would show that the scholastic period of iconophile theory had opened before that time.

An even earlier *terminus ante quem* may be inferred from the above-mentioned commentary on the Gospel of St. John, written, as has been seen, before the year 812.[3] There can be no question that the unknown author of this work was thoroughly familiar with the scholastic theory of religious images.[4] He distinguished, for example, the natural from the artistic image.[5] God's actual image, Jesus Christ, differs from any artistic image in that the former bears the full truth of the Father, while the latter resembles its original in form but not in matter.[6] It is equivocal but not synonymous with the original and therefore does not possess truth.[7] With regard to archetypes and derivatives, the destruction of the effects (icons) destroys the causes (Jesus Christ, or other persons represented on icons), just as, on the other hand, honour and worship rendered to the effects affect the causes.[8] Images and archetypes enter into existence together and cancel

---

[1] Cf. ibid. 1589c: ἐπεὶ καὶ κατὰ φιλοσοφίας λόγον (variant: ὅρον) ὁμώνυμά ἐστι διδασκόμεθα, ὧν ὄνομα μόνον κοινόν· ὁ δὲ κατὰ τοὔνομα λόγος τῆς οὐσίας ἕτερος· οἷον αὐτὸς Χριστός, καὶ ὁ γεγραμμένος, with Aristotle, *Cat.* 1 a 1: ὁμώνυμα λέγεται ὧν ὄνομα μόνον κοινόν, ὁ δὲ κατὰ τοὔνομα λόγος τῆς οὐσίας ἕτερος, οἷον ζῷον ὅ τε ἄνθρωπος καὶ τὸ γεγραμμένον.

[2] G. Cereteli, 'Wo ist das Tetraevangelium von Porphyrius Uspenski aus dem Jahr 835 entstanden?', *B.Z.* ix (1900), 649–53, esp. 649 f. The author read the number of the indiction ζ as six instead of seven so that he arrived at the year 813. Grumel, loc. cit. 186, has corrected the error tacitly.

[3] Above, p. 98.

[4] Hansmann, *Kommentar zum Johannesevangelium*, pp. 45–53.

[5] Ibid., p. 184, 32–35.

[6] Ibid., p. 187, 25–33.

[7] Ibid., p. 188, 6–8: ὅπου δὲ παντελὴς ταυτότης οὐκ ἔστιν ἀλλ' ἑτερότης οὐσίας τε καὶ μορφῆς, οὐδὲ τῆς ἀληθείας ἡ ὕπαρξις καὶ κλῆσις ἔχει χώραν τὸ σύνολον. This was a nuance which was not stressed by the Iconophiles in their debates with the Iconoclasts, but was indispensable to the commentator on the Gospel of St. John where 'Truth' plays a large role.

[8] Ibid., p. 190, 34–38.

each other.[1] From these illustrations it will be seen that the
author was acquainted with the scholastic theory of images. Since
the commentary was written before the end of the Moechian
Controversy in 812,[2] it is clear that this scholastic theory of
images was fully developed by that date. It is interesting, however, that the author makes a very peculiar use of this theory.
His real concern is not with religious images but with the
Moechian party and its views. The theory of religious images is
never brought in for its own sake but only to support the author's
contentions with regard to the Moechian Controversy. For him
the scholastic theory of images is no longer (and not yet) questionable, it is an accepted set of data to be used at discretion
for comparisons and analogies in the matters with which he is
concerned in his commentary. For example, when he discusses
Jesus' words: 'If you abide by what I teach, you are really
disciples of mine, and you will know the truth and the truth will
set you free' (John viii. 32), he utilizes the doctrine of religious
images to stress the superiority of Jesus, who is Truth and God's
natural image, over all artistic and changeable images which are
not Truth.[3] To this commentator, then, the scholastic theory of
images is not a new discovery, it is a well-established line of
argumentation, the truth of which is beyond doubt, and which
can therefore be used to illustrate and prove a different set of
propositions. Under these circumstances it is hard to believe that
this theory was of very recent origin. It is more plausible to
assume that by the time when the commentary was written, i.e.
shortly before 812, the scholastic theory of images had become
traditional. In all probability it was developed in the decade
following the Seventh Council of Nicaea.

Who was the author of this theory? Since it happens to be used
in a commentary on St. John written by an unknown member
of the Studite circle,[4] then in a letter and several treatises of

---

[1] Ibid., p. 191, 5–9: . . . αἱ τεχνηταὶ καὶ πολλῷ δὲ μᾶλλον αἱ φυσικαὶ τῶν πραγμάτων
εἰκόνες συνεισφέρουσι καὶ συναναιροῦσι τῶν ἀρχετύπων τὰς σχετικὰς ὑπάρξεις (εἰκόνος
γὰρ οὔσης φαίνεται καὶ τὸ ἀρχέτυπον ἐξ ἀνάγκης, ἀναιρουμένης δὲ ταύτης συνανήρηται
καὶ τὸ ἀρχέτυπον ᾗ πέφυκεν ἀρχέτυπον πάντως . . .) . . .. It will be seen (below,
p. 202) that Nicephorus was not always as cautious as this commentator and often
forgot the clause printed here in italics.

[2] Hansmann, *Kommentar*, 76, speaks of the year 811, but the Moechian Controversy was not settled until 812; see Grumel, *Regestes*, no. 388.

[3] John viii. 32; Hansmann, *Kommentar*, 187–90.

[4] Ibid. 84.

Theodore of Studios, one is inclined to consider it a Studite invention. This can, however, hardly be the case. It will be shown presently that it reappears in the writings of the Patriarch Nicephorus, whose relations with Theodore and his circle were never intimate. It is best to suppose therefore that the anonymous commentator, Theodore, and Nicephorus reproduced a theory which had been developed by Byzantine schoolmen.

Of Nicephorus' writings neither his Letter to Pope Leo III nor the *Apologeticus Minor* contain any trace of scholastic arguments, a fact possibly to be explained by their official character. From the *Apologeticus atque Antirrhetici* on, however, Nicephorus' writings are replete with the same scholastic arguments which figure so prominently in the works of Theodore of Studios and in the anonymous commentary on the Gospel of St. John.[1]

The Patriarch Nicephorus was well equipped with all the paraphernalia of scholastic logic. He operated with concepts such as those of essential qualities (οὐσιώδεις ποιότητες)[2] and indicative properties (παραστατικὰ ἰδιώματα).[3] Where Constantine V, after discussing the two natures in Christ whom he calls the image of God, undertook by a veritable *tour de force* to draw certain conclusions purportedly valid for all images, Nicephorus branded this procedure as 'specification by generalization' (καθολικὸς προσδιορισμός).[4] The definitions of the schools and their theories played a major role in the works of Nicephorus. Constantine V had denied that Christ was circumscribable (περιγραπτός). In his answer, Nicephorus held that the iconoclastic thesis in effect denied Christ's full human nature. In his reasoning he made use of a number of traditional definitions, notably that of man, horse, &c.:

What, I ask you, gives you this power to disregard the other specific properties (ἰδιώματα) of Body, namely that of being shaped, tridimensional, tangible, provided with organs, and the others from which it sbeing circumscribable is being inferred . . .? For if a man

---

[1] It needs be emphasized that the remarks following in the text are meant to be selective and do not claim to exhaust the scholastic material contained in Nicephorus' works.

[2] *Apologeticus Maior*, 22 (*P.G.* c. 588D). Cf. Iohannes Damascenus, *Dialectica*, 51 (*P.G.* xciv. 636D–637A).

[3] *Apologeticus Maior*, 35 (*P.G.* c. 617B), said of the distinctions made in the Old Testament between Jews and pagans).

[4] Constantine, frg. 1 (Ostrogorsky). Cf. Nicephorus, *Antirrheticus*, i. 14 (*P.G.* c. 225A).

would not retain his [property of] being rational, he would not be man. Similarly if his mortality, or his erect walk, or his moving, or his being animate, or any of the other properties which combined constitute the nature and definition of man, were lacking, he would not be a man. And if somebody take away the ability to neigh from the horse, or that to bark from the dog, there will be neither horse nor dog. Therefore the humanity of Christ if bereft of one of its properties is a defective nature, and Christ not a perfect man, or rather not Christ at all, but is lost altogether if He cannot be circumscribed and represented in art.[1]

In discussing the difference between painting (γραφή) and circumscription (περιγραφή) Nicephorus was in agreement with the schoolmen in distinguishing definitions proper (ὅροι) from descriptions (ὑπογραφαί): 'Often descriptions are used in place of definitions wherever it is appropriate, and they are named descriptive definitions.'[2] Of the key term, εἰκών, he offered not one but three alternative definitions:

The pattern (ἀρχέτυπον) is an existing beginning and exemplar of a form shaped after it, and the cause of the likeness of the similitude. Of the image, however, the following definition says what one might say about objects produced by art: an image is a likeness of an archetype (ἀρχέτυπον) which reproduces in itself by way of resemblance the entire form of what is impressed upon it, and which differs from it merely by the difference of substance with respect to matter. Or: an imitation and similitude of a pattern differing in essence and substratum. Or: an artifact shaped in imitation of a pattern but differing in substance and subject; for if it does not differ in some respect, it is not an image nor an object different from the model. Thus an image is a likeness and a figuration of things being and existing.[3]

If these three definitions of the image are compared with that found in the writings of John of Damascus, a distinct change in form is apparent.[4] What John of Damascus had tagged on to his definition as an afterthought and in non-technical language, the

---

[1] Ibid. i. 20 (*P.G.* c. 244B–C).
[2] *Refutatio et Eversio*, Paris. Gr. 1250, fol. 285ʳ πολλάκις ὑπογραφαὶ ἀντὶ ὅρων ἐν οἷς χρὴ παραλαμβάνονται καὶ ὅροι ὑπογραφικοὶ προσαγορεύονται. On 'descriptive definitions' see John of Damascus, *Dialectica*, 8 (*P.G.* xciv. 553B).
[3] *Antirrheticus*, i. 28 (*P.G.* c. 277A–B).
[4] *De imaginibus*, iii. 16 (*P.G.* xciv. 1337A–B): 'An image is a likeness, and a pattern (παράδειγμα, corruption?), and an imprint of something showing in itself what it represents.' Then Iohannes goes on to demonstrate, in non-technical language, that pattern and image are not alike in all respects. Cf. also i. 9 (1240C).

essential difference between original and image, had now been incorporated into the definition; in other words, the technical character of the definition had been intensified. Few things show as clearly as this comparison the work done by the Byzantine schools since the days of John of Damascus.

Like his contemporaries, Nicephorus referred repeatedly to the Aristotelian doctrine of categories to refute his iconoclastic opponents. One of the most characteristic passages occurs in the *First Antirrheticus*:

I believe it will not be inappropriate to our present purpose to add this further point that the image is related to the pattern and is the effect of a cause. Therefore necessarily it belongs to, and is called, a relative [notion] (τῶν πρός τι). Relatives are said to be such as they are from their being *of* some other thing, and through their relation they are mutual correlatives (ἀντιστρέφει τῇ σχέσει πρὸς ἄλληλα).[1] A father, for instance, is called the son's father. . . . Thus a pattern is called the pattern of an image, and an image the image of a pattern, and nobody will call the image of an individual an unrelated image; for the one and the other are introduced and contemplated together. If somehow the pattern should disappear, the relation does not end together with it: the law of mutual cancellation[2] does not pertain to all such [notions], for sometimes the relations remain and survive although deprived of their object; as for instance in the case of father and son and in similar cases; for by the similarity and remembrance and form, it [the image] shows even the deceased as if he were present and it preserves the relation as time goes along. Now likeness is an intermediate relation and mediates between the extremes, I mean, the person represented and the representation. It unites and connects [them] through the form even though they differ in nature; for although they are different objects according to their nature, they are not different subjects and the image is another self (ἄλλος δὲ αὐτὸς ἐκεῖνος); for the knowledge of the primary form is obtained through the figure [image], and in it the hypostasis of the person represented can be discerned. This [relationship] one cannot observe in any other of these [notions, i.e. relatives], as in father, or son, or friend; for here we have the opposite case: each one of those is not a different object since they participate in the same essence but a different subject, and they differ in otherness of the hypostases. And if the relation does not perish in the case of these [father, son, friend] although they are separated, it will be preserved all the more in that other case [image].

[1] Aristotle, *Categories*, 7, 6 a 37 f., cf. 6 b 29 ff.
[2] Ibid., 7, 7 b 15–8 a 12.

In addition, likeness bestows also equivocalness, for the appellation is the same for both; for even the image of the king is called 'king'. . . . This was said by us in order to illustrate the character of the images which relates it to the pattern: it does not have identity of essence, nor can we in all respects predicate what is predicated of the pattern as pattern also of the image derived from it. If the one happens to be animate, the other is inanimate; if the one happens to be endowed with reason and moving, the other unreasoning and unmoved, the two are not identical, but on the one hand they resemble each other in form and on the other hand they differ in essence. Now, inasmuch as the image belongs to the relative [notions], it is praised alongside with the original, and conversely it is dishonoured alongside with it. Now since on the basis of both reasoning and definition, the difference is thus realized to lie in these points, and as pictorial representation is an external factor, and has nothing in common with the definition of the essence, why do our opponents stir in vain and boast that henceforth there will be separated what is naturally united?[1]

This long passage had to be rendered in full because it is a good illustration of the scholastic method. Nicephorus wished to disprove Constantine's thesis that by pictorial representation the Iconophiles established a new person of Christ according to the flesh, separated from His divine existence. He proceeded by applying to the image of Christ the corollaries derived from its being a relative term in the sense of scholastic logic. Thus he arrived at an essential difference between image and model which precluded the christological implications made by the Iconoclasts. Nicephorus' deductions, with their clumsy connexions between the various stages of the demonstration by the ubiquitous γάρ and οὖν, certainly lack the tight reasoning which distinguishes the works of the Aristotelian school; but as an application of the traditional logic to a contemporary theological problem the reasoning is perhaps not unimpressive.

In a passage in the *Refutatio et Eversio* Nicephorus handled the

---

[1] *Antirrheticus*, i. 30 (*P.G.* c. 277c–280c). Another reference to the category of relation occurs early in the *Refutatio et Eversio* where Nicephorus combats the heretical contention that the images are 'useless', Paris. Gr. 1250, fols. 182ᵛ 25–183ʳ 5:
ἀλλὰ καὶ τῶν πρός τι ἡ εἰκών ἐστι καὶ τοῦτο πᾶσιν ἂν οἶμαι διωμολογῆσθαι οἷς τὸ ἐν διανοίαις ἀκέραιον διασώζεται, ἐπεὶ καὶ σχέσις αὐτῇ πρὸς ὃ λέγεται πρόσεστι καὶ δι' ἑαυτῆς ἐμφανίζει τὸ ἀρχέτυπον καὶ τὴν γνῶσιν αὐτοῦ παρέχεται. δηλώσει καὶ ὁ κατ' αὐτὴν ὁρισμός· καὶ γὰρ ἀφομοίωσις πρὸς τὸ πρωτότυπον εἶδος εἶναι πέφυκε καὶ ταὐτὸν ἐκείνῳ παρὰ τὸ τῆς οὐσίας διάφορον, ἐξ οὗ καὶ τοῦ ὀνόματος μεταλήψεται· πρὸς δέ γε καὶ ἀντιστρέφει ταῦτα πρὸς ἄλληλα κατὰ τὸν λόγον τῶν πρός τι καὶ τὴν ἑαυτῆς σχέσιν σχοίη δ' ἄν τινα καὶ μέθεξιν ὡς παρὰ αἰτίου αἰτιατόν.

argument from the category of relation in a less satisfactory way.[1] There he argued against the iconoclastic contention that pictorial images of Jesus Christ are 'spurious' (ψευδώνυμος). Image and prototype are relative terms, Nicephorus wrote, and as such they come into being together and disappear together. If one is spurious, the other must be spurious too. Therefore, if the Iconoclasts call Christ's image spurious, they imply that Christ was a spurious Christ and a spurious king; in other words, that He does not exist at all. No image is spurious unless it has no archetype, and by their contention the Iconoclasts deny the Incarnation.

This line of argument is erroneous because an image can be 'spurious' not only if the original does not exist but also if the image distorts or otherwise misrepresents its features. In fact the author of the *Categories* himself had given examples where one of the correlatives could be removed without affecting the other: objects of knowledge or perception may exist without anybody knowing or perceiving them. Likewise, one may attack the veracity of a particular image without, in the framework of logic, questioning the original.[2]

Elsewhere Nicephorus referred to other categories, quality and substance, to disprove the iconoclastic view of the identity of essence between original and image:

For whereas he [Constantine] should have operated with the words 'similar' and 'dissimilar' which are inherent in the aforesaid, and are referred to [the category of] quality, as the devotees of these studies

---

[1] *Refutatio et Eversio*, fols. 223ʳ–224ᵛ, esp. 223ᵛ 20–224ʳ 15: ἐντεῦθεν λοιπὸν ἐφ' ὧν τὰ ὅμοια πρόκειται τῷ κοινῇ μετέχειν τῆς σχέσεως συνεισάγεσθαι ὡς τὰ πολλὰ καὶ συναναιρεῖσθαι κατὰ τὸ εἶδος τοῦ λόγου τούτου συμβήσεται. καὶ εἰ πρὸς θάτερον τὸ ψεῦδος ἐπιφημισθείη, καὶ τὸ ἕτερον ὡσαύτως τὸ ψεῦδος ἂν ἀπενέγκοιτο· εἰ δὲ τὸ ἕτερον τἀληθὲς ἔχοι, καὶ θάτερον δήπουθεν. ὡς φέρε εἰπεῖν ἡ τοῦ βασιλέως εἰκὼν ὁμοία τῷ βασιλεῖ ἐστιν ὅστις ποτὲ ὢν αὐτὸς τυγχάνει. οὐκοῦν εἰ ὁ εἰκονιζόμενος ἀληθὴς βασιλεὺς ὑπάρχει, ἔσται καὶ ἡ ἐκεῖνον εἰκονίζουσα ἀληθὴς εἰκών. εἰ δὲ ψευδὴς ὑπάρχει, καὶ ἡ κατ' αὐτὸν εἰκὼν ψευδὴς ἐξ ἀνάγκης δειχθήσεται. καὶ εἰ δεῖ τἀληθέστερον φάναι, οὐ μᾶλλόν ἐστιν εἰπεῖν τοῦ ὁπωσοῦν ψεύδους τὴν εἰκόνα ψευδῆ ἢ μηδὲ εἶναι τὸ παράπαν εἰκόνα, οἷάπερ εἰσὶ τὰ πλαττόμενα, ἱπποκενταύρους λέγω καὶ τραγελάφους, ἃ μὴ ὑφεστῶτα τῶν πλασσόντων ἐλέγχει τὴν κακοδαιμονίαν εἰδωλικοῖς προσανεχόντων φάσμασιν. οὕτω τοίνυν κατὰ τὸ ἀκόλουθον τοῦ λόγου, ὁπήνικα οἱ ψευδιεροὶ τὰς τοῦ μεγάλου βασιλέως Χριστοῦ καὶ Θεοῦ εἰκόνας ψευδωνύμους ἀποκαλεῖν τολμῶσιν, πᾶσα ἀνάγκη, ἐπειδὴ ἀλλήλων ἐστὶ δηλωτικὰ καὶ τὰς ἐμφάσεις ἀλλήλων κέκτηνται, αὐτὸν τὸν Χριστὸν ψευδῆ Χριστὸν καὶ ψευδῆ βασιλέα τυγχάνειν αὐτοὺς ἀποφαίνεσθαι. καὶ δογματισθήσεται αὐτοῖς ἐμφανέστερον καὶ Χριστὸς ψευδώνυμος μηδαμῇ μηδαμῶς ὤν· τὸ γὰρ ψεῦδος μὴ ὄν ἐστι παντί που δῆλον.

[2] Aristotle, *Categories*, 7, 7 b 15–8 a 6. It was seen above (p. 197 and n. 1) that in other passages Nicephorus himself was aware of this point.

would say,[1] whence somehow and gradually he might have reached the enquiry into these matters, he produces here [the notion of] identity which is matched by [the notion of] otherness and which is considered under [the category of] substance. Of these [notions, i.e. identity and otherness] there is no need in the aforesaid discussion. It seems to me that in such matters this same man [Constantine] does not postulate (?) the difference of object (τὸ ἄλλο καὶ ἄλλο) which distinguishes natures, but introduces the difference of subjects (τὸ ἄλλος καὶ ἄλλος) inasmuch as he determines hypostases which change the identity of subjects, and assumes necessarily many hypostases and as many Christs as there are images. . . .[2]

This supplemented an earlier discussion of the same problem where Nicephorus had expounded the absurd consequences which would follow from the iconoclastic view of the true image. If image and prototype, so he argued, were consubstantial, they would partake of the same definition. Thus if man be defined as a reasonable and mortal animal capable of thought and knowledge, the same would have to be true of his image. In reality, an image would cease to be image if it were consubstantial with the original, it would be identical with the latter. Identity of image and original exists only as to form but not as to substance.[3] If Constantine were right, one and the same thing could be both one and two (archetype and image), the terms archetype and image would be interchangeable, man could be said to resemble his image just as the image would resemble man. The relation between them would become a correlation and one might speak of the 'man of an image' as well as the 'image of a man'. One would, furthermore, be at a loss to say which of the two is the cause and which is the effect. Apparently Nicephorus was here operating with the scholastic concept of identity and its corollaries, yet the precise source from which he derived his remarks is difficult to identify. It need hardly be said that they were wide of the mark: Constantine had never claimed identity of archetype and image but merely consubstantiality.

In addition to logic Nicephorus availed himself of the physical

[1] Aristotle, *Categories*, 8, 11 a 15.
[2] *Antirrheticus*, i. 31 f. (*P.G.* c. 281A). Substance and quality are also discussed by our author where he attacks Eusebius' claim that after the resurrection Christ was changed into light (Pitra, i, chs. xxviii, xxx, pp. 418 and 420).
[3] Ibid. i. 17 (*P.G.* c. 228D): . . . οἷς (image and original) τὸ ταὐτὸν εἴδει μόνον, ἀλλ' οὐ τῷ ὑποκειμένῳ ἐμφαίνεται.

science of the schools.[1] Repeatedly he referred to the scholastic
doctrine of causation because, according to him, prototype and
image are related as cause and effect. In his effort to disprove
iconoclastic contentions Nicephorus used Aristotle's *Physics* and
Metaphysics (or writings derived from them). According to Nicephorus the word 'cause' (αἴτιον) has five connotations: efficient
(ποιητικόν), instrumental (ὀργανικόν), exemplary (παραδειγματικόν), material (ὑλικόν), and final (τελικόν) causes. This, Nicephorus said, holds for works of art. A person's image (ἡ τινός
εἰκών) is due to these causes. Now the exemplary cause (to speak
of this one only) of Christ's image is Christ or His form (ἤτοι τό
κατ' αὐτόν εἶδος), and hence the Iconoclasts destroy the bodily
form of Christ by calling His image 'spurious'.[2] While it may well
be that Aristotle's notion of a formal cause is applicable to Christ
as the formal cause of an image, the conclusion Nicephorus has

---

[1] I cannot resist the temptation of calling attention to a curious piece of meteorological lore although it has no connexion with the theory of images. Towards the
end of the *Third Antirrheticus* Nicephorus criticizes the notion that the Empire was
prosperous under Constantine V. He reports all sorts of celestial visitations and
continues (*Antirrheticus*, iii. 66, *P.G.* c. 497B): 'In this matter let none avail himself
[of the theories of] the experts on astronomical phenomena (τὰ μετέωρα), and refer to certain smoky and thick exhalations. With them the air surrounding the
earth is filled, then lifted upwards through its own impetus and poured out over the
ethereal space. It changes because of the combustion and forms the so-called shoot-
ing-stars, the meteors, the so-called torches, also comets, bearded stars, and whatever forms arise and shine. . . .' Cf. Aristotle, *Meteorologica*, 341 b. The comparison
with the natural phenomena after Christ's death (497c) makes it possible that
Nicephorus took this meteorological discussion from a Good Friday homily. A
similar explanation of the star over Bethlehem occurs in Basil the Great (?),
Homilia in sanctam Christi generationem, 6 (*P.G.* xxxi. 1472B).

[2] *Refutatio et Eversio*, fols. 224ᵛ–225ʳ: τὸ αἴτιον τῶν πολλαχῶς λεγομένων. οἱ περὶ
τὰ τοιαῦτα ἐσχολακότες φασὶν ποιητικόν τε γὰρ εἶναι καὶ ὀργανικὸν παραδειγματικόν τε
αὖ καὶ ὑλικὸν καὶ ἔτι πρὸς τούτοις τελικόν, καὶ εἴ τι ἕτερον ἐνταῦθα συναναφαίνεται· καὶ
ταῦτα θεωρεῖται καὶ ἐπὶ τῶν χειροτεύκτων ὡς τὰ πολλὰ καὶ ὑπὸ τέχνης κατὰ τὸν βίον
ἀποτελούμενα τὸν ἀνθρώπειον. ἐν οἷς καὶ ἡ τινὸς εἰκὼν παρὰ τοιούτων αἰτίων προάγεται.
ἐπεὶ οὖν καὶ ἡ τοῦ Σωτῆρος ἡμῶν Χριστοῦ εἰκὼν τεχνητή ἐστι καὶ χειρόκμητος, ἵνα
τἆλλα παρῶμεν, νῦν παραδειγματικὸν αἴτιον οὐχ ἕτερόν τι ἢ αὐτὸν τὸν Χριστὸν
κέκτηται ἤτοι τὸ κατ' αὐτὸν εἶδος. οἱ τοίνυν τοῦ ψεύδους καθηγημόνες διὰ τῆς φωνῆς
ταύτης λυμαίνονται τῷ τοῦ αἰτίου λόγῳ, ταὐτὸν δὲ εἰπεῖν ἀναιροῦσι τὸ σωματικὸν εἶδος
αὐτὸ καθ' ὅ ἡ τοιαύτη γραφὴ διακεχάρακτα. For Aristotle's four types of causes see
Physics, ii. 3, 194 b 16–195 a 3 (= *Metaphysics* Δ 2, 1013 a ff.) where Aristotle
himself uses εἶδος and παράδειγμα as synonymous to denote the formal cause. The
separate mention of an instrumental cause (ὀργανικόν) ought to make it possible
to define the particular handbook of philosophy used by Nicephorus and his contemporaries. In the *Antirrheticus*, iii. 35 (*P.G.* c. 432B) he mentions only the effective cause.
Yet the final cause (τὸ δι' ὅ γέγονεν) is mentioned immediately afterwards and the
term ὅ τινος ἕνεκεν γέγονεν probably refers to the instrumental cause in this passage.

drawn here is certainly bold, to say the least. It presupposes that the falsehood of the effect implies that of the cause, and that presupposition is as faulty as the one discussed in connexion with the category of relation.[1]

In another context Nicephorus turned to the concept of change. Eusebius, in his letter to Constantia, had claimed that in the Ascension 'the form of a servant was changed completely into His light'. This provided Nicephorus with an opportunity to discuss change. He did so by borrowing from John of Damascus' chapter περὶ κινήσεως (or its source) almost literally:

Nicephorus, *Contra Eusebium*, 27, p. 416 Pitra:

πᾶν τὸ μεταβαλλόμενον ἢ καθ' αὑτὸ ἤτοι κατ' οὐσίαν μεταβάλλεται (ὃ δὴ περὶ γένεσιν καὶ φθορὰν θεωρεῖται) ἢ κατά τι τῶν ἐν αὐτῷ. καὶ τοῦτο διχῶς· ἢ γὰρ κατὰ τὸ ποσὸν μεταβάλλεται, καθ' ὃ ἡ αὔξησις καὶ μείωσις δείκνυται· ἢ κατὰ τὸ ποιόν, ἐξ οὗ ἐμφαίνετα ἡ ἀλλοίωσις. παρετέον τὰ νῦν τόπου γε εἵνεκεν λέγειν ἢ χρόνου ἢ τινος ἄλλου τῶν ἐν κινήσει θεωρουμένων. . . .

Iohannes Damascenus, *Dialectica*, 61, 649D–652A:

πᾶν γὰρ μεταβαλλόμενον ἢ καθ' αὑτὸ μεταβάλλεται, ἢ κατά τι τῶν ἐν αὐτῷ, ἢ κατά τι τῶν περὶ αὑτό· καὶ εἰ μὲν καθ' αὑτό, ποιεῖ γένεσιν καὶ φθοράν· εἰ δὲ κατά τι τῶν ἐν αὐτῷ, ἢ κατὰ τὸ ποσὸν καὶ ποιεῖ αὔξησιν καὶ μείωσιν, ἢ κατὰ τὸ ποιὸν καὶ ποιεῖ ἀλλοίωσιν. εἰ δὲ κατὰ τὸ περὶ αὑτό, ποιεῖ τὴν κατὰ τόπον μεταβολήν. . . .

In this case not only is it evident that Nicephorus was using Aristotelian philosophy but even the source of his information can be identified.

What followed was not taken from the same authority but betrays its ultimate basis, Aristotle, by its style. Nicephorus proceeded to refute each alternative of the trilemma as applied to Eusebius' statement. If Eusebius meant that change took place κατὰ τὸ ποιόν or by alteration (ἀλλοίωσις), this would not change Christ *completely* as Eusebius claimed, 'for alteration is a transfiguration of some characteristic, or a separate or associated variation concerning some feature of the substance'. The same holds true for quantitative change as it does not represent complete change either. The remaining alternative, essential change, i.e. coming-to-be and passing away, would imply a complete annihilation of Christ's human form. This would indeed be a complete change, but it would do away with Christ's humanity.[2]

---

[1] p. 202 above.

[2] *Contra Eusebium*, ed. Pitra, i. 416. Cf. for example *Physics*, iii. 1, 200 b 33: μεταβάλλει γὰρ ἀεὶ τὸ μεταβάλλον ἢ κατ' οὐσίαν ἢ κατὰ ποσὸν ἢ κατὰ ποιὸν ἢ κατὰ τόπον κτλ.

As was said before, the direct source for the definition of qualitative, quantitative, and essential change used in these deductions cannot be ascertained, but they are in keeping, both as to style and content, with the medieval Aristotelian system.

Nicephorus explored yet another line of argumentation. In his *Apologeticus atque Antirrhetici* he proposed several times to elaborate the differences between circumscription (περιγραφή) and painting (γραφή) which his opponents had equated.[1] He touched on the subject of circumscription when he criticized Constantine's assertion that Christ could not be circumscribed:

Where in the world has an incircumscribable body ever been heard of? Especially as circumscription is a *condicio sine qua non* of bodies. For as a body does not exist without place or time, thus does it not exist without circumscription. For place circumscribes and contains the body, if it is true that 'space is the limiting surface of the body continent, in which it contains the body contained'. Now to say that the body is not circumscribed is identical with saying that it is not in a place. What, however, is not in a place, is not a body.[2]

This definition of place was taken from Aristotle's *Physics*, yet not in the faulty and deficient form in which the passage now appears in medieval manuscripts but in something like its entirety, as it was read by the medieval commentators.[3] Nicephorus dealt once again with the problem of circumscription in his *Second Antirrheticus*. The Emperor Constantine V, at the end of his second πεῦσις, had announced further writings in which he would deal with religious images other than those of Christ. These were not available to Nicephorus, but he tried to imagine what the Emperor might have set down in them. The angels he would have called uncircumscribable (ἀπεριγράπτους). So they are, said Nicephorus, but not altogether. They are circumscribable first of all in time; for they have a beginning. But they are furthermore

---

[1] e.g. *Antirrheticus*, i. 7 (*P.G.* c. 213D); ii. 7 (*P.G.* c. 345D).

[2] *Antirrheticus*, i. 20 (*P.G.* c. 241A).

[3] Aristotle, *Physics*, iv. 4, 212 a 7. Nicephorus: τόπος ἐστὶ πέρας τοῦ περιέχοντος ἐν ᾧ περιέχει τὸ περιεχόμενον. *Antirrheticus*, ii, ch. 18, 369B he defines: τόπος γὰρ πέρας ἐστὶ τοῦ περιέχοντος καθὸ περιέχει τὸ περιεχόμενον καὶ πέρασι διείληπται καθ' ἃς ὁρίζεται σχέσεις. Manuscripts of Aristotle: ἀνάγκη τὸν τόπον εἶναι . . . τὸ πέρας τοῦ περιέχοντος σώματος. Simplicius, Themistius, Philoponus, as well as the Arabic-Latin translation and the second and third Basel editions add: καθ' ὃ συνάπτει τῷ περιεχομένῳ. Iohannes Damascenus, *De Fide Orthodoxa*, i. 13 (*P.G.* xciv. 849C) has: καθ' ὃ περιέχεται τὸ περιεχόμενον.

circumscribable by apprehension (καταλήψει), 'for inasmuch as they are intellects (νόες), they share naturally in each other's thoughts and mutually know to some extent their nature; for one form of circumscription is apprehension . . .'.[1] The passage concluded with a statement that this whole discussion was beside the point and that the real question was not whether the angels are circumscribable (περιγράφεσθαι), but whether they can be represented in art (γράφεσθαι καὶ εἰκονίζεσθαι). Indeed, in a subsequent chapter, Nicephorus addressed himself explicitly to the distinction between painting and circumscription. He began by defining the two meanings of the Greek noun γραφή (writing and painting) and then argued:

Circumscription (περιγραφή), on the other hand, it is said, is produced in the following ways: either the thing circumscribed is circumscribed by place, or by time and beginning, or by apprehension. It is produced by place, as bodies are, for they are enclosed by place, inasmuch as place is 'the limiting surface of the body continent at which it contains the thing contained'.[2] What did not exist before and began its existence in time is circumscribed by time and beginning: in this way angels and souls are said to be circumscribed. [After a lengthy discourse on angels he proceeds:] and what is apprehended by thought and knowledge is circumscribed by apprehension [example: angels]. Circumscription therefore is the comprehending and limiting of the thing comprehended and limited, or termination of what is begun or moved, or apprehension of what is thought and known. What is contained by none of these is uncircumscribable. Christ, so far as His humanity is concerned, is circumscribable in all three ways.[3]

Having thus introduced these distinctions, Nicephorus went on to develop them. He imagined a portrait painter and set out to prove that such a painter does not circumscribe the person portrayed. First, Nicephorus established a number of important differences between painting and circumscribing. The painter does not enclose the person portrayed, indeed that person need not even be present; this does not hold for circumscription.[4] The painter paints on a wall or on a board, but no reasonable person would claim that circumscription is done in the same place.

---

[1] *Antirrheticus*, ii. 7 (*P.G.* c. 345C).
[2] Aristotle, *Physics*, iv. 4, 212 a 7.
[3] Nicephorus, *Antirrheticus*, ii. 12 (*P.G.* c. 356B–357A).
[4] Ibid. ii. 13 (*P.G.* c. 357B).

Pictorial representation is attained by colours and pebbles (mosaics), but circumscription is attained quite differently (by place, time, or apprehension). Painting presents the bodily shape of the person by moulding his outline and form and likeness, while circumscription limits the enclosed. Painting is related to the pattern through resemblance, is called 'painting of a pattern' and has an independent existence; none of these propositions is valid for circumscription. Painting is confined to one or several places, circumscription accompanies the object circumscribed wherever it goes. The one exists wholly in observation, the other in thought. 'And to sum up, neither does pictorial representation circumscribe the man even if he is capable of circumscription, nor does circumscription represent him pictorially even if he is capable of pictorial representation, for each one will have its own function (λόγος).'[1]

There follows a difficult passage for which only a tentative translation can be offered:

Furthermore pictorial representation is contained in circumscription, but circumscription is not contained in it [pictorial representation] but contains it; therefore they are not reciprocal, for circumscription is the more general term. For if something is painted, that is to say, the subject represented, I mean the man, and the painting itself or the moulded figure, somebody might perhaps call it also circumscript ([the term] with which we are dealing now) *and* it [this term] is to be distinguished altogether [from the term 'painted']— because we are not discussing the difference in process. It is not conversely true that if a thing is circumscript, it is likewise painted.[2]

This last point Nicephorus illustrated with a wealth of examples. The year, the Law of Moses, idolatry, sovereignty and power over a people, human life, diseases (especially one-day fevers), flowers, Jacob's descent into Egypt and the return of his progeny, the Babylonian exile, the aerial breeze, speech—all these are circumscribed but not painted.[3] If sometimes one finds personification of the Virtues, this is not a pictorial representation in the proper sense because images as relative terms require the previous

[1] Nicephorus, *Antirrheticus*, ii. 13 (*P.G.* c. 357B–360A).
[2] Ibid. ii. 13 (*P.G.* c. 360A–B). Migne's text may be corrupt in one or more places. Cf. Iohannes Damascenus, *Dialectica*, 15 (*P.G.* xciv. 577B–580A) where the terms ἐπὶ πλέον and ἀντιστρέφειν are explained.
[3] Nicephorus, ibid. ii. 13–15 (*P.G.* c. 360B–361D).

existence of a model.[1] The Iconoclasts ignore the fundamental
difference between pictorial representation and circumscription,
and where they speak of circumscription, the real problem is one
of pictorial representation.

These long quotations and excerpts were given advisedly
because they seem unique in the literature of the Controversy.
The clear distinction between circumscription and religious art
was Nicephorus' own contribution to the doctrine of images.
The definition of circumscription was related to that developed
by John of Damascus in connexion with his doctrine of angels.[2]
Yet the scholastic *distinguendum est* as such must have been
Nicephorus' own. It was appended to Nicephorus' discussion of
the writings of Constantine as an elaboration of what had been
adumbrated several times already. The context does not make it
clear what specific statement of the Iconoclasts Nicephorus had
in mind when he wrote his refutation. It is obvious, and Nicephorus
said so expressly, that his main thesis was that the *painting of
Christ does not imply His circumscription*. It follows that he accused
the Iconoclasts, and Constantine in particular, of holding the
contrary view: *painting of Christ implies His circumscription*. Now
an image of Christ could only be said (by the Iconoclasts) to
circumscribe Christ Himself if Christ and His image were identified. If the image and Christ were mere relatives and, as the
Iconophiles held, of a different nature and essence altogether, it
cannot be understood how Christ's image could affect the person
of Christ Himself. This shows that, to Nicephorus' mind at least,
Iconoclasts and Iconophiles started from a different conception
of the image. With the former it was in some way identical with
the person represented, with the latter there existed only a relation between the two.

This fundamental difference was commented on, though in a
different connexion, by Ostrogorsky.[3] According to him this
difference in the notion of image was evident from the writings
of Constantine himself. He based his view on Constantine's
calling the image consubstantial with Christ and the Eucharist
the true image of Christ.[4] Thus the Iconophiles in general did

---

[1] Ibid. ii. 15 (*P.G.* c. 361D–364A).

[2] Cf. Nicephorus, ibid. ii. 12 (*P.G.* c. 356B–C) with Iohannes Damascenus, *De
Fide Orthodoxa*, i. 13 (*P.G.* xciv. 852C–853B); ii. 3 (ibid. 869A–C).

[3] *Studien*, 40–45.

[4] Ibid., frgs. 2 and 19–22 respectively (pp. 8 and 10 f.). H. Barion, 'Quellen-

not merely misunderstand or misrepresent the Iconoclastic point of view in this connexion; there was a fundamental philosophical difference in the two conceptions of the image, and this difference permeated the doctrinal system of both parties.

What did Nicephorus do to shake that fundamental position of his enemies? At first glance it would seem that his discussion represents a convincing refutation of Constantine's powerful attack. Constantine had claimed that by painting Christ you either circumscribe a mere man, or you circumscribe the divine nature together with the human. Nicephorus replied that this was to confuse the issue: painting is not circumscribing, and if we paint Christ, we do not circumscribe either one of His natures.[1] But soon after stating that painting does not imply circumscription, he contradicts himself by adding that circumscription is the broader term and that a γραπτόν might possibly be called also περίγραπτον.[2] This second statement, it is true, was formulated in a rather cautious way and presented only as a possible position (φήσειεν ἄν τις τάχα που). Still on this point Nicephorus' argumentation must be called confused.

On closer examination Nicephorus' reply to Constantine's attack reveals an even more serious weakness. It is based on the

kritisches zum byzantinischen Bilderstreit', *Römische Quartalschrift*, xxxviii (1930), 78–90, did not accept Ostrogorsky's demonstration on this point, but I cannot share his objections. Barion's basic error seems to be that he fails to recognize the *fragmentary* character of Nicephorus' quotations from the writings of Constantine. From fragments 3, 7, and 10 he infers that according to Constantine 'ein Bild muß durch entsprechende Darstellung der Hypostase einen Schluß auf die Ousia erlauben', which no artistic image could do for Christ's divine nature. Real identity of essence (ὁμόουσιος), according to Barion, Constantine V did not expect of the image. But Barion overlooks the fact that fragments 7 and 10 are part of the famous Constantinian dilemma where the imperial author tried to reduce *ad absurdum* the idea of a pictorial image of Christ and therefore accepted temporarily the views of his opponents, viz. that an image *represents* (frg. 10 δηλοῦσαν) rather than *is* the person represented. Fragment 3 has come down to us in so mutilated a state as to defy syntax and sense. Barion himself admits (p. 81) that 'am meisten für O[strogorsky] spricht die Behauptung der Bildergegner, daß das einzig wahre Bild Christi das Abendmahl sei'. His counter-arguments concern, if they are valid, the Council of 754, not the writings of Constantine V. For Constantine the Eucharist and the image of Christ are not merely comparable, for him the consecrated bread of the Eucharist *is* the image of Jesus Christ (frgs. 21 and 22). In addition Ostrogorsky's thesis is supported by the constant identification, in the writings of Constantine, of γραφή and περιγραφή (frgs. 5, 7–9, 13, &c.). This identification presupposes the identity of image and Christ.

[1] *Antirrheticus*, ii. 13 (*P.G.* c. 357A–B).
[2] Ibid. (*P.G.* c. 360A–B), passage translated above, p. 208.

view that circumscription could occur only by virtue of place, time, or apprehension. This, as was said above, Nicephorus took over from an earlier source and therefore was protected by authority. Yet it is precisely here that he disagreed with the Iconoclasts. Constantine's dangerous alternative rested on a premiss diametrically opposed to that of Nicephorus, namely, that there existed a fourth type of circumscription (περιγραφή), that is, pictorial representation (γραφή). The dilemma which Constantine presented in such a powerful way to his opponents is built on this supposition. Nicephorus advanced his own thesis, buttressed by authority against that of his opponent, but in spite of all the array of learning he did not even attempt to refute it. To sum up, one might say of the Iconophiles what Ostrogorsky said of the Iconoclasts: they and their opponents talked at cross-purposes.[1] Nicephorus' comments miss the point—a phenomenon which is not rare where fundamental tenets are at stake and which is perhaps the surest criterion that such is the case. What remains true is that they are scholastic from beginning to end. From the first warning of the *distinguendum est* (γραφή and περιγραφή) to the careful definitions borrowed from the highest theological authority (John of Damascus), terminology and argumentation are coloured with the scholastic dye.

Finally, the subject of pictorial images lent itself to excursions into the field of aesthetics. Thus Nicephorus, on at least two occasions, discussed the superiority of the sense of sight, as exercised by the beholder of a pictorial image, over that of hearing used by the congregation when listening to the reading of the Gospel. In one of these passages Nicephorus said:

For we all know that sight is the most honoured and necessary of the senses and it may allow apprehension of what falls under perception more distinctly and sharply; for 'it is the nature of that which is heard to travel less quickly than that which is seen',[2] and seeing will attract faster than the other senses since it also has the attractive power to a larger degree.[3]

[1] *Studien*, p. 45.
[2] Pseudo-Aristotle, *De Mundo*, 4, 395 a 17.
[3] *Refutatio et Eversio*, fol. 273ᵛ: ἴσμεν γὰρ δήπου ἅπαντες ὅτι γε ὄψις τῶν αἰσθητηρίων τὸ τιμιώτατον καὶ ἀναγκαιότατον τρανέστερόν τε καὶ ὀξυωπέστερον τῶν ὑποπιπτόντων αἰσθήσει σχοίη ἂν τὴν ἀντίληψιν· καὶ γὰρ τὸ ἀκουστὸν ὑπὸ τοῦ ὁρατοῦ πέφυκε φθάνεσθαι καὶ θᾶττον ἐφελκύσεται τῶν ἄλλων ἡ ὅρασις, ὅσῳ καὶ μᾶλλον τὸ ἐπαγωγὸν ἔχει (the words τῶν ὑποπιπτόντων ... ἀντίληψιν are omitted in Paris. Gr. 1250 and have been

This high estimate of the sense of sight went back, in the last
resort, to passages of Aristotle, such as the famous beginning of
the *Metaphysics*,[1] even though when comparing seeing and hearing Aristotle himself had arrived at a more complex appreciation
in other writings.[2] Yet medieval authors clung to the simpler
statements; John of Damascus, for instance, declared seeing to be
the first sense.[3] All this, and especially the literal quotation from
the *De Mundo*, proves the scholastic inspiration of the passage.

This scholastic type of reasoning had been altogether absent
from the discussion on religious images during the preceding
centuries, particularly during the eighth. It is of course true that
in the Byzantine Middle Ages, when all higher education was
based on the Aristotelian system, an application of this training
to a burning issue like that of the Christian images was inevitable.
It is all the more striking that it took Byzantine theologians
roughly a century before they used this seemingly obvious weapon.

This was not the first time that scholasticism had invaded the
discussion of theological problems. On the contrary, sooner or
later all religious problems in the Middle Ages were subjected to
the scholastic treatment. As early as the fourth century the trini-
tarian issue had forced the theologians to discuss such notions as
essence, nature, &c. The christological controversies had been
marked by the scholastic stamp as early as Cyril of Alexandria
and had been pressed fully into the scholastic system with Boethius
in the West and Leontius of Byzantium and Iohannes Philoponus in the East. About this last writer of the sixth century
Usener remarked: 'Sein Verdienst, die Scholastik angebahnt zu
haben, hat er mit der ewigen Verdammnis als Ketzer gebüßt.
. . . Schon um das Jahr 600 ist die Klappermühle der klerikalen
Philosophie im Gang. . . .'[4] This point of view seems one-sided.
With regard to religious feeling and thought, the intrusion of the
schoolman into the Church may mark a decline, but it is an

added in the margin). A more elaborate passage occurs in *Apologeticus Maior*, 62
(*P.G.* c. 748D–749B). In this last place Nicephorus states that the sense of sight,
as compared with that of hearing, produces the more durable impressions and
is more effective in leading the uneducated from sensible symbols to intelligible
transcendentals. See also *Contra Eusebium et Epiphanidem* (Pitra, iv. 301 f.).

[1] A 1, 980 a 24 ff.

[2] Cf. *De Sensu*, 1, 437 a 3. Theophrastus (apud Plutarchum, *De Recta Ratione
Audiendi*, 2) called *hearing* τὴν παθικωτάτην of all the senses.

[3] *De Fide Orthodoxa*, 18 (*P.G.* xciv. 933D).

[4] Hermann Usener, *Kleine Schriften*, iii. 210.

inevitable consequence of dogmatic controversy. Moreover, from the point of view of the School, the spreading of intellectual habits and processes from the schoolroom to other spheres, and the application of the knowledge acquired in school to the vital issues of the day, may well realize the highest and most justified ambitions of an educational system.

The scholastic defence of image-worship was an argumentation developed by the iconophile party prior to the new outbreak in 815. In the course of the 120 years of actual Controversy and after many more centuries of discussion, the theorists of image-worship were twice successful in transplanting the entire issue from one level to another. First, Constantine had lifted it from the traditional level to the christological, and the image-worshippers were forced to meet him on his own ground. Then the iconophile dogmatists of the late eighth or early ninth century strengthened the christological structure, erected by their predecessors, by scholastic reasoning. It is surprising, however, that the Iconoclasts of the ninth century should not have counter-attacked with scholastic weapons. Perhaps the above-mentioned letter of Theodore of Studios to John the Grammarian is sufficient evidence to prove that such an attempt was at least contemplated.[1]

[1] Above, p. 195.

IX

CONCLUSIONS

1. *'The Images before Iconoclasm'*[1]

FROM the Synagogue the Early Church inherited its hostility to religious art, which both identified with paganism. The Christian Apologists of the second and third centuries of the Christian era attacked the cult statues of the pagans roughly on the same grounds as the great Hebrew prophets had done a millennium earlier: the statues consist of matter and are made and unmade by human hands. The writings of the Christian Apologists, as well as of the pagan defenders of cult statues, show how paganism met these criticisms on the part of its Jewish and Christian contemporaries, as well as the scruples which had arisen in pagan hearts. To thoughtful pagans of all periods, and especially to those of the Late Roman Empire, the cult statues were not gods, nor were the gods thought to inhabit them. They were merely set up to honour the gods, to remind mortal man of their existence and power, and to ensure that sacrifices and prayers presented to the statues would reach the gods themselves. This symbolical view of religious statues grew more complex as time went along until authors like Porphyry and Julian systematized the idea of divine representation. According to them, since the gods were incorporeal and man corporeal, the gods can be worshipped only through bodily likenesses. The first images of the gods were the stars, and the cult statues as representations of the stars were thus twice removed from the invisible gods.

Meanwhile the Christian Church had begun to modify its original position. The 'argumentative' and 'symbolic' art of the Catacombs demonstrated *ad oculos* of the converts the biblical and liturgical guarantees of their new faith. Even here the earliest representations show a notable reluctance to portray Jesus Christ. This funerary art, however, which after the Christianization of the Empire influenced the decoration of basilicas and churches, is less important, in the context of this book, than the representa-

[1] I am borrowing this phrase from the article by N. H. Baynes, *Harvard Theological Review* xliv (1951) 93–106.

tions of Christ and the Saints on portable objects. These 'icons', which are mentioned as early as the fourth century and of which specimens from the sixth and later centuries are preserved, are not so much realistic portraits as attempts to recapture the spiritual essence of the person represented. Enlarged and staring eyes, subtle distribution of light and shade and other devices make these religious images appear to be morsels from the Kingdom of God caught up in earthly matter. On the physical side, it was, at least originally, their bodily contact with a holy place or a Saint which made them *res sacrae* of a secondary kind. At the same time, however, Eastern Christianity, so concerned with the problem of death and immortality, saw in these icons mediators and guarantors of another world which they claimed to represent. From the fourth century on then, if not earlier, the images became part and parcel of personal piety and as visible signs of invisible grace all but rivalled the sacraments of the Church. They thus entered the Church 'from below' in a wide process of 'paganization' of Christianity. The new converts of the fourth and later centuries were no longer satisfied with listening to the word of God as found in Scripture and with worship in spirit and in truth, but wanted in addition to see and possess what they worshipped. The hierarchy of the Church, and particularly the theologians, were slow in adapting themselves to these innovations introduced by the masses. No Church Father prior to the fourth century approved of Christian religious art. Those of the Alexandrian school of theology, as for example Clement and Origen, who were influenced in this matter by a pagan philosophic tradition represented by Porphyry and others, considered artistic images nothing less than a pagan abomination. They held that the Christian equivalent to the pagan cult statues was the Christian virtues developed in a Christian soul.

Even after the icons had conquered for themselves an important position in church and home, many bishops and theologians continued to object. These objections were based not only on the Old Testament prohibitions but also on christological considerations where the images of Jesus Christ were concerned; for other icons the doctrine of the virtuous soul as the true cult statue, as expounded by the Alexandrian theologians and others, was drawn upon. The more a particular theologian emphasized Jesus Christ's godhead, the less would he be inclined to permit artistic representations. Origenists like Eusebius, Monophysites like Philoxenus of Hierapolis, or persons with quasi-monophysitic leanings like the Emperor Constantine V, actively campaigned against religious images. Armenia, which was divided and disputed between the Byzantine and Persian empires, even witnessed the emergence of a schismatic group with iconoclastic tendencies. There, at the turn from the sixth to the seventh century, a small number of monks who had become disgusted with the quarrels between an anti-Chalcedonian and a rival pro-Chalcedonian hierarchy, settled in the desert on the southern slopes of the Caucasus. Following a tradition represented particularly by the theologians of Alexandria, they preached that holiness was a prerogative of ascetics like themselves and that no object made by human hands, such as icons, deserved worship. They also refused to hold communion with the secular clergy, and thus within one generation slipped from schism into heresy. This iconoclastic tradition remained active in Armenia until the eve of the Iconoclastic Controversy in the Byzantine Empire.

In the meantime most theologians in the Empire had yielded to the pressure of popular piety. The Cappadocian Fathers, in the fourth century, had authorized religious art as a vehicle of biblical and religious instruction. In the sixth century Hypatius of Ephesus (531–8), overriding the scruples of one of his suffragan bishops, and again under the impact of popular worship, had condoned the use and perhaps even the worship of religious sculpture as well as paintings in his archdiocese. Yet he was aware of objections based on the Old Testament and on the teachings of the Alexandrian theologians. He also maintained for himself and other learned men the superiority of the written and spoken word of God over the icons. However, as a concession to simple souls, he legitimized religious art because of its 'anagogical' function; the unlearned would be guided by it 'towards the intelligible beauty and from the abundant light in the sanctuaries to the intelligible and immaterial light'. Somewhat later, when the Persian and later Arab conquests put Judaism in the conquered lands once again on an equal footing with Christianity, the Christian disputants in theological discussions at times would feel embarrassed by the existence of Christian images. By this time paganism outside the Church had become a *quantité négligeable*, while the Synagogue had unexpectedly reasserted its vitality and missionary zeal. Under these circumstances an unknown Christian, perhaps a member of the circle around the Patriarch John the Compassionate of Alexandria (610–19), took a natural though bold step; he applied the arguments traditionally used by pagans in defence of their cult statues to Christian images. These arguments are found regularly in the anti-Jewish and anti-Pagan dialogue literature from the seventh century onward. In fact the symbolic theory was eminently suitable to the art of the icons, which had developed a technique designed primarily to guide the onlooker towards spiritual realities. It is in this same literature, to be precise in fragments preserved from the writings of John of Thessalonica (610–49) and later in the eighty-second canon of the Quinisextum (692), that an appeal is made to Chalcedonian christology, particularly to Christ's complete human nature, as a means of legitimizing artistic representations of Christ.

2. *The Iconoclastic Controversy in the Byzantine Empire*

It will be clear that the ultimate cause of the outbreak of the Iconoclastic Controversy in the eighth century lay in the old tradition of hostility to religious art, which the Church had inherited from the Synagogue and which had survived in some circles to the eighth century. The problem is not so much why the conflict broke out in the eighth century but why it had not broken out centuries earlier. There is little need to point to similar movements in other parts of the medieval world to explain the origin of the Iconoclastic movement. It is true that under the Ommayyad Khalifs Umar II (717–20) and Yazid II (720–4) Christian and Jewish images had been destroyed or mutilated. Leo III, the first of the iconoclastic emperors of Byzantium, was a native of Germanicea (Marash) in Syria, which during his youth was repeatedly occupied by the Arabs and had a large Arab population. It is, therefore, not impossible that the personal Iconoclasm of this emperor was in some direct or indirect way due to Moslem influence. Yet Byzantine Iconoclasm seems to have had a motivation quite different from that prevailing in the Moslem dominions. It was not based on hostility towards the representation of living creatures only, as was the case in the Khalifate, but arose from opposition to any kind of religious art. The support which Leo received from the Byzantine clergy is explicable only in terms of the old tradition within the Christian Church which opposed the icons. While the proximate cause of the outbreak may therefore in some way be connected with Leo III and events in Moslem lands, the inspiration of the iconoclastic party seems to have come from within the Eastern Church.

The first generation of Iconoclasts, whose reasoning can be gathered from the writings of John of Damascus († 749?) and of Germanos Patriarch of Constantinople (715–30), relied on the Old Testament prohibitions and other biblical and patristic texts. Otherwise the early Iconoclasts argued as, in the anti-Jewish and anti-Pagan literature of the Early Church, the Jewish or Christian interlocutors had done for centuries: the icons consisted of matter and were the product of human craft. To these objections the defenders of image worship replied in kind by using the traditional arguments adduced in earlier centuries by pagans in defence of their statues, in short by recourse to the symbolic theory of religious images.

In the second generation of Iconoclasm the contending parties emphasized the christological implications of portraits of Christ. This shift was due to the activities of Leo's son, the Emperor Constantine V (741–75). Constantine, born to the purple and raised in the iconoclastic views of his father's court and empire, was himself passionately interested in theological problems and endowed with formidable gifts of dialectics, oratory, and propaganda. He succeeded in imposing much of his thinking, though not always his formulations, on the hierarchy of the Empire. There was a natural correlation between a christology minimizing Christ's human nature and opposition to artistic representations of Jesus Christ; in Constantine V these two tendencies were indeed combined. His avoidance of the Chalcedonian formula 'in two natures', his postulate of essential identity for original and image, and the Apollinarian origin of his famous dilemma that artistic representation of Jesus either separated or confused the two natures in Christ—all these features reveal the quasi-monophysite tendencies in Constantine's thought. With his dilemma Constantine followed his opponents on to the terrain of their own choosing, namely christology, and thus neutralized their most effective weapon. The Iconoclastic Council of Hiereia (754), attended by most of the bishops in the Empire, by and large corroborated Constantine's iconoclastic theses. It repeated the argument from idolatry traditional in anti-Jewish literature, adopted and adapted Constantine's argument from christology, and rejected artistic images of the Mother of God and of the Saints on the ground that they could never represent their essential holiness.

After Constantine's doctrine had been approved by the Council of Hiereia, the Emperor began to destroy images and to persecute dissidents. Most of the secular hierarchy was won over to the teachings of the Council, yet there remained vigorous opponents and many martyrs and confessors in the monasteries. Large numbers of iconophile monks fled to the West and to outlying regions of the Empire or found refuge among the Moslems. Constantine's views, and even more so the legends and apocalyptic tales which soon began to form around his name, were to influence the people of the Empire for many generations. The length and economic prosperity of his reign as well as his military successes over Bulgarians and Arabs seemed to bestow divine approval upon his iconoclastic theories. At the same time the espousal of Iconoclasm by the majority of the clergy led to a serious cleavage between secular and monastic clergies which was to assert itself throughout the later course of the Controversy and which survived even the definitive restoration of image-worship (843). Finally, it was in the time of Constantine that the Papacy placed itself under Frankish protection and that the Illyricum was put under the ecclesiastical jurisdiction of the Patriarch of Constantinople.

Constantine's son and successor, Leo IV, continued the iconoclastic policies of his father. He did, however, appoint abbots to the archbishoprics. By this device the government was able to put pressure on the monasteries to follow its theological directives —a policy which was to prove profitable during the second period of Iconoclasm in the ninth century.

The spiritual and political strength of the Iconoclastic movement was far from exhausted when, through a series of strategic blunders of the first magnitude (the passive attitude towards Irene's plans of restoration of image worship in the first seven years of her rule, the acquiescence to the removal of the iconoclastic garrison from Constantinople and its subsequent discharge at Malagina) the iconoclastic party allowed its opponents to deprive it temporarily of its military strength. Thereupon image worship was restored at the Seventh Ecumenical Council of Nicaea (787).

In the interval between the Council and the new outbreak of the Iconoclastic Controversy in 815 a number of important developments took place. In the first place, the Iconophiles, who were now for the first time since the days of Leo III in a position to argue their case freely, buttressed their views by references to the Aristotelian philosophy as taught in the schools. This scholastic theory of images is found in almost identical terms in works of the early ninth century, notably in a recently discovered commentary on the Gospel of John by an unknown member of the Studite circle, and in the writings of Theodore of Studios and of the Patriarch Nicephorus. They all insist on furnishing careful definitions of key terms such as image, painting, and circumscription. They avail themselves of the doctrine of equivocal terms (τὰ ὁμώνυμα) and of the categories, notably of the category of relation, to prove that what affects the equivocal or relative term (the image) will also affect the correlative (Christ). In a similar vein they operate with the Aristotelian doctrine of causation and show that a successful attack on the effect (the image) will necessarily invalidate its cause (Christ). The concepts of space and change also play a role in this kind of reasoning.

In addition to the formation of this scholastic doctrine of religious images, the thirty years' interval between the Seventh Ecumenical Council and the new outbreak of Iconoclasm witnessed a continuation and intensification of the conflict between secular and regular clergy which had begun in the days of the persecution. At the Council of Nicaea the differences between the two parties had to some degree been reconciled to make the restoration of image worship possible. In the following years the affair of the Simoniac bishops, and even more the issue of Constantine VI's second marriage (the Moechian Affair), had shown the power and determination of the monastic party led by Theodore of Studios. These monks were favoured by Irene, were in opposition under the Emperor Nicephorus (802–11), and in control of the government under his devout and weak successor Michael I Rangabe (811–13). Under the Emperor Nicephorus they opposed the elevation of his namesake to the patriarchate on the ground that he was a layman. They criticized with increasing severity the restoration to the priesthood of Joseph of Kathara, who had blessed the adulterous union of Constantine VI and Theodote. This they did although Constantine VI himself was now dead, although his marriage had been severed posthumously by imperial fiat, and although Joseph had in the meantime deserved well of the Empire by having prevented a civil war.

After Theodore of Studios had been condemned by a local synod in 809, the Studites continued to undermine the authority of the hierarchy by accusing of schism and even of heresy all those who were in ecclesiastical communion with Joseph. Under Michael I Rangabe they attempted to transform the Byzantine Empire into the Studite version of the Kingdom of Heaven. In 812 they prevented, against the advice of the Patriarch and of the archbishops of Nicaea and of Cyzicus, the conclusion of a peace treaty with the Bulgarians by opposing the extradition of refugees from Bulgaria. They demanded and obtained the cancellation of the death penalty (decreed by a local synod at Constantinople as well as by imperial edict) against Paulicians and Athinganoi on the ground that a heretic might yet be converted to orthodoxy. Finally they may well have inspired the mass discharge, without pensions or land allotments, of large parts of the garrison at Constantinople probably because they had iconoclastic leanings; this was reminiscent of Irene's treatment of the Constantinopolitan garrison in 786/7. While the issues involved in the Bulgarian treaty and in the death penalty against Paulicians and Athinganoi are not sufficiently clear to permit an informed judgement as to the morality, wisdom, and legality of the Studite interventions, their opposition to the restoration of Joseph and the mass dismissal of unprovided veterans involved no basic religious principles and were acts of irresponsible folly. The Studite position on Joseph deepened the gulf between secular and monastic clergy to such an extent that the Church was split into two warring factions to the days when the storm of Iconoclasm was to threaten it for a second time. The discharged soldiers who, unlike their predecessors of 786/7, owned no farms to which they could retire, were driven to despair. 'Accustomed to yearn for the worse, they hate the *status quo* at all times and rejoice at innovation and strive after revolutions', as the Patriarch Nicephorus put it. It was this social stratum which gave the strongest support to the iconoclastic policy of Leo V the Armenian (813–20).

There was one other crucial development that occurred prior to the new outbreak of Iconoclasm. On Christmas Day 800 the Papacy formalized its dependence on its Frankish protectors; at St. Peter's King Charles was recognized *de iure* as what the Frankish king had been *de facto* for some time: Emperor of the Romans. Then war broke out between Charlemagne and Byzantium. The latter recognized the imperial title of the Frankish ruler only in 811. From that year dates a delayed letter of enthronement from the Patriarch Nicephorus addressed to Pope Leo III. In it the former compares the pressure exerted by the late Emperor Nicephorus I on himself with the compulsion allegedly suffered by Pope Leo in connexion with the events of Christmas Day 800—an interesting, early, and hitherto unnoticed testimony for the 'imperial coronation' of Charlemagne.

There are indications that the second outbreak of Iconoclasm (814/15) constituted a popular protest against the régime of Michael I Rangabe and his monkish *directeurs de conscience*. The weird shout: 'Let the bones of the images be exhumed', which Nicephorus reports he had heard in 814/15, allows of no other explanation. In its theological aspects the iconoclastic doctrine of the Council of St. Sophia (815) was dependent upon the pronouncements of Hiereia (754). The second iconoclastic council expressly abandoned the argument for idolatry, but reasserted the arguments from christology and from holiness in somewhat vaguer terms than had been done at Hiereia. In fact, the Council of St. Sophia expanded the argument from holiness by making it applicable to images of Christ and the Saints. The patristic quotations, which form the core of the document preserved from the Council of St. Sophia, were selected by a committee of six men. This Committee was appointed by the Armenian Emperor Leo V in 814 and two of its six members were Armenians. Since in Armenia opposition to religious images had for a long time been based on the hostility of saintly ascetics towards the competition of sacred objects (*res sacrae*), the emphasis of the Council of St. Sophia on the argument from holiness seems connected with the traditions of Iconoclasm in Armenia. In the last resort, however, this argument can be traced back to early Christianity, notably to the essential theory of the image held by men like Clement and Origen of Alexandria.

The Patriarch Nicephorus had resigned his august office before the Council of St. Sophia assembled, and resided until his death (828) in the monastery of St. Theodore which he had founded near Chalcedon. After the meeting of the Council there began a persecution of Iconophiles. It was not limited to Constantinople. There were a few martyrs and many confessors in all parts of the Empire. In contrast to the iconoclastic persecution of the eighth century there were now bishops who remained faithful to image worship, perhaps because this time image-worship had behind it the authority of an Ecumenical Council; there were now also monks who had become converts to Iconoclasm, presumably because Leo IV's policy of appointing archbishops from among the abbots had placed the episcopal *omophorion* within the reach of the monk. Iconophile exiles and prisoners were not molested if, like the ex-Patriarch Nicephorus, they kept quiet and lived as private citizens. On the other hand, if they continued, as did Theodore of Studios, to preach in favour of image-worship, to meet with other iconophile leaders, and to correspond with their fellow-Christians abroad, they suffered privations and even torture. Theodore appealed not only to the monks of Egypt, Syria, Palestine, and Rome, but even to Pope Paschal I and through him to the Western Emperor Lewis the Pious, to intervene on behalf of image worship.

The atmosphere changed under Leo's successor Michael II (820–9), the founder of the Amorian dynasty. The ex-Patriarch Nicephorus attempted in a letter to demonstrate to Michael the iconophile dogma, but Michael was unwilling to go beyond neutrality in the matter of images. With this one exception Nicephorus abstained from any intervention in ecclesiastical matters to the day of his death. When in 821 Theodore of Studios came to visit him in the monastery where he was residing, Nicephorus politely but pointedly refused to discuss either past or present matters of Church policy.

The two great leaders of the Iconophiles died within two years of each other. The persecution of the Iconophiles was revived under Michael's son, the Emperor Theophilus (828–43). There is evidence that under this emperor a third Iconoclastic Council was held at Blachernae, either under the Patriarch John the Grammarian (837–43), or under his predecessor Antonius (821–37). This Council once again declared the Eucharist to be the true image of Christ. Furthermore, Iconoclasm under Theophilus appeared to be combined, at least in some quarters, as it had been already under Constantine V, with a denial of the effective intercession of the Saints.[1] The Controversy came to an end when orthodoxy was restored by a council of 843.

These last remarks have led beyond the lifetime of the Patriarch Nicephorus and consequently beyond the subject-matter of this book. In his exile the Patriarch Nicephorus undertook to rebut in the *Refutatio et Eversio* the *Definition* and *florilegium* issued by the Council of St. Sophia. There can be little question that this latest and most mature work of the Patriarch was written to be of use to some future council's restoration of image worship, which Nicephorus, like other Iconophiles, confidently expected. However, when this Council met in 843, fifteen years after Nicephorus' death, his *chef-d'œuvre* does not seem to have played an important part.[2] Nicephorus' *Refutatio et Eversio* was directed against the iconoclastic pronouncements of Constantine V and of the Council of St. Sophia. These iconoclastic pronouncements had been replaced by the decrees of a new iconoclastic council assembled during the reign of Theophilus. From the point of view of the Council of 843 Nicephorus' literary works, learned and orthodox as they were, were unsuitable for the simple reason that they were directed against iconoclastic formulations of which one was obsolete (Constantine's writings) and the other only of ephemeral importance (the Council of St. Sophia). It is not surprising, therefore, that Nicephorus' works were but rarely copied and quoted and soon fell into oblivion. These last remarks illuminate one facet of Nicephorus' fate; the story of Nicephorus the man remains yet to be summarized.

---

[1] *Epistula ad Theophilum*, ed. L. Duchesne, *Roma e l'Oriente*, v (1912–13), 222–39, 273–85, 349–66, esp. p. 358: καὶ ὁ θεήλατος Ἀντώνιος, μετὰ τὴν ψευδώνυμον θεομάχον σύνοδον αὐτῶν ἐν ἀσθενείᾳ βαρυτάτῃ περιτρυχωθεὶς . . ., ἔτι ζῶν σαπρίαν σκωλήκων τῶν μελλόντων ἀκοιμήτων διαδοχὴν προμηνυόντων. *Synodicon Vetus* (above p. 87, n. 1), p. 416: καὶ Θεόφιλος υἱὸς Μιχαὴλ αὐτοκράτωρ γενόμενος τελευτήσαντος Ἀντωνίου τὸν λεκανομάντιν πρόεδρον Ἰωάννην προχειρισάμενος μειζόνως τοῖς εὐσεβέσιν τὸν διωγμὸν ἀνερρίπισε καὶ ἄθεον ἐν Βλαχέρναις κατασκευάσας συνέδριον τοὺς προσκυνητὰς τῶν σεβασμίων εἰκόνων ἀνεθεμάτισεν. V. Grumel, 'Recherches récentes sur l'iconoclasme', *Échos d'Orient*, xxix (1930), esp. p. 99; *Dumbarton Oaks Papers*, vii (1953), p. 57, n. 42.

[2] The Acts of this Council are not preserved. Yet if Nicephorus' *Refutatio et Eversio* had been used or even read, there would be references to and quotations from it in the literature of the ninth century. This is not the case, however.

3. *Nicephorus' Personality and Achievement*

Nicephorus was a tragic figure in more senses than one. This was due partly to circumstances, partly to his personality. The issue of image-worship had inflicted sufferings on his parents and must have clouded his childhood, as it was to darken the days of his patriarchate and exile. Equally serious was the hostility of the monks towards the secular hierarchy, which had developed during the iconoclastic persecution of the eighth century and was to outlive Nicephorus. To solve these momentous issues the Patriarch could rely on his faith, on his excellent education, intellect, and scholarly inclinations, and finally on his previous experience in the imperial and ecclesiastical administration. However, during his conduct of the patriarchal office, these positive sides of his personality were offset by a flaw, the weakness of his character. If Nicephorus' career is reviewed, it is found that only rarely did he act on his own initiative. Sometimes when he had made the correct choice originally, he was forced to act wrongly by the Emperor or by the Studite monks.

Although under Constantine V Nicephorus' father had lost his position of Imperial Secretary and had been exiled because of his iconophile views, the young Nicephorus obtained the same office which his father had held before him, and simultaneously received his education in a school connected with the iconoclastic palace. During this period he must have manœuvred with some difficulty between the iconoclastic policies of the court and the iconophile tradition of his family. It was probably in this period, under Leo IV or during the first years of the rule of his widow Irene, that he wrote his *Breviarium*, a chronicle which extended from the murder of Maurice (602) to the marriage of Leo IV and Irene (769), and was designed to continue the *Histories* of Theophylactus Simocatta. This work reflects the conflicting loyalties which at the time of its composition troubled both the author and his times. In the *Breviarium* Nicephorus roundly denounced the iconoclastic policies of the Emperors Leo III and Constantine V, but unlike the later chronicler Theophanes, who used the same iconophile source for these reigns, Nicephorus gave credit to these emperors for their military and diplomatic exploits. Nicephorus retained his position in the Imperial Secretariate after the Chief Secretary Tarasius had been promoted by Irene to the Patriarchate (784). At the Seventh Ecumenical Council of Nicaea Nicephorus was charged by the imperial government with a minor yet delicate task. He remained at the court under Irene and Constantine VI for a number of years but seems to have met with disgrace, perhaps in 797 because he had sided with Constantine VI against his mother Irene. Nicephorus spent the time of his fall from favour in ascetic practices and founded a monastery outside Constantinople. Probably soon after Irene's overthrow in 802 Nicephorus reappeared in the capital, this time in a semi-ecclesiastical capacity: he was appointed director of the largest poorhouse in Constantinople. When after the death of the Patriarch Tarasius (806) the electors could not agree on a successor, the Emperor appointed Nicephorus. Under imperial pressure Nicephorus became a monk a week before his solemn enthronement, was rapidly ordained to the diaconate and presbyterate a few days later, and finally on Easter Sunday 806 was installed as Patriarch of Constantinople.

Nicephorus owed his appointment primarily to the favour of the Emperor Nicephorus I. It was ominous that he became Patriarch against the opposition of the Studite monks whose leaders Plato and Theodore were even imprisoned for twenty-four days prior to the ceremony of enthronement. The new Patriarch thus began as the protégé of the Emperor Nicephorus I and came to be opposed by the leaders of the monastic clergy. Under this emperor the actions of the Patriarch conformed to the wishes of his imperial lord and master. Under compulsion from the Emperor he refrained even from sending the traditional letter of enthronement to Pope Leo III.

In the very first year of Nicephorus' patriarchate a local synod at Constantinople presided over by the Patriarch restored the stormy petrel of the Moechian Controversy, Joseph of Kathara, to the priesthood. This was done to repay a debt of gratitude which the Emperor had contracted towards Joseph at the time of the rebellion of Bardanes Turcus (803). Thus opened the second stage of the Moechian Controversy. Once again, as under Constantine VI, the Studites protested, were exiled, and even anathematized by a synod (809). They replied by accusing the Emperors, the Patriarch, and all who held communion with Joseph of schism and even of heresy. The Patriarch Nicephorus might not have foreseen the full intensity of Studite opposition when he agreed to the restoration of Joseph, yet he could hardly have failed at the time to consider the possibility of Studite hostility. He was probably sincere when he sent to the exiled Theodore the message: 'I envy you.' As Patriarch he could not, like Theodore, afford the luxury of opposing the Emperor's demand for the restoration of Joseph. This was true not only because he had little support except from the Emperor but also because as the official custodian of Church unity he could not risk a conflict between ecclesiastical and secular power over an issue which, to modern minds at least, involved no basic tenet of Christian faith or ethics. He could have said to Theodore what after the Emperor's death he wrote to Pope Leo III by way of an explanation for the long delay in sending off his letter of enthronement: 'it is not easy to oppose the powers that be which are carried away by their own wishes and strive to fulfil their desires'.

One would imagine that the Patriarch moved with greater freedom under Nicephorus' successors. This was indeed the case in his relations with the Emperors Stauracius and Michael I Rangabe, but the Patriarch now found that his authority was undermined by the Studite party. Under Michael, Joseph of Kathara was deposed a second time, and the Patriarch Nicephorus was forced to apologize to the Studites. He explained that his hands had been forced by the late Emperor Nicephorus. Theodore of Studios also overruled the Patriarch Nicephorus with regard to the death penalty to be meted out to Paulicians and Athinganoi and on the issue of the Bulgarian Peace Treaty.

The attitudes of Nicephorus and Theodore to the tragic events which brought Leo V the Armenian (813–20) to the throne are not clear. Once Leo's accession had been secured, the problem of image-worship quickly began to overshadow all other issues. As the new iconoclastic campaign developed, Leo contrived to isolate the Patriarch from his partisans and finally to keep him *incommunicado*. Nicephorus, separated from his clergy and weakened by disease, felt that this time the Christian faith was endangered and that concessions were out of the question. Orally and in writing he attempted to convert the Emperor and his entourage to image-worship, but in vain. When he came to realize the futility of his efforts, his mind was made up. He abdicated and went into exile.

The rest of his life—he died in 828—was entirely devoted to the literary refutation of Iconoclasm. With great fortitude he rejected several attempts on the part of the Emperors Leo V and Michael II to persuade him to accept Iconoclasm or at least to adopt a neutral attitude. With equal dignity he turned a cold shoulder to Theodore of Studios' proposals that he should act as the official head of the Church-in-Exile. He seems to have felt that his enforced abdication had delivered him from responsibilities which he had always loathed and that he could be of greater help to his cause by laying the theological and philosophical foundations for the future restoration of image-worship for which he hoped and prayed. His treatises written in exile were theological polemics. They were directed against the theses of Constantine V, which he considered fundamental, and against the *Definition* and *florilegium* of the Council of St. Sophia. As theological polemic they have considerable merit. Nicephorus, like his predecessor Tarasius whose *Refutation* became the model for Nicephorus' *Refutatio et Eversio*, realized that his iconoclastic opponents could be answered effectively only if their point of view was authentically represented. Accordingly Nicephorus quoted or paraphrased the pronouncements of the iconoclastic party and preserved in this way precious fragments of the works of Constantine V, the *Definition* and *florilegium* of the iconoclastic Council of St. Sophia (815), as well as numerous quotations from otherwise lost Church Fathers and heresiarchs. Where the text or context of a particular quotation adduced by the Iconoclasts was uncertain Nicephorus often took considerable pains to secure authentic and complete manuscripts.

Nicephorus' writings reveal the strength and weakness of his skill as a controversialist. He is at his best where he can engage with his opponents in a duel of authoritative quotations. He takes delight in explaining what he believes to be the true meaning of a patristic text cited by his opponents, by referring to a parallel text of the same Church Father. He excels in casting doubt on the authenticity of an iconoclastic quotation by confronting it with another passage belonging unquestionably to the author to whom the Iconoclasts attributed the passage. Or finally, if the wording and attribution of the quotation do not permit either of these gentler approaches, he compares it with heretical passages and demonstrates its heterodox inspiration. While in this duel of authoritative quotations Nicephorus is occasionally not averse to relying on a text of doubtful authenticity, he shows on the whole considerable learning and sureness of judgement. On the negative side it must be admitted, however, that Nicephorus' works show little depth and originality. In his dogmatic and philosophical statements he adheres to the scholastic theory of images. A few applications of this approach, like the distinction between painting and circumscription, may be his own, but on the whole he follows the established lines. Furthermore, the historian would desire more information of a factual nature about the stirring events which the Patriarch witnessed. But this can hardly be expected from a theological polemicist. The historian must therefore resign himself and be grateful for the occasional glances which Nicephorus casts at the historical landscape, as in the case of the data on the social composition of the iconoclastic party.

It is certainly true to say that a tragic fate deprived even Nicephorus' literary efforts of their full effectiveness. Nicephorus did not and could not foresee that a third outbreak of Iconoclasm and a new Iconoclastic Council under the Emperor Theophilus would render his works obsolete. He was fortunate in finding an admirer in the ninth century, possibly the Patriarch Methodius, who commissioned an edition of Nicephorus' theological works in two volumes. He might have deserved a better fate, however, at the hands of his modern editors, who either destroyed the sequence of his argument by disarranging the order of some of his treatises (Mai, Pitra) or, in the case of the *Refutatio et Eversio*, were compelled by lack of sponsors (Banduri) or by political upheavals (Andreev) to postpone their project to the Greek calends.

In many periods can be found a pair of historical figures who approached identical problems on the basis of diametrically opposed sets of principles and with different temperaments. Themistocles and Aristides, Octavian and Antony, Danton and Robespierre, Jefferson and Hamilton, Gladstone and Disraeli come most readily to mind. In such situations the key to the understanding of the period often lies in a comparison of these 'parallel lives', their standards and their characters. This is also the case in the early decades of the ninth century when the Patriarch Nicephorus and Theodore the abbot of Studios were the recognized leaders of the Eastern Church. Nicephorus is in many ways the typical Byzantine Patriarch: highly educated, passionately interested in theological issues, obedient to the wishes of his imperial masters, yet determined to suffer martyrdom rather than condone attacks on Christian faith and dogma. Theodore of Studios, on the other hand, reminds one of the militant leaders of the Western Churches, of St. Jerome, St. Francis, Savonarola, Martin Luther. Theodore militantly set out to impose Christian ethics in their purest form on a Byzantine Empire steeped in the traditions of the Greek City State and Roman Law. In some instances this objective may have had beneficial effects, as in his intervention on the occasions of the Bulgarian Peace Treaty and of the death penalty for Paulicians. In other cases, however, it was disastrous. This was most notably so in Theodore's unrelenting distrust of the secular hierarchy, which divided and weakened the Church, and, if the inferences here presented are correct, in his successful agitation for the discharge of the iconoclastically inclined garrison troops under Michael I Rangabe.

The author of an all-too-sober book will perhaps be forgiven if, at the end of his labours, he indulges in some daydreaming. Suppose that after the Council of Nicaea in 787 the leaders of the monastic party had buried the hatchet. The Moechian Controversy would probably have arisen just the same, but given a more conciliatory attitude on the part of the monks it might have been less bitter and its sequel under the Emperor Nicephorus could have been avoided. In the critical year 813, when Michael I Rangabe was defeated by the Bulgarians at Versinicia, the Church could then have looked back on a generation of co-operation between bishops and monks. Under such circumstances no potential Iconoclast like Leo V could have counted on the latent hostility of the two sectors of the Church. Along the lines of this day-dreaming it may be assumed that no mass dismissal of the garrison forces would have taken place under Michael I Rangabe. The battle of Versinicia *might* have been won if the Byzantine commander could have had the surviving veterans of the Emperor Nicephorus' campaign against the same enemy two years earlier to rely upon, and not inexperienced conscripts. In that case there would have been no usurpation by Leo V. But let it even be granted that the battle of Versinicia would have been lost even if the Emperor Nicephorus' veterans had been there. A usurpation then might or might not have taken place. Even if there had been an usurper, is it likely that he could have embarked upon an iconoclastic campaign as was in fact done by Leo V? This emperor derived his strongest support from the discharged veterans who were loitering in the streets of Constantinople and literally did not know where they would eat their next meal. If they had still been in the army, they would have returned from the battle-field to their barracks, would have lived under military discipline, housed, fed, and clothed by the government. It is highly doubtful if the new iconoclastic movement could have gained strength except with the help of the revolutionary ferment provided by the economic despair of defeated and unprovided veterans.

The Studites had sown the seeds of folly, but the entire Eastern Church was to eat the bitter fruit. The same heartaches, the same privations, and the same persecution beset iconophile monks and bishops alike. The Christian Commonwealth of which the Studite leaders had dreamed seemed to disintegrate into the dominion of the Antichrist. The great proponents of image-worship were to die and an entire generation was to pass before the churches of God were once again decorated with images in an Empire transformed, chastened, and rejuvenated by wise and foolish acts and omissions of pious men during the Great Controversy.

NOTES

CHAPTER I

Note A, p. 4.

On the icons, as well as on other subjects, I have profited greatly from the synthesis by Louis Bréhier, *La Civilisation byzantine* (Paris, 1950), esp. 266 ff. See also his article 'Les Icones dans l'histoire de l'art. Byzance et la Russie', *L'Art byzantin chez les Slaves*, deuxième recueil dédié à la mémoire de Théodore Uspenskij (Paris, 1932), 150–73, and the monumental illustrated work of Oskar Wulff and Michael Alpatoff, *Denkmäler der Ikonenmalerei* (Hellerau, 1925). These works are to be supplemented by G. A. Sotiriu's publication of two magnificent sixth-century icons from Mt. Sinai, the first of the Theotokos Enthroned (*Bulletin de Correspondance hellénique*, lxx (1946), 552–6) and the second of St. Peter (*Mélanges Grégoire, Annuaire de l'Institut d'Histoire et de Philologie orientales*, x (1950), 607–10). Bréhier, *Civ. byz.* 33, remarks: '. . . les familles les plus humbles avaient leur iconostase, oratoire où étaient suspendues les saintes images.' His evidence for the iconostasis in private homes is late, but at the height of the persecution under Constantine V the wife of Stephen the Younger's jailer kept three icons of Mary with the Child, of Peter, and of Paul hidden and locked up in her own chest and subsequently smuggled them into the prison (*P.G.* c. 1164A). Similarly, the monks of Studios could upon the order of their abbot Theodore make a procession with their icons (*P.G.* xcix. 185B). Eusebius' letter to Constantia: *P.G.* xx. 1545–50 and the article by George Florovsky, 'Origen, Eusebius and the Iconoclastic Controversy', *Church History*, xix (1950), 77–96. The exact nature of the image is not clear but the wording (περί τινος εἰκόνος ὡς δὴ τοῦ Χριστοῦ γέγραφας, εἰκόνα βουλομένη σοι ταύτην ὑφ' ἡμῶν πεμφθῆναι . . . οὐκ οἶδα πόθεν αὐτὴ ὁρμηθεῖσα τοῦ σωτῆρος ἡμῶν διαγράψαι εἰκόνα προστάττεις κτλ.) seems to suggest a demand for a copy of an icon to which Eusebius had access (in his diocese, the Palestinian Caesarea?—see above, p. 44, n. 1). *Doctrina Addai*, Dobschütz, *Christusbilder*, 171.* The remarks in the text about the icons as actionless portraits have been suggested to me by Professor Ernst Kitzinger.

Note B, p. 8.

De Vaux dates the mosaics themselves, on stylistic grounds, between 550 and 650 (p. 256) and the mutilation in the reign of Umar II († 9 February 720) rather than in the early months of that of Yazid II, largely because he doubts the authenticity of Yazid's 'edict'. I am inclined to accept his dating, but for different reasons: (1) If the destruction at Maïn had taken place under Yazid, one would have to assume that Yazid's orders were issued and conveyed to Transjordania and that the mosaics were mutilated and repaired, all between February and August 720. (2) The initiation of an iconoclastic campaign is in harmony with what is known about the religious zealot Umar II. This would be especially true if the correspondence attri-

buted by the Armenian historian Ghevond to Umar II and the Byzantine
Emperor Leo III is genuine; see Arthur Jeffery, 'Ghevond's Text of the
Correspondence between 'Umar II and Leo III', *Harvard Theological
Review*, xxxvii (1944), 269–332, esp. pp. 278, 322. Perhaps the somewhat
guarded defence of image-worship in the letter attributed to Leo III is an
additional (Jeffery, pp. 330–2) argument in favour of authenticity: (1) Leo
emphatically distinguishes the worship of the Cross from that of images
which according to him is a different kind of worship. (2) Leo states that
image-worship is not ordered by Scripture. (3) Explicitly Leo approves only
of the images of the Apostles 'which have come down to us from their times
as their living representation'. What he says about Christ and the Saints is
ambiguous. An Iconophile would have interpreted it as a defence of images
of Christ and of the Saints, while an Iconoclast could have pointed out that
no images are mentioned. The passage is so interesting that I reproduce it
(in Jeffery's translation): 'As for pictures, we do not give them a like respect,
not having received in Holy Scripture any commandment whatsoever in
regard to this. Nevertheless, finding in the Old Testament that divine
command which authorized Moses to have executed in the tabernacle the
figures of the Cherubim, and animated by a sincere attachment for the
disciples of the Lord, who burned with love for the Saviour Himself, we have
always felt a desire to conserve their images, which have come down to us
from their times as their living representation. Their presence charms us, and
we glorify God who has saved us by the intermediary of His only-begotten
Son, who appeared in the world in a similar figure, and we glorify the saints.
But as for the wood and the colors, we do not give them any reverence.'

Note C, p. 8.

In searching for a motive one may think of biblical texts like Deut. iv.
15 ff. or of the Moslem *Traditions* (*ḥadith*) forbidding the representations of
living forms (Creswell, pp. 161 f.). De Vaux 256 remarks: the mutilations
of the floor mosaics at Maïn 'apparaissent plutôt comme l'exécution d'une
mesure prise par un gouvernement central'. The Moslem government may
have had Christian or Jewish allies who would then have had their own
reasons, but it would be difficult to explain the simultaneous appearance of
these tendencies in churches and in synagogues unless they had been initiated by the Moslems. See de Vaux, p. 257: 'Pas de persécution violente . . .
mais une série de vexations et un effort pour faire respecter même dans les
milieux chrétiens certaines prescriptions musulmanes.' In that case the
Moslem *Traditions* (*ḥadith*) would have to be dated prior to A.D. 720. Creswell, pp. 161 f., thought that the *Traditions* did not exist prior to the end of
the eighth century. He based his conclusion on the silence of John of
Damascus on Moslem Iconoclasm. Yet in *De Haer.*, *P.G.* xciv. 768D–769A,
John of Damascus is aware that the Moslems consider the Christian worship
of the Cross an act of idolatry. More important, the Patriarch Germanos,
c. A.D. 725 (Grumel, *Regestes*, no. 330), knew that the Moslems criticized
Christian image-worship, see his letter to Thomas of Claudiopolis (*P.G.* xcviii.
168c): Σαρρακηνοῖς δέ, ἐπεὶ καὶ αὐτοὶ τὸ τοιοῦτον (religious images)

ἐπισκήπτειν δοκοῦσιν, ἀρκετὸν εἰς αἰσχύνην καὶ ἐντροπὴν προσαγαγεῖν τὴν μέχρι τοῦ νῦν ἐν τῇ ἐρήμῳ τελουμένην παρ' αὐτῶν λίθῳ ἀψύχῳ προσφώνησιν τήν τε τοῦ λεγομένου Χοβὰρ ἐπίκλησιν καὶ τὰ λοιπὰ τῆς ματαίας αὐτῶν πατροπαραδότου ἐκεῖσε ἀναστροφῆς ὡς ἐν ἐπισήμῳ ἑορτῇ παιγνιώδη μυστήρια. If the correspondence attributed to Omar II and Leo III by the Armenian historian Ghevond (see Note B) is genuine, this would be the earliest preserved instance of Moslem criticism of Christian image-worship. The condition of the floor mosaics, as well as the texts cited, thus would date the *Traditions* before A.D. 720.

Note C*, p. 8.

P.G. c. 1120C–D. See André Grabar, *L'Empereur dans l'art byzantin* (Paris, 1936), 166–72.

Note D, p. 8.

Apparently it was felt in some quarters that the edict of Yazid II did little to explain the outbreak of Iconoclasm within the Empire. The *Adversus Constantinum Caballinum* (*P.G.* xcv. 336C–337A) tells how Iconoclasm began with Konon who called himself Leo and became Emperor (Leo III, 717–41). A Jew promised him a long reign if he agreed to destroy the images, and Leo, ten years after his accession, admitted the Jew to the palace and carried out his promise. This tale is absent from the earlier versions of the *Adversus Constantinum Caballinum* (Melioranski, *Georgii Kiprianin*, &c., p. 81) and must therefore have been added between 767 and 787. If it is compared with that read by John of Jerusalem at the Seventh Council (see p. 6 and p. 7, n. 1), one notices two things: (1) John's account contains a great deal of precise information on Ommayyad history which can be checked (Omar II's recall of Maslama after the unsuccessful siege of Constantinople in 717/18, Yazid's short reign, Walid II the son of Yazid I) while the account in the *Adversus Constantinum Caballinum* is distinguished by vague and unverifiable data about the private life of Leo III. (2) The tale in the *Adversus Constantinum Caballinum* has an apocalyptic flavour: the Hebrew is referred to as ὁ βύθιος δράκων, of Leo it is said that before he became Emperor he changed his name from Κόνων to Leo. Now Theophanes, p. 407. 23, makes the Patriarch Germanos refer to a report (p. 407. 18) that the images would be destroyed by a certain Konon who would be the forerunner of the Antichrist. Theophanes therefore knew of a text where Leo was referred to as the forerunner of the Antichrist and which consequently dealt with Constantine V as the Antichrist himself. On Constantine V in apocalyptic literature see Wilhelm Bousset, *Der Antichrist* (Göttingen, 1895), 46, and 'Beiträge zur Geschichte der Eschatologie', *Zeitschrift für Kirchengeschichte*, xx (1899), 103–31, 261–90, esp. 274–7. Since Theophanes and the *Adversus Constantinum Caballinum* refer to Leo as Konon, it is likely that both are based on the same apocalyptic text. If this hypothesis is correct, this apocalypse equating Constantine V with the Antichrist would either have been influenced by the story of Forty-Cubits-High and Yazid II, or both the apocalypse and the story go back to a (lost) apocalyptic tradition of a Hebrew prophet and a wicked king. The latter seems more likely, as it is hard to imagine, in the eighth century, a

Palestinian Jew with a name of perfectly good Byzantine formation (see Heinrich Moritz, *Die Zunamen bei den byzantinischen Historikern und Chronisten*, ii. Teil, Progr. des K. Humanistischen Gymnasium in Landshut für das Schuljahr 1897/8).

Note E, p. 9.

On the whole question of foreign or native inspiration of the Iconoclastic Controversy see George Florovsky, loc. cit. (above, note A), esp. 21 f.: 'It has been usual to interpret the Iconoclastic movement as an Oriental or Semitic reaction and resistance to an excessive Hellenization of Christian art and devotion. . . . But we find nothing specifically 'Semitic' in Iconoclastic theology . . . the main inspiration of the Iconoclastic thought was Hellenistic.' Also K. Schenk, 'Kaiser Leons III Walten im Inneren', *B.Z.* v (1896), 257–301, esp. 272–89; and J. Starr, 'An Iconodulic Legend and its Historical Basis', *Speculum*, viii (1933), 500–3. Schenk rejects foreign influences on Leo, primarily because the story of the Jew Tessarakontapechys (Forty-Cubits) was unknown to Leo's contemporaries and does not make its appearance before the Council of 787, while Starr equates the Tessarakontapechys of the legend with Leo's principal assistant Beser (Theophanes, 402). If Beser had really been a 'Syrian freedman' and if 'even during his period of servitude under Christian captors, he remained a faithful Mohammedan' as Starr asserts (p. 502), this would be concrete evidence for Moslem influence on Leo III. Yet Starr seems to have misinterpreted Theophanes. According to the chronicler (p. 402) Beser had been a Christian, had been captured by the Arabs (not by the Christians, as Starr thinks) and converted to Islam. After much time had elapsed he was freed, probably in the course of one of the exchanges of prisoners usual in the wars between Byzantines and Arabs. He returned to the Empire and won the respect of Leo by his physical strength and iconoclastic views. Not a word is said, as Starr claims, that he remained a Moslem; one must assume on grounds of general probability that he abandoned Islam at the time of his return. On Beser's career see also L. Bréhier, 'Beser', *Dictionnaire d'histoire et de géographie ecclésiastiques*, viii (Paris, 1935), 1171 f. Grumel, *Regestes*, no. 327, p. 3, identifies Beser with the 'apostate' and 'forerunner of impiety' over whose fall the Patriarch Germanos and Pope Gregory II rejoiced in their correspondence (*P.G.* xcviii. 148B–149A).

CHAPTER V

Note F, p. 127.

The Armenian descent of John the Grammarian, patriarch of Constantinople under Theophilus, had been suggested by Saint Martin in his edition of Lebau's *Histoire du Bas-Empire*, xiii, p. 14, n. 3. It has been accepted by S. Der Nersessian, *Armenia and the Byzantine Empire* (Cambridge, Mass., 1945), 24 and N. Adonts, 'Role of the Armenians in Byzantine Science', *Armenian Review* (published by the Hairenik Association, Boston, Mass.), iii (1950), 55–73, esp. 61–66. However, the identity of the lector John, who in 814 was entrusted by Leo V the Armenian with the task of making preparations for the Iconoclastic Council of St. Sophia, with the patriarch John Grammaticus was questioned by V. Grumel, 'Jean Grammaticos et saint Theodore Studite', *E.O.* xxxvi (1937), 181–9. If I understand Grumel correctly, he agrees that the Byzantine sources identify the two figures, but suggests that they are wrong. 'Il y a tout lieu de croire', he writes, 'qu'il y eut à cette reprise de l'iconoclasme deux agents d'importance inégale du nom de Jean, confondus dans la suite en un seul, le patriarche Jean Grammaticos' (p. 181). Grumel's principal arguments in favour of distinguishing two iconoclastical leaders called John are the following. In the first place the *Scriptor Incertus de Leone Armeno* mentions the lowly origins of the John who was active in 814/15 (*P.G.* cviii. 1025 A), while the Continuators of Theophanes state explicitly that the Patriarch John belonged to the noble family of the Morocharzamioi (*P.G.* cix. 169A). Secondly, the *Scriptor Incertus* speaks of John as lector, whereas the future Patriarch was abbot of SS. Sergius and Bacchus even prior to 815 and was then according to Grumel at least a deacon. Grumel's first argument certainly reveals a discrepancy in the sources but it hardly justifies his thesis. Nothing is more common than the attribution of a distinguished ancestry to a person of lowly origin. Even if the Patriarch John did in fact belong to the Morocharzamioi, it may well be that what was an obscure family to Leo's patrician advisers appeared an august lineage to a late chronicler. As to Grumel's second argument there is no reason why John should not have been abbot of SS. Sergius and Bacchus in 814/15 and at the same time held the rank of lector. If Theodore of Studios addresses John Grammaticus as τῇ ἁγιωσύνῃ σου (*Epistulae*, ii. 168, *P.G.* xcix. 1531C), this proves in no way, as Grumel suggests, that the addressee 'était déjà dans les ordres, c'est-à-dire au moins diacre'. This is simply Theodore's way of addressing another abbot (e.g. *Epistulae*, i. 26, ibid. 920; i. 39, ibid. 1045E; i. 56, ibid. 1109B). Grumel's arguments thus are not convincing. Furthermore, even an author who visited Constantinople in 814/15 and witnessed the beginnings of the second outbreak of Iconoclasm implies the identity of the lector John with the persecutor of the Iconophiles. Theosterictus, author of the *Vitae Nicetae*, completed his work between 829 and 840 (cf. p. 126, n. 2 above) and referred to the lector as Γραμματικὸν τὸν νέον Τέρτυλον (*AA. SS. Aprilis*, i, App., p. xxiv; cited p. 127, n. 1 above). What would be the point of comparing the lector with the orator Tertullus of Acts xxiv if Theosterictus had in mind merely John's participation in the preparations for the Iconoclastic Council of St. Sophia? This comparison becomes intelligible if the lector had denounced Iconophiles as Tertullus had denounced St. Paul. The same text tells, a little later (p. xxvi), how after Easter 816 Leo handed Nicetas over to τῷ σοφιστῇ τῶν κακῶν Ἰωάννῃ ᾗ βούλοιτο ἐπινοίᾳ κολάσαι αὐτόν. Any reader of the text will identify this John with the grammarian John mentioned before by the hagiographer. Now the persecutor of the Iconophiles is, as Grumel (p. 182) himself concedes, the future Patriarch (cf. the abundant material quoted by Dvornik, *Les Légendes*, 74 f.). The author of the *Vita Nicetae* clearly thinks of the lector John as the person who was to be the chief persecutor of the iconophile confessors and who from 837 to 843 was Patriarch of Constantinople.

CHAPTER VI

Note G, p. 138.

Paul J. Alexander, 'The Iconoclastic Council of St. Sophia (815) and its Definition (*Horos*)', *Dumbarton Oaks Papers*, vii (1953), 35–66, esp. 58–66. In this paper I tried to establish (1) that the *florilegium*, and in a much vaguer form the Dogmatic Definition, of St. Sophia rejected artistic representations of Christ and the Saints and held that their true image was the virtuous Christian worshipping God in his heart; and (2) that this thesis, though derived from Early Christian or even pagan concepts, was for the first time connected with Christian images at the Council of St. Sophia. The second of these conclusions was challenged by Milton V. Anastos, 'The Ethical Theory of Images as Formulated by the Iconoclasts of 754 and 815', ibid. viii (1954), 151–60. Professor Anastos used the term 'ethical theory of images' to designate the first of the points mentioned above and insisted that it 'first appeared and was strongly emphasized . . . in 754'. He based his view primarily on the fact, already noted in my earlier article, that the sixteenth anathema of the Council of Hiereia-Blachernae expressed the 'ethical theory'. Anastos added, however, the valuable observation (which had escaped me) that this anathema agreed in wording and thought with a passage from Theodotus quoted in the *florilegium* of the same council. The agreement of quotation and anathema is all the more remarkable as this is the only anathema dealing with images of the Saints (rather than of Jesus). The weakness of Anastos's demonstration lies in the fact that the Dogmatic Definition of Hiereia-Bachernae consisted of four parts: a 'Doctrine' (δόγμα, cf. Mansi, xiii. 280D, printed ibid. 208–77); a biblico-patristic *florilegium* (ibid. 280–313); disciplinary canons (ibid. 324–32); and anathemas or 'detailed definitions' (ὅροι κεφαλαιώδεις, ibid. 333–52). Mr. Anastos does not consider the question whether the 'ethical theory' was contained in the 'Doctrine', in the biblical part of the *florilegium*, or in the disciplinary canons. Yet Anastos's view carries conviction only if it could be shown that the principal part of the Definition, the 'Doctrine', an elaborate and detailed dogmatic pronouncement, contained the 'ethical theory'. A detailed re-examination of the evidence, especially of the Dogmatic Definition, has led me to the conclusion that in this matter there is a need for subtler distinctions than have been proposed by either Mr. Anastos or myself. What follows is a highly condensed account of my position as modified in the light of Anastos's article.

Note H, p. 138.

Argument from idolatry: Mansi, xiii. 212E–225D. Argument from christology: ibid. 240C–269D.

Note I, p. 138.

The argument from holiness is summarized from Mansi, xiii. 273B–277E. Unless I am mistaken, this passage has not been explained satisfactorily in the literature of the Iconoclastic Controversy, except for helpful remarks by Karl Schwarzlose, *Der Bilderstreit* &c. (Gotha, 1890), 88, and Louis Bréhier,

La Querelle des images etc. (Paris, 1904), 44. Milton V. Anastos, 'The Argument for Iconoclasm as presented by the Iconoclastic Council of 754', *Late Classical and Medieval Studies in Honor of Albert Mathias Friend* (Princeton, 1955), 177–88, esp. 181, summarizes but does not explain the relevant passages.

Note J, p. 139.

Only a few indications can be given on this point. The biblical part of the *florilegium* (Mansi, xiii 280D–285C) is designed to buttress the argument from idol-worship, as do the quotations from Athanasius (ibid. 300E). The quotation from Eusebius (ibid. 313A) is closely related to the argument from christology. The remaining patristic quotations (attributed to Epiphanius, Gregory Nazianzen, John Chrysostom, Amphilochius, and Theodotus) illustrate the argument from holiness. The anathemas are related either to the argument from christology or to that from holiness. The third part of the *Dogmatic Definition*, the disciplinary canons, by its very nature, does not contribute to the theory of Iconoclasm.

Note K, p. 139.

Pp. 39–43 above. This is especially clear if one considers the 16th and 17th anathemas. The 16th anathema (Mansi, xiii. 345C) is claimed by Professor Anastos to give expression to the 'ethical theory of images'. Yet the very next anathema (ibid. 348D), which like its predecessor speaks of Saints, does not mention images at all but declares all Saints to 'have pleased God and to be honoured before Him in soul and body'. Even the wording is an echo of the 'Doctrine', see ibid. 276D: 'for the Saints have pleased God and are honoured by Him with the dignity of sainthood.' I am therefore hesitant to accept Mr. Anastos's term 'ethical theory'. The thinking behind this argument was speculative or metaphysical rather than ethical. It rested on the premiss, best expressed by the Emperor Constantine V, of the essential identity of image and original (pp. 209 f. above). The artistic image was unable to render the essence of holiness or sanctity of the prototypes and consequently was rejected. The term 'ethical theory' would tend to emphasize the moral (and positive) consequences of an argument that in Byzantine eyes was basically metaphysical (and negative).

Note L, p. 139.

Argument from christology: frg. 13 (I cite the Dogmatic Definition of St. Sophia according to the numbering of my edition, in the article quoted on p. 237, n. 6 above) and Ostrogorsky, *Studien*, 57. The argument from holiness is referred to even more vaguely (if at all). Where the *Horos* of St. Sophia speaks of the Seventh Council and of the Empress Irene, it states that the Empress 'set forth that the all-holy Mother of God and the Saints sharing His [the Son's] form should be set up and worshipped by means of the dead visions of the figures' (frg. 9). The concept of the Saints sharing the Son's form, derived ultimately from *Phil.* iii. 21, is an echo of the argument from holiness as formulated at Hiereia-Blachernae (Mansi, xiii. 277D). Further, the reference to the 'dead visions of the figures' brings to mind the contrast, emphasized by the Doctrine of Hiereia-Blachernae (ibid. 276D, 277D) between the living Saints and the dead art and matter of painting.

Note M, p. 144.

Guillaume de Jerphanion, *Une Nouvelle Province de l'art byzantin, les églises rupestres de Cappadoce*, 2 vols. (each in two parts) and 3 vols. of plates, Paris, 1925–42. In vol. ii, part ii, 412–14, will be found a summary discussion of decorative elements (sculptured crosses, geometric and floral motifs) which point to iconoclastic influences. See especially the description of the Chapel of Zilvé (col. i, part 2, 582 and plate 26 no. 4 with the crosses in relief); also Chapel 2 (ibid. 583, with inscription no. 112 celebrating the Cross). Coloured reproduction of geometric motifs at Gueurémé, plate 33. Most curious is the decoration of Hagios Vasilios at Elevra where in the apse three crosses have the names of Abraham, Isaac, and Jacob inscribed and where in the nave crosses with definitely iconoclastic inscriptions are found together with the images of two saints (vol. ii, part 1, 105–11 and plates 154 and 155 no. 1). Jerphanion suggests (vol. ii, part 1, 110) that this represents a compromise between an iconoclastic donor and the iconophile monks of the region. At Hagios Stéphanos near Djemil (vol. ii, part 1, 146–55) there is a similar mixture of iconophile and iconoclastic motifs, with the difference, however, that here the iconophile decoration prevails. Jerphanion (p. 146) explains this as the work of Iconophiles who, in order to be cautious or to obey the iconoclastic authorities, permitted some iconoclastic motifs. Most remarkable is a painted cross (plate 158, no. 1) which an inscription calls 'the Cross of St. Euphemia' (p. 147). Since on the one hand the Saint is not represented and, on the other hand, the inscription presupposes the return of her relics under Irene and Constantine VI, Jerphanion dates this decoration 'pendant la deuxième crise iconoclaste, dans la première moitié du neuvième siècle' (p. 148). Jerphanion also remarks (pp. 148 f.) that underneath the floral motifs there is an older layer where there were figures of Saints and concludes (p. 149): 'Ces peintures antérieures . . . peuvent avoir été faites après le rétablissement des images par Irène; puis masquées par prudence lorsque la persécution reprit sous Léon l'Arménien.'

CHAPTER VII

Note N, p. 158.

The Vatican Version was fully edited by de Boor (see p. 157, n. 2). The Vat. Gr. 977 itself is a manuscript of the eleventh to twelfth century, but the *Histories* of Theophylactus were written by a scribe different from that of the *Breviarium*. The British Museum Add. MS. 19390, of the late ninth century, was first mentioned in *Catalogue of Additions to the Manuscripts in the British Museum in the years 1848–1853*, p. 228. Described in E. M. Thompson, *Catalogue of Ancient Manuscripts in the British Museum*, Part I: *Greek* (London, 1881), 13–15 (with a facsimile plate 15). Another facsimile: *The Palaeographical Society, Facsimiles of Manuscripts and Inscriptions, First Series*, vol. ii (London, 1873–5), plate 231. The *Londinensis* was discussed in a basic article by Aug. Burckhardt, 'Der Londoner Codex des Breviarium des Nike-phoros P.', *B.Z.* v (1896), 465–77. More recently it has been studied, partly collated, and partly edited by Lajos Orosz, *The London Manuscript of Nike-phoros' Breviarium*, Magyar-Görög Tanulmányok no. 28, Budapest, 1948 (with facsimile). Orosz showed that, in the first part of the *Breviarium* down to the time when Heraclius opened his great offensive against Persia (p. 15: 2 de Boor), the Vatican version shows far-reaching stylistic changes as com-pared with the London Version. Orosz further pointed out that in this part Nicephorus used a source written in iambic trimeters, perhaps a lost work by George of Pisidia (but cf. Franz Dölger, *B.Z.* xliii (1950), 56), which he translated into prose. After the dividing line (p. 15: 2 de Boor), the changes are slight. Burckhardt, loc. cit., had thought that the London Version was not written by Nicephorus but contained excerpts made by Nicephorus from two lost sources. Orosz (pp. 9–11) attempts to disprove the thesis by postu-lating that if Burckhardt were right it would be natural for the London Version to stand closer to Theophanes than the Vatican Version. However, the mistakes in the London manuscript cited by Orosz (p. 10) are either differences of spelling, especially of proper names, which prove nothing, or omissions and corruptions which can be explained as scribal errors having occurred in the copying of the London manuscript. It is therefore still an open question to what degree and extent the *Breviarium* is more than a stylistic adaptation of earlier sources. My guess is that Nicephorus was indeed the author of both versions.

Note O, p. 162.

Recently, E. E. Lipshits, 'Nikifor i ego istoricheskii trud', *V.V.*, N.S., iii (1950), 85–105, attempted to describe the development of the author on the basis of certain observations concerning the *Breviarium*. After summarizing briefly Burckhardt's results, she proceeded to demonstrate (against Burck-hardt and similarly to Orosz whose work she did not know) that the London Version is an earlier version of the chronicle written by Nicephorus himself. She then showed that when dealing with the Emperors Heraclius, Con-stantine IV, Justinian II, and Constantine V, Nicephorus suppresses certain facts unfavourable to the Byzantine armies or embarrassing to the govern-ment. (I mention in passing that the case mentioned by Miss Lipshits in connexion with Heraclius is not one of literary suppression but of scribal omission due to a homoioteleuton, see Burckhardt, loc. cit., 470). Miss Lipshits further contrasted this apologetic attitude of the *Breviarium* with the violent attacks of the *Third Antirrheticus*. She explains these different attitudes by constructing a rather elaborate hypothesis. According to her, Nicephorus developed from a social revolutionary into a reactionary. In his youth Nicephorus belonged to a group which, unlike the Studites, did not protest against the measures taken by the iconoclastic emperors against monastic landholdings, but collaborated with the moderate Iconoclasts, sym-pathized with the social reforms introduced by the iconoclastic emperors, and did not deny the Emperor an influence over the Church. Only under Michael I Rangabe, the Patriarch Nicephorus decided to speak his mind openly. He now objected to the social reforms of the iconoclastic emperors, as well as to their confiscation of monastic lands. The evidence adduced by Miss Lipshits for this last thesis is Nicephorus' attack upon Jews, Montanists, and Manicheans (see above, p. 99). I myself do not see in what sense this agitation can be used in support of Miss Lipshits's thesis and would suggest a much simpler explanation than the theory of an evolution from social revolutionary to reactionary. Nicephorus wrote his *Breviarium* in all probability as a layman—to be exact, as an imperial official. The purpose of his work was much more limited than that of Theophanes, in particular he was much less interested than Theophanes, as Uspenskií (*Ocherki*, p. 424) has shown, in foreign affairs. It may be that Nicephorus, out of patriotism, suppressed a few embarrassing facts. Such a suppression, which as Miss Lipshits herself has shown, occurred in the case of perfectly orthodox emperors, would not prove anything beyond misguided patriotism. More particularly, it does not prove that he ever approved of the social policies of the iconoclastic emperors: in fact it has been shown (above, pp. 159–62) that he condemned certain aspects of their economic policy. There can be no doubt that when Nicephorus wrote his *Breviarium*, he was opposed to Iconoclasm and to the economic policy of the iconoclastic emperors, but coloured his reporting of military and foreign affairs in a 'patriotic' sense. Later on, after Iconoclasm had been anathematized by the Council of Nicaea and after he had become Patriarch of Constantinople, he felt it his duty to speak out more clearly against Iconoclasm in the *Third Antirrheticus*.

APPENDIX

Summary of Nicephorus' 'Refutatio et Eversio'

(Cf. pp. 180 ff. above)

NOTE: The following is a paraphrase of Nicephorus' unpublished treatise. At a few important points I have translated Nicephorus' words and indicated this by using quotation marks. Where small print is used, Nicephorus quotes from the *Dogmatic Definition* issued by the Iconoclastic Council of St. Sophia (815). Numerals in parenthesis normally refer to the folios of the Parisinus Graecus 1250. Where this manuscript is deficient, the folio numbers are those of the Coislinianus 93 and are marked as such.

TITLE: 'Criticism and refutation of the lawless, undefined, and truly spurious *Horos* set forth by men who abandoned the Catholic and Apostolic Church and adhered to foreign thought to destroy the saving dispensation of the Word of God' (173^r).

At the beginning of his work Nicephorus states that to obtain salvation men ought to follow the definitions of piety. From such an attitude result a peaceful life and correct dogmatic opinions. Those, on the other hand, who attempt to upset eternal boundaries will have a perverted mind and a disturbed life. They will rise up against the glory of God and the righteousness of their fellow-men. This holds true particularly of those in power. At the time of the divine judgement they will be held responsible not only for what they have done themselves, but also what they have forced others to do (173^v).

This, according to Nicephorus, is happening at present. There was a time when there was orthodoxy and peace in the Church, when the symbols of Christ's dispensation shone everywhere in the form of the sacred paintings, and when even princes preferred piety to the diadem. Then shameless people attacked the Holy Creed and carried out the plans devised by Christ's enemy. The altar will proclaim his end, the altar which he profaned during his life and which he defiled even more with his blood when he was slain (174^r).[1]

How did he plan, Nicephorus asks, to carry out his impious enterprise? At first he approached the members of the Church to see whether he could not achieve his purpose quietly, but in vain. Then he imitated Constantine,[2] assembled all the priests and tried by all means to win them for his plans. The élite of the clergy resisted, were imprisoned, and afterwards exiled. The more simple-minded mem-

---

[1] Allusion to the Emperor Leo V the Armenian, 813–20. See p. 183 above.
[2] The Emperor Constantine V, 740–75.

bers he won over by money, promises, prospects of political influence, and threats. From their ranks he assembled what he thought was a council;[1] he himself was the councillor or chairman, or rather the forerunner of Antichrist (174^v).

Nicephorus declares that the abomination which speaks boastingly against the sacred dispensation is appearing for a second time in the temple of the Lord. Should this not be called a 'synod of barbarians' (βαρβαροσύνοδος), because of the barbarian or foreign mind of him who assembled it, or 'wicked synhedrion' rivaling that of Caiaphas? Evidently it could not be called a priestly synod. First, how could a synod be composed of men who violated the promise given on the holy altar in the presence of God, the angels, and the entire clergy, men who trampled upon the writings to which they had prefixed the sign of the Cross and their own names and according to which it was not permissible for them to assemble in holy synods? (175^r)[2] Secondly, it was assembled against the ecclesiastical laws and canons. The highest sees, Rome and the others, were not represented, and without them it is illegal to assemble a synod to pronounce on a dogmatic issue. One might repeat what one of the ancient sages said of a large army without an intelligent leader: 'what a beast not to have a head'. They too were numerous, but they were deprived of the Holy Spirit. For what do they attempt but to insult Christ, the head of the Church and His entire dispensation? (175^v)

The ancient heresy turned the members of the assembly away from the faith and its priests. Urged on by audacity and profaneness he who gathered them asserted his own idle opinion. They revived what had been condemned long before and dared to set forth an altogether un-defined 'Definition' (*Horos*). In reality they did not define (ὁρίζειν) anything, but destroyed the established definitions (176^r).

At the beginning of this *Horos*, Nicephorus reports, the Iconoclasts did not reveal their impiety but appeared disguised under the cloak of piety as is customary with heretics. Later they took off the mask. Nicephorus decides to omit their chatter and to turn to the more vital points in need of a refutation. Since the Iconoclasts have misled some of the more simple-minded, he will attempt for their benefit a refuta-tion. The Iconoclasts refer to Leo the Isaurian (τὸν ἐκ τῶν Ἰσαύρων . . . ὁρμώμενον) and his son Constantine, of whom they say:

'These[3] considering the piety of orthodox faith to be the salvation of life sought the honour of Him for whose sake they received their kingship

---

[1] The Iconoclastic Council of St. Sophia, 815.
[2] Allusion to the oath taken at each ordination after the Seventh Council of Nicaea, see p. 114 above.
[3] The Emperors Leo III (717–41) and Constantine V (741–75).

and assembled a synod much frequented by spiritual fathers and bishops beloved by God . . .' (177ʳ).

Like this beginning the whole of their argumentation is false and mendacious. Either from ignorance or impudence they fight against what is even now remembered by the majority and what is still repeated by everybody in house and market-place; for no council ever assembled during the lifetime of Leo[1] who laid the foundation of this heresy and deposed the Patriarch[2] who had anointed him.[3] Still more impious and ungodly was his successor Constantine[4] who gathered together the bishops who were subjected to him. They said many idle things against the glory of Christ and His Incarnation; for they laid down as a dogma that the Church had worshipped idols. This was their prejudice and their recent disciples were glad to accept it. They even dared to call it a synod (there follows a long series of invectives). To sum up, the Iconoclasts trampled upon and upset ancient tradition, custom, and laws (177ᵛ).

According to Nicephorus, the Iconoclasts of 815 continued as follows:

'They condemned the making and worship of images, which is unwarranted by authority and tradition, or rather unprofitable, preferring worship in spirit and in truth.'

This passage shows their hidden cunning and the meanness of their procedure; for they do not state whose images they mean lest they might reveal from the very beginning that they are fighting against things sacred and the Incarnation of Christ. The word 'image' belongs to the class of relative concepts ($\tau\hat{\omega}\nu$ $\pi\rho\delta\varsigma$ $\tau\iota$ $\tau\delta$ $\check{o}\nu o\mu a$). They can never be conceived of separately, but only together with the concept to which they refer. The Iconoclasts should have stated accurately whose image and likeness they mean. This is an artifice of their knavery and an invention of their diabolical craft. They do not wish to upset their audience from the very beginning by stating that they are waging war against Christ Himself. But a little later they reveal their craft by inferring from the fact that Christ is not circumscribable ($\dot{a}\pi\epsilon\rho\iota\gamma\rho a\pi\tau o\varsigma$) that He cannot be represented by an image ($\mu\dot{\eta}$ $\epsilon\dot{\iota}\kappa o\nu\iota\zeta\epsilon\sigma\theta a\iota$). This is docetism (178ᵛ). Emmanuel Himself is the source of the painting of images as the images 'not wrought by human hand' ($\tau\dot{a}$ $\dot{a}\chi\epsilon\iota\rho\delta\tau\epsilon\upsilon\kappa\tau a$) show (179ʳ). One of them our Saviour Himself is said to have impressed on linen and

---

[1] Leo III.   [2] Germanos, 715–30.

[3] 177ʳ: τὸν ἐπιθέντα χεῖρας αὐτῷ [Leo III] καὶ χρίσαντα ἱεράρχην τὸν ἱερώτατόν τε καὶ ὁσιώτατον τοῦ θρόνου τοῦ ἱερατικοῦ μετὰ πολλῆς καθεῖλε τῆς ἀδοξίας καὶ ὕβρεως. This passage proves that the ceremony of anointing an emperor was known at Byzantium at the latest in 828, see Bréhier, *Institutions*, 13 f.

[4] Constantine V.

sent to the ruler of Edessa. From that time dates this practice, and if the Iconoclasts call it 'not warranted by tradition', they forget Christ. How could the painting of images be 'unwarranted by tradition?' (179ᵛ). What is not handed down by tradition cannot exist. What does not exist cannot be condemned. How could it be condemned if it did not prevail? How could something be unwarranted which has spread wherever the Gospel is known? But these enemies of Christ are impressed neither by what they see nor by tradition.

Why do the Iconoclasts, Nicephorus asks, call the sacred objects 'unprofitable'? (ἄχρηστος) (180ʳ). This might make sense if they were talking of the gods of pagans or barbarians (180ᵛ). How could sacred objects be unprofitable if images of Christ are meant? With their condemnation they have revealed themselves to be idol-worshippers, they have condemned themselves by ignoring the worship of the Creator, and all this they have confirmed by their *Horos* in which they praise the iconoclastic tyrants as liberators from the devil and the demons (181ʳ). Instead of confessing their sins to the holders of the more important sees (τοῖς ἐπὶ μείζοσι θρόνοις), instead of repenting and doing penance (ἐπιτιμίοις ὑποπίπτειν), they condemn the orthodox. When the Council met, the throne of the Patriarch of Constantinople was vacant, towards the end the Emperor Constantine appointed his namesake[1]—a measure which was repeatedly objected to by the Pope of Rome (181ᵛ).

This verbal condemnation of images was followed by their destruction in the palace and in all the churches and by the persecution of the orthodox (182ʳ). Why do the Iconoclasts condemn, of all our sacred objects, the image alone? All things existing have a cause (λόγον ἔχει καθ' ὃν γίνεται καὶ ὑφίσταται): the purpose of Heaven is to proclaim God's glory, that of the sun is to distinguish the day from the night, &c. The cause of the image of Christ is its resemblance to the original, the manifestation of Christ Incarnate, and the commemoration of the name which is inscribed upon it. If that is so, how can anybody call it 'unprofitable'? Furthermore, the image belongs to the class of relative objects (τῶν πρός τι ἡ εἰκών ἐστι), it is a similitude of the original, it is identical with it except for its matter, it even shares its name, and, as relative objects, original and image are correlatives (ἀντιστρέφει πρὸς ἀλλήλα). How then can a person who insults the image of our Saviour still be called a Christian? (183ʳ) If the image were 'unprofitable', why did the early Iconoclasts create such a stir about it?

The Iconoclasts of 815 declare:

'We have approached the images like gods.'

But according to Nicephorus nobody ever did that, and if the

[1] The Patriarch Constantine II, 754–66.

Iconoclasts ever saw some simple soul make such a mistake, they should have set him straight, but should not have condemned the image (183ᵛ).

'This synod confirmed and strengthened the God-inspired dogmas of the holy Fathers, it followed the six holy synods and set forth most holy canons.'

If they had really followed the decisions of the six ecumenical councils, they should have acted as the Sixth Council did[1] and not have condemned image-worship (184ᵛ). The Fathers of the Sixth Council knew that preference was due to adoration in the spirit and truth, but preference for something superior does not mean condemnation of things inferior. Examples: archangels—angels, Peter—other apostles, Emperor—consuls, things divine—things human, virginity—child birth (185ʳ). If images were reminders of something different, the argument of the Iconoclasts might have some force, but since the images represent our Saviour, they are wrong (185ᵛ). Where did they learn that Christians hold original and image in equal honour? If image-worship were condemned because adoration in spirit and truth is preferred, the logical consequence would be to destroy every sacred object. The real reason for their attack is not the preference due to worship in spirit and in truth, but the fact that they desire nothing but the goods of the world, prosperity, glory, and long life (186ʳ). Divine justice has triumphed over their wicked deeds. Do they believe that none of the former rulers ever cared for the worship of God? They followed the opinion of the shepherds of the Church who were entrusted with its government; for according to Paul only prophets, apostles, and leaders were established.

Nicephorus continues with an elaborate statement of the creed, with special emphasis on the Incarnation and on the 'anagogical' function of the image. Since the Iconoclasts claim that they are following the six ecumenical councils, Nicephorus proposes to examine the conciliar decrees (188ʳ). To begin with the first Council of Nicaea, the position of its members on the image problem is made clear by the church built in their honour and adorned, together with other images, with splendid mosaics of those holy fathers of Nicaea and of Constantine the Great. Furthermore, would they have condemned Arianism as creature-worship if they had seen Christians committing the much more serious sin of idol-worship? There follow similar observations on the Second, Third, Fourth, Fifth Ecumenical Councils as well as a lengthy discussion of the Sixth Council (189ᵛ); the doctrine of the two wills and two energies shows that Christ's human nature subsists even after His resurrection, consequently He can be represented by an image (190ʳ).

All this, in Nicephorus' opinion, constitutes blasphemy inasmuch as the Iconoclasts charge the Word of God with being unable to save men from idol-worship (192ʳ). The Iconoclasts attack Holy Scripture

---

[1] Canon 82, see pp. 45 f. above.

by declaring idols the golden cherubim above the mercy seat, the images in Solomon's temple, the vision of Ezekiel. Jesus honoured the Jewish temple, even the image of the heathen Caesar. How can they say that they are following the Fathers and the Councils? (193ʳ) The latter worshipped images; the Iconoclasts started a persecution of images and image-worshippers. They followed the wishes of depraved men whom they call 'teachers sent for our education' (193ᵛ). How could they be called priests since they turned over to laymen matters referring to the priesthood and to the evangelical canons?

'Therefore the Church of God has remained calm for not a few years and the subjects were kept in peace' (194ʳ).

How can they dare say this? Do they forget the persecution of the image-worshippers? Nicephorus proposes to give a brief description of it (194ᵛ). Immediately after the Council of Hiereia 'the proclamations and notices of the imperial impiety (τὰ προγράμματα καὶ προθέματα τῆς βασιλικῆς ἀθεΐας) were sent to every region and town'. The most terrible punishments took place, images were destroyed by breaking them upon the heads of their owners (some of those who suffered this punishment are still alive), most cruel types of death penalty were devised. Churches were destroyed, sacred objects were burned, monasteries were used as barracks for the troops or sold, the so-called Catholic churches were assigned as stables for the cavalry;[1] inside of the fane there remained lying even until today the remainder of the dung-stained beams 'which we saw with our own eyes and cleared away with our own hands' (195ʳ). Everybody knows that they roused slaves against their masters and made them denounce their owners as image-worshippers. He[2] influenced the army against the orthodox, in particular those detachments which he had recruited for the capital from the herdsmen. He made them attack the Church and even asked them to take an oath never even to associate with monks or greet them and to imprison them unless they foreswore orthodoxy and put on lay dress. That is why the monks received their new name of 'those not to be remembered' (ἀμνημόνευτοι) (195ᵛ). Once he even forced monks to marry nuns in the Hippodrome. Divine Justice punished him by all sorts of catastrophes: earthquakes, freezing of the sea, floating ice even damaging the walls of Constantinople, finally the bubonic plague[3] and shooting stars (196ʳ). Eyewitnesses of these events, Nicephorus says, survive at the time of his writing.[4] This is the kind of 'calm' and 'peace' which was to be found in the Church under Constantine.

---

[1] αἴ τε λεγόμεναι καθολικαὶ ἐκκλησίαι ὅπως εἰς χρῆσιν ἱπποστασίων τῶν ἐκ τῆς στρατιωτικῆς ἀλογίας χρηματίζουσαι συγκεχώρηνται.

[2] The Emperor Constantine V.   [3] A.D. 747.

[4] ὧν τὰ πολλὰ καὶ μέχρι τοῦ δεῦρο ἀπαγγέλλουσιν ἄνθρωποι, κήρυκες τῶν ἐπὶ τοῖς παρανομοῦσι παθῶν περισωζόμενοι.

'Until the Empire was transferred from men to a woman, and the church of God was ruined by womanly simplicity; for she assembled a witless gathering and followed completely uneducated bishops.'

Many of the Iconoclastic emperors were men indeed, but only in their attacks on the Church (196ᵛ). They strove for long life (πολυχρο-νιότης) and all but said: 'We shall do evil that the good may come!' (Rom. iii. 8). Their entire reign was filled with civil strife and disturbance. 'Womanly simplicity', on the other hand, was profitable to the state (197ʳ). Not only did she[1] find the Church divided in itself, but Christians subject to the other patriarchs did not hold communion with the see of Constantinople because of its impiety and revolted. Irene brought about unity (197ᵛ). The Patriarch Paul,[2] very clever and orthodox, retired to a monastery not far from St. Sophia. At this the Empress was angry and the population disturbed (198ʳ). All the dignitaries assembled before Paul, he chastised their impiety and said that he refused to be bishop over heretics and to be separated from the other patriarchs. Soon afterwards Paul died. From that time on orthodoxy began to revive so that the abdication of the high priest from his throne became the revival of orthodoxy[3] (198ᵛ). Tarasius became Patriarch[4] and all (senators, dignitaries, soldiers) agreed that an ecumenical synod should be held (199ʳ). The customary messages were sent to the Patriarch in the West and those in the East who all sent representatives equipped with γράμματα συνοδικὰ καὶ κανονικά (199ʳ). The council[5] approved image-worship and condemned the iconoclastic council of 754. 'She assembled a thoughtless gathering and followed most uneducated bishops.' With these words they[6] condemn themselves, in Nicephorus' opinion, for they criticize their own archbishops and teachers who consecrated, taught, and appointed them (201ʳ). They who are thus raging against the holy Council had approved it previously with their own signature when they were ordained, and had anathematized all those who would ever transgress its *Horos* (203ʳ). If their assertion is true, then their own ordination is null and void. If on the other hand they are lying, they have forfeited their priesthood by their lie. In consequence they should neither enjoy the privileges of a Christian nor assemble in synods. Therefore their assembly should not be called a council.

Nicephorus foresees that malicious critics may turn his argument against the iconophile cause and claim that the teachers ought to be blamed for the shortcoming of their disciples (203ᵛ). But there was

---

[1] The Empress Irene.   [2] Paul IV, 780–4.

[3] ὥστε τὴν παρὰ τοῦ ἱεράρχου γενομένην τοῦ θρόνου παραίτησιν τῆς εὐπιστίας γενέσθαι ἀνάστασιν.   [4] 784–806.

[5] Seventh Ecumenical Council of Nicaea, 787.

[6] The Iconoclastic Council of St. Sophia, 815.

fault neither in the teachers nor in their teachings, it was only in the bad intentions of the pupils. Some of them deserted the faith because they had previously committed dishonourable deeds, others who had violated the canons and were ousted from the priesthood were honoured with the presidency over the vain assembly (204^r).[1] They will have to confess that they had been worshipping idols, and therefore they are excluded from the Church until they have done penance for the pre-scribed period (204^v). How could such men assemble in councils? It has escaped them that they are fighting against their own teachers. 'She followed completely uneducated bishops.' On the contrary, says Nicephorus, they were wise, experienced, the best of their time (205^r). The purpose of the Empress was to restore peace in the Church. She did not use coercion, quite unlike the rulers of the present genera-tion when turmoil has overtaken the entire Roman Empire[2] (205^v). Instead of following the apostolic teaching, the Iconoclasts have sub-mitted themselves to secular rulers. They have changed with surprising ease from Christians into barbarians. Like the Jews they honour the golden image, but refuse to worship the image of Christ (206^r).

'She established as a dogma the painting of the incomprehensible Son and Word of God in His Incarnation by means of worthless matter.'

As Nicephorus proposes to explain later on in his treatise, this is the view of a certain Epiphanides and his docetic followers which the Iconoclasts have adopted just as their predecessors did (206^r). If the above words are interpreted to mean that incomprehensibility is predi-cated of God the Word even after His Incarnation, then this view is Manichean. If, however, Christ is considered a man after the Incar-nation, then in accordance with the doctrine of the two natures this view is concordant with the teaching of the Church and there is no obstacle to pictorial representation (207^r). The teachings of the Council of Nicaea represent no innovations, nor are they the teaching of the Empress; she merely co-operated with the Council (σύνδρομος τῇ συνόδῳ καὶ ὀπαδὸς καὶ σύμψηφος), but she did not say as Mamonas did: 'If we shall have convinced you with respect to this one image' (the image of Christ is meant) 'that our view is right, then we intend to lay once more before you considerations (σκόποι) concerning the other images, and (it shall be) as you decide' (207^v).[3] The Iconoclasts object not only to the matter, but also to the art of painting. Yet not the arts are to be blamed, but those artists who use the art for a wicked purpose. And if the Iconoclasts blame matter, let them think that the forms of crosses, of bibles, and of all other sacred objects also are made of matter.

---

[1] προεδρίοις ἐπὶ τῆς τοῦ συνεδρίου αὐτῶν τετίμηνται ματαιότητος.
[2] ὁ πᾶσαν τὴν ὑπὸ Ῥωμαίοις ὑπολαβὼν θόρυβος.
[3] Ostrogorsky, *Studien*, p. 11, frg. 24.

'. . . And heedlessly she decreed to set up and worship by the dead visions of figures the all-holy Mother of God and the Saints sharing in his likeness (τοὺς συμμόρφους αὐτοῦ ἁγίους). She offended against the fitting doctrine of the Church itself, disturbed our adoring worship, and stated her opinion that what is due to God should be offered to the soulless matter of the icons.'

These are again the teachings of Epiphanides, a weak authority indeed (208ʳ). How can the Iconoclasts speak of adoring worship in connexion with images of the Mother of God and the Saints, since not even the originals can claim it? How can anybody be prevented from painting men who lived among us, since even those who distinguished themselves in war or otherhow are judged worthy of this honour? There is even more reason to paint images of the Saints. The Iconoclasts refer to the 'considerations' of Constantine; for it is clear to anybody that it is Constantine who is speaking through them:

'. . . foolishly she dared to declare them full of divine grace, and she led astray the simple-minded by ordaining the kindling of candles and the fragrance of incense together with worship by constraint' (209ʳ).

Nicephorus reciprocates in kind. According to him many people still remember how Constantine, so fond of horse races, honoured the famous horse race (ἀνθιππασία) with all sorts of sacred objects taken from the churches (209ᵛ). They were given to the chariot-horses and their drivers, and the clergy had to kindle candles and torches in church processions. Nobody accused him of idol-worship for such acts, but now they bitterly accuse the Saints. The faithful are forbidden to offer to sacred objects the honour which is bestowed even upon unreasoning animals. It is not true that force was used to induce people to worship images.

'If the Lord had not assembled us[1] and taken pity on the world about to be shipwrecked in a flood of sin and had not given the Christians a second Noah[2] who laboured to make blunt the storm of the heresy together with the Devil's acting' (Coisl. 93, fol. 35ʳ).

In reality [Leo V] released the flood against the Christians. One might say that unless the Lord had taken pity on the orthodox and had unexpectedly quieted down the hurricane and had removed him who wasr esponsible for all these evils,[3] all his subjects would have suffered a most serious shipwreck (Coisl. 93, fol. 35ᵛ).

Nicephorus then states that he is omitting certain sayings of the Council of St. Sophia. The Council further lists the six ecumenical councils and declares that it follows their teachings (210ʳ). It should be noticed, says Nicephorus, that they do not mention among the ecumenical councils 'the harlot's crew which now has brought them forth', i.e. the Council of Hiereia. In their enumeration of councils and of the heresies which they condemned they remark:

[1] Text corrupt.   [2] The Emperor Leo V, 813–20.
[3] Allusion to the murder of Leo V, see p. 183.

'But those who offer worship to the soulless images gladly welcomed these heresies as a starting-point for their former nonsense, either by circumscribing even the uncircumscribable in the image, or by separating the flesh from the godhead, thus attempting to correct one evil by another; for trying to avoid nonsense they fell into nonsense' (210ᵛ).

This, says Nicephorus, is not heresy but apostasy. The holy councils approved image-worship, in particular the sixth. '. . . by circumscribing even the uncircumscribable in the image or by separating the flesh from the godhead.' Never has it been said that the godhead is circumscribed (211ʳ). How can men who call the images 'spurious' assign them such great power as to perform a confusion or separation of the natures in Christ? (211ᵛ) '. . . attempting to correct one evil by another; for trying to avoid nonsense they fell into nonsense' (212ʳ). No, the Church unbrokenly has held the same opinions, it is rather the Iconoclasts who proceeded from evil to worse. Before this they ignored the promises which they deposited on the altar, now they even accuse those who consecrated them, and even Christ Himself, by removing the sacred decorations (212ᵛ). The Iconoclasts put forward the word ἀπερίγραπτος as an attack against the orthodox faith (213ʳ). They do not know the difference between γραπτός and περίγραπτος, between γράφειν and περιγράφειν, and they are confusing them constantly. One can speak of γραφή in two senses: (1) γραφή by means of letters, syllables, words, (2) γραφή by the art of painting with the help of colours. Περιγραφή, on the other hand, can occur in three different ways: (1) in space, (2) in time, (3) by apperception (καταλήψει). Now the painter when painting (γράφειν) a human being does not circumscribe (περιγράφειν) his model in either of the three ways indicated above, nor does he who circumscribes somebody in one of these three ways paint him. Christ was circumscribed not by men—for that would be beyond human power—but by Himself by virtue of His dispensation (οἰκονομία). Men paint, but do not circumscribe. What are the Iconoclasts going to say about the Body which God the Word assumed from the Mother of God in her womb? Was the Word circumscribed along with the Body? Or was it separated from it? Perhaps they are even going to follow their teachers to the extent that they will claim confusion of the two natures, or claim that Christ was seen in appearance and imagination only.

To put it more elaborately: While Christ was staying at Jerusalem in the body doing His miracles in the Temple, He was not at the same time in Galilee in the body, but as God He was everywhere (214ʳ). Thus His godhead is neither painted nor circumscribed when He is painted or circumscribed in the body, nor is His godhead separated from His manhood. When has anybody ever heard of a body which cannot be painted or circumscribed? περιγραφή is part of the definition of 'body'. If Christ's Body is not γραπτός, then He did not possess a human body. According to the dogma of the Catholic Church, Christ consists of two opposed natures. If the divine nature has the qualities of ἄγραπτος and ἀπερίγραπτος, the human nature has the opposite qualities (215ʳ). Why should the difference be preserved with all other pairs of opposites, but perish with respect to these two? If the Iconoclasts claim that because of its union with the godhead the body of Christ is ἀπερίγραπτος, then the consequence is that all the sufferings of the body likewise affect the godhead. A further contradiction is that while they declare Christ ἀπερίγραπτος, they state that simple-minded persons circumscribe Him together with His image. Thus they declare Him to be both περίγραπτος and ἀπερίγραπτος. Their aim is to deny the Incarnation by this one word ἀπερίγραπτος.

After completing this analysis, Nicephorus turns to quotations (ἐπὶ τὰς φωνὰς ἐκείνας μετελεύσομεν) (215ʳ), in order to reveal the sources from which the Iconoclasts and their intellectual fathers arrived at such impiety. He cites:

1. A docetic fragment said to come from Valentinus.[1]
2. A fragment from Marcion.[2]
3. A fragment from a later writer, the Messalian Markianos.[3]
4. Mani, Letters to Oddas and to Scythianos.[4]
5. Quotation from Eusebius' *Letter to the Empress Constantia*.

With respect to this letter Nicephorus refers to a previous work of his, clearly the *Contra Eusebium et Epiphanidem* (216ᵛ).

Against these passages from heretics who declare Christ to be ἀπερίγραπτος, Nicephorus proceeds to line up the orthodox authorities (217ʳ). The *florilegium* which now follows (217ʳ–222ʳ) is designed to support the thesis that Christ is circumscribable.[5]

'Therefore we embrace this straight doctrine and banish from the Catholic Church the illegitimate making of the spurious images which has been recklessly proclaimed as doctrine' (222ʳ).

---

[1] A. Hilgenfeld, *Die Ketzergeschichte des Urchristentums urkundlich dargestellt* (Leipzig, 1884), 283–316.

[2] Also quoted in *Contra Eusebium*, ed. Pitra, i. 406, see A. von Harnack, *Marcion: Das Evangelium vom fremden Gott*, &c., *T.U.* xlv. 287*.

[3] Pitra (*Spicilegium Solesmense*, i. 406) could identify neither the writer nor the fragment, which is quoted also in the *Contra Eusebium* as ἐκ τῆς συγγραφῆς Τιμοθέου πρεσβυτέρου. On the Messalians see M. Wellnhofer, 'Die thrakischen Euchiten' &c., *B.Z.* xxx (1930), 477–84; S. Der Nersessian, 'Une Apologie des images du septième siècle', *Byzantion*, xvii (1945), 61 f., n. 17.

[4] Also quoted in *Contra Eusebium* (ed. Pitra, i. 405 f.). See P. Alfaric, *Les Écritures manichéennes* (Paris, 1919), ii. 73.

[5] Except for minor matters such as introductory formulas, arrangement, &c., this *florilegium* is identical with the one that was appended to the *Third Antirrheticus*.

Concerning the images the Iconoclasts are using again the expression of Epiphanides: spurious (222ᵛ). Nicephorus replies that it would be absurd to permit one kind of pictorial representation and to forbid another. By calling the image ψευδής, they deny the existence of the original (223ʳ). If they call the image false, they should be asked: If you see an image with an inscription, do you not think of the person it represents? Clearly, then, Emmanuel Himself appears to us in His image (223ᵛ). Another approach: a portrait (εἰκών) is a likeness resembling the person which it represents (etymologically the word is derived from εἴκω which is equivalent to ὁμοιῶ), therefore it would be said by a logician to belong to the class of relative concepts (τὰ πρός τι), and it is the relation (σχέσις) which connects image and original. Through their common participation in the relation,[1] each of the two is 'false' if the other is false (224ʳ). Image and archetype are correlatives and as such they come into existence together and disappear together. Therefore if the Iconoclasts dare to call Christ's images 'spurious', they declare that Christ is a false Christ and a false King. If they call the images of Christ false, they necessarily call Christ false too, and since the false is non-existent, they deny the existence of Christ. Thus the term 'spurious' denies the entire dispensation of Christ (224ᵛ).

The shamelessness of the Iconoclasts forces Nicephorus to rely on secular authors. According to them the word 'cause' has several meanings; effective, instrumental (ὀργανικόν), exemplary (παραδειγματικόν), material, and final cause. Everything made by hand has Christ as its exemplary cause. The cause of the image is Christ Himself, therefore they destroy Christ by calling His image false. They accuse the Catholic Church and thereby they prove that the images are worshipped all over the inhabited world. Thereby they 'banish' themselves rather than the images from the Church (225ʳ)

'Not by an injudicious judgement, but by just judgement we decide against the worship of images injudiciously proclaimed by Tarasius. We refute and invalidate his Council for having bestowed, as we have said before, excessive honour upon the hues.'

They invalidate not the Council but themselves (225ᵛ).

' . . . for having bestowed excessive honour on the hues, the kindling of candles and lamps, offerings of incense, in one word: the worship of adoration' (σέβασμα λατρείας).

(pp. 177 f. above) and which was edited by Pitra, i. 343–52. Even the formulas introducing a quotation are the same in some cases, and at the end (222ᵛ) there is a clear reference to the second part of the florilegium attached to Nicephorus' *Third Antirrheticus* (Pitra, i. 352–70) which proves that Christ is both perfect God and perfect Man. Under these circumstances it was not necessary to summarize the florilegium.　　　　　　　　　　　[1] τῷ κοινῇ μετέχειν τῆς σχέσεως.

In reply to these words Nicephorus considers it sheer madness to believe that honour is offered to religious paintings. What is the right measure of honour that the impious are willing to bestow upon images? (225ᵛ) They have not stopped at any measure, but are holding the images in complete contempt. A Christian does not worship paintings, but through the images, which are, as it were, the gateway to the sacred sanctuaries, his mind is led towards higher things.

'We gladly accept the holy council assembled at Blachernae in the temple of the Immaculate Virgin under the late pious Emperors Constantine and and Leo[1], as supported by the doctrines of the Fathers. We preserve its decrees unaltered and declare the making of images to be neither venerable nor profitable, but we refrain from calling them idols, for there are also different degrees of evil' (226ᵛ).

How can they call 'council', Nicephorus asks, a gathering foreign to all Church discipline? How dare they speak of the temple of the Immaculate Virgin since they removed from it her image through which this Church has enjoyed so much honour? They have omitted to mention the lofty plane-trees (πλατάνους) outside the city-walls where this gathering assembled.[2] Therefore the synod should be called πλατανίτης since it remained sterile like that tree. The Fathers of whom they speak must be Eusebius, Epiphanides, and their ilk. Any other passages are either torn from their context or forgeries (227ʳ). To prove that the iconoclastic *Horos* does not conform to the six Ecumenical Councils Nicephorus gives a history of these Councils (227ᵛ–229ʳ).[3] Contrary to its claim, the iconoclastic Council is not following the doctrine established by the six Ecumenical Councils (Coisl. 93, fol.57ʳ). Its *Horos* is entirely negative and has no positive content. Nicephorus demonstrates its disagreement with that of the First Ecumenical Council by referring to the existence, at Nicaea, of the church which is named after those who assembled the first holy Council; their statues are preserved down to Nicephorus' time.[4] The Council is just as much out of step with the other Ecumenical Councils. Its 'Definition' is

---

[1] Constantine V and his son Leo IV.

[2] Were there plane-trees in the neighbourhood of the palace of Hiereia?

[3] Edited from the *Paris Gr.* 1250 by J. B. Pitra, *Juris Ecclesiastici Graecorum Historia et Monumenta* (Rome, 1868), ii. 317–20.

[4] I reproduce the text for the benefit of historians of architecture: . . . μαρτυρεῖ τὸ ἱερὸν τέμενος ὃ ἐπ' ὀνόματι τῶν τὴν πρώτην ἁγίαν συγκεκροτηκότων σύνοδον ἀνεγήγερται τὰς αὐτῶν ἐκείνων μέχρι καὶ σήμερον στήλας προβαλλόμενον, μονονουχὶ τὴν παρ' αὐτῶν ὁμολογίαν καὶ τὸ φρόνημα σαφῶς διακεκραγυίας εἰς ἔνδειξιν τῆς ὑγιοῦς πίστεως τοῦ θεοκινήτως συγκεκληκότος θεοφιλοῦς βασιλέως· ἃς ἤδη καὶ καθελεῖν πειραθέντες οἱ τῆς καταστροφῆς ἄνδρες ὅμως οὐ συγκεχώρηται τὴν εἰς τοῦτο παρανομίαν ἀνύσαι. This passage is lost in the *Graecus* 1250, but preserved in Coisl. 93, fol. 57ʳ, in the above (somewhat corrupt) form. This is clearly the same church as that mentioned before, fol. 188a (see p. 246 above) and by Theophanes, 406. 2. (where

truly undefined. What image does the Council want to set up since it rejects that of Christ? (Coisl. 93, fol. 58ᵛ) That of the Antichrist? Perhaps the Iconoclasts follow Constantine V and declare the Eucharist to be the image of His body? But Christ Himself called it His body, not the image of His body (230ʳ). While they reject image-worship, the orthodox follow the Seventh Council of Nicaea and accept it (230ᵛ).

'But we refrain from calling them idols' (231ʳ).

Here, in Nicephorus' opinion, the wise men are contradicting them-selves. Did they not announce that they were following unswervingly the council of the plane-trees? (231ʳ) Still it had called the images idols. Here is an inconsistency; they are forgetful of the doctrines of their teachers (232ᵛ). If they hesitate to apply the word 'idols' to Christian images, they certainly treat them as such. If they are idols, they should call them idols; and if they are not, they should anathema-tize the council held by Constantine V (233ʳ). Just as the entire *Horos* of St. Sophia consists of negative criticism only, so here too they do not accept the word 'idols', but do not agree equally to give them their orthodox name (233ᵛ). Slyly they are speaking of images without mentioning that the images of Christ are meant.

'For there are also different degrees of evil' (234ʳ).

Now the Iconoclasts are calling the images an evil and 'lesser idols' (ἥττονα εἴδωλα) (234ᵛ). Then Christ would have come in vain. The Iconoclasts are unable to distinguish between things sacred and pro-fane (235ʳ). They should not be called Christians at all (235ᵛ). The rashness of their judgement and its fickle nature are shown clearly in that now they call the images 'idols' and now they hesitate to do so.

At this point Nicephorus turns towards the second part of the Dog-matic Definition issued by the Council of St. Sophia. This Council collected useless quotations (χρήσεις ἄχρηστοι) to establish its fictitious contentions, yet the Iconoclasts have not achieved more than their teacher Constantine. Some quotations they have changed, the majority of their authorities are heretical. They have misinterpreted others, or altered their attributions in order to deceive the simple-minded with resounding names. These quotations Nicephorus plans to contrast with orthodox passages. He feels confident that he will triumph over the contradictions of his opponents. The very first of these iconoclastic quotations puts to the test their above-mentioned assertion that they refrain from calling the images idols; for it is directed against idols.

unfortunately the text is corrupt, see Anastasius' translation in the apparatus which is not satisfactory either). I am not able to decide whether the church mentioned by Nicephorus and Theophanes (and their common source?—see pp. 158 ff. above) is identical with the church of St. Sophia or with the Koimesis Church (see Cabrol et Leclerq, 'Nicée', *Dictionnaire d'Archéologie chrétienne et de Liturgie*, xii. 1, 1183–211).

1. The first quotation is supposed to come ἐξ ἀποστολικῶν διατάξεων.[1] Nicephorus states that the full passage was directed against
idol-worship and quotes from [Pamphilus], *Ex Apostolorum in Antiochia
Synodo*.[2] Had the Apostles objected to Christ's image, they would have
contradicted Christ's own action with regard to King Abgar (238ʳ).
Why did they not destroy the monument set up by the woman with
the issue of blood? Then follows a discussion of the images of Christ
and the Virgin Mary at Rome, painted by the Apostle Luke, other
images at Jerusalem also painted by Luke, images depicted by Peter
and Paul at Rome, and the image 'not made by hands' at Lydda.
Nicephorus adds several long passages from the life of Pancratius,
bishop of Tauromenium in Sicily, by his successor Euagrios, according
to which St. Peter had portraits made of Jesus Himself, and of Pancratius.[3] Nicephorus briefly mentions that the Apostle Thomas likewise
took paintings to all the places where he preached the Gospel. If some
people object to this evidence because they have no complete manuscript of these texts, they should blame the Iconoclasts who burned
and mutilated many manuscripts and in particular those containing
the *Life* of St. Pancratius.

2. Asterius of Amaseia, *Homilia de Divite et Lazaro*[4] is expressly
termed the second iconoclastic quotation (241ᵛ). According to
Nicephorus the Iconoclasts interpret the passage incorrectly. The
full text, as quoted by Nicephorus, does not contain a prohibition of
images, but admonishes the rich to spend their money on charity
rather than on costly paintings. An accurate analysis shows that
Asterius believed Christ to be γραπτός. To demonstrate Asterius'
friendly attitude towards images Nicephorus cites Asterius, *Homilia
in Iairum et mulierem sanguinis profluvia laborantem*,[5] and he promises to
quote later from an enkomion of St. Euphemia by the same author (see
p. 258 below). Nicephorus adduces Antipatros of Bostra, *On the woman
with the issue of blood*,[6] and mentions that even the impious Eusebius
of Caesarea accurately describes the image of Paneas.[7]

---

[1] This fragment which enjoins an embroiderer to represent the Cross and to
avoid unseemly adornment is not contained in F. X. Funk, *Didascalia et Constitu-
tutiones Apostolorum* (Paderborn, 1905).

[2] Ed. J. B. Pitra, *Iuris Ecclesiastici Graecorum Historia et Monumenta* (Rome, 1864),
i. 92.

[3] This text is unpublished in the Greek, but an old Georgian translation was published by A. Khakhanov, *Bagrat episkop tavromeniiskii* &c., Trudy po vostokovedenyu
izdavaemye Lazarevskim Institutom Vostochnych Yazykov xix (1904). See, furthermore, E. von Dobschütz, *Christusbilder, T.U.*, n.f., iii (1899), 109* (Greek fragments)
and p. 12, n. 2 above. I remember with pleasure the (unpublished) lecture given
on this text by the late Professor R. P. Blake at one of the Dumbarton Oaks
symposia.   [4] *P.G.* xl. 168ʙ.

[5] Mentioned by Photius, *Bibliotheca*, cod. cclxxi, *P.G.* civ. 221ᴀ.

[6] *P.G.* lxxxv. 1793ᴅ.   [7] *Hist. Eccl.* vii. 18.

3. Next the Iconoclasts quote 'a certain Leontius' (246ʳ), from an unnamed work. The point of the quotation is that the painters paint different images of Jesus; that Leontius is frightened by anybody who claims to possess a likeness (ὁμοιωσίδιον) of the Lord; that Christ's likeness must be acquired in Man's soul; and that it is impossible to represent Christ in a pictorial image. Nicephorus replies that the painters do indeed paint different images of Christ, that is however quite natural since Christ was a complete man, grew older, &c. Leontius' inference that Christ cannot be painted is illogical. Against this obscure Leontius, Nicephorus arrays Leontius of Neapolis, *Contra Iudaeos*.[1] Nicephorus announces that he could quote also from other works written against Jews and Gentiles, such as Anastasius from Mount Sinai or from Antioch (ὁ κατὰ τὸ Σιναῖον ὄρος ἤτοι τῆς Ἀντιοχέων προεδρεύσας), John of Thessalonica, Sergios, Moschos, or Constantine, deacon and chartophylax of St. Sophia, but that he does not wish to shoot wide of his mark (254ᵛ).

4. The next quotation is from Theodotus 'of Galatia'. According to tradition Christians should not paint the Saints, but should imitate their virtues and thus become their animate images (254ᵛ). Nicephorus states that the author is not identical with Theodotus of Ancyra whose *Homilia In Sanctam Deiparam et in Simeonem*[2] permits images of Christ. Nicephorus infers that the iconoclastic quotation must be spurious. Usually the Iconoclasts attack the image of Christ, this passage is directed against images of Saints. If Theodotus claims that images are not warranted by tradition, Nicephorus is going to refute him by some genuine patristic passages:

(*a*) John Chrysostom, ἐν τῷ εἰς τὸν Ἰὼβ λόγῳ (256ᵛ).[3]

(*b*) Idem, *Homilia in Meletium*.[4]

(*c*) From a *Vita Iohannis Chrysostomi*.[5]

(*d*) Basil the Great, *Homilia in Barlaam martyrem*.[6]

(*e*) Gregory of Nyssa.[7]

(*f*) Idem, *In Sanctum Theodorum*[8] (258ʳ–259ʳ).

(*g*) Idem, εἰς τὸν ἅγιον μάρτυρα Βασιλίσκον.[9]

---

[1] *P.G.* xciii. 1597–1610. [2] *P.G.* lxxvii. 1393ᶜ.

[3] This is a puzzling attribution. Part of it was quoted already at the Seventh Council (Mansi, xiii. 9ᴀ) but there it was said to come from John Chrysostom, *Homilia de Legislatore*; it is indeed found in this homily (*P.G.* lvi. 407).

[4] *P.G.* l. 516 = Mansi, xiii. 8ʙ.

[5] Quoted by Iohannes Damascenus, *De Imaginibus Oratio*, i, *P.G.* xciv. 1277ᶜ.

[6] *P.G.* xxxi. 489ᴀ = Mansi, xiii. 80.

[7] A fragment quoted in Mansi, xiii. 9ᶜ from περὶ θεότητος υἱοῦ καὶ πνεύματος, καὶ εἰς τὸν Ἀβραάμ.

[8] *B.H.G.* 1760, *P.G.* xlvi. 737ᶜ–740ʙ.

[9] Not identified.

(h) Gregory Nazianzen, Carmina.[1]

(i) Asterius of Amaseia, In Euphemiam Martyrem[2] (259ʳ–260ᵛ).

Having thus refuted Theodotus' contention solely from such authorities as the Iconoclasts themselves had called to their aid, Nicephorus proceeds to another sentence of this quotation (261ʳ). Theodotus' hostile attitude against images can be explained only by the fact that he is a Judaizer. It is senseless to recognize a Saint's virtues as his 'animate images' yet to prohibit painted images (262ᵛ). If Theodotus does not see any useful purpose served by the images, he will be refuted again from those authors whom the Iconoclasts have invoked:

(a) Basil the Great, Homilia in Sanctos Quadraginta Martyres.[3]

(b) Gregory Nazianzen, Carmina (263ᵛ).[4]

(c) Short references to the above passages from Gregory of Nyssa, John Chrysostom, and Asterius of Amaseia (264ʳ).

If anybody wanted to go beyond the authors cited by the Iconoclasts, he would find material in the Life of the Patriarch Eutychius of Constantinople,[5] the writings of Sophronius of Jerusalem, and the acts of the martyrs. The images remind men of the content of the Bible (264ᵛ), as is shown by the above passage from Basil the Great, and another passage from John Chrysostom which the Iconoclasts themselves adduce (p. 261 below). Since the Bible is not an 'animate image' either, Theodotus' argument would reject the Bible as well as the images (265ʳ). On the contrary, the Fathers and the Saints all approved of image-worship (265ᵛ).

5. Next the Iconoclasts refer to a passage from Basil of Seleucia (266ʳ) which, like that from Theodotus from Galatia, rejects painted images in favour of written records of the Saints' virtuous deeds. Nicephorus declares it to be spurious. Against it he cites a genuine passage of this author: a letter to the Emperor Leo concerning the martyr Thecla (266ᵛ–267ᵛ).[6]

6. Furthermore they quote Amphilochius of Iconium (267ᵛ), Ἐγκώμιον εἰς τὸν μέγαν Βασίλειον (267ᵛ).[7] It opposes painted images

---

[1] ii. 119, vv. 47–52, P.G. xxxviii. 75A.

[2] B.H.G. 623, Mansi, xiii. 16–18, cf. also 308A and p. 256 above.

[3] P.G. xxxi. 508D–509A.

[4] ii. 10, vv. 793–807, P.G. xxxvii. 737 sq., cf. Mansi, xiii. 13B.

[5] B.H.G. 657.

[6] Basil of Seleucia wrote the Acta (B.H.G. 1717) and Miracula (B.H.G. 1718) of Thecla, and there exists a letter of his to the Emperor Leo, see E. Schwartz, Concilium Universale Chalcedonense, v (Berlin and Leipzig, 1936), 46, but none of the three seems to contain the passage quoted by Nicephorus.

[7] This passage is preserved in Syriac translation, see K. V. Zetterstéen, 'Eine Homilie des Amphilochius von Iconium über Basilius von Cäsarea', Oriens Christianus, xxxi (1934), 68 f., see Mansi, xiii. 301D.

of the Saints, but enjoins the imitation of their good deeds and the preservation of their memory in writing. Nicephorus warns his readers not to believe their first impression (268^r). Its true meaning is shown by the prologue to the whole work, from which Nicephorus quotes a long section (268^r–268^v) : if the populations of the cities honour their temporal rulers by images, Christians must honour the Saints all the more in this way. This latter passage proves how the former should be interpreted : it does not condemn the painting of images, but since Amphilochius is proceeding to honour Basil by the art of the word, he declares that for this purpose of his he does not need the art of painting (268^v–269^r). Amphilochius means that an enkomion is neither the right occasion nor time for the art of painting (271^r). Whoever refuses to honour the likeness of the bodies of the Saints refuses to honour the Saints themselves : for it was in their bodies that their steadfastness appeared (273^r). As Amphilochius is more interested in the art of the word, so a painter may be more interested in the art of painting. A painter would say that the two faculties of hearing and seeing are at least of equal importance, and that he (the painter) has no need for the art of the word, but that would not mean that the art of the word is useless. If Amphilochius were alive nowadays, he would in Nicephorus' opinion be a vigorous advocate of image-worship (274^r). If, therefore, the quotation is genuine (and Nicephorus professes to have no judgment on this question), it should be interpreted along the lines indicated. The fact is that the Iconoclasts have committed several forgeries, and Nicephorus has been unable to find even a single manuscript of the text, not even one of recent date, because he was already in prison (275^r).[1]

7. Their next quotation (275^v) is said to come from Basil the Great, ἐκ τοῦ περὶ τῆς τοῦ ἀνθρώπου γενέσεως εἰς τὸ κατ᾽ εἰκόνα λόγου πρώτου.[2] Nicephorus has some doubts as to its genuineness since, according to Gregory of Nyssa, Basil's *Hexaëmeron* was left unfinished.[3] At any rate the passage is in favour of images rather than against them (276^r) : if, as the passage asserts, the painter is generally admired rather than the image, that happens only if the image as such is admirable (276^v). Basil's true ideas are expressed in other works which are undoubtedly authentic :

(a) *Liber de Spiritu Sancto*.[4]
(b) *Homilia contra Sabellianos et Arium et Anomoeos*.[5]

---

[1] ἡμῖν γὰρ οὐκ ἐξεγένετο καίτοι πολλὰ καμοῦσιν ὅτι μὴ μόνῳ ἀντιγράφῳ, καὶ τούτῳ νεογράφῳ, περιτυχεῖν, ἐν φρουραῖς ἀσφαλεστάταις ἤδη ἐγκαθειργμένοις καὶ μηδαμοῦ ἐλευθεριάζειν συγκεχωρημένοις, οὐ μὴ οὐδὲ πόδα προτείνειν πώποτε.

[2] It is attributed to Gregory of Nyssa in *P.G.* xliv. 253A–B, but see *P.G.* xxx. 32B.

[3] Cf. Gregory of Nyssa, *De hominis opificio*, *P.G.* xliv. 125C.

[4] 18, *P.G.* xxxii. 149C.   [5] 4, *P.G.* xxxi. 608A.

(c) Short references to the *Laudatio XL Martyrum Sebastenorum* and *In Barlaam Martyrem*.[1]

8. Their next quotation is said to come from Gregory of Nyssa :[2] it is an admonition not to represent (ἀνατυποῦν) or to adore (προσκυνεῖν) the corporeal shape of Christ, but Christ glorified and deified (278ʳ). Nicephorus claims that this does not refer to an image of Christ but to the human nature which Christ assumed. Gregory was arguing against the Arians who were worshipping the creature. Besides, Nicephorus reports that certain manuscripts have a different reading (279ᵛ). If his opponents should pretend that Christ has thrown off His body, he refers them to

(a) Gregory of Nyssa, *Homilia in Ascensionem Christi*.[3]
(b) Gregory of Nyssa, *in Stephanum Protomartyrem*.[4]
(c) Gregory Nazianzen, *Oratio in Sanctum Baptisma*.[5]
(d) Idem, *Oratio in Pentecostem*.[6]

Therefore Christ's resurrection concerned also His body. On this subject Nicephorus quotes in addition (281ᵛ):

(a) Athanasius.[7]
(b) Epiphanius, *Ancoratus* (282ʳ).[8]
(c) *Phil.* 2. 6.
(d) John Chrysostom (282ʳ).[9]
(e) Fifth Ecumenical Council, as quoted before.

9. Their next quotation comes (282ᵛ) from Gregory Nazianzen, ἐκ τῶν 'Επῶν αὐτοῦ: It is *hybris* to put one's faith in hues and not in the heart.[10] This passage has already been explained properly by earlier leaders of the orthodox,[11] still the Iconoclasts are not ashamed of using it again. It does not refer to images, but to faith manifesting itself in words only, as may be seen from other citations from Gregory,

(a) ὁ πρῶτος τῶν 'Επῶν λόγος (283ʳ).[12]
(b) ὁ εἰς τὰ 'Εγκαίνια λόγος.[13]
(c) *Homilia in Sanctum Baptisma*.[14]

---

[1] *B.H.G.* 1205 and 223 respectively.   [2] I cannot trace it.
[3] *P.G.* xlvi. 693B.   [4] *P.G.* xlvi. 713C.
[5] *P.G.* xxxvi. 424C.   [6] *P.G.* xxxvi. 436B.
[7] Not identified.   [8] li, ed. K. Holl, p. 60.   [9] Not identified.
[10] *Carmina Moralia*, 31, 39 f., *P.G.* xxxvii. 913, cf. Mansi, xiii. 297A–B.
[11] fol. 282ᵛ: τῆς γὰρ τοιαύτης χρήσεως καὶ πάλαι ἀναπτυχθείσης καὶ τὴν δέουσαν ἐξάπλωσιν καὶ ἑρμηνείαν τῆς διανοίας εὐσύνοπτον παρὰ τῶν πρὶν τοῦ ὀρθοῦ λόγου προεστη-κότων εἰληφυίας, τῆς δὲ ἀμαθίας καὶ δυσσεβείας τῶν κακῶς καὶ ἀνοήτως χρησαμένων ἐληλεγμένης οὐ καταδύονται οἱ ἄθλιοι ὑπ' ἀνοίας καὶ ἀναιδείας πάλιν ἐν τοῖς αὐτῶν συνείρειν λόγοις. This is a reference to Tarasius' *Refutation* of the Definition of the Council of Hiereia, pp. 20 f. above.   [12] Not identified.
[13] Not identified.   [14] *P.G.* xxxvi. 405A and 421B.

These passages prove that Gregory's alleged attack against images was only an allegory: Nicephorus interprets Gregory to mean that just as colours are perishable, so the audience was fickle (283ᵛ). Gregory's real views on the image problem may be gathered from the fact that he set up an image of Basil the Great (?, ἐλέγξει τοὺς ἄφρονας ἡ παρ' αὐτοῦ εἰς τὸν μέγαν Βασίλειον ἀνατεθεῖσα εἰκών) and from his reaction to an image of the martyr Polemon (284ʳ).

10. Their next quotation is John Chrysostom, *In Romanum Martyrem Oratio.*[1] The context, according to Nicephorus, shows that the author is not speaking of Christ being painted but of Christ being circumscribed within the walls of a church. It is the old distinction of γραφή and περιγραφή which Nicephorus has discussed elsewhere.[2]

11. Then follows a quotation, again from John Chrysostom, Λόγος εἰς τὸν Ἀβραάμ.[3] The fact that pagans in Palestine made statues of the angels visiting Abraham does not prove that Christians should not paint images, rather the contrary (289ʳ).

12. Another passage is alleged to come from John Chrysostom, Εἰς τὸν δεσμοφύλακα (290ᵛ).[4] According to Nicephorus, Constantine Mamonas was obliged to delete certain quotations from the *florilegium* assembled by the Council of Hiereia–Blachernae and he would have done so most of all with this one, had not the most prominent member of the clergy persuaded him not to do so (291ʳ).[5] The latter claimed that otherwise the Iconoclasts might be accused of accepting only such texts as were in their favour. Again this passage is not directed against images, it merely attempts to show that the Saints are present by means of their words and of what is written about them (291ᵛ). John Chrysostom was interested only in the words of the Saints as images of their souls, but he does not prohibit artistic images of their bodies (293ʳ).

13. The next quotation (293ᵛ) hardly deserves a refutation, for it had been rejected almost thirty years ago,[6] namely the Letter of Nilus to Olympiodorus.[7] It suffices to contrast this quotation with the full text of the letter (294ᵛ–295ʳ) to see what the impious do to orthodox writings. Nicephorus quotes, furthermore, from Nilus' letter to Heliodorus Silentiarius.[8]

14. To crown their impious undertaking, the Iconoclasts adduce last of all certain quotations which they allege to be derived from

---

[1] *P.G.* l. 616.
[2] *Antirrheticus,* ii. 12–15, *P.G.* 356A–364C, also pp. 206 ff. above.
[3] Not published among the works of St. John Chrysostom.
[4] *P.G.* lv. 521, see Mansi xiii. 300A–B.
[5] Presumably Theodosius of Ephesus who presided at the Council.
[6] Here is another (see p. 260, n. 11 above) reference to Tarasius' *Refutation.*
[7] iv. 61, *P.G.* lxxix. 577–80, cf. Mansi, xiii. 32–36.
[8] iv. 62, *P.G.* lxxix. 580–2.

Epiphanius of Cyprus (295^v), but which cannot belong to him. Nicephorus has shown this already in another work of his (pp. 176 f. above) but will present his arguments again in a shorter form (συνοπτι-κώτερον.). What follows (296^r–330^r) agrees so closely, in some cases even literally, with Nicephorus' earlier discussion of the quotations from Epiphanius in his *Contra Eusebium et Epiphanidem* that it may be permissible to refer to that text and its analysis.[1] The only significant difference is that here, in his *Refutatio et Eversio*, Nicephorus includes a document which he had omitted in his earlier work: Epiphanius' *Letter to John of Aelia*.[2] Nicephorus declares it to be a work not of Epiphanius but of some docetist (329^r).

Nicephorus' work concludes with the advice to the reader to follow the path of truth and to reject the impious teachings of the Iconoclasts which are disapproved by East and West alike and thrive only in the wicked Empire (330^r–332^r).

[1] Pitra, iv. 292–376. See pp. 176 f. above.
[2] On this letter see P. Maas, 'Die ikonoklastische Episode in dem Brief des Epiphanios an Johannes', *B.Z.* xxx (1930), 279–86.

CHRONOLOGICAL TABLE

Where advisable reference is made to the *pages* of this book.

ca. A.D. 200	Earliest catacomb paintings.
300–500	Use of images spreading in Church.
Fourth century	Cappadocian Fathers approve certain religious images as instruments of Christian instruction.
Sixth century	Rapid progress of image worship.
ca. 600	Beginning of Iconoclastic movement in Armenia.
610–49	In the writings of John of Thessalonica, arguments used earlier by pagans in defence of their cult statues appear in support of Christian icons. Christ's perfect human nature is first adduced in support of artistic images of Christ.
692	Can. 82 of Quinisextum prohibits symbolic (Lamb) representation of Christ and orders His portrait in human form.
717–41	Leo III Emperor of Byzantium.
723/4	Ommayyad Khalif Yazid II decrees destruction of Christian images.
724	Beginning of iconoclastic agitation among bishops of Asia Minor.
730	Emperor Leo III decrees destruction of icons.
c. 700–49(?)	John of Damascus.
715–30	Germanos Patriarch of Constantinople.
741–75	Constantine V (Copronymus) Emperor of Byzantium.
754	Iconoclastic Council of Hiereia and Blachernae.
756/7	Constantine V transfers Eastern Illyricum, Sicily, and Calabria from the ecclesiastical jurisdiction of the Pope to that of the Patriarch of Constantinople (p. 103).
758	Birth of Nicephorus.
764	St. Stephen the Younger suffers martyrdom. General persecution of Iconophiles begins.
775–80	Leo IV the Khazar Emperor of Byzantium.
c. 775(?)–97	Nicephorus Imperial Secretary.
780–97	Constantine VI and his mother Irene Emperors of Byzantium.
780–7	*Breviarium* of Nicephorus.
784–806	Tarasius Patriarch of Constantinople.
786	Assembly of Seventh Ecumenical Council at church of the Holy Apostles in Constantinople broken up by the garrison troops.
787	Seventh Ecumenical Council of Nicaea.
795–7	First stage of Moechian Controversy.
797–802	Irene 'Emperor' of Byzantium, Nicephorus in retirement (pp. 61 ff.).
800	'Imperial Coronation' of Charlemagne at St. Peter's.

802–11	Nicephorus I Emperor of Byzantium.
802?–6	Nicephorus in charge of poorhouse at Constantinople (p. 63).
803	Revolt of Bardanes Turcus.
806–15	Nicephorus Patriarch of Constantinople.
806–11	Second stage of Moechian Controversy.
806	Local synod of Constantinople anathematizes those who refuse to hold communion with Joseph of Kathara (esp. the Studites, who go into exile).
809–11	Anonymous commentary on Gospel of John (pp. 98 f., 196 f.).
811	Byzantine army defeated by Bulgarians and death of Emperor Nicephorus I; his son Stauracius though fatally wounded proclaimed Emperor.
811–13	Michael I Rangabe Emperor of Byzantium, under influence of Studites.
811–12	Nicephorus' Synodal Letter to Pope Leo III (pp. 106–8, 163.)
811–13	Large sections of Constantinopolitan garrison discharged, probably on Studite intervention because of Iconoclastic leanings (p. 121).
811	Joseph of Kathara ousted, Nicephorus apologizes to Studites.
811	Death penalty against Paulicians and Athinganoi announced by synodal and imperial decrees. Measure supported by Patriarch Nicephorus, withdrawn on Studite intervention.
812	Studites veto peace treaty with Bulgarians.
813	Defeat of Michael I at Versinicia by Bulgarians.
813–20	Leo V the Armenian Emperor of Byzantium.
814	Committee of six appointed by Emperor to compile patristic florilegium in favour of Iconoclasm.
814–15	Leo V attempts to convert Patriarch Nicephorus and clergy to Iconoclasm. Nicephorus organizes iconophile resistance and composes *Apologeticus Minor* and *De Magnete*.
815	Synodal decision unfavourable to Nicephorus (contents unknown). Nicephorus abdicates, exiled first to his monastery of τὰ Ἀγαθοῦ, afterwards to monastery of St. Theodore near Chalcedon.
815–21	Theodotus Cassiteras Patriarch of Constantinople.
815, after Easter	Iconoclastic Council of St. Sophia, *Definition* and patristic florilegium preserved. Followed by a general persecution of Iconophiles.
818–20	Nicephorus completes *Apologeticus atque Antirrhetici, Contra Eusebium et Epiphanidem*, and *Adversus Iconomachos*.
820	Murder of Leo V.
820–9	Michael II of Amorium Emperor of Byzantium.
820–8	Nicephorus writes a lost work on Leo V, as well as his *Refutatio et Eversio*.

821–34	Antonius Patriarch of Constantinople.
826	Death of Theodore of Studios.
828	Death of Nicephorus.
829–43	Theophilus Emperor of Byzantium.
830–4	Third Iconoclastic Council at Blachernae, persecution of Iconophiles renewed.
843	Council of Constantinople restores image worship.

BIBLIOGRAPHY

I. SOURCES

(1) Unpublished Material

Bodleianus Laudianus Graecus 69, fols. 306–24, containing a Life of Euthymius of Sardis by Metrophanes (see p. 130, n. 2). (I inspected the manuscript at Oxford on 3 August 1939, and took notes.)

British Museum Add. MS. 19390, fols. 24–55, containing the *Breviarium* attributed to Nicephorus (see II, under OROSZ).

Parisinus Graecus 1250, fols. 173–332, containing the "Έλεγχος καὶ Ἀνατροπή of Nicephorus.

Coislinianus 93, fols. 1–159, likewise containing the "Έλεγχος καὶ Ἀνατροπή of Nicephorus.

(2) Works of Nicephorus (genuine and dubious)

Breviarium, ed. C. de Boor, *Nicephori Archiepiscopi Constantinopolitani Opuscula Historica* (Leipzig, 1880), 3–77 (see II, under OROSZ).

Χρονογραφικὸν Σύντομον, ibid. 79–135.

Epistula ad Leonem, P.G. c. 169–200.

Apologeticus Minor, ibid. 833–50.

Apologeticus atque Antirrhetici (above, pp. 167 ff.), ibid. 533–831 and 205–533.

Contra Eusebium et Epiphanidem, ed. J. B. Pitra, *Spicilegium Solesmense complectens Sanctorum Patrum Scriptorumque Ecclesiasticorum Anecdota hactenus Opera etc.* (Paris, 1852–8), i. 371–503 and iv. 292–380.

De Magnete, ibid. i. 302–35.

Adversus Iconomachos, ibid. iv. 233–91.

"Έλεγχος καὶ Ἀνατροπή, see above under (1).

Book of Dreams, ed. F. Drexl, 'Das Traumbuch des Patriarchen Nikephoros', *Festgabe Albert Ehrhard* (Bonn und Leipzig, 1922), 94–118.

(3) Other Sources

Acta Graeca Davidis, Symeonis et Georgii Mitylenae in insula Lesbo, ed. H. Delehaye, *A.B.* xviii (1899), 209–59.

Acts of the Second Council of Nicaea, J. D. Mansi, *Sacrorum Conciliorum Nova et Amplissima Collectio*, vols. xii and xiii (Florence, 1766 and 1767).

AGAPIUS OF MENBIDJ, *Kitāb al-'Unvān* (= *Universal History*), ed. and transl. by A. Vasiliev, *P.O.* vii and viii (1911–12).

ANASTASIUS SINAITA, *Disputatio adversus Iudaeos*, P.G. lxxxix. 1203 ff.

Annales Regni Francorum, edd. G. H. Pertz et F. Kurze (Hannover, 1895).

APOLLINARIS OF LAODICEA, ed. H. Lietzmann (Tübingen, 1904).

ASTERIUS OF AMASEA, *P.G.* xl.

BAR HEBRAEUS, *Chronography*, transl. by E. A. W. Budge, *The Chronography of Gregory Abû'l Faraj*, &c. i (London, 1932).

BASILIUS, *Notitia episcopatuum*, ed. H. Gelzer, *Georgii Cyprii Descriptio Orbis Romani* (Leipzig, 1890).

Celsi ΑΛΗΘΗϹ ΛΟΓΟϹ, ed. O. Glöckner, Kleine Texte für Vorlesungen und Übungen 151 (Bonn, 1924).

Commentaria in Aristotelem Graeca, 23 vols. (Berlin, 1882–1909).

CONSTANTINE PORPHYROGENNETUS, *De Ceremoniis Aulae Byzantinae*, ed. J. J. Reiske, *C.S.H.B.* ix and x; for Book I, see also the edition of Albert Vogt, *Constantin VII Porphyrogénète, Le Livre des Cérémonies*, 2 vols. ('texte' and 'commentaire') (Paris, 1935).

De exilio et translatione Nicephori, by Theophanes Presbyter (= *B.H.G.* 1336 and 1337), ed. Theophilus Ioannu, *Mnemeia Hagiologika* (Venice, 1884), 115–28.

Dialogue between a Christian and a Jew, ed. A. C. McGiffert (Marburg, 1889).

DIONYSIUS OF TELL-MAHRE, *Chronicle*, Part IV, ed. and transl. by J. B. Chabot, *Bibliothèque de l'École des Hautes Études*, fasc. cxii (1895).

Doctrina Patrum de Incarnatione Verbi, ed. F. Diekamp (Münster in Westf., 1907).

EINHARD, *Vita Karoli Magni*, ed. and transl. by L. Halphen (Paris, 1923).

ELIAS OF NISIBIS, *Chronicle*, transl. by L. J. Delaporte, *Bibliothèque de l'École des Hautes Études*, fasc. clxxxi (Paris, 1910).

Epistula ad Theophilum Imperatorem, *P.G.* xcv. 345–86; another version published and transl. by L. Duchesne, 'L'Iconographie byzantine dans un document grec du ixe siècle', *Roma e l'Oriente*, v (1912/13), 222–39, 273–85, 349–66.

EUSEBIUS, *Letter to Constantia*, *P.G.* xx. 1545–50.

—— *Praeparatio Evangelica*, ed. and transl. by E. H. Gifford, 4 vols. (Oxford, 1903).

GENESIUS, *Historia*, *P.G.* cix. 991–1155.

GEORGE (Bishop of the Arabs), *Letter to Presbyter Isho*, transl. by V. Ryssel, *Theologische Studien und Kritiken* lvi. (1883), 278–371.

GERMANUS PATRIARCHA, *Opera*, *P.G.* xcviii.

GHEVOND, transl. by G. V. Chahnazarian, *Histoire des guerres et des conquêtes des Arabes en Arménie* (Paris, 1856). See also II, under JEFFERY.

HIEROCLES, *Commentarius in Aureum Carmen*, ed. Mullach, Fragmenta Philosophorum Graecorum i (Paris, 1883), 416–84.

IBN KHURDADHBAH, *Liber Viarum et Regnorum*, ed. M. J. de Goeje, *Bibliotheca Geographorum Arabicorum*, vi (Leyden, 1889).

IOHANNES OF DAMASCUS, *Orationes tres adversus eos qui sacras imagines abiciunt*, *P.G.* xciv. 1231–1420.

—— (spurious), *Adversus Constantinum Caballinum*, *P.G.* xcv. 309–44.

IOHANNES PHILOPONUS, *De opificio mundi*, ed. W. Reichardt (Leipzig, 1897).

IOANNES VENETUS, *Cronaca Veneziana*, ed. G. Monticolo, *Fonti per la storia d'Italia*, ix (1890), 59 sqq.

JULIAN, *Against the Christians*, ed. C. I. Neumann (Leipzig, 1880).

—— *Works*, transl. by W. C. Wright, Loeb series, 3 vols. (London and New York, 1913–23).

—— *Letters*, ed. J. Bidez *Œuvres Complètes*, tome i, 2e partie: *Lettres et fragments* (Paris, 1924).

Liber Pontificalis Ecclesiae Romanae, ed. L. Duchesne, 2 vols. (Paris, 1886–92).

MANSI, IOANNES DOMINICUS, *Sacrorum Conciliorum Nova et Amplissima Collectio*, &c. Especially vols. xii and xiii (Florence, 1766 f.).

MASUDI, *Le Livre de l'avertissement et de la revision*, transl. by B. Carra de Vaux (Paris, 1896).

MICHAEL THE SYRIAN, *Chronicle*, ed. and transl. by J. B. Chabot, vol. iii, part 1 (Paris, 1905).

Narratio de sanctis patriarchis Tarasio et Nicephoro, *P.G.* xcix. 1849–54.

NAUCRATIUS, *Encyclica de obitu Sancti Theodori Studitae*, *P.G.* xcix. 1825–50.

Patres Apologetici, ed. E. J. Goodspeed, *Die ältesten Apologeten* (Göttingen, 1914).

PETRUS SICULUS, *Historia Manichaeorum*, *P.G.* civ. 1239–1304.

PHILO IUDAEUS, *De congressu quaerendae eruditionis gratia*, ed. and transl. by G. H. Whitaker, Loeb series, vol. iv (London, 1932).

PHILOTHEOS, *Kletorologion*, ed. J. B. Bury, *Imp. Adm. System* (see under II), 131–79.

PORPHYRY, *Against the Christians*, ed. A. von Harnack, Abhandlungen der Kgl. Preussischen Akademie der Wissenschaften, Phil.-Hist. Kl., 1916.

SCHWARTZ, EDUARD, *Acta Conciliorum Oecumenicorum*, 4 vols. (Berlin and Leipzig, 1927 ff.).

Scriptor Incertus de Leone Armeno, *P.G.* cviii. 1009–38.

Synaxarium Ecclesiae Constantinopolitanae, ed. H. Delehaye, *Propylaeum ad AA. SS. Novembris* (Brussels, 1902). (Important review of this edition by Ernst von Dobschütz, *Göttingische gelehrte Anzeigen*, 1905, 544–74.)

Synodicon Vetus, ed. J. A. Fabricius and G. C. Harles, *Bibliotheca Graeca*, ed. nova, xii (Hamburg, 1809), 360–421.

THEODORE OF STUDIOS, *Magna Catechesis*, ii, ed. A. Papadopulos-Kerameus, in Makarios, *Velikiia Minei Chetii*, 11, November, fasc. 7, prilozhenie (St. Petersburg, 1904).

—— *Sermones Parvae Catecheseos*, ed. J. Cozza-Luzi, *N.P.B.* ix, pt. 1 (Rome, 1888).

—— *Parva Catechesis*, ed. E. Auvray (Paris, 1891).

—— *Epistulae, P.G.* xcix. 903–1679; further letters ed. J. Cozza-Luzi, *N.P.B.* viii, pt. 1 (Rome, 1871).

—— *Laudatio Funebris in Matrem suam*, *P.G.* xcix. 883–902.

THEOPHANES, *Chronographia*, ed. C. de Boor, 4 vols. (Leipzig, 1883 and 1885).

THEOPHANES CONTINUATUS, *P.G.* cix. 15–500.

Trophies of Damascus, ed. G. Bardy, *P.O.* xv. 2 (Paris, 1920).

Vita Georgii Amastridos (= *B.H.G.* 668), ed. V. Vasilievskii, *Trudy*, iii. 1–71.

Vita Gregorii Decapolitae, by Ignatius Diaconus (= *B.H.G.* 711), ed. F. Dvornik, *La Vie de Saint Grégoire le Décapolite et les Slaves macédoniens au IXᵉ siècle* (Paris, 1926).

Vita Ioannicii, by Sabas (= *B.H.G.* 935), *AA. SS. Novembris*, ii. 332–83.

Vita Ioannicii, by Petrus (= *B.H.G.* 936), ibid. 384–435.

Vita Iohannis Alexandrini, by Leontius of Neapolis, ed. H. Gelzer, Sammlung ausgewählter kirchen- und dogmengeschichtlicher Quellenschriften 5 (Freiburg i. Br. and Leipzig, 1893).

Vita Ioannis Gotthiae (= *B.H.G.* 891), *AA. SS. Iunii*, vii. 167–71.

Vita Ioannis Psichaitae (= *B.H.G.* 896), ed. P. van den Ven, *Le Muséon*, N.S., iii (1902), 11–32.

Vita Macarii Pelecetes, by Sabas (= *B.H.G.* 1003), ed. I. van den Gheyn, *A.B.* xvi (1897), 142–63.

Vita Maximi Confessoris (= *B.H.G.* 1234), *P.G.* xc. 68–109.

Vita Methodii (= *B.H.G.* 1278), *P.G.* c. 1244–61.

Vita Nicephori, by Ignatius Diaconus (= *B.H.G.* 1335), ed. C. de Boor, *Nicephori Archiepiscopi Constantinopolitani Opuscula Historica* (Leipzig, 1880), 139–217.

Vita Nicetae Mediciensis, by Theosterictus (= *B.H.G.* 1341), *AA. SS. Aprilis*, pp. xviii–xxvii.

Vita Philaretae (= *B.H.G.* 1512), edd. M. H. Fourmy and M. Leroy, 'La Vie de S. Philarète', *Byzantion*, ix (1934), 85–170.

Vita Platonis, by Theodore of Studios (= *B.H.G.* 1553), *P.G.* xcix. 804–50.

Vita Stephani Iunioris, by Stephanus Diaconus (= *B.H.G.* 1666), *P.G.* c. 1069–1186.

Vita Stephani Suroziae (= *B.H.G.* 1671), ed. V. G. Vasil'evski, *Trudy*, iii (Petrograd, 1915), 72–98.

Vita Tarasii, by Ignatius Diaconus (= *B.H.G.* 1698), ed. I. A. Heikel, *Acta Societatis Scientiarum Fennicae*, xvii (1891), 391–439.

Vita Theodori Studitae (i), by Michael (= *B.H.G.* 1754), *P.G.* xcix. 233–328.

Vita Theodori Studitae (ii) (= *B.H.G.* 1755), *P.G.* xcix. 113–232.

Vita Theophanis, by Methodius (= *B.H.G.* 1788), ed. V. V. Latyshev, *Mémoires de l'Académie des Sciences de Russie*, VIIIe série, *Classe Hist.-Phil.* xiii, pt. 4 (1918).

Vita Theophylacti Nicomediae, ed. A. Vogt, *A.B.* l (1932), 67–82.

II. SECONDARY MATERIAL

ADONTZ, N., 'Sur l'origine de Léon V empereur de Byzance', *Armeniaca*, ii (1927), 1–10.

—— 'Les Légendes de Maurice et de Constantin V empereurs de Byzance', *Mélanges Bidez = Annuaire de l'Institut de Philologie et d'Histoire orientales*, ii (1934), 1–12.

—— 'Role of the Armenians in Byzantine Science', *Armenian Quarterly*, iii (1950), 55–73.

ALBERTONI, A., *Per una esposizione del diritto bizantino con riguardo all' Italia* (Imola, 1927).

ALEXANDER, PAUL J., 'Secular Biography at Byzantium', *Speculum*, xv (1940), 194–209.

—— 'Hypatius of Ephesus. A Note on Image Worship in the Sixth Century', *Harvard Theological Review*, xlv (1952), 177–84.

—— 'The Iconoclastic Council of St. Sophia (815) and its Definition', *Dumbarton Oaks Papers*, vii (1953), 35–66.

—— 'An Ascetic Sect of Iconoclasts in Seventh Century Armenia', *Late*

Classical and Mediaeval Studies in Honor of Albert M. Friend Jr. (Princeton, 1955), 151–60.

AMARI, M., *Storia dei Musulmani di Sicilia*, 3 vols. (ed. 2, Catania, 1933–9).

ANASTOS, MILTON V., 'The Ethical Theory of Images formulated by the Iconoclasts in 754 and 815', *Dumbarton Oaks Papers*, viii (1954), 151–60.

—— 'The Argument for Iconoclasm as presented by the Iconoclastic Council of 754', *Late Classical and Mediaeval Studies in Honor of Albert M. Friend Jr.* (Princeton, 1955), 177–88.

ANDREEV, I., 'Sv. Tarasii, Patriarkh Konstantinopol'skii', *Bogoslovskii Vestnik*, 1899, July, 302–46; August, 459–504.

AUSSARESSES, F., *L'Armée byzantine à la fin du VIᵉ siècle d'après le Strategicon de l'empereur Maurice* (Bordeaux, 1909).

BARDENHEWER, OTTO, *Geschichte der altchristlichen Literatur*, vols. iii to v (Freiburg i. Br., 1912–32).

BARION, H., 'Der kirchenrechtliche Charakter des Konzils von Frankfurt 794', *Zeitschrift der Savigny-Stiftung für Rechtsgeschichte, Kanonistische Abteilung*, xix (1930), 139–70.

—— 'Quellenkritisches zum byzantinischen Bilderstreit', *Römische Quartalschrift*, xxxviii (1930), 78–90.

BARONIUS, C., *Annales Ecclesiastici*, xiii (Lucca, 1743).

BAUMSTARK, A., *Geschichte der syrischen Literatur* (Bonn, 1922).

BAUR, P. V. C., 'The Paintings in the Christian Chapel at Dura', *The Excavations at Dura-Europos, Fifth Season* (New Haven, 1934), 254–88.

BAYNES, N. H., 'The Icons before Iconoclasm', *Harvard Theological Review*, xliv (1951), 93–106.

BENEŠEVIĆ, VL., *Ioannis Scholastici Synagoga L Titulorum*, Abhandlungen der Bayerischen Akademie der Wissenschaften, Phil.-hist. Abteilung, N.F., xiv (1937).

BEURLIER, E., 'Le Chartophylax de la Grande Église de Constantinople', *Compte rendu du IIIᵉ Congrès scientifique international des catholiques à Bruxelles*, 5ᵉ section: Sciences Historiques, 1895, 252–66.

BIDEZ, J., *Vie de Porphyre le philosophe néoplatonicien* (Gand et Leipzig, 1913).

BLAKE, R. P., 'Ob otnosheniiakh evreev k pravitel'stvu Vostochnoi Rimskoi imperii v 602–634 gg. po R. Kh.', *Khristianskii Vostok*, iii (1914), 175–94.

—— 'Note sur l'activité littéraire de Nicéphore Iᵉʳ Patriarche de Constantinople', *Byzantion*, xiv (1939), 1–15.

BOAK, A. E. R., 'The Book of the Prefect', *Journal of Economic and Business History*, i (1929), 599–619.

BOUSSET, WILHELM, *Der Antichrist* (Göttingen, 1895).

—— 'Beiträge zur Geschichte der Eschatologie', *Zeitschrift für Kirchengeschichte*, xx (1900), 103–31, 261–90.

BRAIȚANU, G. I., *Études byzantines d'histoire économique et sociale* (Paris, 1938).

BRÉHIER, LOUIS, *La Querelle des images (VIIIᵉ–IXᵉ siècles)* (Paris, 1904).

—— 'Un Patriarche sorcier à Constantinople', *Revue de l'Orient chrétien*, ix (1904), 261–8.

—— 'Normal Relations between Rome and the Churches of the East before the Schism of the Eleventh Century', *The Constructive Quarterly*, iv (1916), 645–72.

BRÉHIER, LOUIS, 'Les Populations rurales au IXe siècle d'après l'hagiographie byzantine', *Byzantion*, i (1924), 177–90.
—— 'Notes sur l'histoire de l'enseignement supérieur à Constantinople', *Byzantion*, iii (1926), 73–94 and iv (1927/28), 13–28.
—— 'Les Icones dans l'histoire de l'art. Byzance et la Russie', *L'Art byzantin chez les Slaves*, Deuxième recueil dédié à la mémoire de Théodore Uspenskij (Paris, 1932), 150–73.
—— 'Beser', *Dictionnaire d'histoire et de géographie ecclésiastiques*, viii (Paris, 1935), 1171 f.
—— 'Sur un texte relatif au début de la querelle iconoclaste', *É.O.* xxxvii (1938), 17–22.
—— 'L'Investiture des patriarches de Constantinople au moyen-âge', *Studi e Testi*, cxxiii (Miscellanea G. Mercati III, 1946), 368–72.
—— *Le Monde byzantin*, vol. i: *Vie et Mort de Byzance*; vol. ii: *Les Institutions de l'empire byzantin*; vol. iii: *La Civilisation byzantine* (Paris, 1947–50), *Évolution de l'Humanité*, xxxii, xxxii *bis*, xxxii *ter*.
BROCKELMANN, Carl, *Geschichte der arabischen Litteratur*, 2 vols., 1 supplementary volume (Weimar, 1898–1902, and Leiden, 1937).
BROOKS, E. W., 'The Campaign of 716–718, from Arabic Sources', *Journal of Hellenic Studies*, xix (1899), 19–33.
—— 'On the Date of the Death of Constantine the Son of Irene', *B.Z.* ix (1900), 654–7.
—— 'Byzantines and Arabs in the time of the early Abbasids', *English Historical Review*, xv (1900), 728–47 and xvi (1901), 84–92.
BROWNE, LAURENCE E., *The Eclipse of Christianity in Asia from the time of Muhammad till the Fourteenth Century* (Cambridge, 1933).
BURCKHARDT, AUGUST, 'Der Londoner Codex des Breviarium des Nikephoros P.', *B.Z.* v (1896), 465–77.
BURY, J. B., *A History of the Later Roman Empire from Arcadius to Irene (A.D. 395 to 800)*, 2 vols. (London and New York, 1889).
—— *The Constitution of the Later Roman Empire* (Cambridge, 1910).
—— *The Imperial Administrative System in the Ninth Century, with a revised text of the Kletorologion of Philotheos*, The British Academy, Supplementary Papers, i (London, 1911).
—— *A History of the Eastern Roman Empire from the Fall of Irene to the Accession of Basil I (A.D. 802–867)* (London, 1912).
—— *History of the Later Roman Empire from the death of Theodosius I to the death of Justinian, A.D. 395–A.D. 565*, 2 vols. (London, 1923).
BUTLER, A. J., *The Arab Conquest of Egypt* (Oxford, 1902).
CANARD, MARIUS, 'Les Expéditions des Arabes contre Constantinople dans l'histoire et dans la légende', *Journal Asiatique*, ccviii (1926), 61–121.
CASPAR, E., *Geschichte des Papsttums von den Anfängen bis zur Höhe der Weltherrschaft*, ii (Tübingen, 1933). (Important review by Ernst Stein, see below.)
—— 'Papst Gregor II und der Bilderstreit', *Zeitschrift für Kirchengeschichte*, lii (1933), 29–89.
—— 'Das Papsttum unter fränkischer Herrschaft', *Zeitschrift für Kirchengeschichte*, liv (1935), 132–264.

CASSIMATIS, G., 'La Dixième Vexation de l'empereur Nicéphore', *Byzantion*, vii (1932), 149–60.

CERETELI, G., 'Wo ist das Tetraevangelion von Porphyrius Uspenskij aus dem Jahre 835 entstanden?', *B.Z.* ix (1900), 649–53.

CHARANIS, P., 'Nicephorus I, the savior of Greece from the Slavs', *Byzantina-Metabyzantina*, i (1946), 75–92.

CHRISTOPHILOPULU, AI., ' Σιλέντιον ', *B.Z.* xliv (1951), 79–85.

CLERC, CHARLY, *Les Théories relatives au culte des images chez les auteurs grecs du IIᵉ siècle après J.-C.* (Paris, 1915).

CLUGNET, L., 'Les Offices et les dignités ecclésiastiques dans l'église grecque', *Revue de l'Orient Chrétien*, iii (1898), 142–50, 260–4, 452–7 and iv (1899), 116–28.

CONYBEARE, FRED C., *The Key of Truth. A Manual of the Paulician Church of Armenia* (Oxford, 1898).

COTLIARCIUC, N., 'Die Besetzungsweise des (schismatischen) Patriarchalstuhles von Konstantinopel', *Archiv für katholisches Kirchenrecht*, lxxxiii (1903), 3–40.

CRESWELL, K. A. C., 'The Lawfulness of Painting in Early Islam', *Ars Islamica*, xi/xii (1946), 159–66.

DANNENBAUER, HEINZ, *Die Quellen zur Geschichte der Kaiserkrönung Karls des Großen*, Kleine Texte für Vorlesungen und Übungen, no. 161 (Berlin, 1931).

DER NERSESSIAN, S., 'Une Apologie des images du septième siècle', *Byzantion*, xvii (1945), 58–87.

—— *Armenia and the Byzantine Empire* (Cambridge, Mass., 1945).

—— 'Image Worship in Armenia and its Opponents', *Armenian Quarterly*, i (1946), 67–81.

DEVREESSE, R., 'La Vie de S. Maxime le Confesseur et ses recensions', *A.B.* xlvi (1928), 5–49.

—— 'Une Lettre de S. Théodore Studite relative au synode moechien', *A.B.* lxviii (1950), 44–57.

DIAKONOV, A. P., 'Vizantiiskie dimy i faktsii (τὰ μέρη) v v–vii vv', *Vizantiiskii Sbornik* (Moscow and Leningrad, 1945), 144–227.

DIEHL, CHARLES, *Études sur l'administration byzantine dans l'Exarchat de Ravenne*, Bibliothèque des Écoles françaises d'Athènes et de Rome, liii (1888).

—— *Études byzantines* (Paris, 1905).

—— 'Une Vie de Saint de l'époque des empereurs iconoclastes', *Comptes rendus de l'Académie des Inscriptions et Belles-Lettres*, 1915, 134–50.

—— 'Leo III and the Isaurian Dynasty', *Cambridge Medieval History*, iv (1923), 1–26.

DIEKAMP, FRANZ, 'Analecta Patristica', *Orientalia Christiana Analecta*, cxvii (Rome, 1938).

DOBSCHÜTZ, ERNST VON, 'Nicephorus' Hauck, *Realencyklopädie für protestantische Theologie und Kirche*, xiv (1904), 22–25.

—— *Christusbilder. Untersuchungen zur christlichen Legende*, *T.U.*, N.F., iii, parts 1 to 4 (Leipzig, 1899).

—— 'Methodius und die Studiten', *B.Z.* xviii (1909), 41–105.

DÖLGER, FRANZ, *Corpus der griechischen Urkunden des Mittelalters und der Neueren Zeit*. Reihe A: *Regesten*. Abt. i: *Regesten der Kaiserurkunden des oströmischen Reiches*. 1. Teil: *Regesten von 565–1025* (Munich and Berlin, 1924).

—— *Beiträge zur Geschichte der byzantinischen Finanzverwaltung, besonders des 10. und 11. Jahrhunderts*, Byzantinisches Archiv, ix (Leipzig and Berlin, 1927).

—— 'Der Kodikellos des Christodulos in Palermo', *Archiv für Urkundenforschung*, xi (1930), 1–65.

—— 'Rom in der Gedankenwelt der Byzantiner', *Zeitschrift für Kirchengeschichte*, lvi (1937), 1–42.

DVORNIK, FR., *Les Légendes de Constantin et de Méthode vues de Byzance*, Byzantinoslavica, Supplementa, i (Prague, 1933).

—— 'The Circus Parties in Byzantium', *Byzantina–Metabyzantina*, i (1946), 119–33.

—— 'The Patriarch Photius and Iconoclasm', *Dumbarton Oaks Papers*, vii (1953), 67–97.

EHRHARD, A., 'Nicephorus', Wetzer and Welte, *Kirchenlexikon*, ed. 2, ix. 249–59.

—— 'Theologie', in Krumbacher, Karl, *Geschichte der byzantinischen Litteratur* (see below), 37–218.

—— *Überlieferung und Bestand der hagiographischen und homiletischen Literatur der griechischen Kirche von den Anfängen bis zum Ende des 16. Jahrhunderts. Erster Teil: Die Überlieferung*, 3 vols., *T.U.* l, li, and lii (Leipzig, 1937–52).

ELLIGER, WALTER, *Die Stellung der alten Christen zu den Bildern in den ersten vier Jahrhunderten*, Studien über christliche Denkmäler, xx (1930).

—— *Zur Entstehung und frühen Entwicklung der altchristlichen Bildkunst*, ibid., xxiii (1934).

—— 'Zur bilderfeindlichen Bewegung des achten Jahrhunderts', *Forschungen zur Kirchengeschichte und zur christlichen Kunst*, Festgabe Johannes Ficker (Leipzig, 1931), 40–60.

FISCHER, F., *De patriarcharum Constantinopolitanorum Catalogis et de chronologia octo primorum patriarcharum*, Commentationes Philologae Ienenses, iii (1894), 263–333.

FLICHE, AUGUSTIN, and MARTIN, VICTOR, *Histoire de l'Église depuis les origines jusqu'à nos jours*, iv to vi (Paris, 1937).

FLOROVSKY, GEORGE, 'Origen, Eusebius and the Iconoclastic Controversy', *Church History*, xix (1950), 77–96.

FORGET, J., 'Conciles', *D.T.C.* iii. 1, 636–76.

FREY, J.-B., 'La Question des images chez les Juifs à la lumière des récentes découvertes', *Biblica*, xv (1934), 265–300.

FUCHS, FRIEDRICH, *Die höheren Schulen von Konstantinopel im Mittelalter*, Byzantinisches Archiv, viii (Leipzig and Berlin, 1926).

GARDNER, ALICE, *Theodore of Studium. His Life and Times* (London, 1905).

GASS, 'Nicephorus', in Herzog and Plitt, *Real-Encyklopädie für protestantische Theologie und Kirche*, x (1882), 537 f.

GEDEON, MANUEL G., *Patriarchikoi Pinakes*, &c. (Constantinople, 1890).

GEFFCKEN, J., 'Der Bilderstreit des heidnischen Altertums', *Archiv für Religionswissenschaft*, xix (1916–19), 286–315.

—— *Zwei griechische Apologeten* (Leipzig and Berlin, 1907).

—— *Der Ausgang des griechisch-römischen Heidentums* (Heidelberg, 1920).

GELZER, H., 'Der Streit über den Titel des ökumenischen Patriarchen', *Jahrbücher für protestantische Theologie*, xiii (1887), 549–84.

—— *Die Genesis der byzantinischen Themenverfassung*, Abhandlungen der Kgl. Sächsischen Gesellschaft der Wissenschaften, xviii, pt. 5 (1899).

GILL, J., 'The Life of Stephen the Younger by Stephen the Deacon. Debts and Loans', *Orientalia Christiana Periodica*, vi (1940), 114–39.

GOOSSENS, R., 'A propos de la légende de Constantin V', *Annuaire de l'Institut de Philologie et d'Histoire Orientales*, iii (1935), 157–60.

GRABAR, ANDRÉ, *L'Empereur dans l'art byzantin* (Paris, 1936).

—— *Martyrium. Recherches sur le culte des reliques et l'art chrétien antique*, 2 vols. and album (Paris, 1943–6).

GRAF, GEORG, *Die christlich-arabische Literatur bis zur fränkischen Zeit* (*Ende des 11. Jahrhunderts*) (Freiburg i. Br., 1905).

—— *Die arabischen Schriften des Theodor Abû Qurra, Bischofs von Harran* (ca. 740–820), Forschungen zur christlichen Literatur- und Dogmengeschichte, x, Heft 3–4 (Paderborn, 1910).

GRÉGOIRE, HENRI, 'Un Nouveau Fragment du *Scriptor Incertus de Leone Armeno*', *Byzantion*, xi (1936), 417–27.

—— 'Les Sources de l'histoire des Pauliciens', Académie Royale de Belgique, *Bulletin de la Classe des Lettres*, xxii (1936), 95–114.

—— 'Sur l'histoire des Pauliciens', Académie Royale de Belgique, *Bulletin de la Classe des Lettres*, xxii (1936), 224–6.

—— 'Notules épigraphiques', *Byzantion*, xiii (1938), 165–82.

—— 'Pour l'histoire des églises pauliciennes', *Miscellanea Guillaume de Jerphanion II* = *Orientalia Christiana Periodica*, xiii (Rome, 1947).

GROSSE, R., *Römische Militärgeschichte von Gallienus bis zum Beginn der byzantinischen Themenverfassung* (Berlin, 1920).

GRUMEL, V., 'L'Iconologie de S. Théodore Studite', *É.O.* xx (1921), 257–68.

—— 'Recherches récentes sur l'iconoclasme', *É.O.* xxix (1930), 92–100.

—— 'Images', *D.T.C.* vii. 1, 766–844.

—— 'La Politique religieuse du Patriarche Saint Méthode', *É.O.* xxxiv (1935), 385–401.

—— *Le Patriarcat byzantin*. Série i: Les Regestes des actes du patriarcat de Constantinople, vol. i: *Les Actes des patriarches*, fasc. ii: *Les Regestes de 715 à 1043* (Chalcedon, 1936).

—— 'Jean Grammaticos et Saint Théodore Studite', *É.O.* xxxvi (1937), 181–9.

—— 'L'Annexion de l'Illyricum Oriental, de la Sicile et de la Calabre au patriarcat de Constantinople', *Recherches de Science Religieuse*, xl (*Mélanges Jules Lebreton II*, 1952), 191–200.

HALPHEN, L., *Études critiques sur l'histoire de Charlemagne* (Paris, 1921).

HAMPE, K., 'Hadrians I. Vertheidigung der zweiten nicaenischen Synode gegen die Angriffe Karls des Großen', *Neues Archiv für ältere deutsche Geschichtskunde*, xxi (1896), 85–113.

HANSMANN, KARL, *Ein neuentdeckter Kommentar zum Johannes-Evangelium*, Forschungen zur christlichen Literatur- und Dogmengeschichte, xvi. 4–5 (Paderborn, 1930).

HARNACK, A. VON, *Die Altercatio Simonis Iudaei et Theophili Christiani, nebst Untersuchungen über die antijüdische Polemik in der alten Kirche*, T.U. i (Leipzig, 1883).

—— *Lehrbuch der Dogmengeschichte*, ii (ed. 4, Tübingen, 1909).

—— *Der Geist der morgenländischen Kirche im Unterschied von der abendländischen*, Sitzungsberichte der Kgl. Preußischen Akademie der Wissenschaften, 1913, 157–83.

HARTMANN, L. M., *Untersuchungen zur Geschichte der byzantinischen Verwaltung in Italien (540–750)* (Leipzig, 1889).

—— *Geschichte Italiens im Mittelalter*, 4 vols. (Leipzig and Gotha, 1897–1915).

HEFELE, CHARLES JOSEPH, and LECLERQ, H., *Histoire des Conciles d'après les documents originaux*, esp. vols. i–iii (Paris, 1907–9).

HEISENBERG, AUGUST, *Grabeskirche und Apostelkirche. Zwei Basiliken Konstantins etc. Zweiter Teil: Die Apostelkirche in Konstantinopel* (Leipzig, 1908).

HELDMANN, K., *Das Kaisertum Karls des Großen. Theorien und Wirklichkeit* (Weimar, 1928).

HERGENRÖTHER, J., *Photius, Patriarch von Constantinopel. Sein Leben, seine Schriften und das griechische Schisma*, vol. i (Regensburg, 1867).

HIRSCH, FERDINAND, *Byzantinische Studien* (Leipzig, 1876).

HOECK, JOHANNES M., 'Stand und Aufgaben der Damaskenos-Forschung', *Orientalia Christiana Periodica*, xvii (1951), 5–60.

HOLL, KARL, *Enthusiasmus und Bußgewalt beim griechischen Mönchtum. Eine Studie zu Symeon dem neuen Theologen* (Leipzig, 1898).

—— *Gesammelte Aufsätze zur Kirchengeschichte*, vol. ii: *Der Osten* (Tübingen, 1928).

HUSSEY, J. M., 'Byzantine Monasticism', *History*, xxiv (1939), 56–62.

IVANKA, E. VON, 'Die Autorschaft der Homilien' etc., *B.Z.* xxxvi (1936), 46–57.

JAEGER, WERNER, 'Der neuentdeckte Kommentar zum Johannesevangelium und Dionysius Areopagites', *Sitzungsberichte der Preußischen Akademie der Wissenschaften*, 1930, 569–94.

JANIN, R., 'Nicéphore de Constantinople', *D.T.C.* xi. 1, 452–5.

—— 'Les Églises byzantines des saints militaires (Constantinople et banlieue)', *É.O.* xxxiv (1935), 56–70.

—— *Constantinople byzantine*, Archives de l'Orient chrétien, 4 (Paris, 1950).

—— *La Géographie ecclésiastique de l'empire byzantin.* Première partie: *Le Siège de Constantinople.* Tome iii: *Les Églises et les monastères* (Paris, 1953).

—— 'L'Église byzantine sur les rives du Bosphore (Côte asiatique)', *Revue des Études byzantines*, xii (1954), 69–99.

JEFFERY, ARTHUR, 'Ghevond's Text of the Correspondence between Umar II and Leo III', *Harvard Theological Review*, xxxvii (1944), 262–332.

JERPHANION, G. DE, 'Ibora-Gazioura', *Mélanges de la Faculté Orientale de l'Université de Saint Joseph de Beyrouth*, v (1911), 333–54.

JERPHANION G. DE, *Une Nouvelle Province de l'art byzantin. Les églises rupestres de Cappadoce*, 2 vols. (each in two parts) and 3 vols. of plates (Paris, 1925–42).

JUGIE, M., 'La Vie et les œuvres de Jean de Thessalonique', *É.O.* xxi (1922), 293–307.

—— 'Jean de Thessalonique', *D.T.C.* viii. 1, 819–25.

—— 'La Pénitence dans l'Église grecque après le schisme', *D.T.C.* xii. 1, 1127–38.

KAUFMANN, C. M., *Handbuch der christlichen Archäologie* etc., 3rd ed. (Paderborn, 1922).

KITTEL, GERHARD, *Theologisches Wörterbuch zum Neuen Testament*, 5 vols. (Stuttgart, 1949–54).

KLEINCLAUSZ, A., *Charlemagne* (Paris, 1934).

KOCH, HUGO, *Die altchristliche Bilderfrage nach den literarischen Quellen*, Forschungen zur Religion und Literatur des Alten und Neuen Testaments, xxvii (1917).

KRUMBACHER, KARL, *Geschichte der byzantinischen Litteratur von Justinian bis zum Ende des oströmischen Reiches (527–1453)*, ed. 2, in I. von Müller, Handbuch der klassischen Altertumswissenschaft, ix, pt. 1 (Munich, 1897).

—— *Miscellen zu Romanos*, Abhandlungen der phil.-hist. Kl. d. kgl. bayer. Akademie der Wissenschaften, xxiv (1909).

KULAKOVSKII, JULIAN, *Istoriia Vizantii*, iii (Kiev, 1915).

LADNER, G., 'Origin and Significance of the Byzantine Iconoclastic Controversy', *Medieval Studies*, ii (1940), 127–49.

LÄHR, G., 'Die Briefe und Prologe des Bibliothekars Anastasius', *Neues Archiv für ältere deutsche Geschichtskunde*, xlvii (1927/8), 416–68.

LANGEN, JOSEPH, *Johannes von Damaskus* (Gotha, 1879).

LEVILLAIN, L., 'Le Couronnement impérial de Charlemagne', *Revue d'histoire de l'Église de France*, xviii (1932), 3–19.

LEVISON, WILHELM, 'Konstantinische Schenkung und Silvesterlegende', *Miscellanea Francesco Ehrle*, ii. *Studi e Testi*, 38 (Rome, 1924), 159–247.

LINGENTHAL, C. E. ZACHARIÄ VON, *Ius Graeco-Romanum*, iii (Leipzig, 1857).

—— *Geschichte des griechisch-römischen Rechts* (ed. 3, Berlin, 1892).

LIPSHITS, E. E., 'Nikifor i ego istoricheskii trud', *V.V.*, n.s., iii (1950), 85–105.

LOMBARD, ALFRED, *Constantin V, Empereur des Romains (740–775)* (Paris, 1902).

LÜBECK, K., 'Die Patriarchenwahl in der griechisch-melkitischen Kirche', *Theologie und Glaube*, vi (1914), 730–40.

LUCZAK, J., *La Résidence des évêques dans la législation canonique* (Paris, 1931).

MAAS, PAUL, 'Die ikonoklastische Episode in dem Brief des Epiphanios an Johannes', *B.Z.* xxx (1930), 279–86.

MANOJLEVIC, G., 'Le Peuple de Constantinople', *Byzantion*, xi (1936), 617–716.

MARÇAIS, GEORGES, 'La Question des images dans l'art musulman', ibid., vii (1932), 161–83.

MARIN, EUGÈNE, *De Studio coenobio Constantinopolitano* (Paris, 1897).

— *Les Moines de Constantinople* (Paris, 1897).

MARKWART, JOS., *Südarmenien und die Tigrisquellen* (Vienna, 1930).

MARTIN, EDWARD JAMES, *A History of the Iconoclastic Controversy* (London, 1930).

MELIORANSKI, B., *Perechen vizantiiskikh gramot i pisem. I. Nieskolko slov o rukopisakh i izdaniakh pisem prepod. Theodora Studita*, Mémoires de l'Académie des Sciences de Saint Pétersbourg, Classe des Sciences historico-philosophiques, iv (1899), no. 5.

—— *Georgii Kiprianin i Ioann Ierusalimlianin, dva maloizviestnych bortsa za pravoslavie v VIII viekie*, Zapiski Istor.-Filolog. Fakulteta Imp. S.-Peterburgskago Universiteta, lix (1901).

MENGES, HIERONYMUS, *Die Bilderlehre des hl. Johannes von Damascus* (Diss. Münster, Kallmünz, 1937).

MERCATI, GIOVANNI, 'Per l'apocritico di Macario Magnete. Una tavola dei capi dei libri I, II e III', *Studi e Testi*, xcv (1941), 49–76.

MILLER, E., 'Fragments inédits de Théodore le lecteur et de Jean d'Égée', *Revue Archéologique*, xxvi (1873), 273–88.

MILLET, G., 'Les Iconoclastes et la croix. A propos d'une inscription de Cappadoce', *Bulletin de Correspondance Hellénique*, xxxiv (1910), 96–109.

—— 'ΠΑΡΑCΤΑCΕΙC CΥΝΤΟΜΟΙ ΧΡΟΝΙΚΑΙ. Essai sur la date', ibid., lxx (1946), 393–402.

MILLINGEN, A. VAN, *Byzantine Constantinople* (London, 1899).

MONNIER, HENRI, 'Études de droit byzantin', *Nouvelle Revue Historique de Droit Français et Étranger*, xvi (1892), 125–64, 330–52, 497–542, 637–72; xviii (1894), 433–86; xix (1895), 59–103.

MONTICOLO, G., 'I Manoscritti e le fonti della Cronaca del Diacono Giovanni', *Bullettino dell' Istituto Storico Italiano*, ix (1890), 37–328.

MORAVCSIK, GYULA, *Byzantino-Turcica*, 2 vols. (Budapest, 1942).

MORDTMANN, J., *Esquisse topographique de Constantinople* (Lille, 1892).

MORITZ, HEINRICH, *Die Zunamen bei den byzantinischen Historikern und Chronisten*, ii. Teil, Progr. des K. Hum. Gymnasiums in Landshut, 1897/8.

MÜLLER, VALENTIN, 'Kultbild', *R.E.*, Suppl.-B. v. 472–511.

NORDEN, EDUARD, *Die antike Kunstprosa*, 2 vols. (Leipzig and Berlin, 1909).

—— *Agnostos Theos* (Leipzig and Berlin, 1923).

OPITZ, H. G., 'Theodorus Anagnostes', *R.E.*, Zweite Reihe, x, 1869–81.

OROSZ, LAJOS, *The London Manuscript of Nikephoros' Breviarium*, Magyar-Görög Tanulmányok 28 (Budapest, 1948).

OSTROGORSKY, GEORG, 'Die Chronologie des Theophanes im 7. und 8. Jahrhundert', *Byzantinisch-Neugriechische Jahrbücher*, vii (1930), 1–56.

—— 'Les Débuts de la querelle des images', *Mélanges Charles Diehl*, i (Paris, 1930), 235–55.

—— *Studien zur Geschichte des byzantinischen Bilderstreites*, Historische Untersuchungen, v (Breslau, 1929). (Important reviews by F. Dölger, *Göttingische Gelehrte Anzeigen*, 1929, 353–72; Henri Grégoire, *Byzantion*, iv (1927–8), 765 ff.; V. Grumel, *É.O.* xxix (1930), 92–100; H. Barion, *Römische Quartalschrift*, xxxviii (1930), 78–90.)

—— 'Theophanes', *R.E.* x. 2127–32.

—— 'Löhne und Preise in Byzanz', *B.Z.* xxxii (1932), 293–333.

OSTROGORSKY, GEORG, und STEIN, ERNST, 'Die Krönungsordnungen des Zeremonienbuches. Chronologische und verfassungsgeschichtliche Bemerkungen', *Byzantion*, vii (1932), 185–233.

OSTROGORSKY, GEORG, *Geschichte des byzantinischen Staates*, Handbuch der Altertumswissenschaft, Zwölfte Abteilung, Erster Teil, Zweiter Band (Munich, 1940).

PARGOIRE, JULES, 'Les Monastères doubles chez les Byzantins', *É.O.* ix (1906), 21–25, reprinted in *D.A.C.L.* xi. 2, 2182–7.

—— 'Saints iconophiles. Michel de Synnades, Pierre de Nicée, Athanase de Paulopétrion', *E.O.* iv (1901), 347–56.

—— 'S. Euthyme et Jean de Sardes', *É.O.* v (1902), 157–61.

—— 'Saint Théophane le chronographe et ses rapports avec Saint Théodore Studite', *V.V.* ix (1902), 31–102.

—— 'A propos de Boradion', *B.Z.* xii (1903), 449–93.

—— *L'Église byzantine de 527 à 847* (Paris, 1905).

PEETERS, P., 'S. Romain le néomartyr († 1 mai 780) d'après un document géorgien', *A.B.* xxx (1911), 393–427.

PERNICE, A., *L'Imperatore Eraclio* (Firenze, 1905).

QUIBELL, J. E., *Excavations at Saqqara 1908–9, 1909–10*, iv (Cairo, 1912).

RAMSAY, W. M., *The Historical Geography of Asia Minor*, Royal Geographical Society's Supplementary Papers, iv (1890).

ROSTOVTZEFF, M., *Gesellschaft und Wirtschaft im römischen Kaiserreich*, 2 vols. (Leipzig, no date).

RUNCIMAN, STEVEN, *The Medieval Manichee* (Cambridge, 1947).

SALAVILLE, ST., 'La Primauté de S. Pierre et du Pape d'après S. Théodore Studite', *É.O.* xvii (1914/15), 23–42.

SCHENK, KARL, 'Kaiser Leons III. Walten im Inneren', *B.Z.* v (1896), 257–301.

SCHLUMBERGER, GUSTAVE, 'Monuments numismatiques et sphragistiques du moyen-âge byzantin', *Revue Archéologique*, xl (1880), 193–212.

—— *Sigillographie de l'Empire byzantin* (Paris, 1884).

SCHNEIDER, ALFONS M., 'Die Blachernen', *Oriens*, iv (1951), 82–120.

SCHNEIDER, G. A., *Der hl. Theodor von Studion. Sein Leben und Wirken*, Kirchengeschichtliche Studien, v, Heft 3 (Münster i. W., 1900).

SCHRAMM, P. E., 'Die Anerkennung Karls des Großen als Kaiser', *Historische Zeitschrift*, clxxii (1951), 449–515.

SCHWARZLOSE, K., *Der Bilderstreit* (Gotha, 1890).

SOKOLOV, I., 'Izbranie archiereev v Vizantii ix–xv v.', *V.V.* xxii (1915/16), 193–252.

SOKOLOV, P. P., *Izbranie patriarchov v Vizantii s poloviny IX do polovinu XV vieka* (St. Petersburg, 1907). (Not available, see *B.Z.* xvii (1908), 267, identical with preceding?)

STARR, J., 'An Iconodulic Legend and its Historical Basis', *Speculum*, viii (1933), 500–3.

—— 'An Eastern Christian Sect: the Athinganoi', *Harvard Theological Review*, xxix (1936), 93–106.

STEIN, ERNST, *Studien zur Geschichte des byzantinischen Reiches vornehmlich unter den Kaisern Justinus II und Tiberius Constantinus* (Stuttgart, 1919).

—— *Geschichte des spätrömischen Reiches*, i (Vienna, 1928).

—— 'Zum mittelalterlichen Titel "Kaiser der Römer"', *Forschungen und Fortschritte*, vi (1930), 182–3.

—— 'La Période byzantine de la papauté', *Catholic Historical Review*, xxi (1935), 129–63 (review of Caspar, *Geschichte*, ii).

STERN, H., 'Les Représentations des conciles dans l'église de la Nativité à Bethléhem', *Byzantion*, xi (1936), 101–52 and xiii (1938), 415–59.

STIGLMAYR, JOSEPH, 'Der Verfasser der *Doctrina Patrum de Incarnatione Verbi*', *B.Z.* xviii (1909), 14–40.

STÖCKLE, A., *Spätrömische und byzantinische Zünfte*, Klio, Beiheft 9 (Leipzig, 1911).

TER MEKERTTSCHIAN, KARAPET, *Die Paulikianer im byzantinischen Kaiserreiche und verwandte ketzerische Erscheinungen in Armenien* (Leipzig, 1893).

TISSERANT, E., 'Philoxène', *D.T.C.* xii. 1509–32.

TIXERONT, J., *Histoire des dogmes dans l'antiquité chrétienne*, iii (ed. 5, Paris, 1922).

TOUGARD, A., *Excerpta Bollandiana. Quid ad profanos mores dignoscendos . . . conferant Acta Sanctorum Graeca Bollandiana* (Paris, 1874).

—— *La Persécution iconoclaste d'après la correspondance de Saint Théodore Studite* (Paris, 1891).

UNDERWOOD, PAUL A., 'A Preliminary Report on Some Unpublished Mosaics in Hagia Sophia', *American Journal of Archeology*, lv (1951), 367–70.

USENER, HERMANN, *Kleine Schriften*, 4 vols. (1912–14).

USPENSKI, F., *Sinodik v nedeliu pravoslaviia* (Odessa, 1893).

—— 'Partiitsirka i dimy v Konstantinopolie', *V.V.* i (1894), 1–16.

—— 'Konstantinopol'skii Eparkh', *Izvestiia Russkago Arkheologicheskago Instituta v Konstantinopolie*, iv (1899), 79–104.

—— 'Voennoe ustroistvo vizantiiskoi imperii', *ibid.* vi (1900), 154–207.

USPENSKII, K. N., 'Ocherki po istorii ikonoborcheskogo dvizheniia v vizantiiskoi imperii v VIII–IX vv. Feofan i ego khronografiia', *V.V.* n.s., iii (1950), 399–438.

VASIL'EVSKI, V. G., *Trudy*, iii (St. Petersburg, 1915).

VASILIEV, A. A., *Histoire de l'Empire Byzantin*, 2 vols. (Paris, 1932).

—— *Byzance et les Arabes*, vol. i: *La Dynastie d'Amorium (820–867)* (Brussels, 1935).

—— *The Goths in the Crimea* (Cambridge, Mass., 1936).

VAUX, R. DE, 'Une Mosaïque byzantine à Ma'in (Transjordanie)', *Revue Biblique*, xlvii (1938), 227–58.

VISSER, A. J., *Nikephoros und der Bilderstreit. Eine Untersuchung über die Stellung des Konstantinopeler Patriarchen Nikephoros innerhalb der ikonoklastischen Wirren* (Haag, 1952).

VORST, CHARLES VAN DE, 'En quelle année mourut S. Théophane le Chronographe?', *A.B.* xxxi (1912), 148–56.

—— 'S. Thaddée Studite', *A.B.* xxxi (1912), 157–60.

VORST, CHARLES VAN DE, Un Panégyrique de S. Théophane le Chronographe par S. Théodore Studite', *A.B.* xxxi (1912), 11–23.

—— 'Note sur S. Macaire de Pélécète', *A.B.* xxxii (1913), 270–3.

—— 'Les Relations de S. Théodore Studite avec Rome', ibid. xxxii (1913), 439–47.

—— 'La Translation de S. Théodore Studite et de Joseph de Thessalonique', ibid. xxxii (1913), 27–62.

—— 'La Petite Catéchèse de S. Théodore Studite', ibid. xxxiii (1914), 31–51.

WELLHAUSEN, JULIUS, *Das arabische Reich und sein Sturz* (Berlin, 1902).

WELLNHOFER, M., 'Die thrakischen Euchiten', *B.Z.* xxx (1930), 477–84.

WENDLAND, PAUL, *Die hellenistisch-römische Kultur in ihren Beziehungen zu Judentum und Christentum* (Tübingen, 1907).

WULFF, OSKAR, and ALPATOFF, MICHAEL, *Denkmäler der Ikonenmalerei* (Hellerau, 1925).

INDEX

OTHER TITLES IN THIS HARDBACK REPRINT PROGRAMME FROM
SANDPIPER BOOKS LTD (LONDON) AND POWELLS BOOKS (CHICAGO)

ISBN 0–19–	Author	Title
8264011	ALEXANDER Paul J.	The Patriarch Nicephorus of Constantinople
8143567	ALFÖLDI A.	The Conversion of Constantine and Pagan Rome
9241775	ALLEN T.W	Homeri Ilias (3 volumes)
6286409	ANDERSON George K.	The Literature of the Anglo-Saxons
8219601	ARNOLD Benjamin	German Knighthood
8208618	ARNOLD T.W.	The Caliphate
8144059	BAILEY Cyril	Lucretius: De Rerum Natura (3 volumes)
814167X	BARRETT W.S.	Euripides: Hippolytos
8228813	BARTLETT & MacKAY	Medieval Frontier Societies
8219733	BARTLETT Robert	Trial by Fire and Water
8118856	BENTLEY G.E.	William Blake's Writings (2 volumes)
8111010	BETHURUM Dorothy	Homilies of Wulfstan
8142765	BOLLING G. M.	External Evidence for Interpolation in Homer
814332X	BOLTON J.D.P.	Aristeas of Proconnesus
9240132	BOYLAN Patrick	Thoth, the Hermes of Egypt
8114222	BROOKS Kenneth R.	Andreas and the Fates of the Apostles
8214715	BUCKLER Georgina	Anna Comnena
8203543	BULL Marcus	Knightly Piety & Lay Response to the First Crusade
8216785	BUTLER Alfred J.	Arab Conquest of Egypt
8148046	CAMERON Alan	Circus Factions
8148054	CAMERON Alan	Porphyrius the Charioteer
8148348	CAMPBELL J.B.	The Emperor and the Roman Army 31 AD to 235
826643X	CHADWICK Henry	Priscillian of Avila
826447X	CHADWICK Henry	Boethius
8222025	COLGRAVE B. & MYNORS R.A.B.	Bede's Ecclesiastical History of the English People
8131658	COOK J.M.	The Troad
8219393	COWDREY H.E.J.	The Age of Abbot Desiderius
8644043	CRUM W.E.	Coptic Dictionary
8148992	DAVIES M.	Sophocles: Trachiniae
814153X	DODDS E.R.	Plato: Gorgias
825301X	DOWNER L.	Leges Henrici Primi
814346X	DRONKE Peter	Medieval Latin and the Rise of European Love-Lyric
8142749	DUNBABIN T.J.	The Western Greeks
8154372	FAULKNER R.O.	The Ancient Egyptian Pyramid Texts
8221541	FLANAGAN Marie Therese	Irish Society, Anglo-Norman Settlers, Angevin Kingship
8143109	FRAENKEL Edward	Horace
8142781	FRASER P.M.	Ptolemaic Alexandria (3 volumes)
8201540	GOLDBERG P.J.P.	Women, Work and Life Cycle in a Medieval Economy
8140215	GOTTSCHALK H.B.	Heraclides of Pontus
8266162	HANSON R.P.C.	Saint Patrick
8581351	HARRIS C.R.S	The Heart and Vascular System in Ancient Greek Medicine
8224354	HARRISS G.L.	King, Parliament and Public Finance in Medieval England to 1369
8581114	HEATH Sir Thomas	Aristarchus of Samos
8140444	HOLLIS A.S.	Callimachus: Hecale
8212968	HOLLISTER C. Warren	Anglo-Saxon Military Institutions
9244944	HOPKIN-JAMES L.J.	The Celtic Gospels
8226470	HOULDING J.A.	Fit for Service
2115480	HENRY Blanche	British Botanical and Horticultural Literature before 1800
8219523	HOUSLEY Norman	The Italian Crusades
8223129	HURNARD Naomi	The King's Pardon for Homicide – before AD 1307
9241783	HURRY Jamieson B.	Imhotep
8140401	HUTCHINSON G.O.	Hellenistic Poetry
9240140	JOACHIM H.H.	Aristotle: On Coming-to-be and Passing-away
9240094	JONES A.H.M	Cities of the Eastern Roman Provinces
8142560	JONES A.H.M.	The Greek City
8218354	JONES Michael	Ducal Brittany 1364–1399
8271484	KNOX & PELCZYNSKI	Hegel's Political Writings
8212755	LAWRENCE C.H.	St Edmund of Abingdon
8225253	LE PATOUREL John	The Norman Empire
8212720	LENNARD Reginald	Rural England 1086–1135
8212321	LEVISON W.	England and the Continent in the 8th century
8148224	LIEBESCHUETZ J.H.W.G.	Continuity and Change in Roman Religion
8143486	LINDSAY W.M.	Early Latin Verse
8141378	LOBEL Edgar & PAGE Sir Denys	Poetarum Lesbiorum Fragmenta
9240159	LOEW E.A.	The Beneventan Script
8115881	LOOMIS Roger Sherman	Arthurian Literature in the Middle Ages
8241445	LUKASIEWICZ, Jan	Aristotle's Syllogistic
8152442	MAAS P. & TRYPANIS C.A .	Sancti Romani Melodi Cantica
8113692	MANDEVILLE Bernard	The Fable of the Bees (2 volumes)
8142684	MARSDEN E.W.	Greek and Roman Artillery—Historical
8142692	MARSDEN E.W.	Greek and Roman Artillery—Technical
8148178	MATTHEWS John	Western Aristocracies and Imperial Court AD 364–425